Advances in Computer Science Applications and Research **5**

This outstanding new series publishes state-of-the-art research spanning the entire spectrum of informatics ranging from foundational topics in the theory of computing to information and communications science and technology. A broad variety of multidisciplinary and interdisciplinary topics are welcome, as well.

While the focus is on publication of peer-reviewed full papers presenting mature work, inclusion of reviewed short papers reporting on work in progress are welcome, too. Besides globally relevant meetings with internationally representative program committees guaranteeing a strict peer-reviewing and paper selection process, conferences run by societies or of high regional or national relevance are also considered for publication.

Publication in ACSAR is free of charge. No royalties are paid, however, we offer registered conference participants temporary free access to the online version of the conference proceedings on SpringerLink (http://link.springer.com) by means of an http referrer from the conference website and/or a number of complimentary printed copies, as specified in the official acceptance email of the event.

ACSAR proceedings can be published in time for distribution at conferences or as post-proceedings, and delivered in the form of printed books and/or electronically as USBs and/or e-content licenses for accessing proceedings at SpringerLink. Furthermore, ACSAR proceedings are included in the ACSAR electronic book series hosted in the SpringerLink digital library at http://link.springer.com/bookseries/7899. Conferences publishing in ACSAR are allowed to use our online conference service (Meteor) for managing the whole proceedings lifecycle (from submission and reviewing to preparing for publication) free of charge.

Publication process

The language of publication is exclusively English. Authors publishing in ACSAR have to sign the Springer ACSAR copyright transfer form, however, they are free to use their material published in ACSAR for substantially changed, more elaborate subsequent publications elsewhere. For the preparation of the camera-ready papers/files, authors have to strictly adhere to the Springer ACSAR Authors' Instructions and are strongly encouraged to use the ACSAR LaTeX style files or templates.

How to start

To start the evaluation of your proposal for inclusion in the ACSAR series, please send an e-mail to acsar@springer.com , or directly to the editor responsible for your region. For more information about the responsible editor for your region please check the **Editors** section.

Van Vung Pham · Bing Zhou ·
Ford Lumban Gaol · Tokuro Matsuo
Editors

Cybersecurity, IoT, Data Science and Digital Forensics

First International Conference, CIDDF 2025
The Woodlands, TX, USA, October 2–4, 2025
Proceedings

Springer

Editors
Van Vung Pham
Computer Science
Sam Houston University
Huntsville, TX, USA

Ford Lumban Gaol
Binus University
Jakarta, Indonesia

Bing Zhou
Sam Houston State University
Huntsville, TX, USA

Tokuro Matsuo
Advanced Institute of Industrial Techno
Tokyo, Japan

ISSN 3091-2954 ISSN 3091-2962 (electronic)
Advances in Computer Science Applications and Research
ISBN 978-3-032-19487-9 ISBN 978-3-032-19488-6 (eBook)
https://doi.org/10.1007/978-3-032-19488-6

This Springer imprint is published by the registered company Springer Nature Switzerland AG
The registered company address is: Gewerbestrasse 11, 6330 Cham, Switzerland

Preface

The 2025 International Conference on Cybersecurity, Internet of Things, Data Science, and Digital Forensics (CIDDF 2025) was held from October 2–4, 2025, hosted by Sam Houston State University. The conference brought together researchers, practitioners, and educators to present and discuss recent advances at the intersection of cybersecurity, IoT systems, data science, and digital forensics, with a strong emphasis on real-world applicability, system-level analysis, and forensic rigor.

The technical program of CIDDF 2025 reflected the breadth and interdisciplinarity of these domains. Several accepted papers focused on digital forensics and security analytics, including forensic techniques for insider threat detection, performance evaluation of widely used digital forensic tools, phishing and social-engineering forensics using machine learning, and hybrid detection of command-and-control communications from real-world network traffic. These contributions highlighted both methodological advances and empirical evaluation in operational security and investigative settings.

A prominent theme of the conference was the use of data science, machine learning, and visualization for security and forensic analysis. Accepted papers addressed topics such as intrusion detection using weighted silhouette ranking of PCA projections, interactive visual forensics for high-performance computing incidents through time-indexed PCA trajectories, and AI-driven analytics platforms for intelligent data insight generation. Together, these works demonstrated how explainable analytics and visualization can support human-centered investigation and decision-making.

The program also included research on multimodal AI and intelligent systems, such as generative reasoning for UML model comparison, bilingual code-switching voice separation using transformer-based architectures, real-time sign language recognition using lightweight deep learning models, and advances in lip-speech synchronization and facial recognition. These papers underscored the growing role of multimodal learning and efficient models in applied AI systems.

In the area of IoT and system security, contributions examined IoT device security configurations using intrusion detection tools, IoT risk management and forensic considerations for large-scale systems, and immersive virtual reality techniques for crime scene analysis and investigation. These works highlighted emerging challenges in securing heterogeneous systems and leveraging novel technologies for forensic reconstruction and analysis.

CIDDF 2025 employed a double-blind peer review process to ensure fairness and high scientific quality. All submissions were handled through the Meteor online submission system, which also provided integrated plagiarism checking. Each paper received at least three independent reviews from members of the Program Committee. Submissions co-authored by committee members were reviewed with appropriate safeguards to avoid conflicts of interest. Specifically, Program Committee members reviewed only papers for which they had no conflicts of interest, and the Program Committee Chairs made the final acceptance decisions after carefully considering the manuscripts and the reviewers' reports.

In total, 42 papers were submitted; 29 papers were submitted for peer review. Following a rigorous evaluation process, 14 full papers were accepted for publication in these proceedings. No short papers or other paper types were included. The selected papers represent a focused and high-quality collection of current research addressing both foundational challenges and applied solutions in cybersecurity, IoT, data science, and digital forensics.

The editors would like to thank all authors for their valuable contributions and for their careful revisions in response to reviewer feedback. We are deeply grateful to the Program Committee members for their expertise and dedication, which were essential to the success of the conference. We also acknowledge the efforts of the organizing team and the hosting institution for their support.

We hope that these proceedings will serve as a useful reference for researchers and practitioners and will stimulate further interdisciplinary collaboration and innovation in cybersecurity, IoT, data science, and digital forensics.

December 2025

Van Vung Pham
Bing Zhou
Ford Lumban Gaol
Tokuro Matsuo

Organization

General Chairs

Bing Zhou	Sam Houston State University, USA
Ford Lumban Gaol	BINUS University, Indonesia

Program Committee Chairs

Van Vung Pham	Sam Houston State University, USA
Tokuro Matsuo	Advanced Institute of Industrial Technology, Japan

Organizing Committee

Fan Liang	Sam Houston State University, USA
Amar Rasheed	Sam Houston State University, Sam Houston State University, USA
Min Kyung An	Sam Houston State University, USA

Program Committee

Adrian Adascalitei	Technical University Gh Asachi Iaşi, Romania
Osayomore Aigbogun	Sam Houston State University, USA
Tosin Akinsowon	Sam Houston State University, USA
Duy Linh Bui	FPT University, Vietnam
Lei Chen	Georgia Southern University, USA
Madhab Chandra Das	Sam Houston State University, USA
Thi Ngoc Lan Dong	Academy of Finance, Vietnam
Hieu Duong	University of Louisville, USA
Pasan Edirisinghe	Sam Houston State University, USA
Chiamaka Femi-Adeyinka	Sam Houston State University, USA
Murat Gunestas	University of New Haven, USA
Chukwuemeka Ihekweazu	Sam Houston State University, USA
Paul Isibor	Sam Houston State University, USA
Razaq Jinad	Sam Houston State University, USA

Contents

Performance Evaluation of Widely Used Digital Forensic Tools on Kali Linux

Erasmus Mfodwo(✉), Juli Dutta, Pacific Stensland, and Cihan Varol

Department of Computer Science, Sam Houston State University, Huntsville, TX, USA
{exm251,jxd148,pts010,cxv007}@shsu.edu

Abstract. This study evaluates the performance of digital forensic tools on Kali Linux across multiple categories, including imaging tools (dd and Guymager), analysis tools (bulk extractor and autopsy), memory dumping (dd and memdump), password cracking tools (fcrackzip and John the Ripper), network scanning tools (Nmap and Nikto) and penetration testing tools (Metasploit Framework and Armitage). Findings reveal variations in tool performance with test time ranging from 0.06 s to 66 s for password cracking, 11 s to 25.23 s for data carving, 25.2 s to 63.28 s for analysis tools, and 1:46:09 h to 3:44:59 h for imaging tools. Most tools utilize terminal interfaces, with a few offering GUI options, and the analysis provides forensic investigators with an overview of tool capabilities, versions, and update status to inform open-source tools selection for digital investigations.

Keywords: Analysis tools · File carving tools · imaging tools · memory dumping · network scanning tools · password cracking tools

1 Introduction

In the current era of digital interactions, digital forensics tools have become an essential toolkit for locating, collecting, preserving, processing, analyzing, and validating evidence vital to corporation investigations, law enforcement investigations, civil litigations, and intelligence gathering [1]. The need for tools has increased due to the complexity and demand of investigating cybercrimes, which has led to the rise of free and open-source solutions with features that address a variety of domains, including imaging, analysis, data carving, memory dumping, password cracking, network scanning, packet capturing, and penetration testing.

These tools are cost-effective, easily accessible, and may substitute for proprietary software. However, selecting a suitable one can be crucial as it may impact the outcome of an investigation [2]. An investigator needs to know the capabilities and strengths of each tool to make the right choice according to each case and the circumstances surrounding the investigation. To share a holistic view, this study measures successfulness, process speed, checksums, progress meter presence, process time, latest version, last updated date, and interfaces of tools on the Kali Linux platform, helping users make the right choice.

V. V. Pham et al. (Eds.): CIDDF 2025, ACSAR 5, pp. 1–10, 2026.
https://doi.org/10.1007/978-3-032-19488-6_1

Open-source tools are different in quality, and here, password cracking, pen testing, network scanning, and memory dump tools were selected, and test samples were created. Each category of tool was tested and observed according to the metrics mentioned above.

The following sections make up the paper: the related work is highlighted in Sect. 2, the experimental design is presented in Sect. 3 along with the test samples and digital forensic tools used in the experiments; the results of the experiments and associated discussions are presented in Sect. 4, and the research work is concluded in Sect. 5.

2 Related Work

Forensic investigators' objective is to gather and examine digital evidence to present it in court or during legal processes. In doing so, forensics tools are needed, and many tools both open source and proprietary have been published depicting their importance in solving crimes. This research aims to measure the performance of open-source tools in imaging, analyzing, data carving, memory dumping, cracking passwords, and more.

A study was conducted by K. Raychaudhuri to juxtapose disk forensics tools, analyzing and extracting exhibits. Tools selected were FTK 7.0 and Autopsy in the Windows environment and it found that the proprietary tool can recover more data from slack space and unallocated space as compared to that of the open-source tool [3].

Padmanaghan et al. presented a paper collating commercial and open-source mobile forensic tools features. TSK with Autopsy, SIFT, MOBILedit Forensic, and UFED Cellebrite Physical extractor were compared and some of the metrics considered were accuracy of extraction, advanced image and video modules, amount of community support, availability of tool, password cracking ability, cloud storage analysis ability, data recoverability, etc. [4]. Concerns have also been raised about the growing use of encryption technology. Although lost encrypted data may be retrieved, there may be issues when attempting to decode it.

G. Kambiz et al. tested the password recoverability of Encase, DFF, Pro-Discover, X-ways Forensics, Quest Changeauditor, COFFE, WindowScope and Bulk extractor and found that Encase, Pro-Discover, X-Ways Forensic, COFFE, and Bulk extractor performed equal and better [5].

In their study of the Metasploit Framework, Raj and Walia draw attention to its application in system exploitation, pointing out that although the internet has made life easier, it has also created security vulnerabilities that hackers take advantage of [6]. Their findings highlight the urgent need for strong cybersecurity practices, especially when it comes to dealing with the always changing terrain of cyber threats and advanced attack methods that keep posing a threat to defenses.

Gerome's project entails configuring a modest office network infrastructure with numerous subnets and devices, employing Medusa for password cracking, Kali Linux for penetration testing, Nmap for scanning, and Legion for vulnerability discovery to effectively map, analyze, and identify potential network security vulnerabilities [7].

A study was conducted to evaluate the capabilities of three digital forensics tools: Sleuth Kit, EnCase, and FTK, specifically examining their ability to identify evidentiary data. The research placed a particular focus on assessing Sleuth Kit across multiple dimensions, including its ease of use, functionality range, and the reliability of its forensic results. The study extended beyond tool performance to examine the practical implications of implementing open-source forensic tools in educational environments. This evaluation provided insights into the relative strengths and applications of these forensic analysis platforms [8].

On a positive note, examining artifact location, collection, and processing ultimately reveals that open-source forensics tools demonstrate some effectiveness and reliability to some proprietary counterparts, challenging to some level the traditional assumptions about commercial software superiority in the digital forensics domain [9]. The digital forensic domain is composed of computer forensics, mobile forensics, network forensics, database forensics, cloud forensics, Internet of Things (IoT) forensics, and operational technology (OT) forensics. Although from literature there are several studies including comparison studies for forensic tools across these domains, there is no research work specifically focusing on broad digital forensic tools' performance evaluation on the Kali operating system to the best of our knowledge.

3 Methodology

The scope and objective of this work is to provide a current assessment of open-source and free tools capabilities from computer forensics, network forensics, penetration testing, and password-cracking domains to help forensic investigators in their tool selection. The experiment was carried out using a newly installed virtual machine with the setup as shown in Table 1. The host machine runs Windows 11 Professional and is equipped with a 16-thread CPU, 32 GB RAM, a 1TB SSD, and a 4GB dedicated graphics card.

Table 1. General setup.

VirtualBox Configuration	
Base Memory	8000 MB
Video Memory	128 MB
CPU	10
Operating System	Kali-linux-2024.3-virtualbox amd64.vdi

Data is collected through screen capture, with a timer to measure command execution time. Command execution is performed 5 times, and their respective times is recorded. Average of these times is calculated and taken as execution time.

3.1 Tools Used

DD and Guymager: DD is a command-line tool used to make bit-by-bit copies of disk media, mostly utilized as an imaging tool during forensic investigations. Guymager is also used to make forensic copies but has a graphical user interface. It is designed to support different file formats with a high-speed multi-threaded engine [10].

Bulk Extractor and Autopsy: Bulk extractor does bulk data analysis instead of file-by-file extraction techniques to quickly process and extract important features from digital media. Its main goal is to detect and extract artifacts by parallelizing and optimizing the scanning of entire storage media streams. Bulk extractor processes raw data directly, in contrast to traditional forensic tools that rely on file system parsing [11]. The Sleuth Kit project created Autopsy, a comprehensive graphical interface that allows forensic investigators to analyze digital evidence. It supports a variety of file system types and offers features like hash set filtering, timeline analysis, keyword searching, and visual file categorization. It enables investigators to create thorough forensic reports, examine surfing histories, retrieve metadata, and recover erased items [12].

Foremost and Scalpel: Scalpel is a quick file carver that can extract matched files from a collection of picture files or raw device files by reading a database of header and footer definitions. File systems such as FAT16, FAT32, exFAT, NTFS, Ext2, Ext3, Ext4, JFS, XFS, ReiserFS, raw partitions, and others can all have their files carved by the filesystem-independent scalpel. Scalpel is a full rebuilt of Foremost 0.69 and may be used for file recovery as well as digital forensics investigations [13].

Metasploit Framework and Armitage: Metasploit Framework is an open-source penetration testing tool. A full range of tools for creating and running exploit codes, creating payloads, and carrying out exploitation tasks are provided [14]. As a graphical user interface for Metasploit, Armitage improves the framework's usability by providing automated exploit recommendations, visual network mapping, and streamlined attack planning, thereby facilitating the completion of complex penetration testing tasks by both inexperienced and seasoned security researchers. When used in tandem, they give security professionals the ability to methodically evaluate and illustrate possible security flaws in target systems, strengthening an organization's overall cybersecurity posture in the process [15].

Nmap and Nikto: Cybersecurity professionals may employ Nmap and Nikto, two important open-source tools for network discovery and scanning. Nmap supports a variety of scanning techniques to find live hosts, open ports, and operating systems. It also has extensive network mapping, vulnerability detection, and security auditing features [16]. Nikto specializes in scanning web servers including their vulnerabilities, checking for outdated software, misconfigurations, and common web vulnerabilities like SQL injection and XSS [17].

Fcrackzip and zip2john+JTR: Fcrackzip, zip2john+JTR are specialized password-cracking tools used in digital forensics and security testing to break password-protected ZIP archives [18]. Fcrackzip is a command-line tool that can brute-force or dictionary attack ZIP file passwords, while zip2john is a preprocessing utility that converts ZIP file hashes into a format compatible with John the Ripper. These tools are primarily used by security professionals and forensic investigators to recover lost or forgotten passwords [19], though they can also be misused for unauthorized access, making ethical usage crucial.

Impacket+JTR and Samdump2+JTR: Impacket is a collection of Python classes for working with network protocols, enabling advanced network exploitation, remote code execution, and credential extraction from the SAM database. Samdump2 is also used for extracting Windows password hashes from SAM (Security Account Manager) database files [20], which can then be processed by John the Ripper. John the Ripper is a renowned password-cracking tool that can use various attack methods like dictionary, brute-force, and hybrid approaches to crack extracted password hashes, making these tools a potent combination for analyzing and potentially recovering Windows system credentials.

Memdump: To preserve volatile system data and possible proof of active processes, network connections, and encryption keys, memdump is a tool made to record and retrieve the contents of computer memory (RAM) at a particular moment in time. By creating a complete snapshot of system memory, memdump allows forensic investigators to capture critical runtime information that disappears when a computer is powered off or restarted [21]. This tool is particularly valuable in cybersecurity investigations, malware analysis, and digital forensics, as it can provide evidence of system state, running applications, and potential security breaches that would otherwise be lost.

3.2 Installation

All tools used are preinstalled in kali-linux-2024.3-virtualbox-amd64.vdi except Armitage.

3.3 Test Samples

The research is conducted by running a standard test across each category. Tools in each category are used to run the same sample or process to ensure comparative consistency and reliability, allowing for precise evaluation of performance metrics across different scenarios.

4 Results and Discussions

4.1 Imaging Category

A USB 3.0 flash drive with a data set of PowerPoint presentations, word documents, image file types of.jpg,.png,.jpeg, a video file of mp4, pdf files, HTML files, and broken files of various file types is prepared. The flash drive is sterile, and FAT formatted. It was attached to the virtual machine with DD and Guymager used to make bit-by-bit forensic copies and performance metrics were recorded.

4.2 Analysis Category

The dd copy obtained has been used as an evidence sample. Bulk extractor and Autopsy have been used to process it and the results of how each performed have been recorded.

4.3 Data Carving Category

Foremost and Scalpel have been used to process the same dd forensic image since it has broken files in the data set.

4.4 Penetration Testing Category

An FTP service vulnerability is exploited using two well-known penetration testing frameworks: Armitage and Metasploit Framework. Initial testing involved enumerating the target system running vsftpd 2.3.4 using the built-in network scanning features of the Metasploit Framework. The behavior of the FTP service was then examined using the framework's exploitation modules. The identical testing sequence, which included service enumeration, vulnerability detection, and exploitation attempts, was carried out independently by Armitage in parallel, and results were recorded for both successful exploitation and test completion time.

4.5 Network Scanning Category

Network identification is conducted by deploying Nmap and Nikto to actively scan and enumerate an active host. Time command is used to measure the duration and provide efficiency of the two scans.

4.6 Password Cracking Zip Files Category

The password cracking performance is investigated by creating an encrypted zip file. The two password cracking tools are used to crack it and each of them is observed based on the developed metrics.

4.7 Password Cracking Windows SAM Category

A SAM file from a Windows PC is used after creating a new user account with a designated username and password. The two tools are then configured to crack the SAM file, revealing the user password while their performance is monitored.

After the completion of experimentations, we analyzed the results, and performance metrics are obtained as shown in Tables II, III, and IV. The performance results highlight clear differences between dd and Guymager. In testing, dd required 3:44:59s to complete imaging at an average speed of 19.3 Mb/s, whereas Guymager finished the same task in just 1:46:09s with a much higher throughput of 31.57 Mb/s, showing nearly double the efficiency. Both tools operate at block level and avoid filesystem parsing, but Guymager adds significant advantages: it supports on-the-fly hashing, while dd does not, and it leverages multi-threading and optimized I/O buffering to maximize hardware performance. Functionally, both provide manual documentation and run in a terminal environment, but Guymager's version 0.8.12–1 offers more modern forensic capabilities compared to dd's slower, single-threaded design. In short, dd is reliable but basic, whereas Guymager is optimized for forensic imaging speed and integrity.

Autopsy and Bulk Extractor take different approaches to forensic work, which explains their contrasting performance profiles. Autopsy, a GUI-based suite, is well-suited for case management, timeline analysis, and file system parsing, but this depth comes at a cost: in tests it took 63.28 s at a throughput of 25.23 Mb/s, slowed by metadata indexing, and GUI overhead. Bulk Extractor, in contrast, is a lightweight terminal-based tool focused on pattern extraction. It completed its run in 25.4 s, though at a lower throughput of 11.2 Mb/s, reflecting its efficiency in quick bursts but narrower scope. Both tools provide manuals and hashing support, but only Autopsy integrates full case management and GUI features. Bulk Extractor lacks hashing which is vital in forensics but comes with progress feedback which is also essential in emergency case scenarios. Ultimately, Autopsy is slower but comprehensive, whereas Bulk Extractor is faster for triage yet limited in scope.

The results show that Scalpel outperforms Foremost in both speed and throughput during file carving. Foremost completed the task in 25.23 s at 21.5 Mb/s, while Scalpel achieved the same in just 11s with a throughput of 44 Mb/s, making it nearly twice as fast. Both tools are terminal-based file carvers with manual documentation, no GUI, and no built-in hashing, but Scalpel's newer version (2.1–01, Oct 2024) includes performance optimizations and improved handling of file carving rules compared to Foremost's older release (1.5.7, Mar 2024). This updated design allows Scalpel to process data more efficiently, explaining its superior speed and throughput in forensic carving tasks.

Different performance characteristics are revealed by running penetration testing and network scanning tools. With an execution time of 0.17 s, Nmap showed the fastest speed, but Nikto took 0.51 s which was far longer due to the default vulnerability scanning feature when scanning for the host. During scanning, Nikto does not only finds host availability and response but also scans for server software version, vulnerabilities to cross-site scripting, SQL injection, file uploads, authentication bypass, and more, hence taking a longer time to complete the test. The performance was mediocre for Armitage and Metasploit Framework, with respective timings of 163.53 and 122.11 s. Each utility maintained up-to-date documentation using Kali Linux resources, and tools were successfully tested with a variety of interface types, from terminal to GUI.

From the password-cracking software perspective, Impacket+JTR displayed longer processing times (1.06 s), while fcrackzip and John the Ripper took 0.06 and 0.09 s respectively. With memory dumping, memdump elapsed time is 0.18 s while the dd used 64.17 s. Here we need to note that memdump has not been updated since October 2022 while the dd's recent version was March 2024 even though the last updated date for memdump is October 2022 and the dd is March 2024.

Based on the experimental results, Guymager proved faster than dd for imaging with built-in hash computation capabilities, while among other forensic tools, Bulk Extractor outperformed Autopsy, Scalpel worked faster than foremost for file carving, Nmap scanned quicker than nikto, and in terms of password cracking, fcrackzip and John the Ripper demonstrated better performance than Impacket+JTR. Armitage and Metasploit have same underlining code, but Armitage were slower than Metasploit framework and this might be because of its graphic overhead (Tables 2, 3 and 4).

Table 2. Performance metrics of imaging, analysis and data carving tools.

Tools vs. Metrics	DD	Guymager	Autopsy	Bulk extractor	Foremost	Scalpel
Test time	3:44:59 s	1:46:09 s	63.28 s	25.4 s	25.23 s	11 s
Speed	19.3 Mb/s	31.57 Mb/s	25.23 Mb/s	11.2 Mb/s	21.5 Mb/s	44 Mb/s

(continued)

Table 2. *(continued)*

Tools vs. Metrics	DD	Guymager	Autopsy	Bulk extractor	Foremost	Scalpel
Test successful?	yes	yes	yes	yes	yes	yes
Hash calculation	no	yes	yes	no	no	no
Version tested	8.32	0.8.12–1	2.24	1.6.0	1.5.7	1.6.0
Latest version	9.4	0.8.12–1	2.24	2.2.1	1.5.7	2.1–01
Last updated date	03/28/2024	Mar-2024	Feb-24	April-2024	Mar-2024	Oct-2024
Documentation	man	man	man	man	man	man
Progress meter	yes	yes	no	no	no	no
Interface	terminal	terminal	GUI	terminal	terminal	terminal

Table 3. Performance metrics of network scanning and penetration tools.

Tools vs. Metrics	Nmap	Nikto	Armitage	Metasploit Framework
Last updated date	Oct - 2024	Dec - 2023	April - 2022	Dec - 2024
Test successful?	yes	yes	yes	yes
Test time	0.17s	0.51s	163.53s	122.11s
Latest version	7.94	2.5.0	20221206-0kali1	6.4.34-0kali1
Interface type	terminal	terminal	GUI	terminal
Progress meter	no	yes	yes	-
Documentation	Man, kali.org	Man, kali.org	Man, kali.org	Man, kali.org
Version tested	7.94	2.5.0	20221206-0kali1	6.4.34-0kali1

Table 4. Performance metrics of memory dumping and Password cracking tools.

Tools vs Metrics	Fcrackzip	Zip2john +JTR	Impacket +JTR	Sam dump2 +JTR	Mem-dump	DD
Last updated date	Aug – 2024	Nov -2021	Nov – 2021	Oct – 2022	10/15/22	Mar – 2024
Test successful?	yes	yes	yes	no	yes	yes
Test time	0.06s	0.09s	1.06s	-	0.18s	64.17s

(continued)

Table 4. (*continued*)

Tools vs Metrics	Fcrackzip	Zip2john +JTR	Impacket +JTR	Sam dump2 +JTR	Mem-dump	DD
Latest version	1	1.9.0 jumbo-1	1.9.0 jumbo-1	4.6.1	4.6.1	Cureutils 9.5
Interface type	terminal	terminal	terminal	terminal	terminal	terminal
Progress meter	no	no	no	no	no	yes
Docu-menta-tion	Man, kali.org	Man, Open wall.com	Man, kali.org	Man, kali.org	Man, kali.org	Man, kali.org
Version tested	1	1.9.0 jumbo-1	1.9.0 jumbo-1	3.0.0	1.01.9	Cureutils 9.4

5 Conclusion

With each tool demonstrating distinct strengths in features like speed, hash computation, interface design, update frequency, and time of process completion, this study emphasizes the significance of choosing the right tools depending on forensic requirements. Most utilities retained functioning across terminal interfaces despite differences in update cycles and performance metrics, with documentation mostly drawn from Kali Linux sites, highlighting the crucial role that open-source tools play in digital forensics.

Using specialized capabilities across several areas, investigators should strategically choose digital forensic tools according to investigative requirements. While guymager offers high-speed acquisition with integrity preservation for disk imaging, Bulk extractor provides a complete forensic analysis platform, with password cracking tools like fcrackzip and John the Ripper being quicker in decrypting files. Performance metrics, update frequency, interface type, computational resources, and evidence preservation integrity are among the crucial selection criteria that highlight the necessity of a flexible, multi-tool strategy to cater to some level of difficulties a forensic investigation may present.

This research presents an opportunity for continuous investigation into proprietary tools' performance in Kali Linux and may be extended to different operating systems like Windows and Macintosh. The investigation can be expanded to systematically evaluate the capabilities, performance, and unique features of commercial forensic tools in these environments. Moreover, the proposed research may develop methodologies to assess proprietary tools, their artifact recovery techniques, metadata extraction capabilities, and overall forensic effectiveness. Finally, a cross-platform analysis may be done, and researchers can gain insights into the strengths and limitations of digital forensics tools across these operating systems ultimately contributing to a more comprehensive understanding of forensic tools and their potential advancements.

References

1. Lwin, H.H., Aung, W.P., Lin, K.K.: Comparison analysis of android mobile forensic tools. In: 2020 IEEE Conference on Computer Applications, pp. 1–6. IEEE (2020)
2. Manson, D., et al.: Is the open way a better way? Digital forensics using open-source tools. In: 2007 40th Annual Hawaii International Conference on System Sciences (HICSS'07). IEEE (2007)
3. Shankar, R.K.: A comparison study of analysis and extraction of digital forensic evidence from exhibits using disk forensics tools. (2019)
4. Padmanaghan, R., Lobo, K., Ghelani, M., Sujan, D., Shirole, M.: Comparison analysis of commercial and open-source mobile device forensic tools. IEEE (2016)
5. Kambiz, G., Vakharia, D.M., Kannaji, K.C., Satyakumar, R.: A study on digital forensic tools. In: 2017 IEEE International Conference on Power, Control, Signals and Instrumentation Engineering (ICPCSI), pp. 3136–3142. IEEE (2017)
6. Raj, S., Walia, N.K.: A study on metasploit framework: a pen-testing tool. In: 2020 International Conference on Computational Performance Evaluation (ComPE), pp. 296–302. Shillong, India (2020)
7. Gerome, M.: Small Business Office Network. Bachelor's thesis (2023)
8. Ismail, I., Ariffin, K.A.Z.: Open-source tools for digital forensic investigation: capability, reliability, transparency and legal requirements. J. Korean Soc. Internet Inf. **18**(9) (2024)
9. Ghafarian, A., Seno, S.A.H.: Exploring digital forensics tools in Backtrack 5.0 r3. In: Proc. Int. Conf. Security Manag. (SAM). The Steering Committee of WorldComp (2014)
10. Kali.org: Guymager open-source tool. https://www.kali.org/tools/guymager/. Accessed: 12 Aug 2024
11. Garfinkel, S.L.: Digital media triage with bulk data analysis and bulk_extractor. Comput. Secur. **32**, 56–72 (2013)
12. Sleuthkit.org: Open-Source Digital Forensics. https://www.sleuthkit.org. Accessed 12 Aug 2024
13. Kali.org: Scalpel open-source tool. https://www.kali.org/tools/scalpel/. Accessed 12 Aug 2024
14. Kesharwani, P., Pandey, S.S., Dixit, V., Tiwari, L.K.: A study on penetration testing using Metasploit Framework. Int. Res. J. Eng. Technol. (IRJET) **5**(12), 239–243 (2018)
15. Filip, H., Horalek, J., Marik, O., Neradova, S., Zitta, S.: Effective penetration testing with Metasploit framework and methodologies. In: 2014 IEEE 15th International Symposium on Computational Intelligence and Informatics (CINTI), pp. 237–242. IEEE (2014)
16. Gurline, K., Kaur, N.: Penetration testing–reconnaissance with NMAP tool. Int. J. Adv. Res. Comput. Sci. **8**(3) (2017)
17. Nikita, K., Mishra, A.K., Khan, D.A.: Comparison of Nikto and Uniscan for measuring URL vulnerability. In: 2019 10th International Conference on Computing, Communication and Networking Technologies (ICCCNT). IEEE (2019)
18. Disha, P., Sidana, P.: Implementing and comparing different password cracking tools. Int. Res. J. Eng. Technol. (IRJET) **8**(5) (2021)
19. Trionfetti, N., Marcantoni, F.: Brute Force: Wordlist, Brute Force Strategies and CUDA (Bachelor's thesis). Università degli Studi di Camerino, School of Science and Technology (2021)
20. Sharma, H.: Exploiting vulnerabilities of Metasploitable 3 (Windows) using Metasploit framework (2020)
21. Jungtaek, S., Lee, S., Shon, T.: A study on memory dump analysis based on digital forensic tools. Peer-to-Peer Netw. Appl. **8**, 694–703 (2015)
22. Thomas, G.: The Next Threat Landscape: Securing America's Cyber-Physical Systems. (2024)

Hybrid Detection of Command and Control Communications Using Flow-Based Features from Real-World Network Traffic

Chiamaka Femi-Adeyinka, Tosin Akinsowon(✉), and Qingzhong Liu

Sam Houston State University, Huntsville, TX, USA
{cjf068,tba015,qxl005}@shsu.edu

Abstract. Command and Control (C2) communications are a persistent and stealthy component of advanced cyber threats, enabling adversaries to maintain remote access, exfiltrate sensitive data, and orchestrate lateral movement within target networks. This study presents a hybrid, flow-based machine learning framework for the intelligent detection and analysis of C2 traffic using two benchmark datasets: CTU-13 and CICIDS2017. A PyCaret-driven pipeline was developed to automate model comparison, training, and explainability, incorporating ensemble models such as Random Forest, Gradient Boosting, and LightGBM classifiers. Cross-dataset validation demonstrated that the trained models generalize well across heterogeneous traffic profiles, achieving over 99% accuracy and recall on unseen CICIDS2017 samples. SHAP-based explainability was used to identify high-impact features, enabling actionable insights into C2 behavior patterns. The results advocate for integrating flow-based anomaly detection and DNS tunneling filters into SIEM pipelines, and reinforce the importance of model interpretability and dataset diversity for real-world cyber defense applications.

Keywords: C2 · Command and Control · Flow-Based · Network · PyCaret · Machine Learning · SHAP · Anomaly · Detection · DNS · Hybrid · Feature Engineering

1 Introduction

Command and Control (C2) communications are a core component of advanced cyberattacks, providing adversaries with persistent access to compromised systems and enabling activities such as data exfiltration, malware propagation, and lateral movement [24]. Detecting C2 traffic is particularly challenging due to its stealthy nature, often camouflaged through techniques like encrypted channels, Domain Generation Algorithms (DGAs), and low-volume beaconing [1]

Recent developments in machine learning (ML) have offered promising directions in network traffic analysis, where flow-based features such as connection

V. V. Pham et al. (Eds.): CIDDF 2025, ACSAR 5, pp. 11–25, 2026.
https://doi.org/10.1007/978-3-032-19488-6_2

duration, byte counts, and DNS query patterns are used instead of payload inspection [14]. Tools like Zeek have emerged as robust solutions for extracting structured flow metadata, enabling efficient and privacy-preserving threat detection pipelines [8].

This paper proposes a hybrid C2 detection system with Zeek-extracted features and multiple real-world datasets. We integrate botnet flows from the CTU-13 dataset with infiltration-based attacks from CIC-IDS2017 to evaluate the generalizability of ML models across environments. Pycaret model are trained and evaluated using cross-dataset metrics to assess their detection accuracy.

The contributions of this study are:

1. Develop a reproducible Machine learning system to pre-process and merge features derived from Zeek with labeled C2 traffic across two datasets.
2. Perform a hybrid performance evaluation across CTU-13 and CIC-IDS2017 to test robustness of the model in generalization,
3. We propose lightweight detection system that can be integrated with Zeek or a Security Information and Event Management (SIEM) systems for real-time deployment.

1.1 Research Objectives and Hypothesis

The primary objective of this research is to investigate the effectiveness of machine learning models in detecting Command and Control (C2) communications within real world network traffic using flow-based features. We aim to evaluate whether flow metadata extracted via Zeek can sufficiently distinguish between benign and malicious C2 traffic without relying on payload inspection.

Based on prior literature and preliminary dataset analysis, we propose the following hypothesis:

Null Hypothesis ($\mathbf{H_0}$). Flow-based machine learning models trained on a single dataset (CTU-13) will not generalize effectively to other datasets, such as CIC-IDS2017, for detecting C2 communications.

Alternative Hypothesis ($\mathbf{H_1}$). Flow-based machine learning models trained on labeled C2 communications in CTU-13 will generalize effectively to identify similar C2 activity in different network environments, such as CIC-IDS2017, when engineered using Zeek logs and evaluated with appropriate feature sets.

The hypothesis will be tested through a cross-dataset evaluation strategy, where models trained on one dataset are validated on the other dataset. Statistical performance metrics such as precision, recall, and ROC-AUC will guide the evaluation and hypothesis validation.

2 Related Work

2.1 Datasets and Evaluation Benchmarks

The CICIDS2017 and CTU13 datasets are widely regarded as realistic benchmarks for modern intrusion detection systems (IDS), covering various attack scenarios like DDoS, botnets, and infiltration. Several studies leveraged these datasets to train and benchmark machine learning models, validating their efficacy across different network attack types. [11] conducted a comprehensive benchmarking of 31 machine learning algorithms on the CICIDS2017 dataset, demonstrating that traditional models like k-NN and Decision Trees perform competitively with lower computational costs compared to deep neural networks. [7] proposed stacked autoencoders for attack detection in SDN environments, achieving high multi-class accuracy on CICIDS2017. [6] highlighted that CNNs outperform LSTM-based models on CICIDS2017 due to better spatial feature extraction. [12] introduced a CNN-LSTM hybrid achieving 99.59% binary classification accuracy, combining spatial and sequential patterns. Additionally, [19] used layered autoencoders to boost classification accuracy on noisy subsets of CICIDS2017.

2.2 Traditional Machine Learning for Botnet/C2 Detection

Early machine learning approaches to botnet detection focused on supervised models such as Decision Trees, Random Forests, and Logistic Regression. [23] optimized botnet detection on CTU-13 using Information Gain and Gini importance for feature selection, demonstrating high performance with lightweight models. [3] applied logistic regression on Bro (Zeek) logs for botnet detection, focusing on lightweight and interpretable detection using flow aggregates. [20] conducted one of the foundational works on flow-based botnet detection, applying Random Forest classifiers to separate botnet and benign traffic across TCP, UDP, and DNS channels.

2.3 Deep Learning and Advanced Models for Botnet/C2 Detection

As botnet traffic patterns became more evasive, deep learning approaches gained traction. [13] proposed a Recurrent Variational Autoencoder (RVAE) to detect sequential anomalies in C2 communication, validated on the CTU-13 dataset. Their model effectively captured sequential C2 behaviors and was capable of detecting previously unseen botnets. In industrial control and IoT environments, [17] proposed a lightweight DNN architecture for intrusion detection with real-time feasibility, [21] integrated Random Forest classifiers with Deep Q-Networks (DQN) to create dynamic, adaptive honeynets based on detected threats.

2.4 Flow-Based and Zeek-Based Detection Approaches

Behavior-based detection strategies that leverage flow-level data rather than payload inspection have been recognized for their privacy-preserving and scalable properties. [15] introduced the Energy-based Flow Classifier (EFC), an anomaly detector based on inverse statistics of network flows, achieving robust results across CTU-13 and ISOT HTTP datasets. [3] utilized Zeek/Bro logs to extract flow features for lightweight logistic regression models, demonstrating efficient C2 botnet detection without relying on payload inspection.

2.5 Feature Engineering and Feature Selection for C2 Detection

Proper feature engineering is crucial for improving C2 detection accuracy while minimizing computational overhead. [10] systematically identified minimal yet effective flow features for detecting different stages of IoT botnet life cycles, emphasizing that network-channel features are critical for detecting the C2 phase. [4] conducted a foundational study analyzing the relative effectiveness of different flow-based features for machine learning-driven botnet detection. [18] emphasized that feature reduction using Information Gain improved model interpretability and detection accuracy.

2.6 Real-Time and Scalable Detection Architectures

Modern large-scale networks require real-time botnet detection mechanisms. [25] proposed BotSifter, a scalable SDN-based framework for real-time C2 channel detection using centralized machine learning with distributed flow monitoring. [2] proposed integrating graph-based features into ML detection pipelines, significantly improving the generalization to zero-day botnets in IoT and CTU-13 environments.

2.7 Early-Stage and Zero-Day Botnet Detection

Addressing the early detection of botnets before they fully form and conduct attacks is critical. [16] proposed an early-stage botnet detection model based on optimal feature selection and ML classification, achieving near-perfect accuracy with low false positives. [2] further demonstrated that graph-augmented models enhance the robustness against previously unseen botnet types, showing promise in zero-day C2 detection.

Despite significant advances in machine learning-based C2 detection, existing research suffers from critical gaps, including overfitting to specific datasets, limited cross-environment validation, computationally expensive models unsuitable for real-time deployment, and lack of focus on interpretable flow-level features. Furthermore, current public datasets like CTU-13 and CICIDS2017, while valuable, individually fail to fully emulate modern, evasive C2 strategies. Our study addresses these limitations by proposing a hybrid detection framework leveraging Zeek-extracted flow features, validated across CTU-13 and CICIDS2017 to demonstrate generalization. The system emphasizes model interpretability, cross-domain robustness, and practical deployment feasibility, offering a scalable solution for modern C2 threat detection.

3 Methodology

The steps carried out in this study are listed as follows and illustrated in Fig. 1.

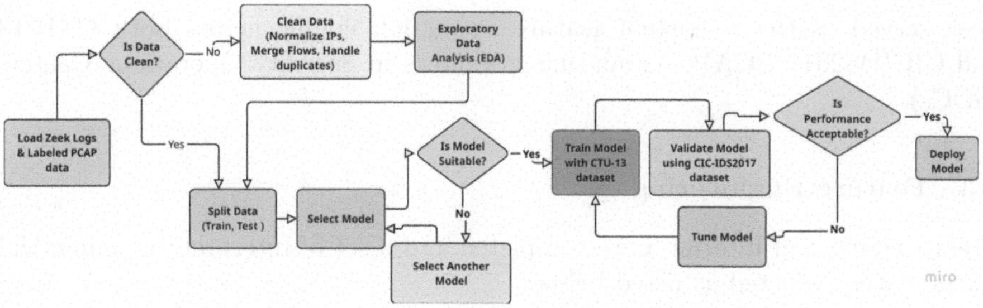

Fig. 1. Methodology

3.1 Dataset Overview

The datasets used for this experiment are the CTU-13 and the CIC-IDS2017 datasets. These datasets are used because they are published, have real-life network capturing of different attack scenarios that are publicly available.

CTU-13. The CTU-13 Dataset [9] is a labeled dataset of botnet traffic captured in the CTU University in Czech Republic, in 2011. It aimed to have a large capture of real botnet traffic mixed with normal and background traffic, it comprises of thirteen scenarios of different botnet samples. In each scenario, the authors [9]executed a specific malware, which used several protocols and performed different actions. It was downloaded from https://www.stratosphereips.org/datasets-ctu13.

CIC-IDS2017. The CIC-IDS2017 dataset [22] was designed by the Canadian Institute for Cybersecurity (CIC) for the development and evaluation of intrusion detection systems (IDS). This dataset showcases the implementation and comparison of different machine learning models for binary and multi-class classification tasks. The dataset was downloaded from https://www.unb.ca/cic/datasets/ids-2017.html.

3.2 Zeek Log Extraction

Zeek, a widely adopted open-source network traffic analyzer, was utilized to process raw packet capture (PCAP) files and extract flow-level metadata for this study. The tool generated structured log files such as conn.log and dns.log, which included key features such as connection duration, byte counts, protocol types, and endpoint addresses.

While a direct merge between Zeek-derived flows and the CTU-13 dataset's NetFlow records was inconsistent due to timestamp alignment issues, we aligned Zeek-extracted flows with the official CTU-13 scenario documentation and labels. With this, it was ensured that the extracted metadata retained correct botnet or normal labels without requiring one-to-one timestamp matching. Thus,

Zeek served as the consistent feature extraction engine across both CTU-13 and CICIDS2017 PCAPs, emulating workflows in Security Operations Centers (SOCs).

3.3 Feature Engineering

Preprocessing and filtering were completed and a set of interpretable numerical features were selected as listed below:

- TotBytes: Total Bytes
- TotPkts: Total Packets
- SrcBytes: Source Bytes
- Dur: Duration
- Sport: Source Port
- Dport: Destination port

Non-numeric values then were converted or removed to ensure compatibility with model input requirements. The final dataset was split into training and testing sets using an 80–20 ratio respectively.

Correlation Matrix. To ensure the selection of relevant and non-redundant features for model training, a correlation matrix was computed for the extracted NetFlow attributes. As shown in 2, the features TotBytes, TotPkts, and SrcBytes exhibit moderate positive correlation among themselves such as TotBytes vs. TotPkts with r = 0.53), which is expected due to their common dependency on flow volume. However, these features are retained because they capture different aspects of traffic behavior, such as size and burst patterns. On the other hand, Sport and Dport show low to moderate negative correlations with the label (r = –0.38 and r = –0.097 respectively), indicating that certain port usage patterns may be indicative of malicious activity. Dur (flow duration) also presents a weak negative correlation (r = –0.074) with the label but is retained due to its interpretability in timing-based attacks such as beaconing. Overall, the selected features offer a balanced combination of volume-based, port-based, and time-based indicators, suitable for training robust machine learning classifiers for botnet traffic detection.

Labeling and Class Distribution. For the labeling and classification, this study grouped the data into Normal and Botnet, where Normal is numerically encoded to 0 and Botnet is 1. After merging the five (5) different binetflow files from CTU-13, the label distribution is as follows:

1. Normal (0) was 4,584,901,
2. Botnet (1) was 230,584

To address the data imbalance, we experimented with stratified sampling and Synthetic Minority Oversampling Technique (SMOTE) to balance training sets by setting the fix_ imbalance parameter to true. Additionally, ensemble models used were configured with class-weight adjustments, reducing bias towards the majority class and improving minority (botnet) recall.

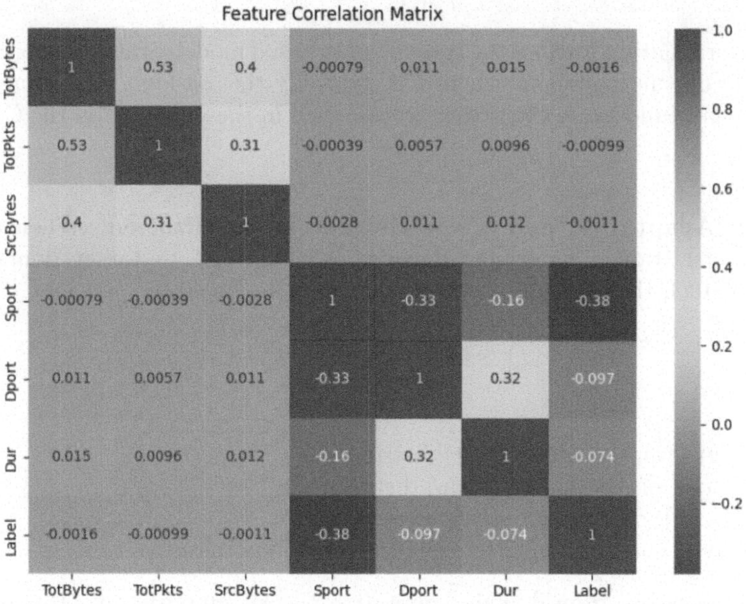

Fig. 2. Correlation Matrix

3.4 Modeling Pipeline

3.5 Cross-Dataset Validation

To evaluate generalization, the trained models were tested on attack traffic from the CICIDS2017 dataset, specifically the **Friday WorkingHours Afternoon DDoS scenario**. Although C2 traffic typically refers to command messages between bots and controllers, we selected this scenario because the DDoS traffic originates from a botnet and reflects coordinated behavior driven by a C2 infrastructure. While the traffic differs from traditional low-rate beaconing, it provides a valuable stress test for cross-environment evaluation of C2 detection models.

3.6 Equation

Supervised Learning Objective. In the given dataset $D = \{(x_i, y_i)\}_{i=1}^{n}$, where $x_i \in \mathbb{R}^m$ and $y_i \in \{0, 1\}$, our goal for the supervised learning is to find a function $f \in \mathcal{F}$ that minimizes the empirical loss:

$$\hat{f} = \arg\min_{f \in \mathcal{F}} \frac{1}{n} \sum_{i=1}^{n} \mathcal{L}(f(x_i), y_i) \tag{1}$$

This formulation justifies the training of the used models (Random Forest and others) in our methodology, where $\mathcal{L}$ is typically the log-loss or Gini impurity. This principle underpins the fitting process used in these models on the CTU-13 dataset.

Domain Adaptation and Cross-Dataset Generalization. When applying a model trained on source domain $\mathcal{D}_s$ (CTU-13) to target domain $\mathcal{D}_t$ (CICIDS2017), the error in the target domain is bounded by:

$$\epsilon_t(f) \leq \epsilon_s(f) + \text{disc}(\mathcal{D}_s, \mathcal{D}_t) + \lambda \tag{2}$$

where:

- $\epsilon_t(f)$: error on the target (test) distribution
- $\epsilon_s(f)$: error on the source (train) distribution
- $\text{disc}(\mathcal{D}_s, \mathcal{D}_t)$: distribution divergence
- λ: minimal combined error of the ideal joint hypothesis

This inequality from domain adaptation theory supports our cross-dataset validation from CTU-13 to CICIDS2017, indicating the importance of reducing distributional divergence [5].

4 Experimental Results

The performance evaluation of the proposed detection models was conducted using standard machine learning metrics, including Accuracy, Precision, Recall, F1-Score, and the Area Under the ROC Curve (ROC-AUC) as shown in Table 1

Ensemble-based classifiers, particularly Random Forest with extra trees, achieved outstanding results with accuracy scores exceeding 99.8%, recall rates above 98%, and near-perfect ROC-AUC values (approximately 0.9998) as shown in Fig. 4. The high F1-scores, which balance precision and recall, further confirm the models' ability to minimize both false positives and false negatives, a critical requirement for operational deployment in Security Operations Centers (SOCs).

Table 1. Performance of Machine Learning Models on CTU-13 Dataset

Model	Accuracy	AUC	Recall	Precision	F1	Kappa	MCC	TT (Sec)
Random Forest (RF)	0.9989	0.9998	0.9855	0.9923	0.9889	0.9884	0.9884	244.717
Extra Trees (ET)	0.9987	0.9999	0.9818	0.9915	0.9866	0.9859	0.9860	73.776
Decision Tree (DT)	0.9983	0.9911	0.9822	0.9817	0.9825	0.9816	0.9816	4.972
LightGBM	0.9972	0.9998	0.9671	0.9742	0.9706	0.9691	0.9692	107.238
K-Nearest Neighbors (KNN)	0.9964	0.9941	0.9653	0.9607	0.9630	0.9611	0.9611	34.558
Gradient Boosting (GBC)	0.9942	0.9992	0.9133	0.9654	0.9386	0.9356	0.9360	285.121
AdaBoost (ADA)	0.9933	0.9988	0.9192	0.9421	0.9305	0.9270	0.9271	89.467
Logistic Regression (LR)	0.9793	0.9781	0.7418	0.8167	0.7774	0.7666	0.7676	24.749
Linear Discriminant (LDA)	0.9597	0.9652	0.6541	0.5758	0.6124	0.5913	0.5926	2.613
Ridge Classifier	0.9513	0.9652	0.0000	0.0000	0.0000	−0.0000	-0.0000	1.198
Dummy Classifier	0.9513	0.5000	0.0000	0.0000	0.0000	0.0000	0.0000	0.938
SVM (Linear)	0.9493	0.4097	0.0000	0.0036	0.0000	−0.0035	−0.0071	4.330
QDA	0.8319	0.9764	0.9773	0.2219	0.3617	0.3066	0.4204	1.538
Naïve Bayes (NB)	0.8241	0.9721	0.9823	0.2147	0.3524	0.2961	0.4129	1.483

4.1 Confusion Matrix and Feature Importance

In addition to standard performance metrics, confusion matrices were generated to visualize classification performance. The results showed a strong separation between benign and malicious traffic classes with minimal misclassifications, reflecting high model precision and recall as shown in Fig. 3.

Feature importance plots, including SHAP-based interpretability analysis, revealed that volume-based features such as TotBytes, TotPkts, and SrcBytes, along with port-based indicators like Sport and Dport, were the most influential in distinguishing botnet-related flows. Although Dur had lower correlation, it was still significant for capturing temporal anomalies associated with command-and-control (C2) behaviors such as beaconing and burst activity.

4.2 Cross-Dataset Generalization

A critical aspect of the experiment was evaluating the generalization capability of models trained on CTU-13 when applied to unseen traffic in CICIDS2017. Despite differences in traffic patterns and volume, the trained classifiers maintained high accuracy, precision, and recall, validating their robustness.

This supports the hypothesis that Zeek-extracted flow-level features encode core behavioral characteristics such as repetitive short flows, abnormal byte volumes, and unusual port usage that persist across environments.

These results highlight the feasibility of deploying such models in live networks for real-time detection of C2 communications, especially when integrated with Zeek-based monitoring pipelines.

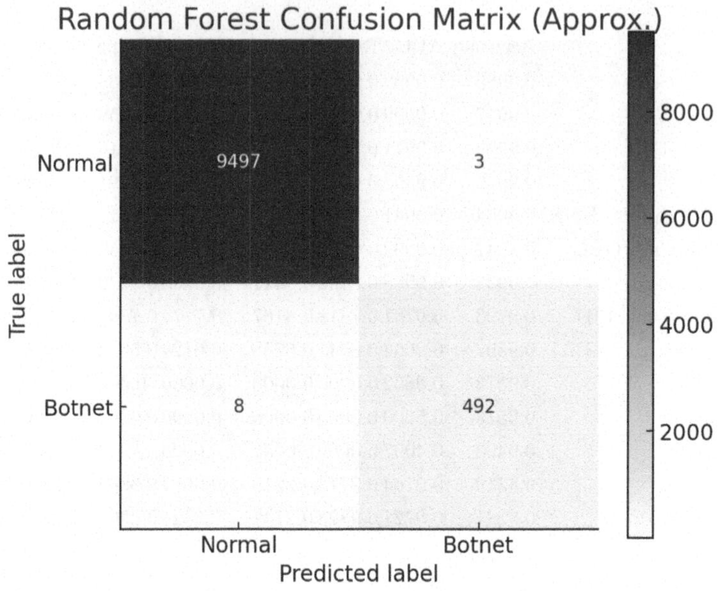

Fig. 3. Confusion Matrix

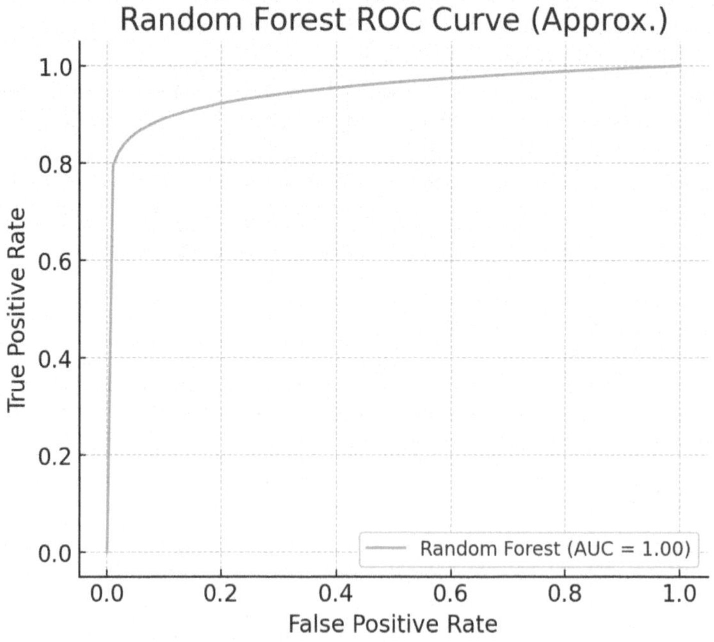

Fig. 4. AUCROC

4.3 Feature Importance and Explainability

To enhance the interpretability of the trained models, feature importance analysis was performed using both global and local explanation techniques. PyCaret internally computed feature importances based on the trained ensemble model, which relies on aggregated impurity reduction across tree nodes. The most significant features identified include `TotBytes`, `TotPkts`, and `SrcBytes`, all of which are volume-related indicators commonly elevated during botnet communications. Port features (`Sport`, `Dport`) also ranked high, consistent with known botnet behaviors using fixed or uncommon ports.

The importance score $I(f)$ for each feature f is defined using the mean decrease in Gini impurity:

$$I(f) = \sum_{t \in T_f} p(t) \cdot \Delta i(t) \tag{3}$$

where:

- T_f denotes the set of all nodes where feature f is used,
- $p(t)$ is the proportion of training samples reaching node t, and
- $\Delta i(t)$ is the impurity decrease at node t.

To understand the model, SHAP (SHapley Additive exPlanations) was used to analyze the contribution of each feature to the prediction. As shown in 5, the Sport and Dport features have the highest SHAP values, indicating a significant influence on model output. These are likely tied to the behavioral patterns of command-and-control (C2) channels and botnet activity. Higher SHAP values indicate greater impact. Red points represent high feature values, while blue represent low.

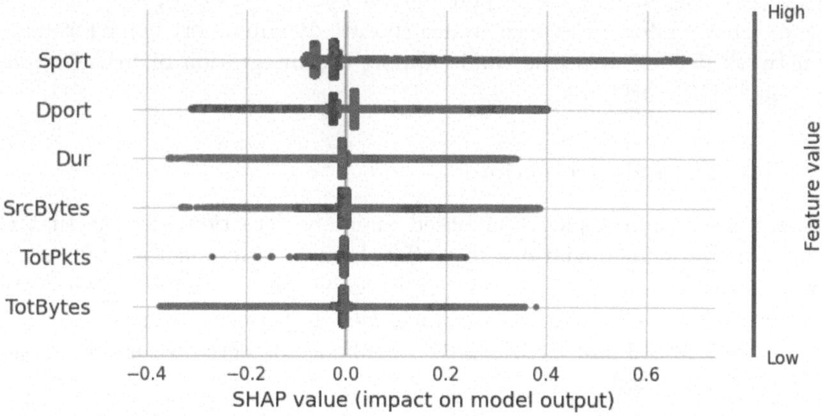

Fig. 5. SHAP summary plot showing the feature importance based on their contribution to the model output

4.4 Threat Attribution and Analysis

Beyond binary classification of traffic, our study explored the potential for threat attribution within the CTU-13 dataset. By mapping C2-related flows to their corresponding botnet families, the analysis enabled a deeper understanding of the specific threats present in the network captures. Indicators of Compromise (IOCs), such as IP addresses associated with malicious command servers, suspicious domain names, and abnormal User-Agent strings observed in HTTP flows, were extracted to support threat hunting and forensic investigations. Furthermore, attack patterns were visualized using time series graphs and connection flow maps, illustrating trends such as repetitive beaconing intervals, sudden spikes in byte transfers, and clustering of anomalous port usage. These visualizations provide security analysts with intuitive insights into botnet behavior, facilitating early detection and response strategies beyond simple binary alerting. By combining flow-level classification with contextual threat attribution, the pipeline supports not only detection but also proactive intelligence gathering for advanced cyber threat mitigation.

4.5 Recommendation for Defense Strategy

The findings from this study underscore the importance of flow-level metadata in detecting sophisticated and stealthy botnet activities. The high detection performance achieved using a small, interpretable set of features demonstrates that volume, port, and time-based behaviors are sufficient to distinguish malicious traffic patterns from benign when properly modeled. Based on these observations, the following defense strategies are recommended to enhance the robustness of an organization's and critical infrastructure networks.

The dominance of Sport and Dport in feature contribution aligns with common C2 patterns, such as use of non-standard or randomized ports for evasion. These insights reinforce the need to incorporate dynamic port behavior analysis into network defense strategies and support the integration of SHAP explainability into SOC workflows.

4.6 Flow Anomaly Detection

Organizations should deploy flow-based anomaly detection systems that continuously monitor for deviations in traffic characteristics such as unusual byte volumes, short repetitive durations, or irregular port activity. These systems can be integrated with machine learning models trained on curated NetFlow datasets like CTU-13 and CICIDS2017 to enhance detection capability without deep packet inspection.

4.7 DNS Tunneling Filters

Since many botnets utilize DNS tunneling for command and control (C2) communication, it is recommended that network administrators implement filters to detect and block abnormal DNS query patterns. These include long TXT queries, high entropy domain names, and query frequency anomalies. Coupling these rules with behavioral models can reduce false negatives.

4.8 Zeek-Based Real-Time Alerting

Zeek can be employed to process live packet captures and generate structured logs for instance conn.log, dns.log, http.log. These logs can be fed into the trained classifier to generate real-time alerts on potentially malicious flows. Given Zeek's flexibility, custom scripts can be written to tag suspicious traffic and generate alerts on indicators derived from trained models.

4.9 Integration with SIEMs and Threat Intelligence Feeds

To further enhance situational awareness, the proposed detection pipeline can be integrated into existing Security Information and Event Management (SIEM) platforms. Model outputs can be used to enrich logs with risk scores or threat labels, which can be correlated with external threat intelligence feeds blacklisted such as IPs, malware signatures for triage and investigation.

In conclusion, by adopting a layered defense strategy combining machine learning, flow metadata analysis, Zeek-based monitoring, and SIEM integration, organizations can proactively detect and respond to advanced botnet and command-and-control threats in real-time.

5 Conclusion and Future Work

This study presents a comprehensive machine learning pipeline for the detection and analysis of sophisticated cyber threats using flow-based metadata from real-world datasets. By aggregating and preprocessing multiple .binetflow files from the CTU-13 dataset, and validating the trained models against CICIDS2017, we demonstrated that a minimal set of interpretable flow features is sufficient to achieve high accuracy in distinguishing botnet traffic from normal activity. Both traditional ensemble models and PyCaret's automated machine learning framework achieved precision and recall rates exceeding 98%, underscoring the effectiveness of flow-level threat detection. Additionally, the integration of correlation analysis, SHAP explainability, and cross-dataset validation strengthens the robustness and transparency of the proposed approach.

In addition to detection, the pipeline supports threat attribution by mapping malicious flows to known botnet families and extracting actionable indicators of compromise (IOCs). Real-time application of this approach is feasible using Zeek-based monitoring and SIEM integration, making it adaptable to both enterprise and research environments.

The integration of explainability methods such as SHAP not only improves model transparency but also supports real-world deployment in Security Operations Centers (SOCs). Analysts often require interpretable evidence when triaging alerts, particularly in high-stakes or regulated environments. By visualizing which features contribute most to a given detection such as abnormally high byte volumes or unusual port usage, SOC teams can distinguish between true positives and false alarms with greater confidence. This reduces alert fatigue and strengthens incident response workflows. In essence, explainability transforms the detection model from a black-box classifier into an actionable decision support tool.

For future work, we propose extending the pipeline with deep learning models capable of detecting novel, zero-day threats using sequential or temporal patterns in network flows. Incorporating NLP techniques to parse payload metadata such as HTTP headers, or DNS queries, may also improve semantic threat interpretation. Furthermore, a distributed architecture leveraging edge detection nodes and federated learning could allow for scalable deployment across large infrastructures while preserving data privacy. Finally, enriching the dataset with additional context, such as operating system fingerprints, geolocation data, or honeypot logs, could enhance threat attribution accuracy and support multi-dimensional threat intelligence analysis.

References

1. Abeshu, A., Chilamkurti, N.: Deep learning: The frontier for distributed attack detection in fog-to-things computing. IEEE Commun. Mag. **56**(2), 169–175 (2018)
2. Alharbi, A., Alsubhi, K.: Botnet detection approach using graph-based machine learning. IEEE Access **9**, 99166–99180 (2021). https://doi.org/10.1109/ACCESS.2021.3094183
3. Bapat, R., Mandya, A., Liu, X., Abraham, B., Brown, D.E., Kang, H., Veeraraghavan, M.: Identifying malicious botnet traffic using logistic regression. In: 2018 Systems and Information Engineering Design Symposium (SIEDS). pp. 266–271. IEEE (2018https://doi.org/10.1109/SIEDS.2018.8374749
4. Beigi, E.B., Jazi, H.H., Stakhanova, N., Ghorbani, A.A.: Towards effective feature selection in machine learning-based botnet detection approaches. 2014 IEEE Conference on Communications and Network Security pp. 247–255 (2014).https://doi.org/10.1109/CNS.2014.6997492
5. Ben-David, S., Blitzer, J., Crammer, K., Pereira, F.: Analysis of representations for domain adaptation. In: Advances in Neural Information Processing Systems. pp. 137–144 (2007)
6. Bhuyan, M.H., Kumari, P.: Deep learning algorithms for intrusion detection: A comparative study. IEEE Access **9**, 45190–45205 (2021)
7. Choobdar, S., Zohrevand, S.: Efficient deep neural network for intrusion detection using cic-ids-2017 dataset. Wireless Pers. Commun. **119**, 3447–3463 (2021)
8. Ghorbani, A.A., Lashkari, A.H.: A detailed analysis of the cicids2017 dataset for network intrusion detection. In: Machine Learning and Data Mining in Pattern Recognition, Lecture Notes in Computer Science, vol. 11318, pp. 172–182. Springer (2019)
9. Imfaisalmalik: Ctu13 csv dataset contains botnet, normal and background traffic. https://github.com/imfaisalmalik/CTU13-CSV-Dataset (2025), Accessed 25 Apr 2025
10. Kalakoti, R., Nõmm, S., Bahsi, H.: In-depth feature selection for the statistical machine learning-based botnet detection in iot networks. IEEE Access **10**, 94518–94535 (2022). https://doi.org/10.1109/ACCESS.2022.3204001

11. Khan, M., Byun, Y.: Benchmarking of machine learning for anomaly-based intrusion detection systems in the cicids2017 dataset. Sensors **21**(4), 1346 (2021a). https://doi.org/10.3390/s21041346
12. Khan, M., Byun, Y.: Cnn-lstm hybrid deep neural network for network intrusion detection system. IEEE Access **9**, 22005–22017 (2021b)
13. Kim, J., Sim, A., Kim, J., Wu, K.: Botnet detection using recurrent variational autoencoder. In: GLOBECOM 2020 - 2020 IEEE Global Communications Conference, pp. 1–6. IEEE (2020). https://doi.org/10.1109/GLOBECOM42002.2020.9348169
14. Lashkari, A.H., Gil, M., Mamun, M., Ghorbani, A.A.: Toward generating a new intrusion detection dataset and intrusion traffic characterization. In: Proceedings of the 4th International Conference on Information Systems Security and Privacy (ICISSP), pp. 108–116 (2018)
15. Lopes, D.A.G., Marotta, M., Ladeira, M., Gondim, J.: Botnet detection based on network flow analysis using inverse statistics. In: 2022 17th Iberian Conference on Information Systems and Technologies (CISTI), pp. 1–6. IEEE (2022). https://doi.org/10.23919/CISTI54924.2022.9820318
16. Muhammad, A., Asad, M., Javed, A.R.: Robust early stage botnet detection using machine learning. In: 2020 International Conference on Cyber Warfare and Security (ICCWS), pp. 1–6. IEEE (2020). https://doi.org/10.1109/ICCWS48432.2020.9292395
17. Qureshi, M.B., Javaid, N.: Efficient deep neural network for intrusion detection using cic-ids-2017 dataset. J. Netw. Comput. Appl. **144**, 102670 (2020)
18. Rahman, M., Ruwanpura, J.: Cicids-2017 dataset feature analysis with information gain for anomaly detection. Int. J. Netw. Secur. **23**, 152–160 (2021)
19. Shah, Z., Patel, R.: Intrusion detection system using hybrid model of denoising autoencoder and ladder variational autoencoder. Int. J. Comput. Appl. **42**, 321–330 (2020)
20. Stevanovic, M., Pedersen, J.M.: An efficient flow-based botnet detection using supervised machine learning. In: 2014 International Conference on Computing, Networking and Communications (ICNC), pp. 797–801. IEEE (2014). https://doi.org/10.1109/ICCNC.2014.6785481
21. Tan, C., Liu, Y.: Research on dynamic honeynet technology based on machine learning. In: 2021 IEEE 5th Advanced Information Technology, Electronic and Automation Control Conference (IAEAC), pp. 2155–2160 (2021)
22. University of New Brunswick: Canadian institute for cybersecurity: Cicids2017 dataset. https://www.unb.ca/cic/datasets/ids-2017.html (2025), Accessed 25 Apr 2025
23. Velasco-Mata, J., González-Castro, V., Fernández, E.F., Alegre, E.: Efficient detection of botnet traffic by features selection and decision trees. IEEE Access **9**, 120567–120579 (2021). https://doi.org/10.1109/ACCESS.2021.3108222
24. Winter, P., Enzinger, R., Hermann, M.: Detection of domain generation algorithms for botnets using machine learning. J. Comput. Virol. Hacking Tech. **14**(3), 145–156 (2018)
25. Zha, Z., Wang, A., Guo, Y., Montgomery, D., Chen, S.: Botsifter: An sdn-based online bot detection framework in data centers. In: 2019 IEEE Conference on Communications and Network Security (CNS), pp. 142–150. IEEE (2019). https://doi.org/10.1109/CNS.2019.8802854

Immersive Technology Virtual Reality (VR) in Crime Scene Analysis & Investigation: A Systematic Review

Chiamaka Femi-Adeyinka(✉) and Bing Zhou

Sam Houston State University, Huntsville, TX, USA
{cjf068,bxz003}@shsu.edu
{cjf068,bxz003}@shsu.edu

Abstract. Virtual Reality (VR) is emerging as a transformative tool in crime scene investigation (CSI), offering immersive training environments and enhanced crime scene analysis capabilities. This paper presents a systematic review of recent advances in VR applications for CSI over the last five years (2020–2025). A total of 27 peer-reviewed studies were analyzed to identify prevailing application domains, methodologies, benefits, and unresolved challenges. Key focus areas include VR-based training simulations for investigators, 3D crime scene reconstruction and walkthroughs, and virtual evidence presentation in courtroom settings. The review finds that VR training systems significantly improve user engagement and skill acquisition, while VR reconstructions enable investigators to revisit and analyze crime scenes with high fidelity, integrating diverse evidence types in a single interactive environment. However, challenges such as technical complexity, validation of accuracy, and legal admissibility of VR-generated evidence remain. To address these gaps, we outline recommendations including the integration of artificial intelligence for automated evidence analysis, development of standard protocols for virtual evidence handling, and user studies to evaluate effectiveness across agencies. The findings underscore VR's considerable potential to augment forensic investigations and training, while highlighting the need for further research to ensure reliability, user adoption, and acceptance in judicial processes.

Keywords: Virtual Reality (VR) · AR · Crime Scene investigation · Crime Scene reconstruction · Forensic analysis · Evidence documentation · 3D · photogrammetry · crime scene detection · Immersive Technology · object detection · systematic review

1 Introduction

Virtual Reality (VR) technology has rapidly evolved and is being embraced in fields ranging from healthcare, education to public safety. In the context of Forensic Science and criminal investigations, VR is increasingly recognized and utilized for its potential to transform how Crime Scene Investigations (CSI) are

V. V. Pham et al. (Eds.): CIDDF 2025, ACSAR 5, pp. 26–52, 2026.
https://doi.org/10.1007/978-3-032-19488-6_3

done. Several studies have proposed VR-based solutions for training investigators and reconstructing crime scenes in immersive detail by creating realistic, interactive crime scene training simulations for both professionals and students [22,33,34]. For instance, [5] developed a mixed reality training system that incorporates 3D laser scans of real crime scenes, allowing trainees to practice evidence collection in a realistic virtual environment. Such applications of VR reiterates the developing and growing interest and need for immersive technology in this field.

Virtual environments offer several unique advantages in CSI such as reducing the risk of contaminating real crime scenes and ability to repeat or rerun scenarios as many times as possible [34,41]. They also reduce cost and logistics as traditional full-scale mock crime scenes are expensive to build and can only be used once [6], whereas a virtual scene can be reused severally by many trainees. With training using VR, there has been reported high levels of engagement, skill development, and user satisfaction [16,34]. The COVID-19 pandemic accelerated the adoption of remote and virtual training solutions in forensics, highlighting the readiness of VR-based approaches [41].

Additionally, VR is increasingly utilized for crime scene analysis and reconstruction by digitally capturing a scene with 3D scanners and photographs, and allowing investigators to later navigate the environment in VR, preserving details and context of the crime scene which might otherwise be lost once the physical scene is cleared [3,33]. Complex scenarios such as post-fire debris fields can be examined safely in VR without any physical risk to investigators or the evidence [41]. VR also enables integration of multiple evidence types like bloodstain patterns, bullet trajectories, laser scans into a single immersive model of the scene [22,32], helping investigators reconstruct the sequence of events and explore hypotheses interactively. This immersive visualization can enhance understanding and collaboration during investigations.

Despite these promising capabilities, VR in CSI is still an emerging field and a lot of research is needed to validate its effectiveness, and also address challenges such as technical limitations and acceptance within the justice system [32,41]. Therefore, a systematic review of recent developments over the last five (5) years is both important and timely. In this paper, we review the state-of-the-art applications of VR in crime scene investigations, the gaps in literature, the current challenges faced by investigators, and discussing their benefits, current limitations, and the future research directions.

The rest of this paper is structured as follows: Sect. 2 discusses the Global Applications of VR, Sect. 3 describes the review methodology, Sect. 4 discusses VR in Crime Scene Investigation, Sect. 5 highlights the Finding and Analysis, Sect. 6 discusses the Future Research Direction and Sect. 7 covers the Discussion and Conclusion.

1.1 Research Questions

To achieve the objective of this Systematic Review, we proposed five (5) research questions to provide a guide in reviewing previous literature which are:

1. What are the current state-of-the-art applications of Virtual Reality (VR) in Crime Scene Investigation (CSI)?
2. What are the trends in research related to VR in Crime Scene Investigations?
3. What are the current gaps in the literature that need to be focused on?
4. What are the future research directions for integrating VR into forensic science, and
5. How can existing technologies be enhanced to better meet the operational needs of investigators and legal practitioners?

2 Global Applications of VR Technology

Virtual Reality (VR) has seen wide adoption across education, healthcare, engineering, and other fields since 2020 to enhance learning, improve design processes, train workers in hazardous tasks, and entertain users in novel ways. This section highlights current applications in several major fields, demonstrating VR's versatility.

2.1 Education and Training

Virtual Reality (VR) has a huge impact in Education and Training. VRs immersive and interactive nature enables experiential learning that can be difficult to achieve in a traditional classroom. This means that Students can be placed in virtual environments that simulate real-world scenarios and allowing learning by doing in a safe space. A meta-analysis carried out by [16] found a significant improvement in student engagement using VR with mean effect size $g = 0.85$ compared to conventional learning.

Ihekweazu et al. [19] proposed integrating virtual reality (VR) into digital forensics education to enhance hands-on learning, especially in institutions with limited resources. By developing a photogrammetric, scenario-based VR environments aligned with standard digital forensics curricula to provide immersive, interactive experiences that improve student engagement, knowledge retention, and practical skills.

In K–12 education, VR has shown promising results in STEM instruction, Naji et al. [36] conducted a systematic review of VR-based interventions in preparatory schools and found small but highly significant improvements in the learning outcomes. Similarly, Lin et al. [4,31] reinforced this through their experiment and showed that VR increases classroom engagement, most especially for students who struggle with traditional learning and teaching methods. These studies emphasized that VR supports diverse learning styles and can make theoretical concepts more meaningful or easier to understand.

Yang et al. [53] conducted a meta-analysis on the effectiveness of VR in science and engineering education and showed that students learning through VR simulations gained better practical skills than those in the traditional settings. These virtual labs allow learners to visualize complex 3D models, repeat experiments safely, and build confidence especially in fields like physics, biology, and engineering.

Beyond the formal education, VR is also widely being adopted in corporate and vocational training. Stefan et al. [49] and Scorgie et al. [49] reviewed VR safety training programs and conducted a meta-analysis which showed that VR is more effective than the conventional methods in improving safety knowledge and compliance as the participants retained higher safety procedures than those trained with lectures or videos.

Furthermore, Abdelhay [1] found that VR improves employee training outcomes by enhancing user engagement and immersion. Cognitive engagement was found to bring together the effectiveness of VR modules, technical and interpersonal development. Across both educational and training domains, studies consistently show more learner satisfaction, higher retention, and effective skill acquisition when using VR. As VR becomes more accessible, it will potentially become a core technology in classrooms, universities, and even workforce development programs.

2.2 Healthcare

VR has become as a transformative tool in healthcare by enhancing medical training, patient rehabilitation, and health monitoring. Recent studies have highlighted the diverse applications and benefits of VR in this sector.

Rajeswaran et al. developed AirwayVR, a VR simulator for endotracheal intubation that addresses limitations of manikin–based training. This was described as an introductory platform to learn and practice intubation in VR for beginners and also a training tool for expert clinicians to mentally practice complex cases.

Ajmera et al. [2] carried out a survey in AR/VR in healthcare and listed practical lessons from VR development, such as immersive simulations requiring different type of infrastructure like the head-mounted displays and tracking than the regular software. They highlighted some challenges such as latency and user discomfort, and suggested that emerging methodologies or techniques such as AI or deep-learning can help smoothen the VR experience for clinical training.

VR has now broadly used in rehabilitation and therapy. A study by Khan et al. [27] on motor rehabilitation after stroke showed that VR is as safe and effective as an substitute to conventional therapy and recommended that there are benefits in the VR recovery exercises and it should be routinely used for upper and lower limb motor recovery.

Interactive VR programs in managing chronic pain have shown high engagement as described by Griffin et al. [14] who piloted a VR intervention known as Fruity Feet; aimed for youth with chronic pain. The participants from the study reported distraction from pain, improved mobility, and also fewer pain behaviors during VR sessions. The authors concluded that VR has great potential as a tool to be used in chronic pain treatment in a manner that is very effective and interactive while providing positive results.

Safikhani et al. [44] reviewed VR for psychiatric therapy and observed that VR exposure and simulation of emotional stressful scenarios such as anxiety resulted in patient improvements compared to conventional therapy, with long term goals. Simulation of the social situations or environments provides patients with a platform to safely practice the coping mechanisms, and this also reflects on how VR is emerging as additional rehabilitation or treatment methods with more research and trials.

An interesting emerging research is also exploring VR in diagnostics and health monitoring such as in the cognitive assessment in dementia. Yondjo et al. [54] states that health professionals see VR diagnostic tools as innovative and offer higher external validity than traditional method of assessment. The result highlighted the benefits in VR while expressing concerns about the cost, time required in creating the systems the validation of new VR tools.

Following this research trend, researchers are developing immersive VR assessment for conditions such as for dementia, delirium, ADHD that can patient behavior and performance in virtual tasks. Approaches like this indicate that VR may become a substitute or even replace traditional diagnostics as Sharma et al. [46] discussed how VR is a promising platform for health monitoring and patient engagement, visualizing that immersive systems that can be built to record patient biometrics during VR experiences and also provide interactive health feedback.

2.3 Entertainment and Media

Virtual reality has redefined user engagement in entertainment from gaming to offering deeply immersive audiovisual experiences. Onderdijk et al. [37] examined a live VR concert experiences and found that users wearing headsets felt significantly more present and emotionally connected to performers than those using 2D video formats. Similarly, Carpio-Alfsen et al. [5] studied interactive VR films and showed that 360° immersive formats brought out higher emotional involvement and enjoyment than the traditional on-screen viewing.

Beyond music and film, VR has transformed journalism and storytelling. Iyer [20] analyzed immersive journalism with COVID-19 in perspective and concluded that VR and 360° news stories enhanced users' sense of reality, credibility, and empathy when compared to conventional formats. These findings support the broader idea that embodied experiences in VR increase engagement.

2.4 Architecture and Design

Virtual and augmented reality technologies have become vital tools in the design and review of architectural spaces. Elbadawy et al. [10] emphasized how VR enables real-time collaboration, spatial walkthroughs, and immersive visualization of buildings before construction begins. This not only improves design accuracy but also enhances stakeholder communication.

In a systematic review by Zhang and Huang [56] found that integrating extended reality (XR) into architectural education improved students' spatial understanding and creativity while Hsu et al. [18] developed a VR-based interactive critique system that allowed users collaborate to annotate 3D designs. The study showed that the participants experienced greater engagement, improved communication, and there were fewer design misinterpretation.

This highlights how the use of VR in architecture improves communication and feedback loops, design iterations, and a more efficient real-world planning.

2.5 Industry and Workforce Training

Industrial sectors have embraced VR and AR for training in respect of their safety, scalability, and interactivity. Morales [35] reviewed XR applications in manufacturing, such as Computer Numerical Control (CNC) machine simulators, and found they reduced reliance on physical hardware while improving trainee competence. These XR tools offer repeatable, self-paced modules in addition to real-time error correction and analytics.

In a separate study on occupational safety, Rahman et al. [38] compared traditional electrical safety training with a VR-based curriculum. The VR group demonstrated higher knowledge retention and hazard recognition accuracy than the traditional training. These findings suggest that immersive VR not only enhances technical skill acquisition but also improves workplace safety awareness.

2.6 Emerging VR Applications

VR is also making positive changes through virtual experiences in tourism, sports, and real estate. In real estate, Xiong et al. [52] found that homes listed in addition with VR tours sold 6.4percent faster and with fewer price negotiations, highlighting how immersive walkthroughs increase a buyer's confidence. In sports, Li et al. [30] reviewed VR applications in combat sports and showed significant progress in athletes' reaction time, technique, and tactical decision-making.

3 Methodology

This paper follows a systematic review of 40 research articles to identify, analyze, and group relevant literature on Virtual Reality (VR) in Crime Scene Investigation (CSI). The methodology was designed to ensure the inclusion of peer-reviewed, high-quality, and recent publications within the target period. This section was performed in the following steps shown in Fig. 1.

3.1 Study Characteristics of Reviewed Papers

The systematic review encompassed 27 studies spanning the years 2020–2025. These included a mix of case studies, prototype implementations, empirical evaluations, and conceptual frameworks. Approximately one-third of the studies were case-based, focusing on specific forensic investigations where VR or 3D reconstruction was applied. Another segment concentrated on prototype systems developed and tested in controlled environments, while several empirical

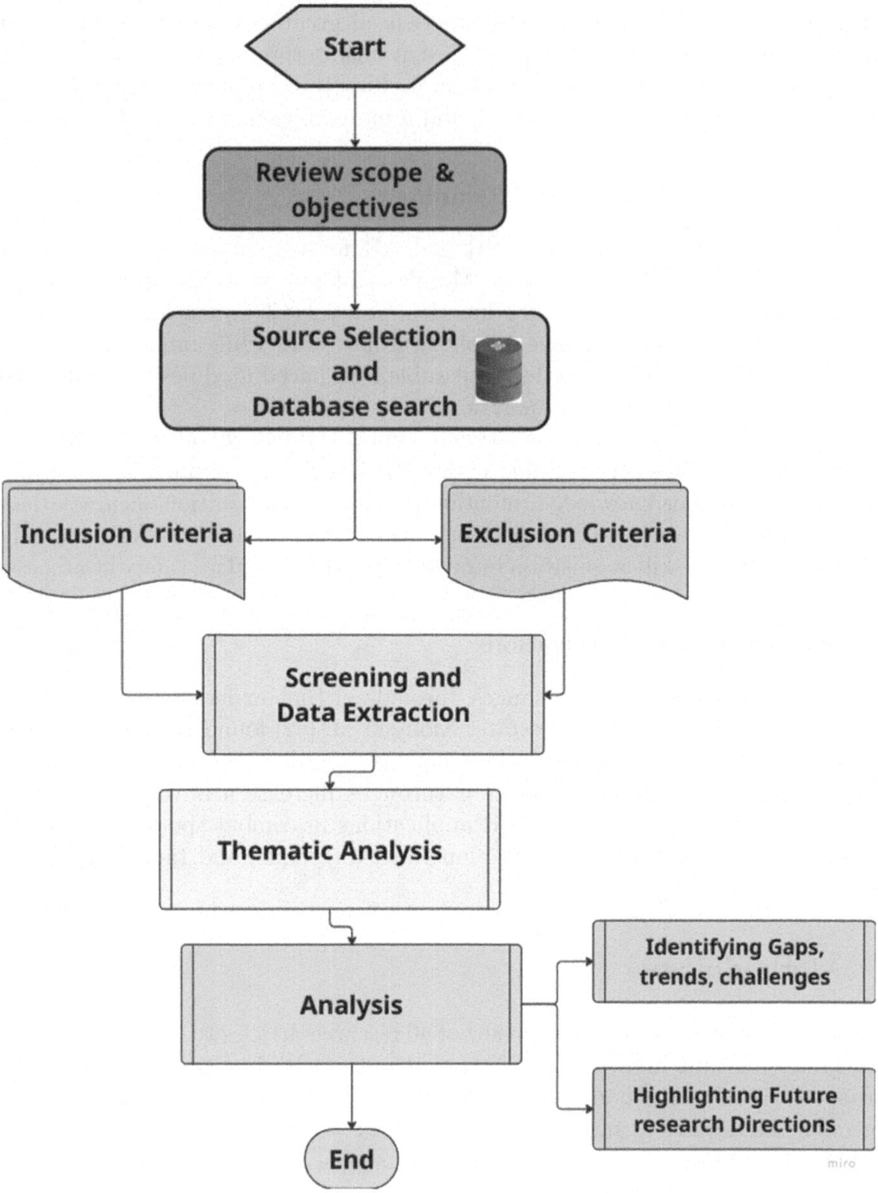

Fig. 1. Methodology for Systematic Review

evaluations assessed the usability and performance of VR tools. In terms of geographical and institutional distribution, contributions were diverse, with research groups spanning North America, Europe, and Asia, reflecting a growing global interest in applying VR to forensic science.

3.2 Definition of Research Scope and Objectives

The review was guided by predefined 5 research questions focused on understanding the state-of-the-art in VR for CSI, identifying existing tools and methods, assessing trends and gaps, and recommending future research directions. The scope was set and limited to peer-reviewed articles published in the last five years 2020–2025.

3.3 Source Selection and Database Search

Relevant literature was collected from the following academic databases: IEEE Xplore Digital Library, ScienceDirect (Elsevier), Springer Nature, ACM Digital Library, and Google Scholar.

The structured search was conducted on 26–28 March 2025 and limited to peer-reviewed English publications from 2020–2025. Representative Boolean queries adapted to each database's syntax were:

> ("virtual reality" OR VR OR "mixed reality" OR XR) AND ("crime scene investigation" OR forensic*) AND (training OR reconstruction OR courtroom OR "evidence presentation")

All retrieved records ($n = 42$) were exported to Zotero and deduplicated ($n = 2$ *duplicates removed*) and then full texts ($n = 13$ *excluded*), arriving at a final record of 27 studies. A PRISMA-style selection flow (Fig. 2) summarizes these stages.

3.4 Inclusion and Exclusion Criteria

The collated papers were screened through the inclusion and exclusion criteria to ensure the articles used matched the research objective and the inclusion criteria, as shown in Fig. 3. Out of 40 articles that were collated, 27 passed the inclusion criteria, and 13 papers were excluded.

3.5 Screening and Data Extraction

Titles and abstracts were screened to assess relevance. Full-text analysis was conducted on selected papers to extract the following key attributes:

- Application domain (training, reconstruction, courtroom use)
- Methods or tools used (e.g., Unity, Unreal, photogrammetry)
- Type of VR system (desktop VR, headset-based VR, mixed reality)
- Presence of standards or validation protocols
- Challenges, limitations, or future directions discussed

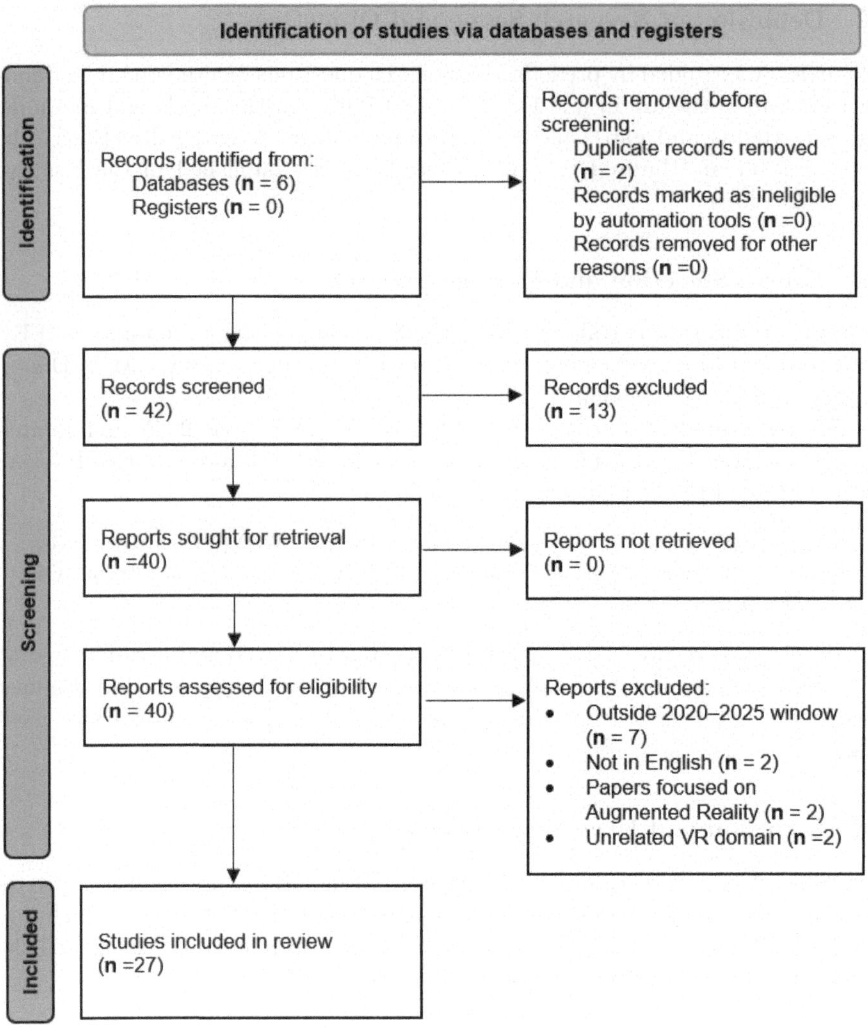

Fig. 2. PRISMA Flow Diagram[15]

Inclusion Criteria	Exclusion Criteria
Peer-reviewed articles and conference papers	Non-peer-reviewed blogs, editorials
Focus on VR in forensic science or CSI	Articles on AR/MR unless combined with VR
Descriptions of tools, methods, frameworks, or validation studies	Papers on VR in unrelated domains such as fitness, pure entertainment etc.
Studies using simulations, object detection, 3D modeling in forensic context	Works published before 2020

Fig. 3. Inclusion and Exclusion Criteria

3.6 Thematic Analysis and Synthesis

The selected papers were grouped into themes:

- Training and simulation
- Crime scene reconstruction and analysis
- Evidence presentation in court
- Standards, Frameworks and Tools
- AI and object detection integration

4 VR in Crime Scene Investigations

Virtual reality (VR) has been widely adopted as a teaching and training tool in forensic science and crime scene investigation education. Several studies highlight the development and evaluation of immersive VR platforms to teach crime scene processing and forensic principles.

4.1 VR-Based Forensic Training and Education

Mayne et al. [34] demonstrated VR crime–scene simulators that allow students to practice evidence collection in photorealistic, interactive environments, alleviating limitations of physical crime–scene labs. Engström et al. [11] and Khalilia et al. [25] mention that multidisciplinary VR training systems, such as the RISEN project, that integrate realistic 3D models of crime scenes and learning exercises showed high student engagement and satisfaction. Likewise, customized VR experiences have been designed for specific domains; for instance Kader et al. [24] built a WebVR crime–scene for chemistry students to explore forensic chemistry concepts, and Ewais et al. [12] implemented VR simulations of a DNA laboratory and a CSI scene in a molecular biology course and found that VR instruction can match or even surpass traditional methods in conveying complex scientific content. Some empirical studies have corroborated the pedagogical value of VR. Hassenfeldt et al. [17] found no deficiency in the learning outcomes when students learned and performed digital forensics tasks in VR vs. real labs, achieving faster task completion in VR, while Chen et al. [6] outline high usability and positive learning apprehension in VR–based forensic courses.

The proposed framework by Ihekweazu et al. [19] for integrating VR into digital forensics education includes modules on crime scene investigation, evidence handling, and legal procedures, while offering a cost-effective and scalable solution to address the shortage of practical training in digital forensics programs. The authors conclude that VR technology can significantly enrich digital forensics education by providing realistic simulations that prepare students for real-world challenges.

In summary, immersive VR allows repeated, costeffective, and safe practice of crime–scene workflows such as evidence tagging, scene sketching, crime scene analysis, and is efficient and enhances students' understanding of the practical CSI skills.

4.2 VR in Crime Scene Reconstruction and Visualization

Another research focus is Crime Scene Reconstruction and analysis using VR tools. Systematic reviews by Maneli et al. [33] emphasize 3D reconstruction techniques for forensic scenes, such as point clouds from LiDAR sensors or photogrammetry and VR visualization. A multi-modal modeling approach by Villa et al. [51] combines victim imaging and 3D room scans to create immersive reconstructions of crime incidents.

Engström [11] highlights how VR presentation using Head–Mounted Displays (HMD) allows investigators to virtually walk through a crime scene with natural navigation and tools for annotation, providing a more intuitive exploration than the traditional 2D media.

Case studies further explain the benefits, as Rinaldi et al. [41] used a photogrammetry–to–VR workflow in an arson crime reconstruction. The study observed that the immersive review improved forensic-related decision–making, and professionals could form more confident hypotheses with fewer caveats when using the VR model. Deshmukh et al. [8] in emerging research focus on integrated advanced sensing and Artificial Intelligence (AI) called CrimeVerse combines LIDAR scanning with VR to document and explore crime scenes, while Zappalà et al. [55] in a similar way proposed a client–server system where a photogrammetric 3D crime scene in VR is paired with deep-learning AI Faster R-CNN (a computer vision algorithm) to automatically identify evidential objects. A review of geospatial VR by Razali et al. [39] similarly reiterates the need to integrate laser scans and point-cloud VR to improve measurement and user experience in CSI. Collectively, these contributions show how VR-based reconstructions have enhanced crime scene comprehension, measurement accuracy, and even data sharing among investigators.

4.3 Advanced VR Technologies and Applications

There is recent research that explores combining VR with emerging technologies and gamified experiences in CSI, such as integrating Augmented reality (AR) into Virtual Reality (VR). Albeedan et al. [3] did a review on VR/AR systems that overlay forensic data, such as bloodstain visualizations, onto the physical or virtual scenes to enrich investigations. On the borderline of AI, Zappalà et al. [55] demonstrated that deep–learning object detection can be integrated with VR reconstructions to automatically highlight and tag evidentiary items, accelerating analysis of complex crime scenes, for example, hazardous crime scenes. Gamification and interactive VR games have also been applied to education in Criminology, as Gerard et al. [13] described the pilot study of the CrimOPS project as an immersive simulation of VR crime operations for criminology students, using gamified scenarios to assess participation and learning. Similarly, Silva et al. [48] built an immersive VR scenario using Unreal Engine for postgraduate forensic courses, where the students could freely roam and tag evidence. The participants found it engaging and highly motivating, thereby improving learning and skills. These approaches can be achieved because VR is versatile and interconnected. An instance of this is CrimeVerse [8], which provides tools to virtually explore the crime scene for evidence documentation; some solutions enable users to reconstruct crime logic using interactive puzzles and clues.

Advanced VR technology and integration of AR, AI and gamification improve the realistic feel, the engagement and analysis efficiency in virtual crime scene applications.

4.4 Tools Used for VR in CSI

There are a wide range of tools used in VR for CSI, providing the investigators with the possibility of using new methods such as photogrammetry and laser scanning to recreate crime scenes to mimic real-world scenes, while making investigation and analysis interactive. Some of the tools that have been used in previous experiments are listed in Table 1, highlighting their function, the component, and how they are relevant.

4.5 Frameworks Used for VR in CSI

Research in VR crime scene investigation (CSI) proposed modular system architectures or workflows in two phases:

- Data Preparation – capturing the scene through photogrammetry or scanning and processing it into a 3D model; and

Table 1. Tools and Components for VR-based Crime Scene Investigation

Component	Tools	Function/Role	Notes
3D Scene Capture	Photogrammetry (DSLR, smartphone + Agisoft, Metashape) [47], Terrestrial/Handheld LiDAR	Captures detailed geometry of scene and evidence	Produces 3D mesh or point cloud models for reconstruction
Portable Capture	iPad Pro (scanning apps), Recap, 3DF Zephyr [47,55]	Mobile, on-site 3D capture	Useful for rapid or field-based documentation
Preprocessing	Leica Cyclone, FARO Scene, CloudCompare [40,41,47]	Mesh/point cloud processing and cleanup	Prepares data for further visualization and analysis
VR Development	Unity3D, Unreal Engine, custom apps [40,55]	VR scene creation and interaction	Supports immersive navigation, evidence annotation, and scenario simulation
VR Hardware	Meta Quest 2, Oculus, Vive, HMDs, Microsoft HoloLens 2 [40,41]	Immersive visualization and interaction	Mixed reality (MR) hardware used for training and collaborative walkthroughs
VR Toolkits/Standards	OpenXR, MRTK 2.0 (for HoloLens) [3]	Platform compatibility and device integration	Ensures cross-device support and standardized development

- Data Utilization – loading the 3D model into a VR application for investigation, analysis or training [47,51].

This workflow includes aligning and scaling 3D models and also many VR CSI systems adopt a client–server setup, where a Unity-based VR client is referred to as the environment laboratory and streams the user interactions to a backend server that manages 3D models and evidence metadata [41]. This architecture also allows multiple users to access and interact with the same crime scene model through a networked database [40,55]. Albeedan et al. [3] presented a mixed-reality training system built in Unity/MRTK, featuring sequential modules like briefing and evidence collection, all connected to a detailed 3D scene. Other conceptual frameworks expand on this by integrating various forensic data types-such as CT/MRI scans, 3D models, and photographs into unified VR toolkits for comprehensive visualization. Additionally, educational frameworks, including experiential learning stages, are often incorporated to enhance the design and effectiveness of VR-based forensic training [3,51].

4.6 Standards for VR in CSI

VR CSI systems are designed to uphold evidence integrity and legal reliability by embedding validation and security measures throughout the workflow. Researchers enhance forensic credibility by attaching original photographs and reference data to 3D reconstructions, maintaining secured repositories with digital certificates, and using open standards like OpenXR to ensure interoperability and cross-platform use [28,40]. While legal standards such as chain-of-custody protocols, Daubert Standard, or ISO/IEC 17025 accreditation are rarely implemented in prototypes, research emphasizes the importance of audit trails, clear evidence labeling, and accurate documentation to support courtroom admissibility and assist jurors in a better understanding of evidence [41]. Additionally, safety and ergonomic guidelines are relevant for training applications, though it is not widely detailed in current literature. Overall, these practices align VR CSI research with established forensic standards, aiming to make virtual reconstructions both admissible and dependable in legal contexts.

4.7 Datasets

Most research in forensic science related to VR relies on custom or synthetic datasets, typically created by capturing mock crime scenes with photogrammetry or laser scanning. These high-detail 3D models, often generated from thousands of images or scans, enable realistic and immersive virtual reconstructions for analysis and training. While a few specialized datasets exist, public access remains limited, and researchers frequently develop their own scene models using standardized protocols. Table 2 describes the different datasets used for CSI research in VR.

4.8 AI Integration and Machine Learning Models in VR CSI

AI-driven object detection is increasingly being integrated into VR-based crime scene investigation, integrating deep learning models like YOLO, Faster R-CNN, and SSD to automatically identify and classify evidence within virtual environments. Studies such as Zappalà et al. [55] have demonstrated the effectiveness of this approach, using a client-server VR system where scene images are processed by a pretrained Faster R-CNN to accurately localize multiple object classes, achieving high detection rates in test scenarios. Similarly, research by Kishore et al. [28] and others highlights the advantages of combining CNN feature extraction with YOLO, enabling real-time, highly accurate detection of forensic objects, which is both fast and suitable for practical applications.

These AI-enhanced systems not only automate the process of identifying weapons, prints, or other key evidence but also reduce the need for manual review and mitigate human bias. By incorporating tools such as virtual rulers and automated measurement, modern VR-CSI platforms streamline scene analysis, improve documentation, and support more efficient and reliable forensic investigations.

Table 2. Datasets and Methods in VR-CSI Research

Study/Source	Scene/Dataset	Capture Method(s)	Main Contribution
Rinaldi et al. [41].	Simulated indoor crime scene	Photogrammetry (1,044 RAW images, Sony ILCE-7SM2)	High-detail 3D model for VR analysis and training
Albeedan et al. [3]	Full-scale training houses	FARO Focus3D X130 laser scanning	Immersive VR environments for CSI training
LRCFS "Udgård III – Portlethen" [29,42,43]	Fire scene reconstructions	LiDAR, Matterport, photos, videos, sensors	Comprehensive fire scene dataset for VR analysis
Sazaly et al. [45]	Indoor mock crime scene	Micro-UAV (DJI Mini 2), photogrammetry	Rapid 3D modeling in confined spaces
CSAFE [7]	Various forensic evidence	Various (not VR-specific)	Open datasets for forensic tool development/validation

5 Findings and Analysis

5.1 Current State-of-the-Art and Trend

Recent research on VR in crime scene investigation centers on three main areas: training and simulation, scene reconstruction and analysis, and evidence presentation. VR-based training simulations have been shown to effectively enhance the skills and preparedness of both professionals and students by providing immersive, interactive crime scene scenarios. Multiple studies highlight the benefits of these VR environments in improving investigative procedures and outcomes [22,33,34].

Training platforms in VR-based crime scene investigation now incorporate highly realistic, laser-scanned replicas of real scenes, allowing trainees to practice evidence collection in immersive, life-like environments[16]. These systems have demonstrated superior trainee engagement and skill development compared to traditional classroom methods, a trend that accelerated during the COVID-19 pandemic as remote and virtual training became essential. Overall, VR tools offer safe, repeatable, and cost-effective practice opportunities, eliminating risks of contaminating real scenes and reducing the need for physical mock-ups [3,34,41].

A growing trend in crime scene investigation is the use of VR for scene capture, reconstruction, and analysis. By integrating technologies such as 3D laser scanning, photogrammetry, and 360° photography, investigators can create highly detailed digital replicas of crime scenes for import into VR systems [33]. This approach not only preserves the spatial context and fine details of the original scene, enabling virtual walkthroughs long after the site is cleared, but also allows for the safe examination of complex or hazardous environments [3]. Additionally, VR platforms encourage the integration of diverse forms of evidence, such as bloodstain patterns, bullet trajectories, and LIDAR point clouds into a single immersive model, supporting comprehensive analysis, event reconstruction, and hypothesis testing [22,32].

Engström's research [11] demonstrates that VR with head-mounted displays enables investigators to navigate and annotate crime scenes more intuitively than traditional photographs or sketches. Case studies, such as Rinaldi et al. [41], show that immersive VR workflows can enhance forensic decision-making by reducing uncertainty during scene analysis. Beyond training and investigation, VR is also being explored as a tool for presenting and sharing crime scene evidence, offering the possibility for investigators and jurors to virtually experience reconstructed scenes in three dimensions.

Although still in its early stages, the use of VR reconstructions in legal settings shows promise for more effectively conveying spatial relationships and evidence layouts compared to traditional 2D photographs. Pilot projects have begun to investigate this application, but widespread adoption in courtrooms remains limited due to unresolved policy and legal standards regarding admissibility and validation [9,21]. Nevertheless, VR enables collaborative inspection of crime scenes, allowing multiple investigators or experts-even those in different locations, to simultaneously examine and discuss the virtual environment, which can enhance the thoroughness and accuracy of forensic analysis.

Zappalà et al. [55] developed a client–server VR system that integrates a pre-trained Faster R-CNN deep learning model to automatically detect and highlight potential evidence within a 3D reconstructed crime scene. Their approach enables faster and more objective identification of relevant objects, assisting investigators-especially those with less experience, drawing attention to items that might otherwise be overlooked, and reducing subjective bias and contamination risk. Experimental results in simulated environments show the system effectively recognizes evidentiary objects, supporting timely and detailed scene analysis, particularly in hazardous or complex cases.

Beyond automated analysis, VR is increasingly being used for interactive and engaging forensic education. Serious games and gamified VR platforms, such as Gerard et al.'s [13] "CrimOPS" and Silva et al.'s [48] Unreal Engine-based interactive crime scene, have demonstrated improved motivation, participation, and learning outcomes among students and trainees. These developments reflect a broader trend of employing VR not just for passive viewing, but as a dynamic, hands-on medium for both investigation and forensic science education.

5.2 Current Gaps and Research

Existing and ongoing studies have highlighted several challenges that prevent the widespread adoption of Virtual Reality (VR) in crime scene investigation (CSI) [3]. Despite VR's promise for enhancing forensic training, scene reconstruction, and evidence analysis, progress is limited by technical, methodological, educational, and legal barriers [40,41]. Table 3 summarizes the key gaps identified in the current literature, highlighting areas that require further research and coordinated effort to realize the full potential of VR in forensic science [45].

5.3 Challenges VR in Crime Scene

Traditional CSI Challenges. Crime scene investigators are often faced with major challenges in evidence handling and documentation due to contamination, human error, and inadequate training. Improper equipment use and poor sterile technique can introduce foreign DNA or damage samples. While standard photography and sketches are affordable and rely on operator skill, advanced 3D laser scanning provides detailed digital records but requires costly equipment and specialized training. Both traditional and modern methods have strengths and limitations, making proper training essential to minimize errors and ensure high-quality evidence [4,50].

Table 3. Key Gaps and Challenges in VR-Based Crime Scene Investigation (VR-CSI) Research

Category	Key Gaps and Challenges
Technical	– VR CSI tools are often custom-built and lack integration with advanced AI analytics. – High-quality 3D data capture (e.g., LiDAR, photogrammetry) is costly and complex. – Scarcity of standardized, high-quality datasets for development and benchmarking.
Methodological	– No widely accepted protocols for virtual scene reconstruction and analysis. – Inconsistent practices complicate system validation and comparison across agencies.
Educational	– Limited scope of studies evaluating VR training's impact on user performance and experience. – Lack of standard frameworks for integrating VR into forensic curricula. – Adoption remains fragmented, mostly isolated pilots rather than broad implementation.
Policy & Legal	– Uncertainty about the legal admissibility of VR-generated evidence due to a lack of validation and judicial guidelines. – Need for standardized procedures to ensure fidelity and objectivity before courtroom use.
Overall Need	– Coordinated research and collaboration needed to advance tool integration, data standards, education, and legal acceptance.

Key traditional challenges include:

1. Preventing contamination is a major challenge, as errors like not using sterile kits or failing to change gloves can cause cross-contamination and jeopardize legal cases. Ongoing hands-on training and strict adherence to protocols are essential to minimize such mistakes [4].
2. Accurate documentation: Recording a crime scene completely and accurately is difficult in the field. Conventional capturing a crime scene accurately is difficult; while 2D photos and sketches are quick and cheap, they often miss spatial details, and advanced 3D tools require expertise and can introduce new errors if misused. Although observers prefer 3D videos, standard photographs currently yield higher correct identification rates [50].
3. Chain-of-custody integrity: Maintaining a complete and unbroken chain of custody is crucial, as any gaps can lead to evidence being excluded in court. Electronic tracking systems and regular audits are recommended to improve traceability and reduce record-keeping errors [4].
4. Resource and training limitations: Many crime scene units lack sufficient equipment, staff, and training, forcing reliance on outdated methods and risking evidence loss or contamination. Budget and staffing shortages can delay scene access and limit the adoption of advanced forensic technologies [26,33].

CSI Challenges with Virtual Reality and Digital Technologies. Digital tools such as VR, AR, and 3D reconstruction provide advanced capabilities for crime scene analysis, enabling detailed virtual environments and collaborative investigations [21]. These technologies can integrate various imaging methods and allow investigators to revisit and analyze scenes from any angle, potentially streamlining casework. However, they are expensive, technically complex, and can be affected by environmental factors that introduce errors or artifacts in the virtual models. To avoid misinterpretation, accurate measurements and verification procedures must be used to ensure virtual scenes accurately reflect reality [23].

1. System accuracy and bias: Technologies like VR and LiDAR are faced with accuracy challenges, having error margins ranging from millimeters to meters, depending on the target size, potentially distorting key evidence measurements. Device inconsistencies also complicate result standardization. Additionally, immersive simulations present the possibility of confirmation bias, as users may over-trust or subconsciously "fill in" gaps in reconstructions. Experts emphasize the need to address these limitations and actively mitigate biases, particularly when presenting 3D visualizations in legal settings [21,23].
2. Data integrity and legal concerns: Digital crime-scene data must be protected just like physical evidence, and maintaining an unbroken digital chain-of-custody is vital for admissibility. In order to address this, researchers are exploring blockchain or NFT-based (Non-Fungible Tokens) ledger systems to timestamp and certify virtual evidence [21]. Theoretically, such systems can

create tamper-evident records of all actions on a piece of digital evidence, but in practice, no solution is foolproof, as adversaries may still exploit vulnerabilities. D'Anna et al. [9] recommended a combination of security measures, such as blockchain and hashing, strong encryption, as well as access controls and audit logs.

3. Operational and adoption issues: Implementing VR and digital tools in crime scene investigations is costly and also requires specific or specialized training; for instance, 3D scanners cost much more than traditional cameras. Also, legal acceptance of VR is still evolving, as jurors often express skepticism about the authenticity of VR reconstructions without clear protocols and expert testimony. The adoption of these technologies demands careful planning, validation, and justification of expenses [9].

6 Future Research Directions

Building on the current state of the art, several directions for future research in VR-based crime scene investigation have been identified:

1. Advanced AI Integration and Automation: One important future direction for VR crime scene tools is the enhanced integration of AI and machine learning to enable automated evidence detection, scene analysis, and hypothesis generation within virtual environments. While early prototypes are promising, further research is needed to improve the accuracy, reliability, and explainability of these AI-driven features so that investigators can confidently trust and adopt them in practice.
2. Augmented/Mixed Reality and Multi-Sensor Data Fusion: Future crime scene investigation platforms are expected to integrate VR and augmented reality, creating a mixed reality continuum that allows investigators to overlay virtual data onto physical scenes or bring real-world context into immersive simulations [3]. This fusion can enhance the investigative process by enabling features like superimposed evidence trajectories or the visualization of missing objects, while also supporting the integration of diverse data sources such as 3D scans, drone imagery, and thermal images with accurate spatial alignment.
3. Standardization and Validation Protocols: A key priority highlighted in the literature is the development of standardized procedures for validating and using VR reconstructions in official investigations. Future research should focus on establishing protocols for verifying the accuracy and fidelity of virtual crime scenes, such as defining acceptable measurement error margins and validating VR simulations against physical evidence [23]. Creating reference datasets, benchmarking scenarios, and formal guidelines-potentially overseen by professional bodies-will support quality assurance, transparency, and effective training, ultimately ensuring that VR-generated evidence is as reliable and trusted as traditional forensic documentation.
4. Security and Chain-of-Custody for Virtual Evidence: As digital reconstruction tools become more prevalent in crime scene investigation, ensuring the

integrity and security of virtual evidence is essential. Future research should explore technologies like blockchain to create immutable, auditable records of every action taken on virtual crime scene models, while also developing secure storage and access control solutions for large 3D datasets [9]. By prioritizing cybersecurity and robust chain-of-custody measures, these efforts will help build trust in VR-based evidence and support its eventual admissibility in court.

5. Expanding Training Efficacy and Adoption Studies: While VR has shown clear benefits for crime scene training in pilot studies, broader research is needed to assess its long-term effectiveness and real-world impact on investigator performance. Future work should focus on integrating VR into standard forensic education, developing assessment tools, and exploring collaborative, multi-agency training scenarios, while also addressing practical barriers like cost, usability, and trainee acceptance. By establishing best practices and documenting successful implementations, researchers can help transition VR training from isolated pilots to widespread, evidence-based adoption in forensic education and law enforcement [39,48].
6. Legal Admissibility and Ethical Considerations: For VR to be routinely used in crime scene investigations, its legal admissibility must be addressed through targeted research and policy development. Collaborations with legal experts and forensic authorities are needed to establish clear protocols for introducing VR reconstructions in court, including guidelines for expert testimony and transparent visualization of evidence [9]. Studies suggest that jurors may be skeptical of virtual evidence without proper context, highlighting the need for standards that ensure accuracy, clarity, and prevent potential bias in courtroom presentations.
7. Ethics and privacy are increasingly important considerations as VR crime scene reconstructions often contain sensitive information and depictions of victims. Establishing clear guidelines on data access, retention, and usage is essential to protect privacy rights and prevent potential misuse or prejudice. Proactive, interdisciplinary research involving technologists, ethicists, and legal experts will be crucial for developing robust ethical frameworks, which can guide responsible policy and facilitate the broader, responsible adoption of VR tools in both investigations and courtroom settings.

Table 4. Comparative Analysis of VR-Based Crime Scene Investigation (CSI) Training Systems

Study	Application Domain	Hardware Used	Platform/ Framework	Evaluation Metrics	Key Outcomes/ Limitations
Albeedan et al. [3]	CSI Training (Mixed Reality)	HoloLens 2	Unity + MRTK	Time to Finish (TTF), TAM, user feedback	High usability and engagement; limited field of view (FOV)
Rinaldi et al. [41]	Arson Scene Review	Meta Quest 2	Unity + OpenXR	Expert validation, qualitative interviews	Enhanced spatial understanding; lacks haptic feedback
Halford et al. [16]	Police Trainee Simulation	Oculus Quest	Unity	Usability ratings, realism scores	Positive user perception; minor motion sickness reported
Ewais et al. [12]	Forensic Biology Education	HTC Vive Pro	Unity	Knowledge retention tests, user surveys	High retention levels; high-cost VR hardware
Gerard et al. [13]	Criminology Education (Game-Based)	Oculus Rift S	Unreal Engine 4	Motivation scale, engagement indicators	Increased motivation; lacks procedural depth
Villa et al. [51]	Victim Scene Training	Desktop VR	Blender + Unity	Expert review, realism scoring	High scene detail; absence of immersive HMD use
Silva et al. [48]	Postgraduate CSI Training	Desktop + VR	Unreal Engine	Observational logs, post-session debriefs	Improved evidence recognition; limited quantitative evaluation

7 Discussion and Conclusion

This review has synthesized the state-of-the-art applications of Virtual Reality (VR) in crime scene investigation (CSI), emphasizing its role in training, scene reconstruction, and evidence analysis. Across the surveyed studies, VR consistently enhances investigative efficiency, engagement, and accuracy while offering controlled, repeatable environments for skill development. At the same time, the findings reveal persistent barriers to large-scale adoption, particularly regarding workflow standardization, legal admissibility, and the validation of AI-integrated features.Table 4 summarizes the core characteristics, reported outcomes, and limitations of each system, offering insights into design choices and research gap.

7.1 Comparative Synthesis of Reviewed Studies

While the preceding sections summarize individual works, a cross-study synthesis clarifies how methods, outcomes, and limitations differ.

- **Methodological contrasts:** From the 27 papers systematically reviewed in this study, about one third relied on photogrammetry (high visual realism, moderate cost), another third used LiDAR or terrestrial scanning (metric accuracy, but higher equipment expense), and the remainder experimented

with game-engine or mixed-reality solutions (rapid prototyping and interactivity). Sample sizes varied widely from small pilot evaluations of fewer than ten participants to large cohort trainings involving more participants, which reflects different priorities in proof-of-concept compared with operational deployment.
- **Outcome variability:** Reported benefits included reduced crime scene processing time (20–60%), improved trainee engagement and retention, and greater accuracy in evidence location and measurement. Yet, [21,55] these gains were not uniform: LiDAR-heavy projects tended to report the strongest spatial precision, whereas low-cost photogrammetry studies focused on accessibility and training reach.
- **Shared limitations:** Across all categories, the authors of the reviewed studies identified common limitations, such as incomplete courtroom validation, absence of universal file standards, and difficulty maintaining an unbroken digital chain of custody. Only a few examined long-term knowledge retention or cross-jurisdictional scalability [9].
- **Implications:** Together, these contrasts highlight that technological choice (photogrammetry vs. LiDAR vs. Mixed Reality) [47] is often dictated by budget, required accuracy, and intended evidentiary use rather than by a single best practice. A more rigorous, comparative research study will help establish when each approach is most appropriate.

7.2 Underlying Causes of Legal and Technical Challenges

Although challenges such as legal admissibility are widely recognized, their root causes remain underexplored. Issues of evidentiary acceptance often arise from the absence of established legal precedents involving VR reconstructions, leading courts to exercise caution in their use as trial evidence [9]. Technical hurdles compound this hesitation: maintaining an unbroken chain of custody in VR-based reconstructions is inherently more complex than in traditional forensic photography [3,53]. Risks emerge at multiple stages: capture, pre-processing, storage, and visualization, where data integrity may be compromised. These combined legal and technical uncertainties explain why, despite promising technological advances, courtroom adoption remains limited.

7.3 User Adoption and Evaluation Metrics

The long-term viability of VR in forensic contexts will depend on practitioner acceptance across domains such as policing, forensic laboratories, and legal institutions. Literature indicates differentiated priorities: law enforcement emphasizes rapid documentation and training, whereas legal professionals focus on reliability, reproducibility, and evidentiary rigor. To bridge these perspectives, adoption should be assessed using standardized metrics including task completion time, accuracy in evidence identification, usability ratings, and perceived cognitive load [16,48]. Furthermore, role-specific evaluation frameworks are essential:

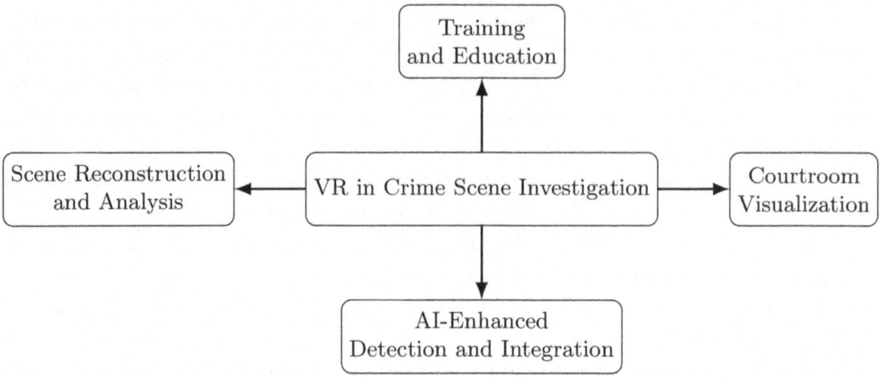

Fig. 4. Proposed taxonomy of VR applications in crime scene investigation.

investigators, prosecutors, and first responders each bring distinct criteria for utility. Embedding such multidimensional metrics into future studies will enable more rigorous validation and foster broader trust in VR forensic applications.

7.4 A Taxonomy of VR Applications in Crime Scene Investigation

To provide a clearer conceptual contribution, this review proposes a taxonomy that organizes VR applications for CSI into four interrelated domains (Fig. 4):

- **Training and Education:** immersive practice environments, skill assessments, and procedural rehearsals for investigators and students.
- **Scene Reconstruction and Analysis:** 3D modeling and interactive walkthroughs for post-incident examination, measurement, and hypothesis testing.
- **Courtroom Visualization:** evidence presentation, jury education, and witness orientation using navigable reconstructions.
- **AI-Enhanced Detection and Integration:** automated object detection, semantic scene understanding, and mixed-reality overlays for real-time decision support.

This taxonomy reflects the progressive flow of forensic work, starting from training and crime scene capture to analytical reconstruction and ultimately courtroom presentation while highlighting where AI can augment each stage. It provides a structured lens for future comparative evaluations and technology development.

7.5 Conclusion

Overall, VR presents significant potential to transform forensic practice by improving investigative accuracy, training realism, and collaborative reconstruction. Realizing this potential, however, requires targeted research into evidentiary standards, technical validation, and end-user adoption. Interdisciplinary collaboration between computer scientists, forensic experts, and legal scholars will be essential to developing forensic-specific protocols and ensuring scientific rigor. With these measures, VR can progress from an experimental technology to an operationally relevant tool that meaningfully advances the practice of digital forensics.

References

1. Abdelhay, S.: The role of virtual reality in employee training and development: mediating role of engagement and immersion, moderating role of organizational culture. Int. J. Res. Hum. Resour. Manag. **6**(2), 292–300 (2024)
2. Ajmera, H., Gonen, B.: Virtual reality in health care. In: IEEE International Conference on Computing, Networking and Communications (ICNC) (2020)
3. Albeedan, M., Kolivand, H., Hammady, R.: Designing and evaluation of a mixed reality system for crime scene investigation training: a hybrid approach. Virtual Reality **28**, 127 (2024). https://doi.org/10.1007/s10055-024-01018-8
4. Alketbi, S.K.: DNA contamination in crime scene investigations: common errors and mitigation techniques. Biomed. J. Sci. Tech. Res. **58**(5), 1–7 (2024)
5. Carpio-Alfsen, R., Baumann, O., Birt, J.R.: Evaluating the viewer experience of interactive virtual reality movies. Virtual Reality **27**(4), 3181–3190 (2023)
6. Chen, Y.R., Chang, C.Y., Chien, T.W.: Forensic science education by crime scene investigation in virtual reality. In: 2021 IEEE International Conference on Artificial Intelligence and Virtual Reality (AIVR) (2021)
7. CSAFE: Forensic science data portal (2024). https://forensicstats.org/data. Accessed May 2024
8. Deshmukh, S., Tyagi, A., Adhikari, V.: Crimeverse: exploring crime scene through virtual reality. In: IEEE ICICT (2023)
9. D'Anna, T., Travaini, F.L., Scarpelli, P., Piras, A., Messina, D., Sessa, G.: The chain of custody in the era of modern forensics: blockchain, nfts, and challenges in digital evidence management. Forensic Sci. Int.: Synergy **5**, 100342 (2023). https://doi.org/10.1016/j.fsisyn.2023.100342
10. Elbadawy, H., Farouk, A.F.A.: Implementation of virtual reality technology in architecture field, and education: a review. Arch. Comput. Methods Eng. **32**(1), 9 (2025)
11. Engström, P., Edgren, F., Strid, A.: Virtual reality for csi training. In: Proceedings of the SPIE 3D Imaging, Modeling, Processing, Visualization and Transmission (2023). https://doi.org/10.1117/12.2664217
12. Ewais, A., Naser, H., Hamouda, A., Jaradat, A.A.: Virtual reality immersive simulations for a forensic molecular biology course–a quantitative comparative study. Appl. Sci. **14**(17), 7513 (2024)
13. Gerard, F.J., Ammerer, K., Mentzelopoulos, M., Economou, D.: Exploring students' experiences in using virtual simulation and gamification principles for authentic learning and assessment in criminal psychology. J. Crim. Justice Educ. 1–19 (2024). https://doi.org/10.1080/10511253.2024.2324179
14. Griffin, A., Stulken, A., Velazquez, R., Lee, K., Mizrahi, C., Rabbitts, D.: Virtual reality in pain rehabilitation for youth with chronic pain: Pilot feasibility study. JMIR Rehabil. Assist. Technol. **7**(2), e22620 (2020)

15. Haddaway, N.R., Page, M.J., Pritchard, C.C., McGuinness, L.A.: PRISMA2020: an r package and shiny app for producing PRISMA 2020-compliant flow diagrams, with interactivity for optimised digital transparency and open synthesis. Campbell Syst. Rev. **18**, e1230 (2022). https://doi.org/10.1002/cl2.1230
16. Halford, E., Keningale, P., Hussain, A.T., Condon, C.: Assessing the utility of a virtual reality arson crime scene investigation simulation. Polic. J. Policy Pract. **18** (2024). https://doi.org/10.1093/police/paae122
17. Hassenfeldt, C., McGough, R., Whitfield, K., Hutt, J.J.: Exploring the learning efficacy of digital forensics concepts and bagging & tagging in immersive virtual reality. Forensic Sci. Int. Digit. Investig. **33** (2020)
18. Hsu, T.W., Chou, Y.J., Hsieh, W.L., Lin, T.W.: Design and initial evaluation of a vr based immersive and interactive architectural design discussion system. In: Proceedings of the IEEE Conference Virtual Reality and 3D User Interfaces, pp. 363–371 (2020)
19. Ihekweazu, C., Shashidhar, N., Ihekweazu, I.H.: Proposed adoption of virtual reality framework in digital forensics curriculum. In: Proceedings of the 2023 ISCAP Conference, vol. 9. Information Systems and Computing Academic Professionals (ISCAP), Albuquerque, NM (2023). https://iscap.us/proceedings/2023/pdf/5935.pdf
20. Iyer, S.R.: Understanding how news content utilizes experiential media (ar, vr, and 360° video) in covid-19 storytelling. Athens J. Mass Media Commun. **9**(2), 85–112 (2023)
21. Jacobsen, C., Lynnerup, N.: A virtual, 3D multimodal approach to victim and crime scene reconstruction. Forensic Sciences **3**(1), 47–61 (2023). https://doi.org/10.3390/forensicsci3010005
22. Jegatheswaran, R., Mohd, H.A., Juremi, J., Thiruchelvam, V., Wei, A.Y.C.: Utilization of virtual reality technology in crime scene investigation. In: Proceedings of the International Conference on Integrated Intelligence and Communication Systems (ICIICS), pp. 1–6 (2023). https://doi.org/10.1109/ICIICS59993.2023.10421600
23. of Justice, N.I.: Crime scene documentation: weighing the merits of three-dimensional laser scanning. Technical report, U.S. Department of Justice (2022). https://nij.ojp.gov/topics/articles/crime-scene-documentation-weighing-merits-three-dimensional-laser-scanning
24. Kader, S.N., Talib, A., Ismail, Z., Karim, A.A.: Building an interactive immersive virtual reality crime scene for future chemists to learn forensic science chemistry. J. Chem. Educ. **97**(9), 2651–2656 (2020)
25. Khalilia, W., Khalil, M.A., Melandri, D., Sani, F., Lamberti, F.: Using virtual reality as support to the learning process of forensic scenarios. IEEE Access **10**, 83297–83310 (2022)
26. Khalilia, W.M., Jarrar, M.Y., Al-Agha, H.A.: Challenges facing palestinian crime scene investigators in evidence collection and preservation. Egypt. J. Forensic Sci. **14**, 13 (2024). https://doi.org/10.1186/s41935-024-00353-w
27. Khan, A., Zhang, R., Chen, P.W., Garza, L., Lee, D.T.: Virtual reality in stroke recovery: a meta-review of systematic reviews. Bioelectron. Med. **10**, 23 (2024)
28. Kishore, P., Giri, K.: Object detection for crime scene evidence analysis using deep learning. Int. J. Commun. Netw. Inf. Secur. **14**, 663–673 (2022)
29. Leverhulme Research Centre for Forensic Science: Udgard iii - portlethen raw dataset. Dataset, University of Dundee (2023). available upon request via LRCFS; includes photogrammetry, lidar, video, and sensor captures from fire scene simulations

30. Li, Y., Zhang, T., Lin, W., Papaioannou, A.G.: Advancements in virtual reality for performance enhancement in combat sports: a mini-review and perspective. Front. Psychol. **16**, 11920182 (2025)
31. Lin, X.P., Chen, Y., Wei, L., Du, S.: The impact of virtual reality on student engagement in the classroom - a critical review of the literature. Front. Psychol. **15**, 1360574 (2024)
32. Ma, J.: Smart tech meets forensics: enhancing crime scene investigation with digital simulations. Forensic Sci. Int. **365**, 112296 (2024). https://doi.org/10.1016/j.forsciint.2024.112296
33. Maneli, M.A., Isafiade, O.E.: 3D forensic crime scene reconstruction involving immersive technology: a systematic literature review. IEEE Access **10**, 88821–88857 (2022). https://doi.org/10.1109/ACCESS.2022.3199437
34. Mayne, R., Green, H.: Virtual reality for teaching and learning in crime scene investigation. Science Justice **60**(5), 466–472 (2020). https://doi.org/10.1016/j.scijus.2020.07.006
35. Morales, R.A.: Extended reality applications for cnc machine training: a systematic review. Multimodal Technol. Interact. **8**(9), 80 (2024)
36. Naji, K.K., Shaban, N.H., Aridi, S.L., Ibrahim, R.S.: Virtual frontiers in stem education: a systematic review and swot analysis of virtual reality-based interventions at the preparatory school level. Comput. Sch. (2025). https://doi.org/10.1080/07380569.2025.2472684
37. Onderdijk, K.E., Bouckaert, L., Maes, P.J.: Concert experiences in virtual reality environments. Virtual Reality **27**(3), 2383–2396 (2023)
38. Pribadi, A.P., Rahman, Y.M.R., Silalahi, C.D.A.B.: Analysis of the effectiveness and user experience of employing virtual reality to enhance the efficacy of occupational safety and health learning for electrical workers and graduate students. PLoS ONE **19**(8), e2024 (2024)
39. Razali, A.F., Mustaffa, N.H., Mohd, M.A.: Exploring the potential of geospatial virtual reality in forensic csi: an overview. J. Teknol. **86**(5) (2024)
40. Rinaldi, V., Hackman, L., Daeid, N.N.: Virtual reality as a collaborative tool for digitalised crime scene examination. In: De Paolis, L.T., Arpaia, P., Sacco, M. (eds.) Extended Reality. XR Salento 2022. LNCS, vol. 13866, pp. 182–197. Springer, Cham (2022). https://doi.org/10.1007/978-3-031-28398-3_15
41. Rinaldi, V., Ljungkvist, E., Thomsen, B., Nic Daeid, N.: Virtual reality aiding fire scene investigation: a thankless endeavor or catalyst for change? WIREs Forensic Science **6**(4), e1518 (2024). https://doi.org/10.1002/wfs2.1518
42. Rinaldi, V., Nic Daeid, N., Yu, S., Thomsen, B., Ljungkvist, E.: Udgard 2021 raw dataset. Dataset, University of Dundee (2021). https://doi.org/10.15132/10000174, available from University of Dundee Research Data Repository
43. Rinaldi, V., Nic Daeid, N., Yu, S., Thomsen, B., Ljungkvist, E.: Udgard ii raw dataset. Dataset, University of Dundee (2023). https://doi.org/10.15132/10000242, available from University of Dundee Research Data Repository
44. Safikhani, S., Pirker, J., Wriessnegger, S.C.: Virtual reality applications for the treatment of anxiety and mental disorders. In: Proceedings of the 7th IEEE International Conference on Immersive Learning Research Network (iLRN), pp. 1–8 (2021)
45. Sazaly, A.N., Ariff, M.F.M., Razali, A.F.: 3D indoor crime scene reconstruction from micro UAV photogrammetry technique. Eng. Technol. Appl. Sci. Res. **13**(6), 12020–12025 (2023). https://doi.org/10.48084/etasr.6260

46. Sharma, M., Kumar, P., Singh, D.K.: Immersive health monitoring: harnessing virtual reality for advanced healthcare solutions. In: Proceedings of the IEEE International Conference on Artificial Intelligence in Health (ICAIIHI), pp. 1–6 (2023)
47. Sheshtar, F.M., Alhatlani, W.M., Moulden, M., Kim, J.H.: Comparative analysis of lidar and photogrammetry for 3D crime scene reconstruction. Appl. Sci. **15**(3), 1085 (2025). https://doi.org/10.3390/app15031085
48. Silva, F.C.E., Alves, J.D.O., de L. Batista, C.A.: Crime scene - vr: immersive learning experience on criminal forensics. In: XXVI Symposium on Virtual and Augmented Reality (SVR) (2024)
49. Stefan, H., Zepf, L.L., Schmidt, N.: Evaluating the effectiveness of virtual reality for safety-relevant training: a systematic review. Virtual Reality **27**, 2839–2869 (2023)
50. Vidoli, G.M., Smith, M.E., Steadman, L.M.: Final report: validating three-dimensional documentation for crime scenes. Technical report. NCJ 302552, National Institute of Justice and University of Tennessee (2020). https://nij.ojp.gov/library/publications/validating-three-dimensional-documentation-crime-scenes
51. Villa, C., Lynnerup, N., Jacobsen, C.: A virtual, 3D multimodal approach to victim and crime scene reconstruction. Diagnostics **13**(17), 2764 (2023)
52. Xiong, C., Cheung, W., Levy, D., Allen, M.: The effect of virtual reality on the marketing of residential property. Hous. Stud. **37**(1), 1–24 (2022)
53. Yang, C., Liu, J., Wang, X., Zhang, L.: The impact of virtual reality on practical skills for students in science and engineering education: a meta-analysis. Int. J. STEM Educ. **11**(28) (2024)
54. Yondjo, J., Siette, J.: 'VR is the Future': perspectives of healthcare professionals on virtual reality as a diagnostic tool for dementia status in primary care. BMC Med. Inform. Decis. Mak. **24**(1), 9 (2024)
55. Zappalà, A., Trovato, M., Manganaro, G., Cutugno, F.: Enhancing crime scene investigations through virtual reality and deep learning techniques. arXiv preprint arXiv:2409.00001 (2024)
56. Zhang, Y., Huang, X.: Integrating extended reality (XR) in architectural design education: a systematic review and case study at southeast university (China). Buildings **14**(12), 3954 (2024)

Evaluating Forensic Techniques for Detecting and Investigating Insider Threats Leveraging Legitimate Access to Systems and Data

Rojeena Khadka(✉), Dorcas Addo, Yvonne Jegede, and Lei Chen

Department of Information Technology, Georgia Southern University, Statesboro, GA, USA
{rk08345,da10782,yj00904,lchen}@georgiasouthern.edu

Abstract. Insider threats continue to pose a significant cybersecurity concern due to the inherent trust and authorized access granted to individuals within an organization. Unlike external attacks, insider threats are often more difficult to detect because they involve users operating with legitimate credentials, making their actions appear routine or authorized. This research presents a forensic framework for detecting insider threats by analyzing behavioral patterns in user email activity. Drawing on the CERT Insider Threat Email dataset, a three-phase process which includes time-based activity analysis, feature extraction, and hybrid anomaly detection was implemented with Isolation Forest and Local Outlier Factor (LOF) algorithms, supplemented by Random Forest classification for user-level evaluation. The system detected over 26,000 anomalous events, with a significant proportion occurring outside standard business hours, indicating possible policy violations or misuse of access. An NLP and sentiment analysis layer was integrated to extract contextual insights from anomalous emails, revealing thematic patterns and potential threat-related language. Results demonstrated strong agreement between Isolation Forest and LOF outputs, highlighting the framework's robustness. While effective in identifying behavioral anomalies without labeled data, limitations included a lack of role-based context and intent determination. Future improvements involve integrating role-informed modeling, and hybrid supervised and unsupervised approaches to enhance accuracy, interpretability, and real-time applicability in operational environments.

Keywords: Insider Threats · Digital Forensics · Anomaly Detection · Machine Learning · Isolation Forest · Email Behavior Analysis · User Activity Monitoring · Cybersecurity · Natural Language Processing (NLP) · Role-Based Access Control

1 Introduction

In the ever-evolving landscape of cybersecurity, insider threats have emerged as one of the most insidious and difficult-to-detect risks facing modern organi-

V. V. Pham et al. (Eds.): CIDDF 2025, ACSAR 5, pp. 53–76, 2026.
https://doi.org/10.1007/978-3-032-19488-6_4

zations. According to recent industry reports, approximately 83% of organizations experienced at least one insider-related security incident within the past year [1]. Unlike external threats, which typically originate outside the organizational perimeter, insider threats stem from individuals who already possess legitimate access to critical systems and sensitive data. These individuals may include current or former employees, contractors, business partners, or third-party vendors [2]. Whether their motives are malicious or negligent, the damage they can inflict is often severe and far-reaching, affecting not only financial assets but also operational stability and corporate reputation [3]. What makes insider threats particularly challenging is the subtlety of their execution. Since insiders operate using authorized credentials, their activities often do not trigger traditional security alarms. Their access is granted, their actions appear routine, and their behavior may blend seamlessly with that of legitimate users. This ability to "hide in plain sight" allows malicious insiders to conduct harmful activities over extended periods without detection [4]. Also, insider threats frequently leave minimal traces, and the evidence they leave behind is often fragmented or obscured, making forensic investigation all the more complicated [5]. Given the high stakes involved, early detection of insider threats is critical to minimizing potential damage. However, traditional security tools such as firewalls, intrusion detection systems, and antivirus software are typically designed to detect external attacks and often fall short in identifying anomalies generated by trusted individuals [6]. This gap in detection capabilities highlights the importance of integrating digital forensic methodologies into cybersecurity frameworks.

Digital forensics involves the systematic identification, preservation, analysis, and presentation of digital evidence [7]. When applied to insider threats, forensic techniques can provide crucial insights into the behavior of users, patterns of unauthorized access, and the timeline of malicious actions. The role of digital forensics in managing insider threats is twofold: it not only aids in post-incident investigations but also enhances proactive threat detection through behavioral analysis, audit trail reconstruction, and real-time monitoring of access patterns [8]. Despite these benefits, current forensic tools and techniques often struggle to keep pace with the increasing complexity of insider tactics and the growing volume of digital data within organizations. Moreover, insider threats are not limited to overt theft of data; they may also include sabotage, intellectual property leakage, fraud, and the abuse of privileges for personal or competitive gain [9]. As such, this research aims to critically evaluate the effectiveness of existing forensic techniques for detecting and investigating insider threats, particularly those leveraging legitimate access to systems and data. It will explore current methodologies, identify their strengths and limitations, and assess how they can be improved or supplemented with emerging technologies such as machine learning, user behavior analytics, and artificial intelligence. By doing so, the research seeks to provide a comprehensive understanding of how digital forensics can be optimized to address one of the most persistent and damaging forms of cyber risk, ultimately contributing to stronger internal defense mechanisms and improved organizational resilience.

2 Background

The increasing digitization of organizational operations has led to a greater dependency on internal stakeholders for maintaining system integrity and safeguarding sensitive information. As digital ecosystems grow more complex, so too does the range of threats they face, not just from external hackers but also from trusted insiders with direct access to networks, databases, and proprietary resources [10].

Although cybersecurity strategies have traditionally focused on erecting barriers against external attacks, there is a growing realization that threats from within may pose an equal, if not greater, risk due to the inherent trust and access these individuals are granted [11]. Historically, insider incidents were often framed as isolated cases of employee misconduct or negligence. However, in recent years, the threat has evolved into a more organized and multifaceted challenge. Insiders may act alone or in collaboration with external actors, leveraging their position to carry out unauthorized data extraction, system manipulation, or operational disruption [12]. In some cases, insider threats are ideologically motivated or driven by grievances, while in others, they may stem from financial incentives or coercion [13].

The sophistication of these attacks has grown, making them harder to trace without in-depth technical analysis. At the core of this challenge is the difficulty in distinguishing between legitimate and illegitimate use of system privileges. For example, an IT administrator accessing sensitive databases may be performing routine tasks or exfiltrating confidential information; both actions can appear identical to standard monitoring tools [14]. This ambiguity complicates the detection and response process and requires more nuanced investigative approaches. Digital forensic science has become an essential discipline in addressing this gap. Unlike general cybersecurity tools that aim to prevent or block intrusions, digital forensics focuses on retrospective analysis, examining logs, reconstructing timelines, recovering deleted files, and identifying patterns that might reveal insider wrongdoing. However, many forensic techniques were originally developed with external attacks in mind and may not be fully optimized for the unique characteristics of insider cases. For example, subtle manipulations of access rights, off-hours data queries, or the use of remote desktop tools may go unnoticed without specialized forensic scrutiny [7].

In light of these developments, there is an urgent need to refine forensic strategies specifically for insider threat contexts. This involves not only improving technological tools but also developing procedural and analytical frameworks that can support early detection, comprehensive investigation, and legal attribution [15]. With the regulatory landscape also placing increasing pressure on organizations to ensure data protection and incident accountability, the role of digital forensics in managing insider threats is becoming more critical than ever [16].

3 Literature Review

3.1 Machine Learning-Based Detection Techniques

Machine learning (ML) remains the foundation of many insider threat detection solutions, enabling the identification of subtle patterns, anomalies, and behavioral deviations in user activity logs. These models range from traditional classifiers to deep learning and ensemble methods.

(i) Supervised Learning Approaches
Supervised learning requires labeled data, making it effective in environments where known insider threat behaviors have been previously recorded. Manoharan et al. [17] benchmarked multiple supervised algorithms—including Random Forest (RF), Deep Neural Networks (DNN), and LSTM Autoencoders—on the CERT dataset. Random Forest performed best, achieving a 95.9% F1-score in balanced conditions; however, its performance dropped under class imbalance, suggesting the need for resampling or synthetic augmentation techniques. Padiet et al. [18] adopted a supervised approach based on user download behavior logs. They applied multiple classifiers and identified Random Tree as the most effective, achieving 98.1% accuracy. The study emphasizes user-centric modeling and behavioral profiling, though it is limited by its reliance on logs without contextual enrichment or adversarial modeling.

(ii) Unsupervised and Anomaly Detection Approaches
In environments where labeled data is scarce, unsupervised learning becomes critical. Wei et al. [19] proposed a proactive forensic investigation framework combining cascaded autoencoders (CAEs), BiLSTM for sequential feature learning, and a hypergraph correction module. This architecture achieved a 0.93 F1-score and significantly reduced false positives on the KDD CUP 99 dataset. Le and Zincir-Heywood [20] contributed an ensemble-based framework using Autoencoder, Isolation Forest, LODA, and LOF. Their method used percentile-based temporal features and achieved AUC scores up to 0.981 on the CERT R6.2 dataset. Notably, the framework outperformed traditional time series models and showed promising generalizability. Kim et al. [21] employed the Discrete Wavelet Transformation (DWT) for feature extraction, combined with decision tree classifiers. Their anomaly detection approach improved detection accuracy, highlighting DWT's utility in reducing noise and enhancing behavioral signal quality.

(iii) Hybrid Approaches and Behavioral-Augmented ML
Alzaabi and Mehmood [22] conducted a comprehensive review of ML-based insider threat detection methods. They argued that rule-based and signature-based models are insufficient to capture nuanced insider behaviors and advocated for integrating NLP, LLMs, and time-series behavioral modeling. Their findings support the need for hybrid models that combine statistical features with contextual metadata.

3.2 Artificial Intelligence and Advanced Analytics

AI provides a more dynamic and scalable foundation for insider threat detection. Modern systems increasingly incorporate predictive modeling, generative models, and explainable AI to improve threat visibility while supporting analyst decision-making. Rhee [23] highlighted the use of AI in intrusion detection and cyber defense. Their study showcased the use of GANs for mitigating data imbalance, NLP for activity classification, and XAI (Explainable AI) for regulatory compliance. These techniques offer greater transparency, particularly in environments requiring auditability, though challenges remain in adversarial robustness.

3.3 Real-Time and IoT-Based Anomaly Detection

Sivaraman [24] conducted a systematic review of real-time anomaly detection systems within federal and IoT contexts. The paper discussed the need for integrating deep learning, forensic analysis, and data privacy protection in environments characterized by decentralized architecture and limited visibility. The key challenges identified include the absence of IoT-specific datasets and the complexity of malware detection in sensor-rich infrastructures.

3.4 Behavioral and Forensic-Oriented Techniques

Manral and Somani [25] introduced the concept of a "Log-of-logs server" to counteract anti-forensic behaviors by superusers, such as system administrators. Their proposed architecture would enforce legitimacy, deny unauthorized access, and preserve forensic trails. Although conceptual, this approach draws attention to compliance and audit challenges often overlooked in technical detection frameworks. Padiet et al. [18] also contribute here by analyzing user downloads as behavioral signals, suggesting the potential to fuse forensic logging with machine learning for more context-rich threat detection.

3.5 Organizational and Human-Centric Strategies

Insider threat detection cannot be solely technological—it must consider organizational culture and human behavior. Sarkar [5] proposed a holistic model integrating HR policy, behavioral analysis, and access control tools. He warned that excessive surveillance could damage morale and advocated for trust-driven frameworks that balance control with employee well-being. Alsowail and Al-Shehari [26] designed a multi-tiered framework combining AI-driven detection, anomaly scoring, and organizational risk assessments. Their model supports early intervention, continuous risk evaluation, and cross-departmental accountability. However, successful implementation depends on strong inter-departmental collaboration and stakeholder participation.

3.6 Gap in the Literature

Although machine learning (ML) and artificial intelligence (AI) techniques have significantly advanced insider threat detection, a major gap persists in the real-world applicability and generalizability of these models. Studies show a high accuracy in detecting insider threats using supervised classifiers on benchmark datasets like CERT, but they often fail to account for model performance in operational settings with evolving behaviors, noise, and partial observability. While data augmentation using GANs and behavioral modeling with large language models (LLMs) are promising, these approaches remain largely untested in dynamic enterprise environments, where false positives and model drift can severely impair usability. Another critical shortfall is the lack of integration between explainable AI (XAI) and detection systems. Despite the rising complexity of ML models, few studies incorporate interpretability in a way that supports human analysts. While some research discusses the role of XAI in enhancing transparency, especially in regulated sectors, applied frameworks that integrate XAI outputs into real-time security workflows are still lacking. At the same time, real-time environments like (Internet of Things (IoT networks remain underserved in insider threat detection. The absence of relevant IoT datasets, combined with the high volume and heterogeneity of sensor data, limits both forensic traceability and accurate anomaly detection. Furthermore, insider threat detection research often neglects cross-disciplinary and organizational dynamics. Some frameworks propose combining HR policies, behavioral monitoring, and access control, yet these approaches are rarely empirically evaluated or adopted at scale. The social, psychological, and policy dimensions of insider threats are frequently siloed from technical solutions, undermining the development of holistic detection systems. Furthermore, while there are several taxonomies, there remains a lack of standardized evaluation frameworks, real-world case studies, and deployment benchmarks; this suggests that researchers and practitioners would still need to find unified guidance for comparing or implementing detection methods across sectors.

4 Methodology

This study utilized the publicly available CERT Insider Threat Dataset v6.2, the email.csv file from Kaggle. The dataset from Kaggle simulates organizational behavior email behavior, such as malicious insider activity [28] across numerous user accounts. The methodology is structured into different phases: Data Collection and pre-processing, Feature Engineering, Anomaly Detection and Analysis and Natural Language Processing based forensic analysis.

4.1 Data Collection and Preprocessing

The dataset is obtained from the CERT repository and extensive data preprocessing is performed using Python (Pandas and Scikit-learn library). The experiment is set up in Google Colab and extensive data preprocessing is performed using the Python 3 Programming language, along with Pandas, Scikit-learn libraries. The steps involved are:

- Data cleaning such as handling missing values, removing duplicates.
- Normalizing timestamps to ensure consistent temporal analysis.
- Feature scaling using `StandardScaler` to align ranges across variables.

4.2 Feature Engineering

The process is then followed by feature engineering, where the features are extracted in different categories.

1 Time-based characteristics [29] such as weekday, hour of sending email, any off-hour indicators is categorized as Temporal features.
2 Behavioral characteristics such as email size, attachment size and number of recipients as Behavioral features.
3 Content characteristics such as Term Frequency-Inverse Document Frequency (TF-IDF) scores, which could not be fully utilized due to scope limitations and keywords flags (threat-relevant terms such as leak, unauthorized, breach) as Content features.

Meanwhile, the Matplotlib used for visualization, helped in identifying common patterns and abnormalities among these features (Fig. 1).

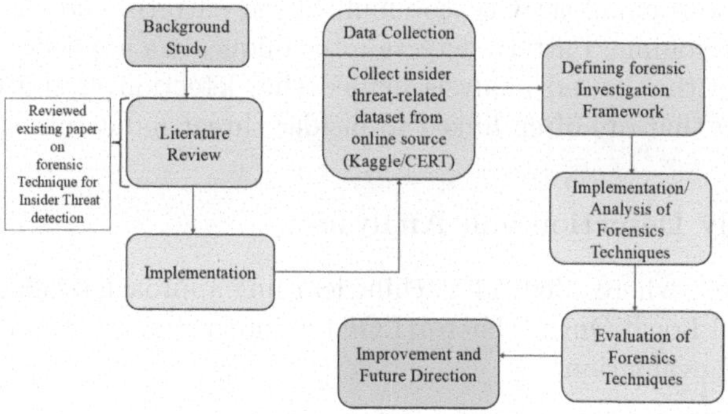

Fig. 1. Overall Workflow/Process for Insider Threat Evaluation

4.3 Insider Threat Detection Framework

A systematic Forensic Detection Framework was applied to detect and examine insider threat behavior based on the CERT Insider Threat Email dataset on

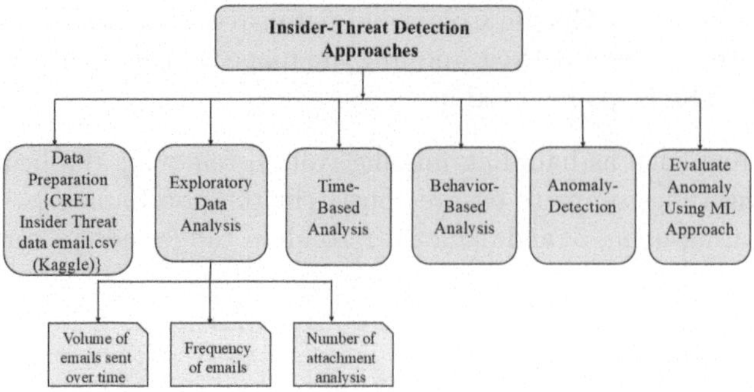

Fig. 2. A diagram showing process involved in Analysis and Evaluation of Insider Threat Email Dataset

Kaggle. The process integrates time-based behavior analysis and anomaly detection per user pattern using machine learning technique [24] (Fig. 2).

(i) Feature Extraction and Pattern Identification
Initially, the experiment focused on time-based email metadata per user. The key features investigated are timestamp, sender ID, number of recipients, and number of emails sent that could help us analyze daily, weekly, and monthly activity patterns. This aggregation helped us establish baseline communication patterns per user.

Then the behavioral features [30] are extracted, which helped to analyze insider threat activities. The main features include the frequency of emails sent over time, off-hour email activity, communication pattern, and change in recipient domains or volume. Pattern detection techniques are applied to identify this behavior, while time-based analysis helped the detection of subtle changes in communication that are often linked to insider threat indicators [31].

4.4 Anomaly Detection and Analysis

The next phase is where a hybrid machine learning approach combining Isolation Forest (IF) and Local Outlier Factor(LOF) is integrated for Anomaly detection and user-based evaluation.

(i) Anomaly Detection Framework
Isolation Forest algorithm [32] is utilized to detect anomalies in the activities. This is an unsupervised method highly capable of identifying outliers based on data points, isolated by tree structure, and best suited for discovering unusual insider threat activity[33].

To ensure a robust comparison and enhance the credibility of results, the Local Outlier Factor (LOF) algorithm was implemented as a secondary unsupervised anomaly detection model alongside the Isolation Forest. While Isolation Forest uses a global isolation approach, LOF detects anomalies by measuring local density deviations relative to the k-nearest neighbors, making it particularly effective for identifying clustered anomalies in user behaviors [34]. The LOF model is applied using `Scikit-learn` in Python on the complete CERT dataset, utilizing the same features as Isolation Forest-email size, number of attachments, number of recipients, hour, and day of the week-after normalization with `StandardScaler`.

For consistency, the parameters are set to `n_neighbors = 20` and `contamination = 0.01` in reference to literature [32–34] on anomaly detection, balancing sensitivity with computational cost and reflecting assumption that 1% represent anomalies in an organizational datasets. Anomalies are labeled as −1 for outliers and 1 for normal instances, with results evaluated through overlap metrics such as Jaccard similarity and visualized using temporal scatter plots, hourly box plots, user-based bar charts, and feature correlation heatmaps generated with `Matplotlib` and `Seaborn`.

The Jaccard similarity is calculated between IF and LOF anomaly sets to evaluate detection consistency.

(ii) "Weakly Labeled" Evaluation

To report standard metrics without human annotation, we constructed a silver (weak) labeled set using policy-inspired heuristics that are independent of model outputs. Emails were labeled as likely anomalies when they exhibited combinations of risk signals. For example, off-hours sending with attachments, very large size, plus links or security terms, or many recipients with attachments. Conversely, business-hours, small size, no attachments, no links/keywords, and few recipients contributed negative votes. Items with insufficient evidence were left unlabeled. We then computed precision, recall, and F1 for Isolation Forest (IF), Local Outlier Factor (LOF), and two simple ensembles—Union (IF ∪ LOF) and Intersection (IF ∩ LOF)—over the $n = 914{,}485$ messages that received a weak label.

4.5 Natural Language Processing and Sentiment Analysis for Contextual Anomaly Insights

To enhance the interpretability of the anomaly detection process, a Natural Language Processing (NLP) and sentiment analysis layer are integrated alongside the metadata-driven anomaly detection framework. This addition is intended to extract deeper semantic patterns from anomalous emails and to determine whether linguistic cues in the content aligned with suspicious behavioral indicators detected by the models. Both the Isolation Forest and Local Outlier Factor (LOF) anomaly sets are examined using this approach, with the objective of identifying recurring phrases, distinctive keywords, and tonal characteristics that could potentially support forensic analysis or threat assessment. This stage of analysis is particularly important when dealing with large-scale email datasets, as metadata anomalies alone may not reveal the underlying contextual relevance or potential security risks embedded in communication content. NLP-based content evaluation allows for the discovery of hidden patterns, thematic clusters, or sentiment imbalances that could help distinguish benign anomalies from those warranting further investigation. In order to add a depth to the forensic analysis a standardized text prepossessing pipeline such as lowercasing and punctuation removal, tokenization and stop word removal are applied. Similarly, three NLP analyses- bigram extraction to reveal thematic phrase pattern, keyword frequency analysis and TF-IDF scoring to identify terms that are excessively common unusual emails are conducted.

5 Results

This section talks about the results of our analysis of email behavior using the CERT Insider Threat Email dataset. The outcome from data visualization and Machine Learning [35] was investigated to identify patterns, anomalies, and possible indicators of insider threat behavior.

5.1 Time-Based Email Patterns

The output shown in "Fig. 3" shows the volume of emails sent over time, which shows a strong concentration of messages occurring between 9:00 AM and 3:00 PM, which hints towards the consistency with organizational norms.

```
print("Email Volume Over Time:\n", email_volume)

Email Volume Over Time:
 date
2010-01-02     350
2010-01-03     390
2010-01-04    7912
2010-01-05    7861
2010-01-06    7924
              ...
2011-05-12    6797
2011-05-13    6723
2011-05-14     321
2011-05-15     319
2011-05-16    6761
Length: 500, dtype: int64
```

Fig. 3. Email volume distribution across workdays(Date/Time). The overall distribution shows communication patterns with peaks during workdays. An unusual spikes or drops may indicates changes or insider activities.

The result from "Fig. 4" indicates that most of the emails are sent between 8:00 AM and 5:00 PM, with a peak email activity recorded from 9:00 AM3:00 PM, aligning with organizational standard working hours. This time-based distribution is a behavioral norm for normal communication patterns. If there has

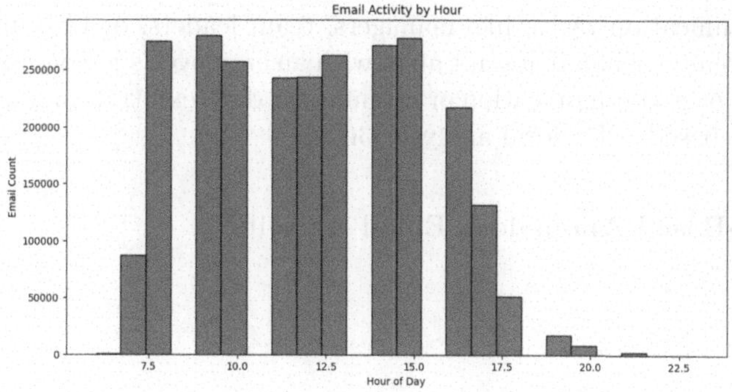

Fig. 4. Time-based emails analysis to identify irregular usages. Deviations from peak working hours (9–3 PM) may hint towards policy voilation, malicious use providing room for forensic investigation.

been any time deviation [33] from this pattern, for instance, emails sent during off-hours, late-night or early morning hours, then it might indicate potential policy violations or malicious activity. And if that activity is repeated by the same senders, then it suggests suspicious behavior, indicating time-based analysis as a key feature in flagging insider threat detection.

5.2 Top 10 Users by Email Activity

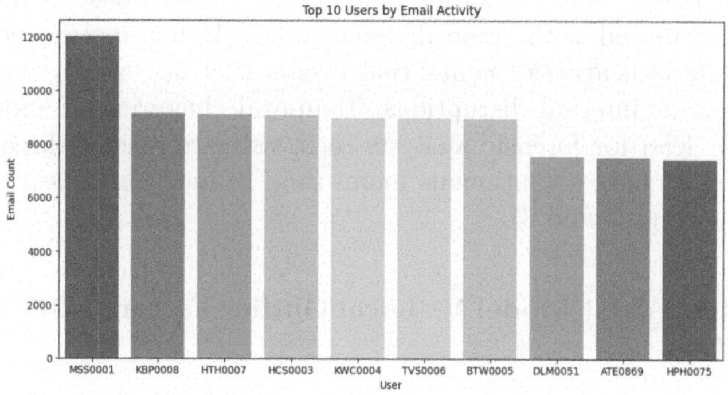

Fig. 5. User-based emails analysis to identify top 10 users. While high activities reflects managerial roles, unusually high activities may indicates misuse of access

As shown in "Fig. 5", the chart shows the top 10 most active users based on the total volume of emails. It indicates that some users, MSS0001 and KBP0008, have significantly more email interactions compared to others. This kind of extreme email usage can naturally be anticipated by those employees who have heavy communication tasks, like managers, team leaders, or IT support. However, if the volume of email doesn't align with an employee's job description, then this suggests over-communication or attempts at data exfiltration, indicating the need for role-based behavioral analysis [36].

5.3 Time-Based Anomalous Email Activity

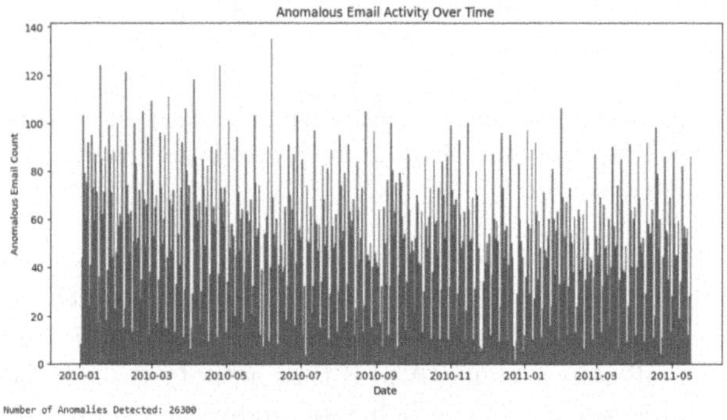

Fig. 6. Temporal distribution of Anomalies (Peaks may indicate periods of heightened insider activity, warranting targeted forensic review)

As shown in "Fig. 6," a red-timeseries plot illustrates anomalies detected across the dataset timeline. The model identified 26,300 anomalous events, and they are evenly distributed with some distinct spikes during specific periods. The spikes could be indicative of contextual events such as employee resignation, policy changes, or internal disruptions. Temporal clustering of anomalies provides a layout lead for forensic analysts to investigate insider threat windows. Similarly, it also enables continuous monitoring rather than passive rule-based static systems (Figs. 7 and 8).

5.4 Isolation Forest Model Vs Local Outlier Factor (LOF) -Anomaly Detection

An Isolation Forest model is applied to identify behavior anomalies on selected email features like email size, attachment count, recipient count, hour of sending, and day of week. The data is normalized using StandardScaler to ensure a consistent scale across features. The model is set to assume 1% contamination as a low percentage of abnormal behavior. The Isolation Forest correctly classified emails as normal (1) or anomalous (−1) while detecting 26,295 anomalies without the need for pre-labeled attack data. This confirms the model's ability to detect behavioral outliers in an unsupervised setting.

```
# Prepare features for anomaly detection
X_sample = data_sample[features]
scaler = StandardScaler()
X_sample_scaled = scaler.fit_transform(X_sample)

# Isolation Forest (as in paper)
iso_model = IsolationForest(n_estimators=100, contamination=0.01, random_state=42)
data_sample['iso_anomaly'] = iso_model.fit_predict(X_sample_scaled)  # -1 for anomaly, 1 for normal
iso_anomalies = data_sample[data_sample['iso_anomaly'] == -1]
print(f"Number of Anomalies Detected by Isolation Forest: {len(iso_anomalies)}")
```

```
Number of Anomalies Detected by Isolation Forest: 26295
```

Fig. 7. Number of Anomalies Detected by Isolation Forest. It highlights user-level and temporal deviations identified through global anomaly isolation.

```
# Local Outlier Factor (added for comparison with Isolation Forest, as per [22])
lof_model = LocalOutlierFactor(n_neighbors=20, contamination=0.01)  # novelty=False for fitting on all data
data_sample['lof_anomaly'] = lof_model.fit_predict(X_sample_scaled)  # -1 for anomaly, 1 for normal
lof_anomalies = data_sample[data_sample['lof_anomaly'] == -1]
print(f"Number of Anomalies Detected by LOF: {len(lof_anomalies)}")
```

```
Number of Anomalies Detected by LOF: 26300
```

Fig. 8. Number of Anomalies Detected by Local Outlier Factor (LOF)- It highlights the anomalies arising from local density differences in communication behavior

The Local Outlier Factor (LOF) algorithm detected 26,300 anomalies, closely matching the 26,295 anomalies identified by the Isolation Forest, with approximately 26,290 overlapping points (Jaccard similarity $\approx$ 0.999) and similar off-hours proportions (47%, or roughly 12,350 for LOF versus 12,345 for Isolation Forest). This indicates strong alignment between the two methods while highlighting LOF's added sensitivity to local clusters.

The temporal overlap scatter plot "Fig. 9" shows dense clustering around mid-2010, with LOF flagging more high-size outliers (greater than 100,000 bytes). Moreover, hourly box plots "Figs. 10 and 11" reveal anomaly medians around 15–16, compared to normals at 11–12, with LOF's narrower interquartile range (10–16) emphasizing extreme-hour outliers. Likewise, User bar plots "Figs. 12 and 13" differ in top-ranked users (e.g., Isolation Forest: ATE0869 $\sim$700; LOF: KBP0008 $\sim$200), suggesting that LOF distributes anomalies more broadly across users. Feature correlation heatmaps "Figs. 14 and 15" highlight LOF's positive hour-recipient correlation (0.059) versus Isolation Forest's negative correlation for size-recipients (−0.32), underscoring LOF's focus on local patterns. Overall, these comparisons validate the anomaly detection framework while enhancing interpretability.

5.5 Precision/Recall/F1 vs. Weak Labels

Against the weak labels, IF achieved very high precision ($\approx$ 1.0) with low recall ($\approx$ 0.08), while LOF exhibited lower precision ($\approx$ 0.7) but higher recall ($\approx$ 0.19). The Union of IF and LOF improved recall to $\approx$ 0.25–0.30 and produced the highest F1 ($\approx$ 0.35–0.38), whereas the intersection attained near-perfect precision with minimal recall ($\approx$ 0.03–0.04). Here, "Fig. 16" summarizes the trade-offs. These results align with the models' low agreement (Jaccard $\approx$ 0.058), indicating that IF and LOF capture different anomaly profiles; combining them

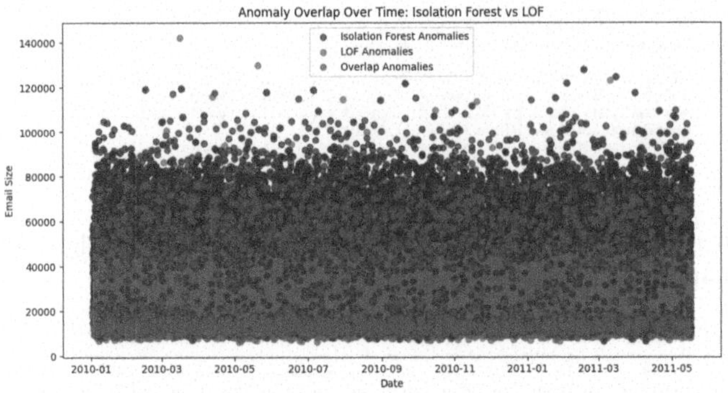

Fig. 9. Anomaly Overlap Over Time: Isolation Forest vs LOF. High similarity indicates robustness and difference suggest distinct risk profile.

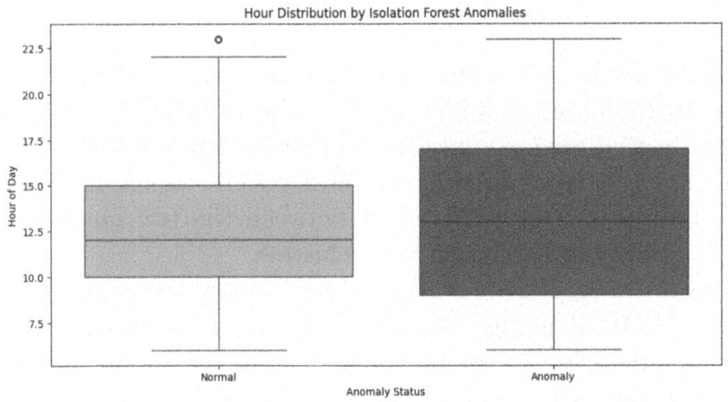

Fig. 10. Hour Distribution by Isolation Forest Anomalies to detect off-hour anomalies

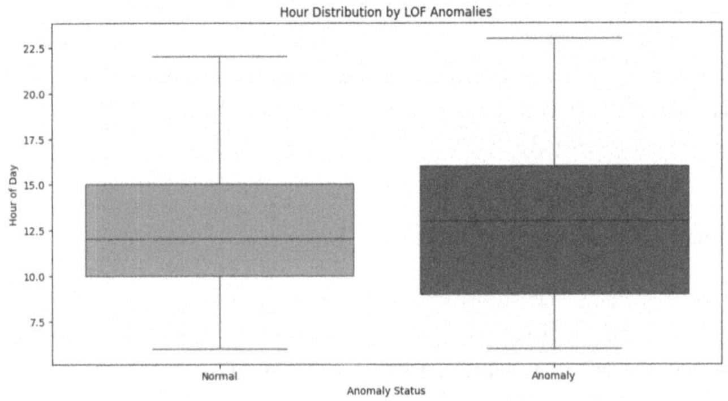

Fig. 11. Hour Distribution by LOF Anomalies to detect off-hour anomalies while LOF methods shows tighter clustering around extreme sending hours.

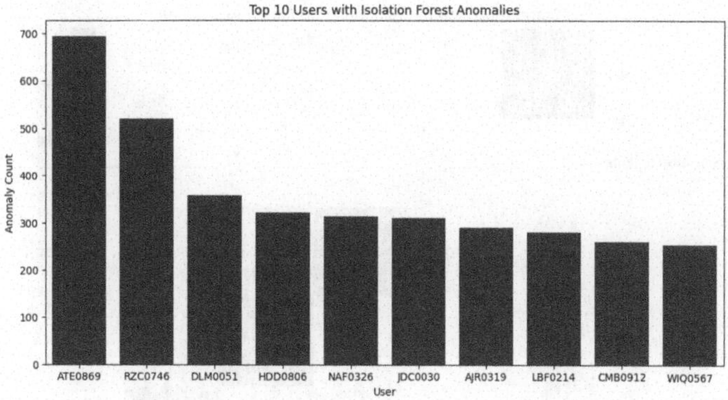

Fig. 12. Top 10 Users with Isolation Forest Anomalies. Different user rankings reveal complementary perspectives on insider risk: IF focuses on Global Outliers

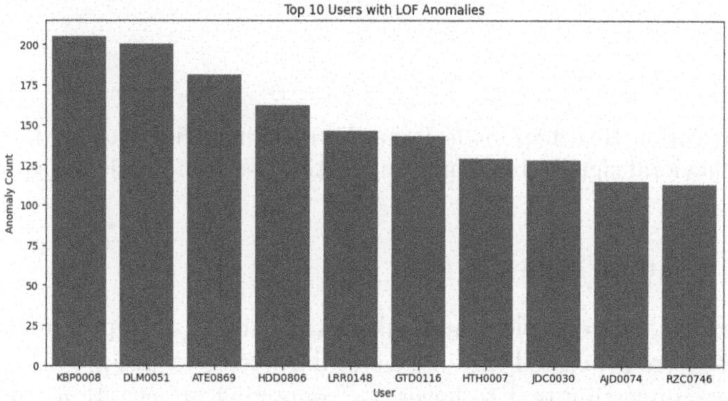

Fig. 13. Top 10 Users with LOF Anomalies. Different user rankings reveal complementary perspectives on insider risk: LOF highlights local clusters

increases coverage, while intersecting them yields a high-confidence alert set. The Jaccard similarity of ≈ 0.999 indicates overlap in anomalies observed by IF and LOF. When comparing models to weak labels, which capture distinct heuristic profiles of risk, the Jaccard coefficient is smaller (≈ 0.058).

While our models detected over 26,000 anomalous events, we acknowledge that not all anomalies correspond to malicious activity. Using programmatically generated weak labels, we found Isolation Forest achieved near-perfect precision but low recall, whereas LOF offered higher recall with some trade-off in false positives. This suggests that a combined approach, intersecting models for high-confidence alerts and union models for broader coverage, can balance accuracy with operational efficiency. In real-world deployments, alert fatigue can be further mitigated through adaptive thresholds, prioritization based on risk scoring, and integration with role-based access data to reduce benign anomalies.

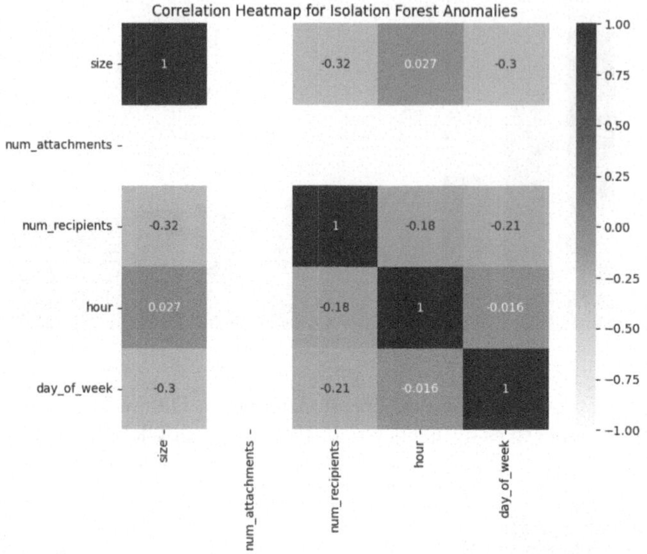

Fig. 14. Correlation Heatmap for Isolation Forest Anomalies showing how IF model interprets behavioral signals differently, supporting use for forensic robustness

5.6 NLP Content Analysis

For both models, the complete anomaly set consisted of approximately 26,300 emails. These were processed through a standardized text pre-processing pipeline that included converting text to lowercase, removing punctuation, and applying tokenization. Three complementary NLP approaches were employed, which are as follows:

(i) Bigram Extraction
The first method involved extracting bigrams, or two-word combinations, from the pre-processed email bodies. This approach helps detect repetitive phrase structures, thematic elements, or unusual word pairings that might be associated with anomalous behavior. The most frequent bigrams in the LOF anomaly set included terms such as "prince prince," "prince ahmose," and "ankh prince." Consequently, although these bigrams are not scan produce misleading high-frequency patterns (Fig. 17, 18).

(ii) Threat Keyword Frequency Analysis To assess whether anomalies contained explicit security-related language, a lexicon of threat-relevant keywords was created, including terms such as leak, unauthorized, breach, confidential, and steal. The anomaly datasets for both LOF and Isolation Forest were scanned for occurrences of these keywords, and the results were aggregated to determine relative prevalence. This step served as a targeted filter to detect direct indicators of potentially malicious intent. While the synthetic dataset limited the frequency of true security terms, the method remains a valuable tool for

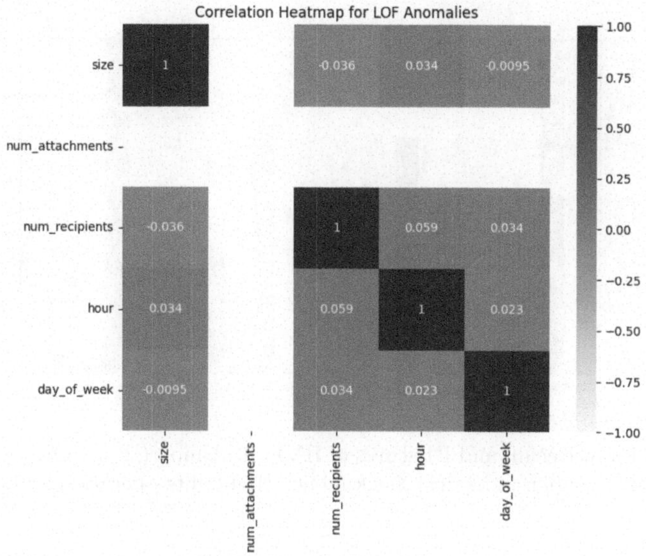

Fig. 15. Correlation Heatmap for LOF Anomalies showing how LOF model interprets behavioral signals differently, supporting use for forensic robustness

use in real-world datasets where direct threat-related vocabulary may be present (Figs. 19 and 20).

(iii) Simplified TF-IDF Approximation The third approach aimed to identify keywords that were disproportionately common in anomalies compared to normal emails. To achieve this, a custom scoring formula is applied which is designed to elevate terms that appear frequently in anomalies but are rare in normal communications. Importantly, an expanded stopword list removed not only standard English stopwords but also dataset-specific artifacts (e.g., "prince," "ahmose," "ankh"), ensuring that results were not dominated by irrelevant synthetic terms. The output was visualized as ranked bar charts for LOF and Isolation Forest anomalies. This allowed for direct comparison of unique anomaly keywords between the two models, revealing differences in the types of terms each model flagged. In the LOF set, for example, words such as "chronicum," "demeans," and "offscreen" ranked highly, while in the Isolation Forest set, terms such as "huxley," "rohmer," and "fishbowl" emerged as distinctive (Fig. 21 and 22).

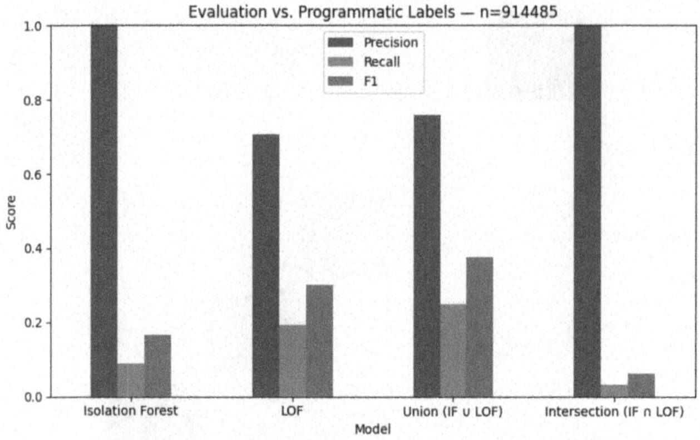

Fig. 16. Precision, Recall, and F1 scores of IF, LOF, Union (IF ∪ LOF), and Intersection (IF ∩ LOF) evaluated against weak labels. Highlights operational implications.

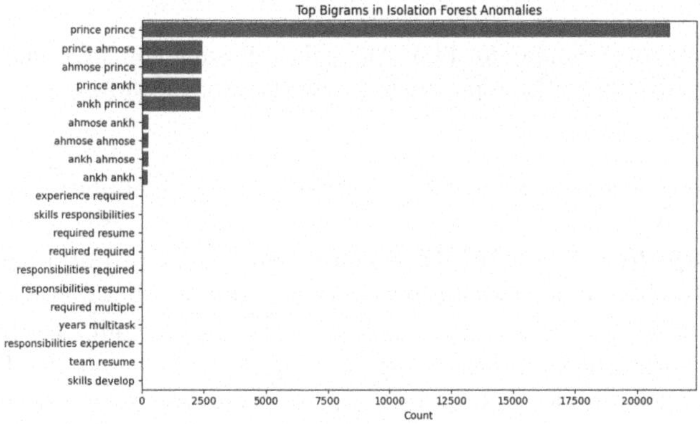

Fig. 17. Top Bigrams extracted from anomalous emails in Isolation Forest

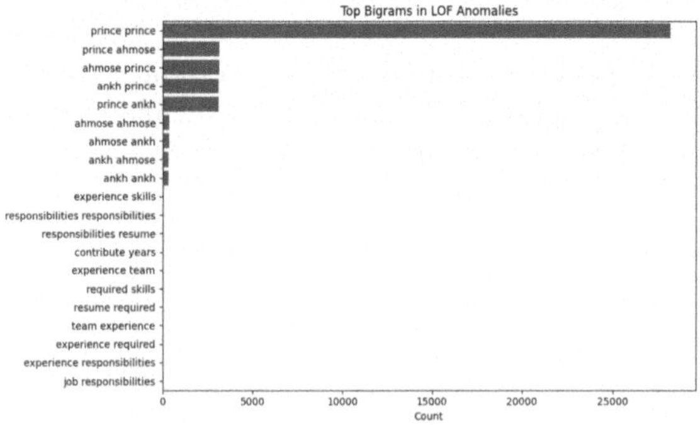

Fig. 18. Top Bigrams extracted from anomalous emails in LOF Anomalies

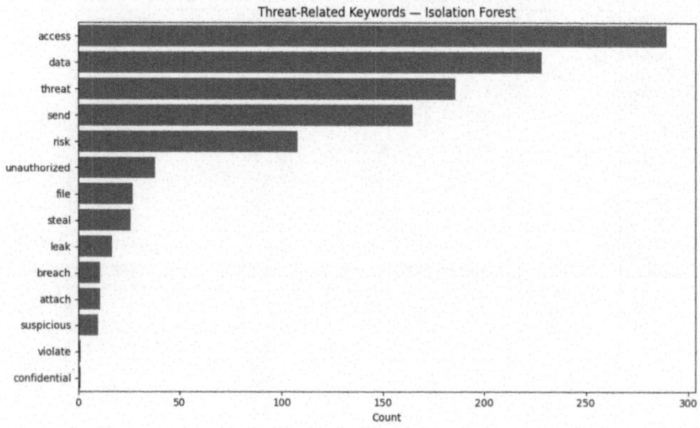

Fig. 19. Threat-Related Keywords—Threat keyword frequency analysis using Isolation Forest

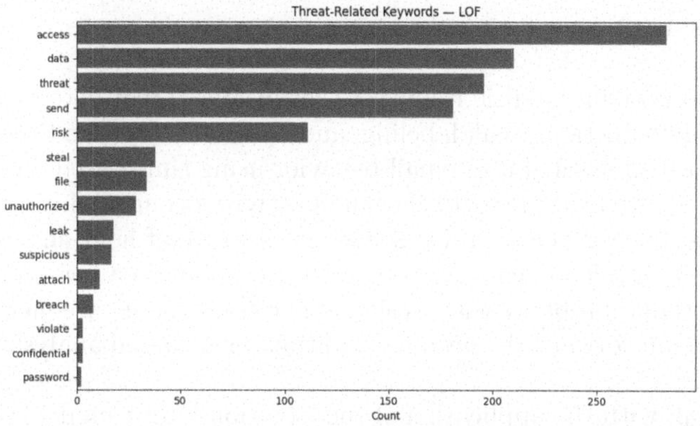

Fig. 20. Threat-Related Keywords—Threat keyword frequency analysis using LOF

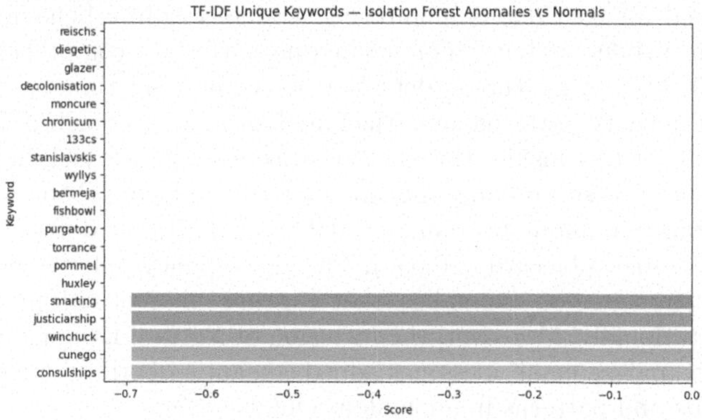

Fig. 21. TF-IDF Unique Keywords in Isolation Forest Anomalies

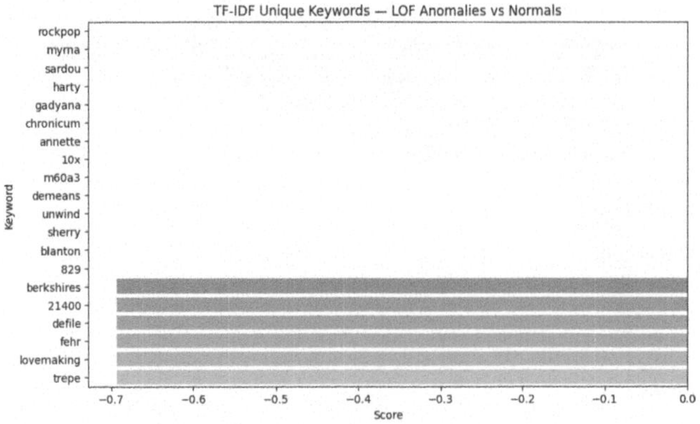

Fig. 22. TF-IDF Unique Keywords—LOF Anomalies vs Normals. Terms highlight contextual cues overlooked in metadata-only analysis.

6 Discussion

This study proposed a forensic framework for insider threat detection that integrates anomaly detection, weak labeling, and Natural Language Processing. The key findings are analysis of user email behavior using time-based and user-based attributes. It showed that most of the email activity occurred during usual work hours that established behavioral baseline and flagged off-hour anomalous activity as high risk. While analysis for top email users showed a few users who have high email activity, probably with explainable roles involving frequent communication, it also put forward the need for additional role-based analysis for context confirmation.

In addition, with the application of the Isolation Forest model [37], an unsupervised anomaly detection technique [38], and feature engineering (e.g., email size, attachments, recipients, time), over 26,000 anomalous events were identified without the need for pre-labeled attack data. These persistent anomalies reflect the need for continuous monitoring to detect subtle behavior deviation and long-term insider activity. This technique outlines a comprehensive forensic framework for insider threat detection by combining time-based behavior analysis, user activity patterns, and Machine Learning approaches. It will allow organizations to detect insider threats that arise from policy violations and misuse of legitimate access, enabling risk mitigation. Similarly, IF and LOF showed good concordance in anomaly counts (≈ 0.999 overlap), but differed when compared to weak lables (Jaccard ≈ 0.058). This discrepancy reflects that while the models generally agree on anomalies, they capture different risk profiles if evaluated computationally. Moreover, the inclusion of Natural Language Processing (NLP) [39] to analyze email messages added semantic depth by unveiling suspicious keywords and patterns in anomalous emails.

7 Conclusion

This research demonstrated a threat detection framework on synthetically generated threat scenarios from the CERT Insider Threat Email dataset on Kaggle. It suggests that Behavior-based anomaly detection using Isolation Forest is effective in detecting potentially malicious email behavior threats without the need for labeled training data. Feature Engineering focuses on time-based activity and the number of recipients to strengthen anomaly detection. Likewise, analysis of the high-activity user also optimized investigation efficiency by emphasizing users with greater forensic value. However, this study lacked a sufficient number of labeled anomalies, which limited the usage of supervised models like Random Forest. The system was also not able to assess the intent or context of email content, and this led to ambiguity in finding anomalies. This suggests the need for context-aware, semantic, and role-informed models in future work.

8 Future Work and Improvement

The current framework successfully identifies anomalous email activity with time-based and user-based attributes. However, there needs to be several enhancements to improve accuracy and practical utilization. If the analysis of the top 10 users by email activity had been integrated with role-based access and job function data, it would have allowed the system to further differentiate between actual high-activity behavior, for instance, managerial or IT role, and malicious intent.

Similarly, this work was evaluated on a smaller-scale dataset, yet the chosen algorithms (Isolation Forest and LOF) are computationally lightweight and amenable to scaling across enterprise-level environments with millions of users. In practice, distributed platforms such as Apache Spark or Dask can parallelize anomaly detection to handle larger data volumes efficiently. Future implementation will also integrate dimensionality reduction and feature selection techniques to maintain performance while reducing computational overhead in massive enterprise systems.

Moreover, Semantic analysis of subject lines, message tone, and keywords could provide much more effective threat categorization than behavior alone [40]. In addition, another area of development is dealing with class imbalance and the unavailability of labeled data. Future research would be facilitated through simulated or synthetic insider threat datasets with ground truth labels to better train and test supervised models. Additionally, hybrid methods combining unsupervised anomaly detection with supervised learning [41] could provide more accurate results. Overall, using this detection model in a real-time monitoring system would offer continuous risk assessment and timely alerts.

8.1 Privacy and Ethical Considerations

Analyzing employee email activity introduces significant privacy and ethical considerations. Any deployment of this framework must adhere to data protection regulations such as GDPR or HIPAA and should be guided by organizational policies on monitoring. Practical safeguards may include focusing primarily on metadata (timestamps, frequency, attachment size) rather than message bodies, anonymizing user identifiers, or applying differential privacy techniques to preserve confidentiality. Moreover, transparency and employee consent mechanisms are essential to ensure that security monitoring does not erode trust or violate ethical standards.

Acknowledgment. This work was supported in part by the National Science Foundation under Grant No. 2321939. Any opinions, findings, and conclusions or recommendations expressed in this material are those of the author(s) and do not necessarily reflect the views of the National Science Foundation.

References

1. Ponemon Institute (2023) Cost of Insider Threats Global Report. https://www.ponemon.org
2. CERT: Insider Threat Center at Carnegie Mellon University (2022). https://insights.sei.cmu.edu/insider-threat/
3. Cappelli, D.M., Moore, A.P., Trzeciak, R.F.: The CERT guide to insider threats: how to prevent, detect, and respond to information technology crimes (Theft, Sabotage, Fraud). Addison-Wesley (2012)
4. Bishop, M., Engle, S., Frincke, D.A., Gates, C., Greitzer, F.L., Peisert, S., Whalen, S.: A risk management approach to the "insider threat". Insider Threats Cyber Secur., 115–137 (2010)
5. Sarkar, K.R.: Assessing insider threats to information security using technical, behavioural and organisational measures. Inf. Secur. Tech. Rep. **15**(3), 112–133 (2010)
6. Colwill, C.: Human factors in information security: The insider threat–Who can you trust these days? information security technical report **14**(4), 186–196 (2009)
7. Casey, E.: Digital evidence and computer crime: Forensic science, computers, and the internet. Academic press (2011)
8. Bradford, P., Hu, N.: A layered approach to insider threat detection and proactive forensics. In: Proceedings of the Twenty-First Annual Computer Security Applications Conference (Technology Blitz) (2005)
9. Kowalski, E., Conway, T., Keverline, S., Williams, M., Cappelli, D., Willke, B., Moore, A.: Insider threat study: Illicit cyber activity in the government sector (2008)
10. Singer, P.W., Friedman, A.: Cybersecurity and cyberwar: What everyone needs to know . Oxford University Press (2013)
11. Inayat, U., Farzan, M., Mahmood, S., Zia, M.F., Hussain, S., Pallonetto, F.: Insider threat mitigation: systematic literature review. Ain Shams Eng. J. **15**(12), 103068 (2024)
12. Division, C.E.R.T.: Common Sense Guide to Mitigating Insider Threats, 6th edn. Carnegie Mellon University, Software Engineering Institute (2021)
13. Randazzo, M.R., Keeney, M., Kowalski, E., Cappelli, D., Moore, A.: Insider threat study: Illicit cyber activity in the banking and finance sector (2004)

14. Greitzer, F.L., Kangas, L.J., Noonan, C.F., Brown, C.R., Ferryman, T.: Psychosocial modeling of insider threat risk based on behavioral and word use analysis. e-Service Journal: A Journal of Electronic Services in the Public and Private Sectors **9**(1), 106–138 (2013)
15. Johansen, G.: Digital forensics and incident response: incident response techniques and procedures to respond to modern cyber threats. Packt Publishing Ltd. (2020)
16. Grant, O., Agoro, H.: Trends in Network Compliance and Regulatory Challenges (2021)
17. Manoharan, P., Yin, J., Wang, H., Zhang, Y., Ye, W.: Insider threat detection using supervised machine learning algorithms. Telecommun. Syst. **87**(4), 899–915 (2024)
18. Padiet, P., Islam, R., Khan, M.A.: Users' Scenario-Base for Analysing Insider Threat Detection Based on User's Downloads Activity Logs. Future of Information and Communication Conference (2024)
19. Wei, Y., Chow, K.-P., Yiu, S.-M.: Insider threat prediction based on unsupervised anomaly detection scheme for proactive forensic investigation. Forensic Sci. Int. Digital Investigation **38**, 301126 (2021)
20. Le, D.C., Zincir-Heywood, N.: Anomaly detection for insider threats using unsupervised ensembles. IEEE Trans. Network Serv. Manage. **18**(2), 1152–1164 (2021)
21. Kim, D.-W., Shin, G.-Y., Han, M.-M.: Anomaly detection based on discrete wavelet transformation for insider threat classification. Comput. Syst. Sci. Eng. **46**(1), 153–164 (2023)
22. Alzaabi, F.R., Mehmood, A.: A review of recent advances, challenges, and opportunities in malicious insider threat detection using machine learning methods. IEEE Access **12**, 30907–30927 (2024)
23. Rhee, J.B.: Explainable AI for Intrusion Detection Systems: Challenges and Opportunities. Authorea Preprints (2025)
24. Sivaraman, H.: Real-Time Anomaly Detection for Insider Threat Prevention in Federal Systems. ESP J. Eng. Technol. Advancements **2**, 62–67 (2024)
25. Manral, B., Somani, G.: Establishing forensics capabilities in the presence of superuser insider threats. Forensic Science International: Digital Investigation **38**, 301263 (2021)
26. Alsowail, R.A., Al-Shehari, T.: A multi-tiered framework for insider threat prevention. Electronics **10**(9), 1005 (2021)
27. Subhani, A., Khan, I.A., Zubair, A.: Review of insider and insider threat detection in the organizations. J. Adv. Res. Soc. Sci. Humanities **6**(4), 167–174 (2021)
28. Homoliak, I., Toffalini, F., Guarnizo, J., Elovici, Y., Ochoa, M.: Insight into insiders and it: a survey of insider threat taxonomies, analysis, modeling, and countermeasures. ACM Comput. Surv. (CSUR) **52**(2), 1–40 (2019)
29. Tian, T., Zhang, C., Jiang, B., Feng, H., Lu, Z.: Insider threat detection for specific threat scenarios. Cybersecurity **8**(1), 17 (2025)
30. Alsowail, R.A., Al-Shehari, T.: Techniques and countermeasures for preventing insider threats. PeerJ Comput. Sci. **8**, e938 (2022)
31. Liu, L., De Vel, O., Han, Q.-L., Zhang, J., Xiang, Y.: Detecting and preventing cyber insider threats: a survey. IEEE Commun. Surv. Tutorials **20**(2), 1397–1417 (2018)
32. Liu, F.T., Ting, K.M., Zhou, Z.-H.: Isolation forest. In: 2008 Eighth IEEE International Conference on Data Mining (2008)
33. Chandola, V., Banerjee, A., Kumar, V.: Anomaly detection: a survey. ACM Comput. Surv. (CSUR) **41**(3), 1–58 (2009)

34. Mahajan, A.A.: A Novel Hybrid Model Merging LOF and iForest Algorithms for Insider Threats Detection. In: 2024 4th Asian Conference on Innovation in Technology (ASIANCON) (2024)
35. Boutaba, R., Salahuddin, M.A., Limam, N., Ayoubi, S., Shahriar, N., Estrada-Solano, F., Caicedo, O.M.: A comprehensive survey on machine learning for networking: evolution, applications and research opportunities. J. Internet Serv. Appl. **9**(1), 1–99 (2018)
36. Legg, P.A., Buckley, O., Goldsmith, M., Creese, S.: Automated insider threat detection system using user and role-based profile assessment. IEEE Syst. J. **11**(2), 503–512 (2015)
37. Al Farizi, W.S., Hidayah, I., Rizal, M.N.: Isolation forest based anomaly detection: a systematic literature review. In: 2021 8th International Conference on Information Technology, Computer and Electrical Engineering (ICITACEE) (2021)
38. Singh, A., Rakhra, M., Singh, D., Kaur, B., Kaur, H.: Improving Insider Threat Detection with User and Role-Based Behavior. In: 2024 11th International Conference on Reliability, Infocom Technologies and Optimization (Trends and Future Directions) (ICRITO) (2024)
39. Haq, M.A., Khan, M.A.R., Alshehri, M.: Insider threat detection based on NLP word embedding and machine learning. Intell. Autom. Soft Comput. **33**(1), 619–635 (2022)
40. Ryciak, P., Wasielewska, K., Janicki, A.: Anomaly detection in log files using selected natural language processing methods. Appl. Sci. **12**(10), 5089 (2022)
41. Yi, J., Tian, Y.: Insider threat detection model enhancement using hybrid algorithms between unsupervised and supervised learning. Electronics **13**(5), 973 (2024)

Dynamic Analysis of Malware Detection Using Customized Payloads in Web Applications: Examining The Effectiveness of Manual and Automated Approaches

Jiban Krisna Das[1(✉)], Lei Chen[2], Christopher Kadlec[2], Atef Mohamed[2], and Yiming Ji[1]

[1] Kennesaw State University, Marietta, GA 30060, USA
jdas4@students.kennesaw.edu, YJi9@kennesaw.edu
[2] Georgia Southern University, Statesboro, GA 30458, USA
{LChen,ckadlec,amohamed}@georgiasouthern.edu

Abstract. The study introduces a novel approach that uses custom payloads to examine the effectiveness of manual and automated malware detection techniques. The dynamic blended approach can effectively generate attack payloads and identify vulnerabilities in a website, ultimately strengthening the security measures of the websites. This research focuses on dynamic analysis in a controlled environment while testing and analyzing SQL and XSS payloads under varying security conditions. This quantitative analysis involves crafting targeted payloads to bypass Web Application Firewall (WAF) filters and security controls, considering the detection accuracy, response times, false positives and false negatives. The study findings reveal that basic manual payloads are effective against lower security levels, while customized advanced or adaptive payloads could successfully evade detection using obfuscation or encoding techniques. Additionally, in various security constraints, time-based and error-based SQL injections demonstrated significant effectiveness in detection. Automatic scanning using OWASP ZAP identifies common vulnerabilities, but is often ineffective during complex or obfuscated injections. This research underscores the importance of hybrid or blended approaches that combine automated and customized payload techniques for the detection of advanced malware attacks to enhance web application security. This integration of custom payload design with manual and automated scanning approaches can improve detection accuracy and speed up the investigation process to mitigate zero-day vulnerabilities.

Keywords: Dynamic analysis · SQL injection (SQLi) · Cross-site scripting (XSS) · Web application firewall · WAF · OWASP ZAP · Custom payload · Cyber-attacks · Zero-day attacks

V. V. Pham et al. (Eds.): CIDDF 2025, ACSAR 5, pp. 77–101, 2026.
https://doi.org/10.1007/978-3-032-19488-6_5

1 Introduction

In the evolving landscape of advanced technology, critical challenges in cybersecurity have emerged in the web application security. Mitigating these crucial issues are becoming a real challenge for cybersecurity researchers, developers and professionals. Due to the increasing integration of data transactions online, business operations and services occurring online have drastically increased the sophisticated malware threats such as injection-based attacks and malware-driven intrusion. According to the OWASP top ten vulnerability list, cyber attackers, prime targets remain to exploit malicious attacks on web applications. Some vulnerabilities include SQL injection (SQLi), Cross-site Scripting (XSS), Cross-Site Request Forgery (CSRF) and Server Side Request Forgery (SSRF) which result in unauthorized data access, data breaches, access control violations and disrupted systems vulnerability [6]. These cyber threats accelerate the need for the development and implementation of manual and automated methods specifically designed to minimize such vulnerabilities. This research evaluates and compares the efficiency and accuracy of custom payload approaches between automated and manual penetration testing methods to identify SQL injection and XSS attacks in web applications. The study conducts both traditional and advanced penetration testing using customized Python-based payloads on different web applications in simulated environments. Automated testing could be accomplished by using different vulnerability scanning tools such as SQLMap, OWASP ZAP and Burp Suite for identifying SQLi and XSS attack vulnerabilities. Manual testing includes different methods such as code review, payload injection and other methods. This study provides a comparative analysis to determine the accuracy and comprehensive results based on custom payload testing and existing methods to provide actionable insights for organizations to optimize the strategies and policies for web vulnerability management.

2 Background

In this digital world, due to the increasingly connected devices of web applications, cybersecurity has become one of the most critical domains. The main goal of cybersecurity is not only to prevent unauthorized access, but also to identify vulnerable entry points, including mitigation techniques to preempt malware execution. The continuous evolution of modern web applications to satisfy business goals and meet consumer needs makes them prime targets by expanding the cyber-attack surface. Web applications that are improperly secured serve as security entry points for cyber attackers to exploit vulnerabilities such as SQL injection, Cross-Site Scripting (XSS) or other OWASP top ten security threats.

SQL injections and XSS have been proven to be the most persistent attacks in web applications where SQL injections may occur due to improper input sanitization, allowing attackers to manipulate backend database queries. Additionally, XSS vulnerabilities allow cyber attackers to input malicious scripts into web applications. In modern attack patterns, three main types of XSS vulnerabilities exist: stored, reflected and DOM-based XSS (which have different severity levels depending on how they are exploited on the DOM). According to the OWASP top ten vulnerabilities list, SQL injection and XSS have consistently been found to be prevalent attack vectors that cybersecurity researchers must address and mitigate by developing advanced customized detection tools and testing frameworks.

To mitigate vulnerability detection gaps, cybersecurity researchers explored hybrid methods that combine dynamic and static analysis. Some studies focused on improving malware detection and identification in Android applications using the sandboxing mechanism through behavioral-based profiling, which can determine better results in complex environments [17]. Malware analysis also integrates framework employing Fuzzy AHP and TOPIS methods to evaluate the effectiveness of static and dynamic analysis and reverse engineering techniques. Reverse engineering was found to be most effective in identifying complex malware in web applications [12].

This background analysis focuses on determining the challenges of malware detection in web applications, which is evidence that customized payload-based testing approaches are necessary for dynamic malware analysis to effectively identify potential threats in web applications. This research seeks to validate the effectiveness of malware analysis approaches using customized payloads to detect injection vulnerabilities and provide insightful recommendations to improve the detection strategies of traditional and automated techniques.

3 Literature Review

Abikoyel et al. [1] proposed a pattern-based detection system which follows a Knuth-Morris-Pratt (KMP) string-matching algorithm that integrates parse-tree analysis for detecting SQLi and XSS vulnerabilities. In a similar study, Alsaffar et al. [4] introduced a Delphi-based vulnerability detection tool capable of detecting stored, reflected and DOM-based XSS vulnerabilities. Although the KMP-based method demonstrated 95% detection accuracy for XSS and 92% for SQLi and found a low false positive rate of 3%, on the other side Delphi-based system detected 99.47% detection accuracy including 100% precision and 81% recall for detecting XSS vulnerabilities. Overall, both the studies highlighted the importance of pattern-based recognition techniques for detecting injection-based vulnerabilities.

Correa et al. [9] developed a hybrid methodology combining static (SAST) and dynamic (DAST) for detecting web application security vulnerabilities. The comparative results determined that static analysis often ignored potential detection of SQL and XSS vulnerabilities while the dynamic validation approach indicated significant reduction in false positives. Similarly, Tudela et al. [14] investigated SAST, DAST and Interactive Application Security Testing (IAST) security analysis tools according to the OWASP benchmark analysis. IAST tool showed best performance on reducing false positives and better in true positive rate. Moreover, the combination of DAST and IAST achieved 100% recall rate and 0% false positive rate.

Han et al. [11] provided another hybrid concept known as "Mallnsight". This framework used static and dynamic systematic profiling techniques for effective malware detection. Additionally, ML classifiers decision tree, random forest and XGBoost were used for accurately profiling malware to overcome the current obfuscation challenges. Likewise, Abhishek and Fawaz [16] emphasized hybrid systems using a Fuzzy Analytical Hierarchy Process (Fuzzy-AHP) framework for prioritizing the malware analysis methods. The "Mallnsight" proved 99.76% detection rate for known malware and 97.21% accuracy for unseen samples whereas Fuzzy-AHP method combining static and dynamic methods showed priority weight of 26.92% and network traffic analysis is 18.26% and Machin-level analysis is 13.18%. Collectively, both the methods highlighted that hybrid methods can minimize false negatives providing more comprehensive, modern and ideal platform for complex analysis of malware in web applications.

Rane and Qureshi [18] highlighted the effectiveness of automated and manual penetration testing tools and determined which methods provide more accurate and comprehensive vulnerability detection in web applications. DREAD threat modeling methods were employed to assess the severity of attack vulnerabilities. The study observed that the automated tool Netsparker able to detect SQL injection and XSS attack vulnerabilities while manual penetration testing detected it as a false positive. Overall, manual penetration testing found more comprehensive which could detect critical vulnerabilities. Similar research conducted by Anaoval et al. [7] also analyzed that manual method is effective to bypass authentication in 80% of cases while automated methods detected fewer vulnerabilities and failed to protect some exploits. Additionally, Alanda et al. [2] explored the automated and manual penetration testing tools, that are used to uncover the weaknesses in different web applications. The black-box testing methods determined the effectiveness of SQL injection vulnerabilities in bypassing security systems across multiple websites. Among 10 websites tested, 80% were detected as vulnerable to SQL injection attacks that allowed the penetration testers to reveal sensitive data from the database. To summarize, these results prove that despite the efficiency of automated penetration testing methods, manual or human expertise is crucial for gaining overall effectiveness specifically for logic-based or multi-step vulnerabilities.

Shah [19] compared four automated tools OWASP ZAP, Burp Suite, Nikto and Arachni. Among other automated tools, Burp Suit identifies 26 and ZAP identifies 18 vulnerabilities on the OWASP benchmark. In contrast, performance of Arachni and Nikto is significantly poor and lower in vulnerability detection. A similar study by Sharma [20] evaluated the performance of similar vulnerability scanners (OWASP ZAP, Acunetix and Burp Suite). Although both study results highlighted that Burp Suite and OWASP ZAP demonstrated superior performance and were found to be the most effective in detecting vulnerabilities, but a later study showed limitations in identifying DOM-based XSS. In further research, Matti [15] focused on analyzing three open source web vulnerability scanners to evaluate their effectiveness in detecting SQLi and XSS attack vulnerabilities. OWASP ZAP showed superior performance while detection of both SQL injection and XSS attacks, while Vega and Wapiti showed inconsistent performance, indicated missing some XSS vulnerabilities.

Parvez et al. [17] analyzed the performance of four black-box scanners such as ZAP, BurpSuite, Wapiti, and Nessus essential were tested on two vulnerable testbeds Wackopicko and Scanit. According to the tool analysis results, none of the scanners successfully detected stored SQL injection and multi-step stored XSS attack vulnerabilities. ZAP and Burp suite were able to detect stored XSS attacks without login pages, but could not detect stored SQLi attacks. Similarly, Althunayyan et al. [5] analyzed the effectiveness of five black-box tools Burp Suite, OWASP ZAP, Nikto, Arachni and Wapiti were tested on the OWASP Juice Shop platform to identify SQLi, NoSQL and SSTI in modern web applications. Burp Suite and OWASP ZAP detect around 40% of SQLi vulnerabilities and 25% of NoSQL and SSTI vulnerabilities. To sum up, both the analysis highlighted the weaknesses and limitations of black-box scanning tools in detecting SQLi, XSS, NoSQL and XSS vulnerabilities which reinforce the need for layered testing methodologies.

Alazmi et al. [3] conducted a systematic literature review approach to examine 90 academic publications and identified 30 web vulnerability scanners. The study analyzes each scanner based on platform capability, user interface type and detection capability of OWASP top ten vulnerabilities. The survey revealed that most of the automated scanners showed inconsistency in their performance of detecting SQLi and XSS vulnerabilities and detection rates from 0% to 100%. Among all other scanners Acunetix and IBM AppScan demonstrated better and variable performance. Altulaihan et al. [6] also discussed the limitations and capabilities of various penetration testing tools and methods such as Netsparker, Acunetix, Vega, OWASP ZAP and Wapiti. Netsparker and Acunetix displayed a significant accuracy in detecting SQL injection while OWASP ZAP demonstrated excellent results in detecting XSS attacks. To summarize, despite better detection rates of automated scanners, both the study analysis recommends emphasizing the need for manual and automated methods to consistently detect complex vulnerabilities.

Lakshmi et al. [13] mentioned that various effective tools and techniques are used to identify SQLi and XSS vulnerabilities such as Burp Suite, OWASP ZAP and some manual testing techniques. Another study by Tudela et al. [14] explored the advantages of static, dynamic and interactive testing tools and technologies for increasing detection rates of OWASP vulnerabilities. Sharma [20] addressed some other vulnerability scanners such as Acunetix, Netsparker and Wapiti which were found effective in terms of detection accuracy and performance rating depending on the complexity of web applications. However, some vulnerability testing tools missed complex malware vulnerabilities in web applications where custom input validation or JavaScript-based logic was implemented.

Garn et al. [10] examined a structured grammar-based testing methods using the SQLIjector+ tool. This tool was designed to automatically submit the attack vectors and to determine injection success considering the structure of query and database response. This tool successfully identified all known SQL injection vulnerabilities evaluated on various web applications including WAVSEP and DVWA. The results showed the SQLIjector+ against WAVESEP achieved 100% injection and execution rate comparing SQLMap, wapti and w3af. In similar research, Auricchio et al. [8] designed a modular testing framework that can integrate several types of attacks and techniques for web application penetration testing. The result demonstrated 100% precision rate, 97.36% recall and F-score was 98.66% and the SQLi and blind SQLi detection rate was 100% where no false positives and false negatives were found. The overall performance of the framework outperforms traditional frameworks such as WAPTI, ZAP, ARCHNI and Nessus. Overall, these grammar-based and modular testing frameworks validate that customized payloads significantly enhance vulnerability detection when tailored to the application logic.

4 Methodology

The research conducts systematic penetration testing methodology tailoring to compare the effectiveness of manual, automated and customized payloads techniques to identify the SQL injection (SQLi) and Cross-Site Scripting (XSS) vulnerabilities in web applications. The research methods follow a structured quantitative approach, and the entire analysis is conducted in a virtual controlled environment to ensure security and reliability and to maintain cybersecurity laws and regulations.

4.1 Penetration Testing Process

This study follows a structured dynamic penetration testing approach where realistic attack scenarios are simulated, which includes pre-engagement arrangements, vulnerability testing, performance evaluations and result analysis.

4.2 Pre-engagement Arrangements

This is the initial phase of the research testing process where various important aspects must be settled before the actual testing begins, including defining and documenting the scope of the experiments, setting up environments, selection of tools and techniques.

4.3 Objective and Scope

The testing specifically focuses on a virtual lab environment installed in a local machine and the websites are DVWA (Damn Vulnerable Web Application) and OWASP Juice Shop, and a MySQL database is used for detecting SQL injection and XSS vulnerabilities. The scope of the tests deliberately excludes all external websites to ensure ethical compliance and safety.

4.4 Configuring the Test Environment

Oracle VirtualBox is installed with 2GB base memory and 25GB of secondary storage to create an isolated and controlled virtual lab environment. One of the popular cybersecurity attack tools, Kali Linux, is configured in VirtualBox to simulate vulnerability tests in a controlled environment, enabling safe and reproducible testing. After setting up the attack environment, web applications (DVWA and OWASP Juice Shop) are installed on the local Kali machine to simulate virtual testing scenarios.

4.5 Determining Testing Tools

Manual and automated testing tools are installed to identify and categorize SQLi and XSS vulnerabilities in websites. The automated vulnerability testing tools OWASP ZAP (Zed Attack Proxy), Burp Suite (Community Edition) and SQLMap (detecting SQL injection) are installed on Kali Linux. Additionally, manual payloads are tested and executed on the DVWA and Juice Shop websites using a default web browser Mozilla Firefox 128.5.0esr 64-bit. After configuring these automated tools, Python 3.12.8 and various Python libraries such as beautifulsoup 4 4.12.3, Requests, Selenium, and psutil are installed for generating and executing custom Python scripts. Moreover, for extended analysis this study also considers some other Python libraries such as mechanize, lxml, mitmproxy, pyshark, sqlparse, Faker, and urllib3 for enhancing SQLi and XSS vulnerability detection. This Python library is crucial for vulnerability testing in stored and DOM-based XSS attacks where JavaScript is required for execution in a real browser environment. In this analysis, it is used to automate the login to the DVWA website through the Firefox browser, also tracking the custom Python payload execution.

In summary, this research is highly focused on setting up the dynamic attack environment with Oracle VirtualBox and Kali Linux, which provides a controlled and simulated platform for the subsequent vulnerability testing. The above configurations ensure that the experimental results are consistent and that the vulnerability testing and resource optimizations are accurately measured throughout the entire experiment.

4.6 Vulnerability Testing

In this execution phase, three testing methods are implemented for the experimental analysis of SQL injection and XSS vulnerability detection, which includes manual, automated and custom payloads techniques.

Manual Testing. Manual penetration testing is conducted using various SQL injection strings ('OR '1'='1' and XSS scripts (<script> alert ('XSS alert')</script>) which are injected into different vulnerable entry points of DVWA and Juice Shop websites. The execution result includes immediate pop-up alerts, error messages and storing payloads in the back-end database.

Automated Testing. The study also incorporates automated vulnerability testing that are performed using SQLMap and OWASP ZAP. These tools can generate multiple payloads and automatically uncover various injection points of the websites. Burp Suite is used to analyze the results captured from the network requests and responses when the payloads are executed by the automated tools.

Customized Payload Testing. This research introduces a novel testing method that is implemented using custom Python scripts by generating dynamic attack payloads to analyze the critical attack environment and evasive attack patterns. These unique variants of payloads are specifically designed to bypass WAF filters and automatic detection of SQL injection and XSS vulnerabilities.

4.7 Performance Evaluations and Analysis

This is accomplished by collecting the results from the previous testing methods and analyzing the effectiveness of each scanning tool and based on key performance indicators (KPIs) which include detection rate, speed of scanning, resource utilized, false positives and negatives and attack security levels (low, medium, high, impossible). In addition, this study also considered server responses, error logs, HTTP request logs and tools specific reports to validate and maintain credibility of the comparative analysis.

5 Results Analysis

In this research, data are collected from each vulnerability scanner and systematically analyzed based on performance metrics. A systematic analysis of SQL injection and XSS vulnerabilities is categorized as manual, automated and customized payload testing. A summary of quantitative data analysis has been provided to evaluate the insights of each scanner's strengths, limitations and effectiveness in detecting SQL injections (SQLi) and Cross-site scripting (XSS) attacks (as summarized in Table 2 and Table 3). Moreover, the primary focus of this research is to generate custom payloads using Python scripts where necessary Python packages and libraries are installed in Kali Linux.

5.1 Manual SQL Injection Testing

In this stage, the manual SQL injection tests are performed by directly injecting basic and advanced level payloads into the web forms and URL parameters of designated DVWA and OWASP Juice shop web pages. UNION-based SQL injection payloads are executed on a DVWA website SQL entry point at a low security level, which successfully retrieved user information from "users" table of 'dvwa'. The information includes 'First name', and 'surname' in hex encoded format. In Fig. 1 error-based SQL injection payloads are effectively injected and executed at a high security level that tries to force the database to generate an error that includes partial data in the output message. These payloads return 'First name' and 'surname' from all users that exist in the database 'user' table. This also demonstrates the hex-encoding SQL injection payloads in impossible security level to bypass the local filters, which are successfully able to inject the encoded code into the database without showing any warning or alert message on the website and not even in the database. Furthermore, for detailed analysis, the Burp suite tool is incorporated to intercept manually executed SQL injection payloads. Figure 2 captures the Burp suite request header which contains important information on method, user agent, cookie, and connection type and response header provides significant database information including 'Firstname' and 'surname' from the database user table. In summary, manual testing consistently performs better at low-and medium-security levels, which indicates that strict security filters are often impeded by manually injected payloads. Furthermore, manual analysis is vital for further understanding the attack behavior and critical injection points in a website, which helps formulate strategies for customized payload design. Table 1 summarizes the manual SQLi payloads tested on various target Web pages, including the findings of potential vulnerabilities at different security levels. These findings signify the vulnerability assessment of critical injection points on websites.

5.2 Automated SQL Injection Testing

Automated methods include SQLMap and OWASP Zap tools for testing SQLi injection payloads into DVWA and OWASP Juice Shop to detect injection vulnerabilities. SQLMap able to inject the SQLi payload into the Juice Shop with severity level-5 and risk level-3. Although the executed payload effectively shows the injected alerts on the webpage and makes the webpage unreachable, it could not extract any database information from the server. Furthermore, Fig. 3 illustrates the SQLMap payload that contains a session cookie to retrieve the information from the 'dvwa' database table. This payload is successfully executed at the vulnerable injection points of the DVWA and retrieves the table names (guestbook and users) from the 'dvwa' database. Some SQLMap payload is executed but failed to detect any vulnerabilities in the database which encountered connection issues due to stronger validation. Figure 4 shows the automatic testing process of the OWASP ZAP, including important alerts. Table 2 represents the comparative analysis of automated scanning tools, where SQLMap performs significantly well in detecting SQLi attack vulnerabilities.

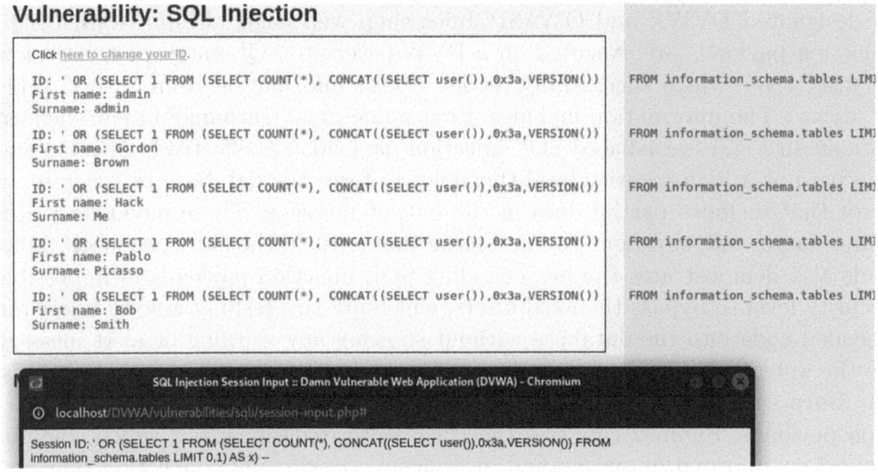

Fig. 1. Error-based manual SQLi payload injection in high security level

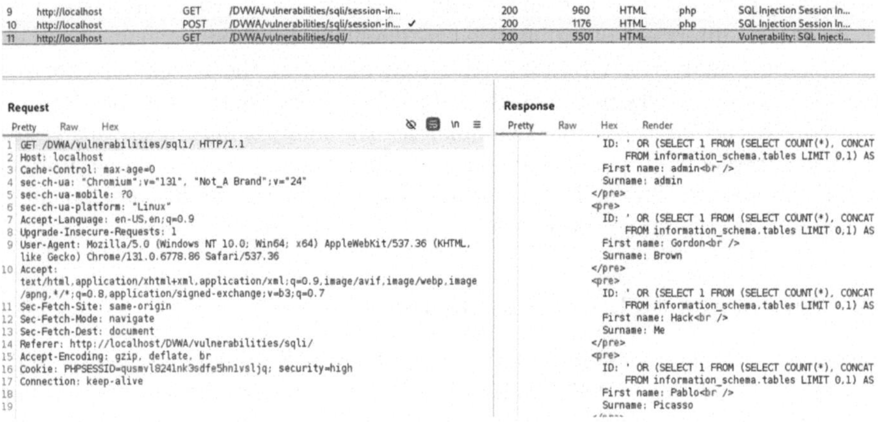

Fig. 2. Request and Response header information while Manual SQL injection captured in Burp suite

5.3 SQL Injection (SQLi) Vulnerability Testing Using Custom Payloads in OWASP Juice Shop and DVWA Websites

The study incorporates customized payload techniques that involved carefully designing custom Python scripts for SQL injection tailored to bypass specific input sanitization and database-specific exploits. Figure 5 shows the custom Python scripts that include dynamic code blocks for admin login credentials (email, password), URL parameters (Base url, Login url and search url) and CSRF token information for automatic login to Juice shop website. In addition, the script also designed with multiple JavaScript payloads including numeric injection ('OR 1=1), simple string-based ('OR '1' ='1' –), basic union-based

Table 1. Results and findings of manual SQLi testing vulnerabilities on different websites

Payloads	Target Website URL	Security Level	Findings
OR '1'='1', OR '1'='1' – null –, 1' AND 1=1 – 1' AND 1=2 – 1' AND SLEEP (5) –	http://localhost/DVWA/vulnerabilities/sqli/	Low	Potential vulnerabilities found including users from MySQL database
OR '1'='1', OR '1'='1' –	http://localhost/DVWA/vulnerabilities/sqli_blind/	Medium	Partial vulnerabilities detected and limited data extraction
'UNION SELECT 1, 2, concat (username, 0x3a, password) FROM users- -	http://localhost/DVWA/vulnerabilities/sqli/	Medium and High	SQLi successful and returns database user information
'UNION SELECT 1, concat (0x41444D494E3A, HEX(password)) FROM users–	http://localhost/DVWA/vulnerabilities/sqli/	Impossible	SQLi executed but no error shown due to stronger input validation

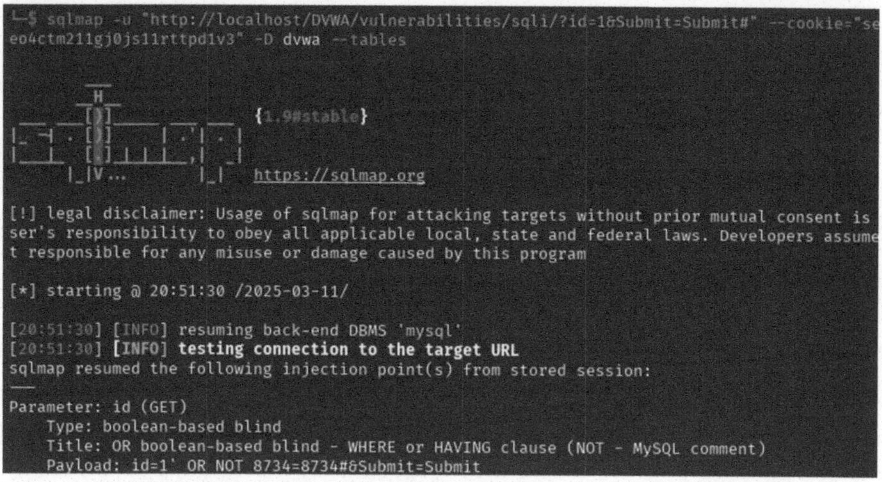

Fig. 3. Successfully Injected SQLMap payload and extracting database information

injections ("UNION SELECT 'a' ,null, null –") and advanced payloads ("—— SELECT GROUPS_CONCAT(name)"). Moreover, during the execution of this Python script, "get_token" function extracts the CSRF token information and admin login information through beautifulsoup4 Python library for successful login. After that, "Request" Python library effectively sends the SQLi payloads to the target website using HTTP GET and POST request. The custom payloads are executed and detected the SQLi vulnerability including active responses from database server and automatically identify the vulnerable entry points of the websites. These results indicate that the custom payloads are significantly effective to inject multiple SQLi payloads into the various vulnerable injection points of the websites as well as exacting important database information.

The dynamic custom Python scripts where contain target_url= ("http://localhost/DVWA/vulnerabilities/sqli), login_url, login information and SQLi payloads. After the execution of the script, the selenium WebDriver automatically load web browser (Firefox) while "url_login" function provides admin credential for login to the DVWA website. Moreover, it automatically redirects to the specific vulnerable target URL which indicates effective SQL injection in the DVWA website. Figure 6 shows that successfully executed payloads are able to interpret backend database version and the website triggers an uncaught "mysqli_exception" which specifies an issue with SQL syntax but it confirms that the requested query reached the backend database. Overall, SQL injection test-

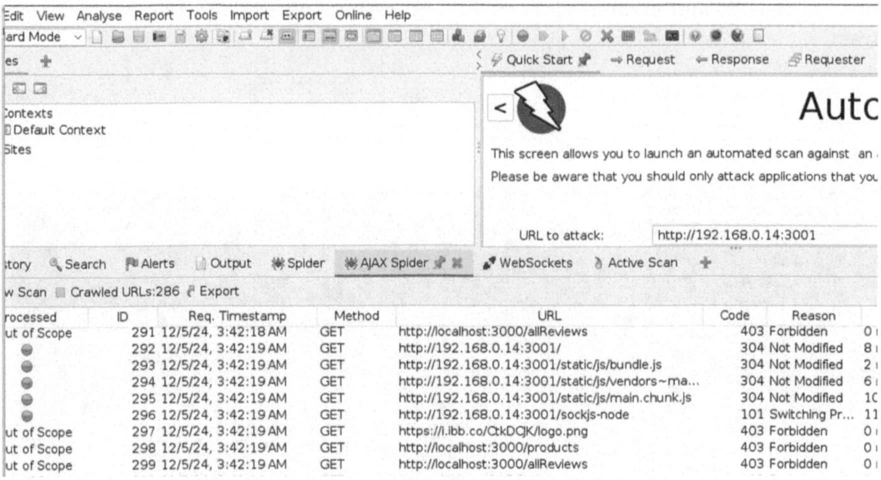

Fig. 4. Automated SQL Injection payload scanning on OWASP ZAP

ing provides a varied analysis and results of the aforementioned methods. Manual testing indicates lower detection accuracy against advanced filters. Additionally, the automated testing using SQLMap outperforms in detection accuracy and speed although it shows partial effectiveness during the detection of SQLi vulnerabilities from the SQLite database. Finally, the customized payload approach provides excellent detection rates and speed and is able to inject multiple payloads at a time. However, some payload execution generates more false positives specifically while testing on the DVWA website due to input sanitizations at the top security level.

5.4 Analysis of Manual XSS Vulnerability Testing

For XSS attacks, some basic payloads (<script>alert('XSS simple test'<script>), <img src= 'x' onerror='alert("XSS vulnerability found")'> and <svg/onload=alert('SVG XSS alert') are tested on DVWA website. These payloads are successfully executed and shows the warning on the webpages (Fig. 7). Additionally, this testing includes some advanced JavaScript payloads such as <iframe src="javascript.alert('Advanced XSS vulnerability alert')">, <svg/onload=setTimeout('alert("XSS detected")', 2000)> and some other stored XSS are also tested on different security levels (Low, Medium, High and Impossible). Although most of the payloads are effectively executed on the websites but some fail to execute XSS vulnerabilities due to high or impossible security levels. Moreover, Significant vulnerabilities are detected after executing advanced stored XSS payloads that create difficulties accessing the website and potential database issues. The study also implements Burp Suite to capture the executed payloads at various security levels and determine some crucial XSS vulnerability information for quantitative analysis. In summary, this man-

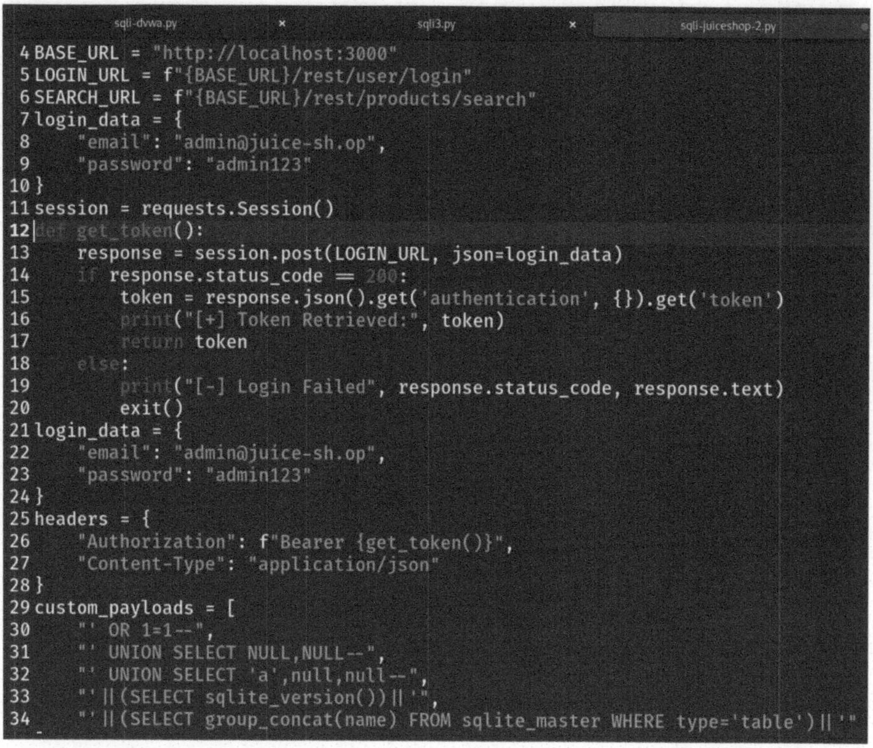

```
sqli-dvwa.py        sqli3.py        sqli-juiceshop-2.py
BASE_URL = "http://localhost:3000"
LOGIN_URL = f"{BASE_URL}/rest/user/login"
SEARCH_URL = f"{BASE_URL}/rest/products/search"
login_data = {
    "email": "admin@juice-sh.op",
    "password": "admin123"
}
session = requests.Session()
def get_token():
    response = session.post(LOGIN_URL, json=login_data)
    if response.status_code == 200:
        token = response.json().get('authentication', {}).get('token')
        print("[+] Token Retrieved:", token)
        return token
    else:
        print("[-] Login Failed", response.status_code, response.text)
        exit()
login_data = {
    "email": "admin@juice-sh.op",
    "password": "admin123"
}
headers = {
    "Authorization": f"Bearer {get_token()}",
    "Content-Type": "application/json"
}
custom_payloads = [
    "' OR 1=1--",
    "' UNION SELECT NULL,NULL--",
    "' UNION SELECT 'a',null,null--",
    "' || (SELECT sqlite_version()) || '",
    "' || (SELECT group_concat(name) FROM sqlite_master WHERE type='table') || '"
```

Fig. 5. Custom python script for SQLi testing on vulnerable websites (DVWA and OWASP Juice Shop)

ual analysis provides an important overview of the attack surface vulnerability assessment which could lead to deeper XSS analysis using customized payloads.

5.5 Analysis of XSS Vulnerability Testing Using Customized Payloads

This section implements Python-based XSS payloads on DVWA websites at different security levels. Figure 8 shows the generated custom Python scripts which include LOGIN_URL, target XSS_URL, and a login function that automatically logsRL into the DVWA website by extracting CSRF token information using the imported Python library beautifulsoup4. Additionally, the code also contains XSS payloads which are tested on the target URL (http://localhost/DVWA/vulnerabilities/xss_s/). The generated custom XSS payloads in Fig. 9 are executed successfully with potential alerts displayed on the web pages. Moreover, some stored XSS payloads are tested on the vulnerable entry points of the DVWA website which are successfully able to insert malicious payloads into the backend database, making the website vulnerable for users. Furthermore, multiple XSS custom payloads are integrated within a

Fig. 6. SQLi custom payloads executed and showing database version

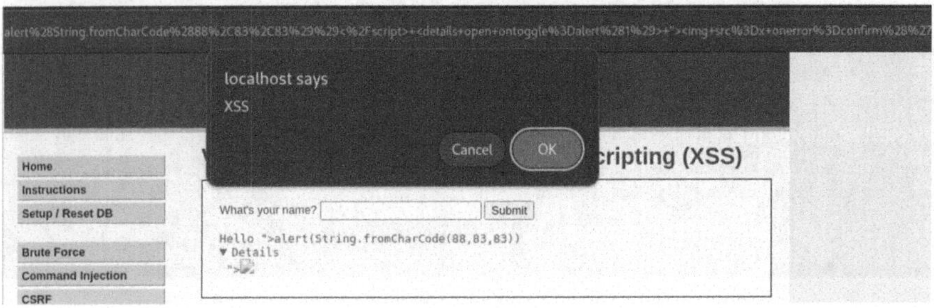

Fig. 7. Manual XSS alert executed in medium security level on DVWA website

Python script which could generate multiple vulnerabilities on a website by executing a single command. These Python scripts are tested in various security levels including low, medium, high and impossible. After execution, XSS payloads are effectively inserted into the database server and displayed the warning in the DVWA webpage. Figure 10 highlights multiple custom XSS payloads are tested on DVWA websites at an impossible security level where the terminal output indicates that the custom payloads are executed but XSS vulnerabilities are not successfully detected. These results can determine that the number of false negatives exist. Although some of the custom payloads cannot detect any vulnerabilities but are executed and stored in the backend database without alerting them the webpage. These results are significant for analyzing the XSS vulnerabilities in impossible security level where strict input validation or other crucial security factors may impede successful execution. All these XSS attacks are also intercepted through the Burp Suite tool for better quantitative analysis of XSS vulnerabilities considering the potential information contained in the request and response headers (Fig. 11). Overall, the performance of customized XSS payloads is significantly high in terms of automatic vulnerability assessment, reconnaissance and penetration testing of any websites. This approach is crucial for identifying the vulnerable injection points well before the attackers compromise the web applications or database servers. This analysis found that stored XSS exhibited better successful detection accuracy than other XSS attack types while common patterns are often triggered but more sophisticated payloads can bypass filters. Some DOM-based XSS failed to trigger alerts due to the high or impossible security level imposed in the DVWA environment. In all three XSS found minimal false positives but moderate false negatives during high and impossible security levels.

```python
import requests
from bs4 import BeautifulSoup
import time

LOGIN_URL = 'http://localhost/DVWA/login.php'
XSS_URL = 'http://localhost/DVWA/vulnerabilities/xss_s/'

USERNAME = 'admin'
PASSWORD = 'password'

payloads_xss = [
    "<script>alert('Stored XSS using custom payloads')</script>",
    "<img src=x onerror=alert('Custom payload XSS')>",
    "<svg/onload=alert('XSS using custom payload')>",
    "\"><script>alert('XSS Break out using custom payloads')</script>"
]
session = requests.Session()
def login():
    response = session.get(LOGIN_URL)
    soup = BeautifulSoup(response.text, 'html.parser')

    token_field = soup.find('input', {'name': 'user_token'})
    token = token_field.get('value') if token_field else None

    login_data = {
        'username': USERNAME,
        'password': PASSWORD,
```

Fig. 8. Customized XSS payloads using Python script for low security level

5.6 XSS Vulnerabilities in OWASP Zap

In this section, the OWASP ZAP tool is used to conduct the automated XSS vulnerability testing, focusing on the target URL (http://localhost/DVWA/vulnerabilities/xss_r/) in the DVWA website. Figure 12 examines the active scanning techniques where header information includes the navigation and scanning structure information which formulates the automated XSS testing. Figure 13 illustrates the potential reflected XSS vulnerabilities are detected and flagged with significant information on the response header including RTT, Size, Method and Timestamp. To summarize, this automated approach by OWASP ZAP provides the fastest actionable insights for security analysts or penetration testers.

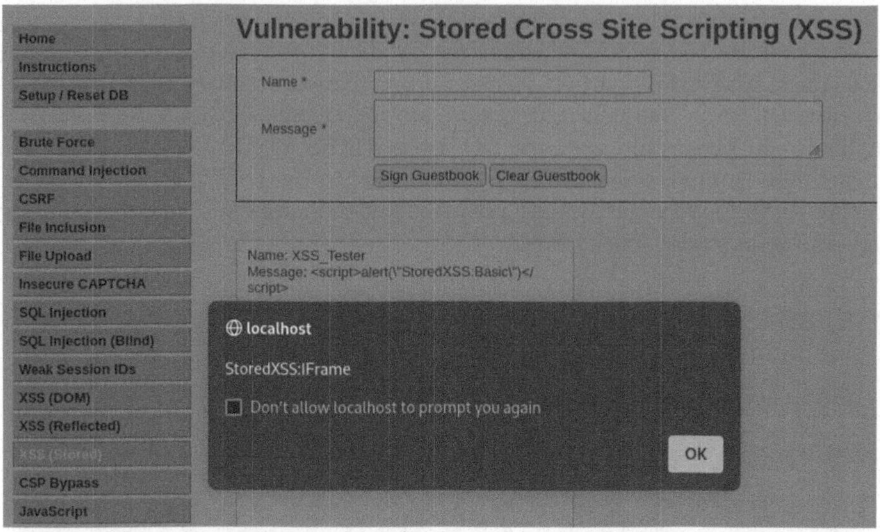

Fig. 9. Successful XSS payload stored in the database and warning in the web browser

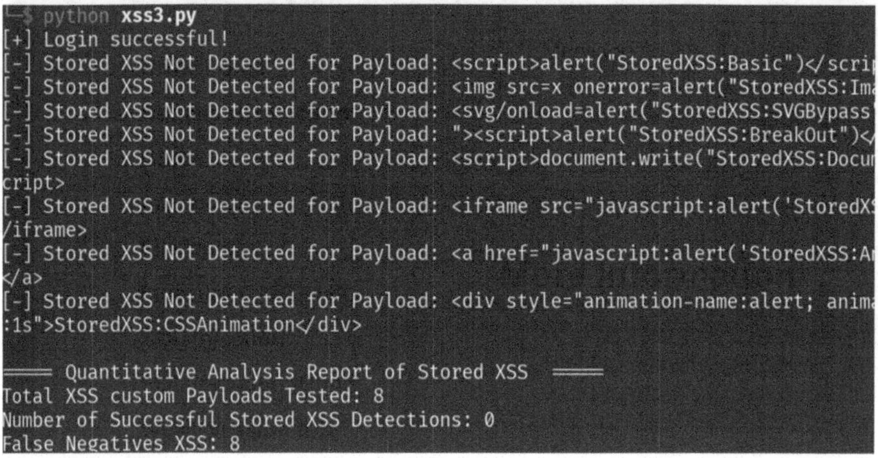

Fig. 10. Multiple XSS payloads not detecting and not showing any alerts on the webpage in impossible security level

Additionally, they could take necessary measures to protect the websites from XSS attacks as well as to implement customized payload approach for enhancing security mechanisms.

Fig. 11. Burp suite captured stored XSS using custom XSS payloads

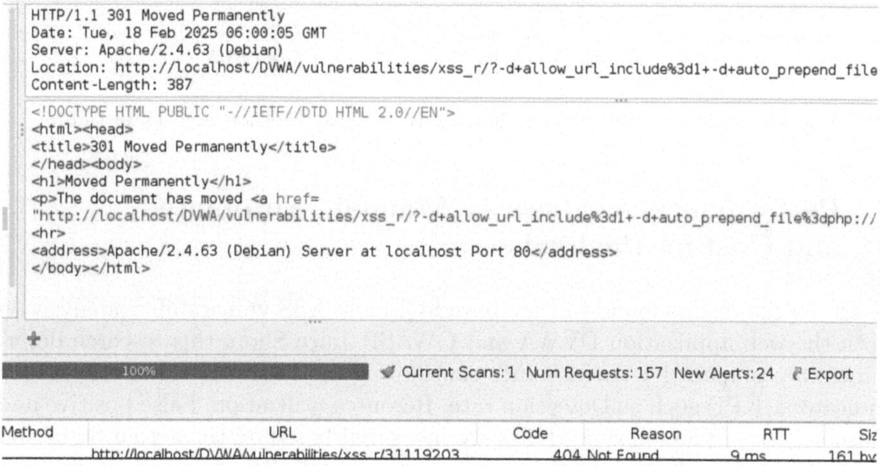

Fig. 12. ZAP request header information for XSS testing on DVWA website

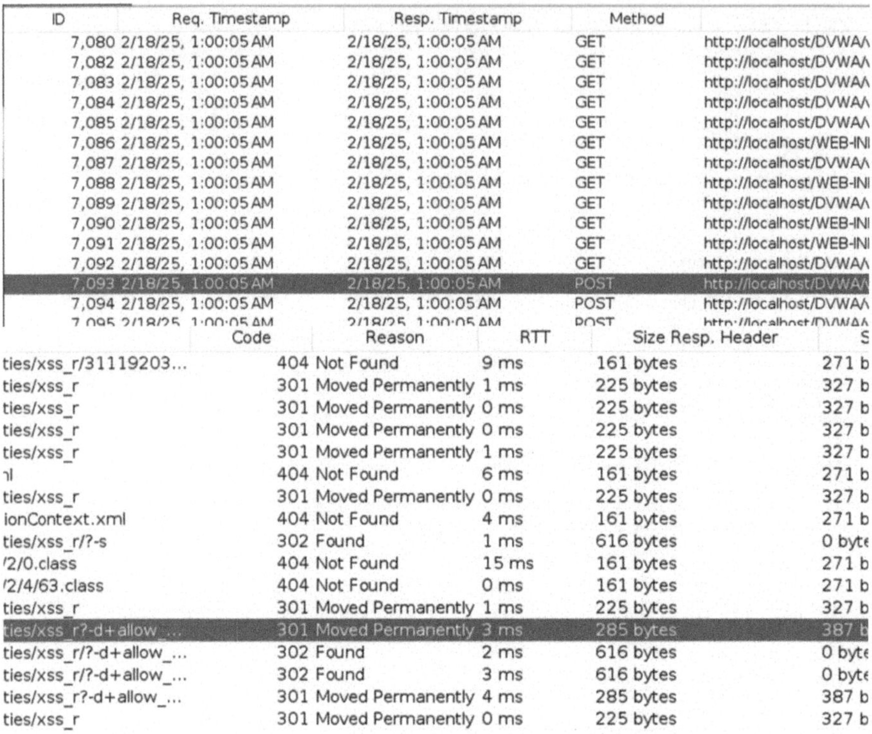

ID	Req. Timestamp	Resp. Timestamp	Method	
7,080	2/18/25, 1:00:05 AM	2/18/25, 1:00:05 AM	GET	http://localhost/DVWA/
7,082	2/18/25, 1:00:05 AM	2/18/25, 1:00:05 AM	GET	http://localhost/DVWA/
7,083	2/18/25, 1:00:05 AM	2/18/25, 1:00:05 AM	GET	http://localhost/DVWA/
7,084	2/18/25, 1:00:05 AM	2/18/25, 1:00:05 AM	GET	http://localhost/DVWA/
7,085	2/18/25, 1:00:05 AM	2/18/25, 1:00:05 AM	GET	http://localhost/DVWA/
7,086	2/18/25, 1:00:05 AM	2/18/25, 1:00:05 AM	GET	http://localhost/WEB-INI
7,087	2/18/25, 1:00:05 AM	2/18/25, 1:00:05 AM	GET	http://localhost/DVWA/
7,088	2/18/25, 1:00:05 AM	2/18/25, 1:00:05 AM	GET	http://localhost/WEB-INI
7,089	2/18/25, 1:00:05 AM	2/18/25, 1:00:05 AM	GET	http://localhost/DVWA/
7,090	2/18/25, 1:00:05 AM	2/18/25, 1:00:05 AM	GET	http://localhost/WEB-INI
7,091	2/18/25, 1:00:05 AM	2/18/25, 1:00:05 AM	GET	http://localhost/WEB-INI
7,092	2/18/25, 1:00:05 AM	2/18/25, 1:00:05 AM	GET	http://localhost/DVWA/
7,093	2/18/25, 1:00:05 AM	2/18/25, 1:00:05 AM	POST	http://localhost/DVWA/
7,094	2/18/25, 1:00:05 AM	2/18/25, 1:00:05 AM	POST	http://localhost/DVWA/
7,095	2/18/25, 1:00:05 AM	2/18/25, 1:00:05 AM	POST	http://localhost/DVWA/

	Code	Reason	RTT	Size Resp. Header	S
ties/xss_r/31119203...	404	Not Found	9 ms	161 bytes	271 b
ties/xss_r	301	Moved Permanently	1 ms	225 bytes	327 b
ties/xss_r	301	Moved Permanently	0 ms	225 bytes	327 b
ties/xss_r	301	Moved Permanently	0 ms	225 bytes	327 b
ties/xss_r	301	Moved Permanently	1 ms	225 bytes	327 b
ıl	404	Not Found	6 ms	161 bytes	271 b
ties/xss_r	301	Moved Permanently	0 ms	225 bytes	327 b
ionContext.xml	404	Not Found	4 ms	161 bytes	271 b
ties/xss_r/?-s	302	Found	1 ms	616 bytes	0 byte
'2/0.class	404	Not Found	15 ms	161 bytes	271 b
'2/4/63.class	404	Not Found	0 ms	161 bytes	271 b
ties/xss_r	301	Moved Permanently	1 ms	225 bytes	327 b
ties/xss_r?-d+allow_...	301	Moved Permanently	3 ms	285 bytes	387 b
ties/xss_r/?-d+allow_...	302	Found	2 ms	616 bytes	0 byte
ties/xss_r/?-d+allow_...	302	Found	3 ms	616 bytes	0 byte
ties/xss_r?-d+allow_...	301	Moved Permanently	4 ms	285 bytes	387 b
ties/xss_r	301	Moved Permanently	0 ms	225 bytes	327 b

Fig. 13. ZAP response header showing RTT, Size, Method and Timestamp

6 Performance Analysis of Manual, Automated and Custom Payloads

Based on the results found in the above SQLi and XSS vulnerability analysis on both the web application DVWA and OWASP Juice Shop, this research determines the comparative performance considering the following Key Performance Indicators (KPI) such as Detection rate, Resource utilization, False positive and False negative. The following KPIs are measured based on the actual SQLi and XSS executed payloads, database error logs, actual CPU resource utilizations and researcher expertise.

Detection Rate(DR): The study analyzed the detection rate considering the total number of payloads tested and the number of successful detections that trigger SQLi and XSS vulnerabilities.

Resource Utilization(RU): Analyze the actual CPU and memory utilized before and after the execution of SQLi and XSS payloads. This study incorporates a Python library such as psutil and top to capture the logs while executing the payloads.

False Positive(FP) and False Negative(FN): Detection of false positives and false negatives is crucial to determine the vulnerability of the executed payloads.

When payloads are detected as vulnerable but do not execute malicious code in the system, they are termed false positives (FP). When payloads are supposed to be detected as vulnerable but are not executed or missed, they are known as false negatives (FN).

Calculations of Detection Metrics

For the experiment, a total of 20 payloads were executed with 4 runs each, producing:

$$\text{Total Attempts} = 20 \times 4 = 80$$

where we found:

$$\text{True Positives (TP)} = 59, \quad \text{False Positives (FP)} = 4, \quad \text{False Negatives (FN)} = 6$$

Detection Rate (DR). Defined as the proportion of successful detections over total attempts:

$$\text{DR} = \frac{TP}{\text{Total Attempts}} \times 100 = \frac{59}{80} \times 100 = 73.75\%$$

False Positive Rate (FPR). In this study, defined as the ratio of false detections to all reported detections:

$$\text{FPR} = \frac{FP}{TP + FP} \times 100 = \frac{4}{59 + 4} \times 100 = 6.35\%$$

False Negative Rate (FNR). Defined as the ratio of missed detections to all actual positives:

$$\text{FNR} = \frac{FN}{TP + FN} \times 100 = \frac{6}{59 + 6} \times 100 = 9.23\%$$

6.1 Performance Analysis of SQL Injection Vulnerabilities

Manual testing is executed using basic and advanced SQL payloads in different security levels on DVWA and Juice shop. This analysis demonstrates moderate detection rates (73%) which are greatly influenced by the penetration tester's knowledge and experience and limitations found in some scenarios where the web applications are protected by input validation or error handling capacities.

Automated SQL Injection consistently maintains higher detection rate (88%) and is able to identify injection points efficiently by injecting various Boolean-based, error-based and time-based payloads. SQLMap is more effective and rapid to detect database vulnerabilities, which provide most accurate insights inside for backend server validation methods. However, due to limitations in parameter validation issues which leading to detect more false positives in a complex attack scenario. Automated testing by OWASP Zap tool shows moderate to high detection rates between 90% which demonstrate highest ability to identify low and medium-risk vulnerabilities. However, this automatic vulnerability tool sometimes faced strong challenges for content filtering mechanism and increase false positives on the testing web applications which can reduce accuracy and reliability. Table 2 summarizes the comparative analysis of tools in detection SQLi vulnerabilities.

Table 2. Comparative analysis of SQLi testing results across manual, automated (SQLMap/OWASP ZAP) and customized payload methods

Method	Payload Tested	Total Runs	TP	DR(%)	RU(%)	FPR(%)	FNR(%)
Manual Testing	20	4	59	73	8	6	12
SQLMap	10	4	35	88	33	5	10
OWASP ZAP	10	4	36	90	23	15	6
Custom Payloads	20	4	72	90	35	8	3

Key Observations on SQLi Detections:
Manual testing: Depends on tester expertise and requires minimal resources.
SQLMap: Require more system resources for large queries.
OWASP ZAP: Effective for common vulnerabilities and less effective for detecting complex injection points, also utilize more CPU/RAM and Tester extensive skills required.
Custom payloads: It has the highest potential for WAF, time-based blind injection and input validation and requires deep understanding of back-end technologies (NoSQL or SQLite), including limited success rate for parameterized queries.

6.2 Performance Analysis of XSS Vulnerabilities

The manual XSS test results indicate a moderate detection accuracy 75%) and are highly dependent on the expertise of the tester to identify injection endpoints and validate the results. The results imply that manual XSS operations are effective in low and medium levels but in impossible security levels most payloads are blocked by security filters.

OWASP ZAP detects XSS vulnerabilities more effectively and quickly and shows a higher detection rate of 85%. However, some limitations are observed due to higher resource utilization in CPU and memory and more frequent false positive rates are also found.

While testing with custom XSS payloads using custom Python scripts that are capable of bypassing moderate to high-level filters (WAF) and demonstrating a high detection rate of 88%. These custom payloads are effective for executing advanced payloads such as error-based, time-based and SVG bypass. Custom payloads provide strong effectiveness during targeted penetration testing scenarios with fewer false negative rates. Table 3 shows the summarized results of the XSS vulnerability testing.

Table 3. Comparative analysis of XSS testing results across manual, automated (OWASP ZAP) and custom payload methods

Method	Payload Tested	Total Runs	TP	DR(%)	RU(%)	FPR(%)	FNR(%)
Manual Testing	20	4	60	75	7	6	11
OWASP ZAP	10	4	34	85	26	15	5
Custom Payloads	20	4	70	88	21	9	6

Key Observations on XSS Detections:
Manual testing: Limited detection at higher security levels and tester expertise required
OWAASP ZAP: Effective in moderate and high security level and Significant false positive rates at higher level security, also require more CPU and memory resources while executing.
Custom Payloads: Reliable and effective in balanced detection accuracy and faster in detection speed, as well as persistence in database retrieval and bypassing filters, but increased false positive rates in higher security level.

7 Discussion

This study demonstrates the critical evaluation of SQL injection (SQLi) and Cross-Site Scripting (XSS) testing methods conducted in a simulated controlled environment. The three different testing methodologies—manual, automated and custom payload-based techniques are analyzed on DVWA and OWASP Juice Shop web applications hosted on Kali Linux environment. The analysis determines that manual testing is effective for discovering hidden or context-specific flaws, whereas automated testing can identify moderate to high-security vulnerabilities, but generates more false positives and sometimes overlooks obfuscated payloads. In contrast, custom payload testing proves to be effective for precision and is able to bypass generic and advanced security filters.

The research hypothesis complies with the outcome of the custom payloads that offer enhanced precision in identifying critical attack vectors whereas manual and automated testing differ significantly in their detection capability of complex or obfuscated vulnerabilities. Additionally, manual testing heavily depends on the tester's intuition and experience which proved time consuming and less scalable during advanced filters. However, automated techniques provide relatively faster scanning and high detection rates in detecting common SQLi and XSS vulnerabilities but occasionally missed context-specific payloads. Overall, the study results of both manual and automated methods demonstrate efficiency in detection, while the custom payloads excel in detection accuracy with minimal false negatives and bypassing strict security filters thereby conforming to the research hypothesis.

Moreover, custom payloads design covers the gaps in detection efficiency between the manual and automated testing methods. This approach injects tailored input to exploit specific application logic and finds the blind injection points that are often missed by traditional techniques. Overall, this novel method not only shows effectiveness in vulnerability detection, but also determines and assesses the behavior and structure of target applications.

Based on the practical viewpoints and analysis, this study recommends a blended approach for web application vulnerability and penetration testing. Organizations and cybersecurity analysts should consider manual and automated methods for regular vulnerability scans, while custom payload-based techniques should be applied for context-specific payload testing during high-risk vulnerabilities and inconsistencies in application logic.

Finally, this research suggests that, to achieve complementary strengths, the combination of tools and techniques is of paramount importance due to the thoroughness of manual payloads, the robustness and speed of automated techniques and the target specific efficiency and multiple attack capability of custom payloads.

7.1 Future Work and Recommendations

Based on the results and findings of this research, there are more opportunities to improve the capabilities of custom payload methods. This research is specifically focused on the need to extend the malware vulnerability detection mechanism to include mitigation strategies and techniques after malware detection in web applications. Therefore, future research has great potential to explore the integration of advanced machine learning models to provide automatic, faster and accurate quantitative analysis of malware detection using custom payloads. In addition, future AI models could automatically and intelligently adapt to evolving threat patterns and incorporate interactive learning from both false positives and negatives. These techniques would significantly improve detection accuracy and rates, leading to more advanced methods to detect zero-day vulnerabilities. By developing a unified framework further synergy could be investigated between manual, automated and custom payload-based approaches that dynamically determine the most effective testing approach considering the attack environment and target application scenario.

8 Conclusion

The analysis determines the effectiveness of three different malware vulnerability detection techniques in web applications (Manual, Automated and Custom payload). Manual methods are found to be effective in identifying vulnerable injection points where hidden application logics are applied. However, this approach is time-consuming and requires certain skills of the tester. Automated tools (SQLMap and OWASP ZAP) have been proven to be efficient in detecting a large number of injection points and detecting common vulnerabilities in web applications. However, this approach generates more false positives and sometimes misses the most critical injection points. The custom payloads demonstrate strong potential for triggering multi-step vulnerabilities and bypassing the security filters. Moreover, custom payload tests achieve the highest detection accuracy in both SQLi and XSS vulnerability testing, as well as showing faster payload execution and consistently demonstrating better performance in complex (time-based and error-based) or high-security environments. Additionally, this technique also provides better adaptability across various application contexts (OWASP Juice Shop and DVWA) and performs significantly well during multi-layered vulnerability detection. However, custom payload also deceives detection rates due to generating some more false positives under varied security conditions.

Overall, in light of the analysis and observations mentioned above, this research confirms that the custom payload-based technique consistently outperforms traditional manual and automated approaches. Thus, this novel technique supports the research hypothesis and proves efficient in malware vulnerability detection specifically SQL Injection and Cross-Site Scripting (XSS) attacks despite generating some detection flaws (False positives).

Finally, this research reveals that a multilayered context-specific approach significantly enhances the detection and mitigation ability of SQLi and XSS vulnerabilities. Future extended studies should include Artificial Intelligence to analyze the effectiveness of AI-based attack detection and mitigation techniques with custom payloads.

Acknowledgment. This work was supported in part by the National Science Foundation under Grant No. 2321939. Any opinions, findings and conclusions, or recommendations expressed in this material are those of the author(s) and do not necessarily reflect the views of the National Science Foundation.

References

1. Abikoye, O., Abubakar, A., Dokoro, H., Oluwatobi, A., Kayode, A.: A novel technique to prevent SQL injection and cross-site scripting attacks using KNUTH-Morris-Pratt string match algorithm. EURASIP J. Inf. Secur. **2020** (2020). https://doi.org/10.1186/s13635-020-00113-y
2. Alanda, A., Satria, D., Ardhana, M., Dahlan, A., Mooduto, H.: Web application penetration testing using SQL injection attack. JOIV: Int. J. Inf. Visual. **5**, 320 (2021). https://doi.org/10.30630/joiv.5.3.470
3. Alazmi, S., De Leon, D.C.: A systematic literature review on the characteristics and effectiveness of web application vulnerability scanners. IEEE Access **10**, 33200–33219 (2022). https://doi.org/10.1109/ACCESS.2022.3161522

4. Alsaffar, M., Aljaloud, S., Al-Shaibani, B., Al-Mekhlafi, Z., Almurayziq, T., Alshammari, A.: Detection of web cross-site scripting (XSS) attacks. Electronics **11**, 2212 (2022). https://doi.org/10.3390/electronics11142212
5. Althunayyan, M., Saxena, N., Li, S., Gope, P.: Evaluation of black-box web application security scanners in detecting injection vulnerabilities. Electronics **11** (2022). https://doi.org/10.3390/electronics11132049
6. Altulaihan, E.A., Alismail, A., Frikha, M.: A survey on web application penetration testing. Electronics **12**(5) (2023). https://doi.org/10.3390/electronics12051229, https://www.mdpi.com/2079-9292/12/5/1229
7. Anaoval, A.A., Zy, A.T., S, S.: Analysis of manual and automated methods effectiveness in website penetration testing for identifying SQL injection vulnerabilities. J. Comput. Networks Archit. High Perform. Comput. (2024). https://api.semanticscholar.org/CorpusID:271715417
8. Auricchio, N., Cappuccio, A., Caturano, F., Perrone, G., Romano, S.P.: An automated approach to web offensive security. Comput. Commun. **195**, 248–261 (2022). https://doi.org/10.1016/j.comcom.2022.08.018. https://www.sciencedirect.com/science/article/pii/S0140366422003267
9. Correa, R.A., Higuera, J.R.B., Higuera, J.B., Montalvo, J.A.S., Rubio, M.S., Magreñán, A.: Hybrid security assessment methodology for web applications. CMES - Comput. Model. Eng. Sci. **126**(1), 89–124 (2020). https://doi.org/10.32604/cmes.2021.010700, https://www.sciencedirect.com/science/article/pii/S1526149220000703
10. Garn, B., Zivanovic, J., Leithner, M., Simos, D.: Combinatorial methods for dynamic gray-box SQL injection testing. Software Test. Verif. Reliabil. **32** (2022). https://doi.org/10.1002/stvr.1826
11. Han, W., Xue, J., Wang, Y., Liu, Z., Kong, Z.: Malinsight: a systematic profiling based malware detection framework. J. Network Comput. Appl. **125** (2018). https://doi.org/10.1016/j.jnca.2018.10.022
12. Kumar, R., Alenezi, M., Ansari, M.T., Gupta, B., Agrawal, A., Khan, P.R.: Evaluating the impact of malware analysis techniques for securing web applications through a decision-making framework under fuzzy environment. Int. J. Intell. Eng. Syst. **13**, 94–109 (2020). https://doi.org/10.22266/ijies2020.1231.09
13. Lakshmi, B.S., Kovvuri, D., Bolisetti, H.N.V., Chikkala, D.S., Karri, S., Yadlapalli, G.: A proactive approach for detecting SQL and XSS injection attacks. In: 2024 3rd International Conference on Applied Artificial Intelligence and Computing (ICAAIC), pp. 1415–1420 (2024). https://doi.org/10.1109/ICAAIC60222.2024.10575599
14. Mateo Tudela, F., Bermejo Higuera, J.R., Bermejo Higuera, J., Sicilia Montalvo, J.A., Argyros, M.I.: On combining static, dynamic and interactive analysis security testing tools to improve OWASP top ten security vulnerability detection in web applications. Appl. Sci. **10**(24) (2020). https://doi.org/10.3390/app10249119, https://www.mdpi.com/2076-3417/10/24/9119
15. Matti, E.: Evaluation of open source webvulnerability scanners and theirtechniques used to find SQL injection and cross-site scriptingvulnerabilities (2021). https://api.semanticscholar.org/CorpusID:263695049
16. Pandey, A., Alsolami, F.: Malware analysis in web application security: An investigation and suggestion. Int. J. Adv. Comput. Sci. Appl. **11**, 2020 (2020). https://doi.org/10.14569/IJACSA.2020.0110725
17. Parvez, M., Zavarsky, P., Khoury, N.: Analysis of effectiveness of black-box web application scanners in detection of stored SQL injection and stored XSS vulnerabilities. In: 2015 10th International Conference for Internet Technology and

Secured Transactions (ICITST), pp. 186–191 (2015). https://doi.org/10.1109/ICITST.2015.7412085
18. Rane, N., Qureshi, A.: Comparative analysis of automated scanning and manual penetration testing for enhanced cybersecurity. In: 2024 12th International Symposium on Digital Forensics and Security (ISDFS), pp. 1–6 (2024). https://doi.org/10.1109/ISDFS60797.2024.10527240
19. Shah, M.P., Iqbal, M.: Comparative analysis of the automated penetration testing tools (2020). https://api.semanticscholar.org/CorpusID:220545356
20. Sharma, S.: A study of vulnerability scanners for detecting SQL injection and XSS attack in websites. Artif. Intell. Appl. **1** (2023). https://doi.org/10.47852/bonviewAIA3202754

System Settings and Security in IoT Devices Using Snort and Suricata

Jeffrey Berg(✉) and Bing Zhou

Sam Houston State University, Huntsville, USA
{jdb118,bxz003}@shsu.edu

Abstract. As Internet of Things (IoT) devices become increasingly integrated into everyday life, their security implications for home networks demand greater attention. This study investigates the effectiveness of two open source intrusion detection systems (IDS), Snort and Suricata, in monitoring IoT device activity using a Raspberry Pi 5 configured as a wireless gateway. By isolating the network environment and connecting devices, which include a Motorola smartphone, iPhone 6 s, Petcube smart camera, and Fitbit Sense 2, to a dedicated Wi-Fi subnet hosted by the Raspberry Pi, all traffic could be captured and analyzed in real time. Both IDS tools were run concurrently with similar rule sets to evaluate their packet capture behavior, detection capabilities, and logging granularity. The results reveal that Suricata, with its default full-packet logging, provides more comprehensive traffic visibility, while Snort's event-based logging requires additional configuration to match this level of detail. Ultimately, this research highlights the practical considerations and configuration trade-offs when deploying IDS solutions for smart home environments.

Keywords: Internet of Things (IoT) · Intrusion Detection System (IDS) · Raspberry Pi · Snort · Suricata · Smart Home Security · Network Monitoring · IoT Forensics · Packet Analysis · Cybersecurity

1 Introduction

The widespread adoption of devices on the Internet of Things (IoT) in modern households has introduced unprecedented convenience, allowing users to monitor their health, automate lighting, control security systems, and manage home appliances with ease. However, this connectivity comes at a significant cost: many IoT devices are poorly secured, lack consistent firmware updates, and often communicate sensitive data over the network, creating multiple vectors for cyber attacks.

Real-world incidents have illustrated the risks associated with insecure IoT ecosystems. For example, in 2016, the Mirai botnet attack exploited thousands of vulnerable IoT devices, such as IP cameras and home routers, using default login credentials to compromise them [7]. The resulting distributed denial-of-service

V. V. Pham et al. (Eds.): CIDDF 2025, ACSAR 5, pp. 102–113, 2026.
https://doi.org/10.1007/978-3-032-19488-6_6

(DDoS) attack disrupted major online platforms including Twitter, Netflix, and GitHub, demonstrating how even consumer-grade devices can be weaponized at scale. More recently, vulnerabilities discovered in Ring doorbells and baby monitors have allowed attackers to gain unauthorized access to video feeds and two-way audio, raising serious privacy concerns for users who assumed these devices were secure out of the box.

As the number of connected devices continues to grow, so does the attack surface of the average home network. With minimal user control over software security, and many manufacturers neglecting long-term patch support, consumers are left increasingly exposed to cyber threats. While some devices receive regular updates and offer security options, many low-cost or lesser-known brands prioritize usability and market speed over robust security protocols. As a result, home networks may be unknowingly hosting exploitable devices that serve as gateways for deeper intrusions.

Given these concerns, this study aims to assess how much information IoT devices reveal through their network behavior and how effectively this traffic can be monitored using intrusion detection systems (IDS). Specifically, a Motorola smartphone, iPhone 6 s, Petcube smart camera, and Fitbit Sense 2 are evaluated to understand their network characteristics under typical usage. A Raspberry Pi 5 is configured to act as both a wireless access point and network gateway, enabling isolation and full monitoring of all device traffic. Two widely adopted open-source IDS tools, Snort and Suricata, are deployed concurrently to compare their effectiveness in capturing and logging IoT traffic.

By examining both the quantity and type of network activity generated by these devices, and analyzing how each IDS handles detection and logging, this study provides insights into how home networks can be better secured against the growing threat posed by insecure IoT devices.

2 Related Work

Ghazi et al. [1] conducted a comparative analysis of Snort and Suricata, highlighting their architectural differences, detection mechanisms, and performance characteristics. Their work situates both IDS tools within broader IoT environments, emphasizing how detection capabilities and efficiency vary depending on traffic volume and protocol usage. This study provides essential context for our experiment, as it highlights why Suricata's multithreaded architecture often excels under high-throughput conditions, while Snort's mature rule set and long-standing community support make it highly reliable for signature-based detection. Building on the foundational comparison of Ghazi et al., our work advances the discussion by moving beyond abstract evaluations and instead applying both IDS tools in a live IoT testbed. By observing real consumer devices under normal and adversarial conditions, we extend their findings to show not only how Snort and Suricata differ in controlled benchmarks, but also how those differences manifest themselves in practice when monitoring IoT devices such as a smartphone, camera, and smartwatch within a home subnet.

Quershi et al. [5] discuss persistent cybersecurity challenges in IoT environments and propose deep learning-based approaches to improve malware detection and forensic analysis. Their work highlights the limitations of traditional forensic methods, particularly against anti-forensic techniques, and categorizes the problem space into IoT security, malware forensics, deep learning, and anti-forensics. While their study emphasizes the potential of machine learning to improve IoT security, our work provides a complementary perspective by focusing on baseline intrusion detection with Snort and Suricata. By directly monitoring real IoT devices in a controlled environment, this study establishes comparative visibility into IoT traffic patterns, producing empirical insights that could inform or serve as training data for future deep learningâĂŞbased IoT forensics and anomaly detection frameworks.

Yalda et al. [6] present a comprehensive study on IoT network security, utilizing open-source IDS tools such as Suricata on various Raspberry Pi models (3B, 4, and 4B). Their work compares multiple setups and evaluates the effectiveness of Suricata in detecting attacks like SSH brute force, Trojan activity, Nmap scans, and SYN flood DoS attacks. They demonstrate Suricata's capabilities in both IDS and IPS modes, showing its utility not only for monitoring but also for actively blocking threats. While their setup focuses primarily on protecting the Raspberry Pi itself as the target of attacks, they note the potential of extending the Pi to function as a gateway for securing other devices. Building on this idea, our work places the Raspberry Pi 5 directly in the network path as a gateway for IoT devices, enabling traffic monitoring from real consumer devices (smartphones, smart camera, smartwatch) under both normal usage and attack scenarios. This distinction allows us to evaluate not only how Suricata performs, but also to compare its detection and logging capabilities against Snort in the context of practical IoT visibility.

Mohd Bakry et al. [4] conducted an experiment simulating IoT devices using a Raspberry Pi, paired with a wireless adapter and a laptop running Kali Linux. They launched three common attack vectors—brute force, man-in-the-middle (MITM), and denial of service (DoS)—using tools such as Nmap, Hydra, Xerosploit, and Bettercap. Their results highlighted how default configurations in IoT environments are easily exploited, while recommending basic mitigation strategies such as stronger passwords and continuous monitoring. Unlike their simulation-focused approach, our study places real IoT devices (e.g., a smart camera and smartwatch) into a controlled network environment and subjects them to similar attacks. By simultaneously monitoring this traffic with both Snort and Suricata on a Raspberry Pi 5 gateway, we extend their work from simulated vulnerabilities toward evaluating how consumer-grade devices behave under real-world conditions and how different IDS platforms capture and report such activity.

Martin et al. [3] explore the rapid expansion of the IoT market and the corresponding rise in malware propagation through compromised smart devices. They deployed a Cowrie honeypot on an Amazon AWS instance to emulate vulnerable SSH and Telnet services, which are frequently exploited by botnets such as Mirai. Within 24 h, the honeypot captured active IoT malware, and over the course of one week it recorded more than 6,500 SSH login attempts across 1,190 devices and 1.3 million Telnet login attempts across 992 devices. Their dynamic and static malware analysis provided valuable insights into attacker behavior and common exploitation methods targeting IoT devices exposed to the public internet. In contrast, our study shifts the focus from external exposures to internal network security, evaluating how consumer IoT devices behave under simulated attacks in a home network and how IDS platforms like Snort and Suricata capture these events. This provides a complementary perspective by examining not just the attacker's methods, but the visibility defenders have within local IoT environments.

Hariawan et al. [2] developed a layered intrusion detection system combining honeypots, Suricata, and packet analysis tools on a Raspberry Pi 4 to monitor malware activity in home networks. Their setup simulated six common attack types—port scanning, brute force, TCP flooding, smurf attacks, UDP flooding, and service exploitation—while leveraging Cowrie and Dionaea honeypots for data collection and Suricata for detection. Network traffic was captured with TShark and analyzed through an ELK stack (Elasticsearch, Logstash, Kibana), enabling detailed visualization of attack patterns. System performance measurements showed that CPU usage spiked significantly during brute force and scanning activity, while memory usage remained largely stable. Unlike their work, which relied heavily on honeypots to attract external threats, our study places real IoT devices (smartphone, camera, and smartwatch) inside a controlled home subnet to evaluate how Snort and Suricata log and detect both normal usage and simulated internal attacks. This approach shifts the focus from attacker-centric data collection to device visibility and IDS performance in realistic consumer IoT scenarios.

All these papers are key to explore the link between IoT devices and malware when it comes to security. A Raspberry Pi 4 is an incredible device when used in conjunction with other software and hardware to trick attackers using honeypots to attract them. This is a great way to see what methods attackers use and explore ways to combat these because honeypots can bring in thousands to millions of attacks for analysis. However, these papers do not utilize real IoT devices for analysis, only simulations using a Raspberry Pi, and one of them (2) used a Raspberry Pi for attacks but wanted to explore real IoT devices in future work but have not so far. These papers show that IoT devices and user information are prime targets for attackers but do not go as far as using devices, only simulations which will not necessarily apply to real devices. I want to compare the results these papers have brought to light alongside some IoT devices I have such as an iPhone 6S, a Motorola phone, a Fitbit watch, and a pet camera to see if these devices are secure. I will be running a closed environment to see if these devices can be disrupted with attacks and if they are, if there is anything a user can do to stop them like changing settings in the apps or on the devices themselves. How real are these simulations and are these IoT devices secure out of the box for users who are tech illiterate?

3 Methodology

To accurately test the security of IoT devices, it is essential to create an isolated and controlled environment. This ensures that only the target devices are connected, eliminating external noise and allowing for precise monitoring of inbound and outbound traffic. As illustrated in Fig. 1, the experimental setup routes internet access through a home router, which is then connected via Ethernet to a Raspberry Pi 5. The Raspberry Pi functions as a dedicated gateway, creating a separate Wi-Fi subnet for the devices under test: a Motorola smartphone, iPhone 6 s, pet camera, and Fitbit watch. This configuration enables complete visibility into network activity while maintaining isolation from other devices on the primary network.

3.1 Devices Used in Experiment

The following devices were selected for testing to evaluate the network behavior of both typical smartphones and IoT devices:

- Motorola G 2022: This Android-based smartphone, running Android 12, was included primarily as a point of comparison against the IoT devices evaluated in this study. While not the focus of the analysis, it serves to contextualize the traffic patterns observed in the IoT devices. Although Android 12 is no longer the latest version, it remains widely used as of 2025, making it a practical baseline for assessing typical smartphone behavior in Snort and Suricata logs.
- iPhone 6 s: Similar to the Motorola device, the iPhone 6 s was used as a comparison platform to highlight differences in traffic behavior between smartphones and IoT devices. Including both Android and iOS platforms allowed the study to capture protocol and flow differences between the two dominant mobile operating systems.
- Petcube Pet Camera: The Petcube is a commercially available smart camera designed for home surveillance and pet monitoring. It communicates via Wi-Fi and integrates with a companion app available on both Android and iOS. Unlike more well-known camera brands backed by large corporations (e.g., Amazon Ring), Petcube offers a cost-effective, third-party solution. This makes it a compelling candidate for assessing the security posture of lesser-known IoT products.
- Fitbit Sense 2: This is a wearable health-tracking device that monitors metrics such as sleep, heart rate, and physical activity. It connects primarily via Bluetooth but occasionally uses Wi-Fi for firmware updates and data synchronization. Although its Wi-Fi usage is minimal, the device was included to investigate whether meaningful network traffic could still be captured and analyzed using Snort and Suricata.

3.2 Raspberry Pi 5

The Raspberry Pi 5 serves as the core of the experimental environment, acting as both a wireless access point and an inline network gateway for all tested

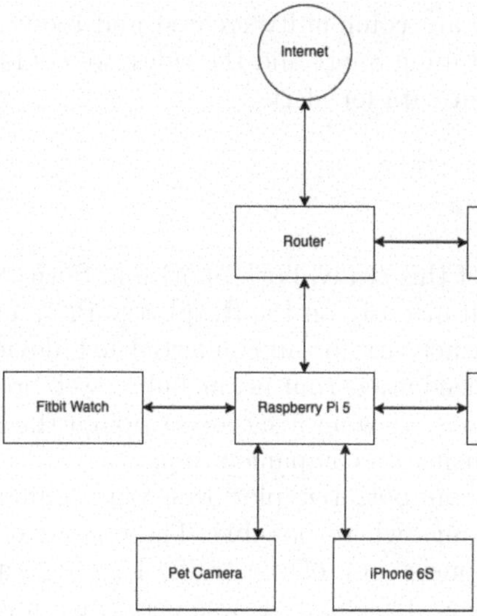

Fig. 1. Layout of experiment

IoT devices. Its compact form factor, affordability, and built-in Wi-Fi capabilities make it a practical alternative to conventional laptops or desktops in constrained environments. By configuring the Raspberry Pi as a Wi-Fi access point and bridging it to an Ethernet-connected router, it is able to assign IP addresses, provide internet connectivity, and route traffic for connected devices. The 8 GB RAM variant offers sufficient computational resources to run intrusion detection systems (IDS) such as Snort and Suricata concurrently with its gateway functions. This setup enables full visibility into all incoming and outgoing traffic for precise data collection and security analysis.

3.3 IDS Programs

The programs that are installed on the Raspberry Pi 5 and used in this paper are two open source IDS's.

- The first one is Suricata, which is easily installable using typical Linux package install and can be started and stopped using the systemctl command. It is a plug-and-play program which comes built with its own rules and config file for the user to change to their rules and alerts. We configured the rules to capture all data incoming and outgoing tied to specific IP addresses linked to each device to easily keep track of the devices used.
- The other IDS we used is Snort which is another common open source IDS and network monitoring tool. However, this tool was not as easily setup as Suricata on the Raspberry Pi 5. The Raspberry Pi Lite OS does not have the most up to date package installer which supports Snort so we had to manually install snort which is not user-friendly. Afterwards we then had to

install snort rules which are community created and required a snort login to even access. After installing Snort and the rules, we could then customize them the same way as Suricata for alerts.

3.4 Experiment

In the experimental phase of this study, both Snort and Suricata were installed and configured to run simultaneously on the Raspberry Pi 5. This allowed real-time monitoring of network activity for all connected IoT devices. Each device was subjected to a standardized usage routine, including web browsing and video streaming on the smartphones, viewing live video through the pet camera, and syncing the Fitbit Sense 2 using its companion app.

To ensure a fair comparison, both IDS platforms were configured with equivalent logging and alert settings where possible. The objective was to evaluate the accuracy, depth, and consistency of the traffic logs generated under typical consumer usage conditions. This analysis was performed under two different configurations: first using each IDS's default rule sets, and then using a shared rule set applied to both tools.

3.5 Default Settings

The initial test was conducted using the default configurations for both Snort and Suricata. Since Snort does not include rules by default, the community rule set 3 was used to enable basic detection capabilities.

Table 1. Snort (PCAP-Based) Traffic Summary by Device

Device	Packets	TCP	UDP	DNS Queries
Fitbit	194	188	6	3
iPhone	96	94	2	1
Motorola	13157	1013	12141	27
Petcube	135	133	2	1

Tables 1 and 2 present a comparison of Snort and Suricata outputs under default configurations. Snort, which records complete packet captures in PCAP format, reported substantially higher packet counts, particularly for the Motorola smartphone (13,157 packets, including 12,141 UDP). Suricata, which logs flow-level metadata in eve.json, produced fewer overall records but captured a greater number of DNS queries across devices (e.g., 42 for the iPhone versus 1 in Snort). Both tools recorded minimal traffic for the Fitbit and Petcube, consistent with their limited Wi-Fi activity, though Suricata reported slightly higher UDP flows. These findings confirm that Snort emphasizes packet-level detail,

Table 2. Suricata (eve.json) Flow Summary by Device

Device	Flows	TCP	UDP	DNS Queries
Fitbit	44	24	22	5
iPhone	168	30	142	42
Motorola	129	45	89	33
Petcube	13	5	14	3

while Suricata provides enhanced visibility into application-layer behaviors such as DNS and flow activity. For IoT visibility, this distinction is significant: Snort is well suited for detecting high-volume packet activity such as floods or scans, whereas Suricata better exposes service-level interactions and device behaviors that are critical to profiling IoT activity.

3.6 Shared Configuration Setting

To enable a more direct comparison, both Snort and Suricata were next configured with identical rules and similar logging parameters. This test aimed to measure how closely the two IDS platforms aligned in terms of packet capture and protocol identification under controlled and matched configurations.

Table 3. Snort Summary per Device (Same Settings and Rules)

Device	Packets	TCP/UDP	DNS Queries
iPhone	25,382	1,351/23,994	34
Motorola	11,656	34/11,610	6
Fitbit	15	11/4	0
Petcube	18,625	64/18,561	1

Table 4. Suricata Summary per Device (Same Settings and Rules)

Device	Packets	TCP/UDP	DNS Queries
iPhone	25,394	1,333/23,993	34
Motorola	11,637	30/11,554	6
Fitbit	36	12/4	0
Petcube	19,311	59/19,223	1

Tables 3 and 4 present a comparative summary of network traffic generated by the four tested devices—iPhone, Motorola phone, Fitbit Sense 2, and Petcube camera under identical settings and rule configurations using Snort and Suricata. The iPhone consistently produced the highest volume of packets, exceeding 25,000 in both IDS systems, with a predominance of UDP traffic and 34 DNS queries. The Motorola generated a moderate amount of traffic, mostly UDP, with six DNS queries recorded. The Fitbit produced minimal traffic overall, with only a handful of TCP and UDP packets and no DNS queries, highlighting its limited network activity. The Petcube camera, while less active than the iPhone, still generated significant traffic exceeding 18,000 packets, again primarily UDP, with a single DNS query. Overall, the results show near-identical traffic patterns between Snort and Suricata, with only minor discrepancies in packet counts, demonstrating consistency between the two IDS tools in capturing device behavior.

3.7 IoT Device Settings

An analysis of the companion applications for the Fitbit Sense 2 and Petcube smart camera revealed a lack of built-in security controls or privacy modes. The Fitbit Sense 2 relied primarily on Bluetooth, even during synchronization events, resulting in minimal Wi-Fi activity. This limited its exposure to network-based monitoring and potential wireless threats. In contrast, the Petcube camera exhibited consistent and persistent Wi-Fi activity, communicating with external servers throughout its operation. This makes the Petcube a more relevant candidate for IDS-based monitoring in typical smart home environments.

3.8 Attacks

To evaluate the resilience of the IoT devices and smartphones under test, we conducted two common types of network-based attacks: a Denial of Service (DoS) attack and a Man-in-the-Middle (MitM) attack. These attacks were carried out using a Kali Linux machine connected to the same isolated subnet as the target devices. While the attacks were in progress, both Snort and Suricata were actively deployed on the Raspberry Pi 5 gateway to monitor and log all traffic. This dual-IDS setup allowed for comprehensive observation and comparison of each system's ability to detect, alert, and log malicious activity in real time (Table 5).

Table 5. Condensed Comparison Between Snort and Suricata

Aspect	Snort	Suricata
Total Packets	26,587	197,609
TCP Packets	26,587	26,532
UDP Packets	0	126,040
Websites Detected	0	60

Snort did not capture any UDP packets or websites detected from the bettercap ARP spoofing the Kali Linux laptop did when it attacked the The analysis of top network endpoints revealed that the most frequent source and destination IP address recorded by both IDS platforms—Snort and Suricata—was 192.168.50.20, which corresponds to the Kali Linux attack machine used during the experiment. This is expected, as the Kali laptop was responsible for launching the simulated attacks, including SYN floods, ICMP floods, port scans, and ARP spoofing. Snort recorded 11,079 packets and Suricata 22,345 packets from this IP as a source, while as a destination, Snort logged 13,612 packets and Suricata captured 66,576. This confirms the high-volume nature of offensive traffic initiated by the attacker system. Furthermore, DNS query analysis showed that Snort did not capture or log any DNS queries, while Suricata successfully recorded multiple DNS-related entries. Notably, any DNS packets that were present was not captured by Snort, highlighting Suricata's advantage in visibility for name resolution traffic and multicast service discovery—key for analyzing IoT behavior.

4 Results

The experiment revealed important differences in how Snort and Suricata capture and represent network activity, which can be traced to their fundamental design choices. Snort, configured to output full packet captures (PCAP), stored every packet observed on the wire. This resulted in larger and more detailed datasets, particularly useful for detecting volumetric behaviors such as DoS floods or repeated scan attempts. Suricata, however, defaults to logging at the event and flow level in its eve.json format. This design emphasizes efficiency and metadata-rich summaries rather than exhaustive packet storage. Consequently, Suricata appeared to record fewer packets and DNS queries overall, though this was not due to missed traffic but rather its aggregation of packets into higher-level events.

Device-specific behavior further reflected expected communication patterns. The Fitbit Sense 2 produced little Wi-Fi traffic, aligning with its reliance on Bluetooth for most functionality, while the Petcube camera generated continuous streams of data to external servers, consistent with its dependency on cloud services. The iPhone 6 s and Motorola smartphone demonstrated typical smartphone traffic, though only the iPhone was successfully ARP spoofed. This may point to platform-level differences in how iOS and Android handle ARP requests and network stack protections. Additionally, the Kali Linux attack machine surfaced as the dominant source and destination IP, as expected, because of the high traffic volumes produced during simulated DoS and MITM scenarios.

These results underscore a deeper phenomenon: Snort's packet-level fidelity favors scenarios where raw traffic inspection is critical, while Suricata's enriched metadata provides greater context about how IoT devices operate within a network. In practice, this means Snort is better suited for detecting traffic saturation and protocol misuse, whereas Suricata more effectively reveals service discovery,

DNS behavior, and device-to-cloud communications. Together, these differences illustrate how IDS architecture influences visibility into IoT environments and explain the complementary strengths of both tools.

5 Conclusion and Future Work

This study explored the network behavior and security visibility of various IoT devices using a Raspberry Pi 5 configured as a network gateway running both Snort and Suricata. Through real-world testing with a Motorola smartphone, iPhone 6 s, Petcube camera, and Fitbit Sense 2, we observed device-specific traffic patterns under both normal usage and simulated attack conditions, including DoS and man-in-the-middle attacks. Unlike the smartphones, which allow user-installed apps and OS-level configurations, the Fitbit Sense 2 and Petcube camera operate as closed systems with limited or no user-level software modification. This restricted our ability to configure or harden them beyond their companion applications. The phones by default have more security, mainly the Motorola such that ARP spoofing wasn't working on it. Our comparison of Snort and Suricata demonstrated that while both IDS tools are capable of detecting high-volume attack traffic, they differ significantly in their default logging behavior and protocol visibility. Snort, when configured with packet capture and a community ruleset, excelled in identifying raw packet activity but lacked insight into DNS and multicast traffic. Suricata, with its event-driven logging, captured richer contextual data such as service discovery and DNS queries, offering greater visibility into IoT device behavior. These findings suggest that for environments focused on IoT device monitoring, Suricata provides a more comprehensive out-of-the-box solution, while Snort remains a powerful tool for targeted traffic inspection when properly configured. Ultimately, understanding the strengths and limitations of each IDS is crucial for building effective and scalable network defenses in smart home or enterprise IoT environments.

Future iterations of this research could explore several directions to expand on the findings of this study:

1) **Expand Device Testing:** Incorporate a broader range of IoT devices such as smart thermostats, doorbells, and lighting systems to evaluate how different device types behave under IDS monitoring.
2) **Explore Attack Scenarios:** Introduce simulated or real-world attack patterns (e.g., ARP spoofing, unauthorized access attempts, or firmware exploits) to assess detection accuracy and false positive rates between Snort and Suricata.
3) **Bluetooth and Zigbee Monitoring:** Extend monitoring capabilities beyond Wi-Fi by including wireless protocol sniffers for Bluetooth and Zigbee, which are commonly used in smart home devices.
4) **Performance and Resource Benchmarking:** Measure CPU, memory, and bandwidth usage on the Raspberry Pi during IDS operation to determine the performance limits of low-cost hardware in real-time detection environments.

5) **Rule Set Optimization:** Develop and test custom IDS rule sets specifically tuned for IoT device behavior to improve detection precision and reduce unnecessary alerts.

References

1. Ghazi, D.S., Hamid, H.S., Zaiter, M.J., Behadili, A.S.G.: Snort versus suricata in intrusion detection. Iraqi J. Inf. Commun. Technol. **7**(2), 73–88 (2024). https://doi.org/10.31987/ijict.7.2.290, https://mail.ijict.edu.iq/index.php/ijict/article/view/290
2. Hariawan, F.R., Sunaringtyas, S.U.: Design an intrusion detection system, multiple honeypot and packet analyzer using raspberry pi 4 for home network. In: 2021 17th International Conference on Quality in Research (QIR): International Symposium on Electrical and Computer Engineering, pp. 43–48 (2021). https://doi.org/10.1109/QIR54354.2021.9716189
3. Martin, E.D., Kargaard, J., Sutherland, I.: Raspberry pi malware: an analysis of cyberattacks towards IoT devices. In: 2019 10th International Conference on Dependable Systems, Services and Technologies (DESSERT), pp. 161–166 (2019). https://doi.org/10.1109/DESSERT.2019.8770027
4. Mohd Bakry, B.B., Bt Adenan, A.R., Mohd Yussoff, Y.B.: Security attack on IoT related devices using raspberry pi and kali linux. In: 2022 International Conference on Computer and Drone Applications (IConDA), pp. 40–45 (2022). https://doi.org/10.1109/ICONDA56696.2022.10000370
5. Qureshi, S.U., et al.: Systematic review of deep learning solutions for malware detection and forensic analysis in iot. J. King Saud Univ. - Comput. Inf. Sci. **36**(8), 102164 (2024). https://doi.org/10.1016/j.jksuci.2024.102164, https://www.sciencedirect.com/science/article/pii/S1319157824002532
6. Yalda, R., Nepal, N., El Hawari, T.: Enhancing IoT security affordably with raspberry pi and open-source ids/ips. In: 2024 IEEE International Conference on Advanced Systems and Emergent Technologies (IC_ASET), pp. 1–6 (2024)
7. Zhang, X., Upton, O., Beebe, N.L., Choo, K.K.R.: IoT botnet forensics: a comprehensive digital forensic case study on mirai botnet servers. Forensic Sci. Int. Digit. Investig. **32**, 300926 (2020)

Generative Reasoning Meets Multimodal Evaluation: A Novel Approach to Activity and Package Diagram Comparison in UML Modeling

Van-Viet Nguyen[1], Huu-Khanh Nguyen[2], Kim-Son Nguyen[1], Thi Minh-Hue Luong[1], Anh-Tu Bui[1], Duc-Quang Vu[1], and The-Vinh Nguyen[1(✉)]

[1] Thai Nguyen University of Information and Communication Technology, Thai Nguyen, Vietnam
{nvviet,nkson,lmhue,batu,vdquang,vinhnt}@ictu.edu.vn
[2] Thai Nguyen University, Thai Nguyen, Vietnam
khanhnh@tnu.edu.vn

Abstract. Large Language Models (LLMs) have been utilized for many downstream tasks such as writing, reasoning and software engineering. However, only a fraction of studies focused on generating code, especially in the field of software requirements. Thus, this paper presents a unique framework that leverages generative reasoning and multimodal evaluation to compare two essential Unified Modeling Language (UML) diagram types: Activity Diagrams, representing behavioral aspects and Package Diagrams, representing structural organization. In the proposed approach, LLaMA 3.2-1B-Instruct was utilized to generate user-oriented prompts, while DeepSeek-R1-Distill-Qwen-32B performs reasoning and automatically produces PlantUML code for diagram construction. To ensure the reliability and accuracy of the generated diagrams, multimodal large models Qwen2.5-VL-3B-Instruct, LLaMA-3.2-11B-Vision-Instruct and Aya-Vision-8B are employed within the MMMU Benchmark for evaluation and scoring. Experimental results demonstrated that the combination of reasoning based generation and multimodal assessment provided significant improvements in diagram consistency, semantic correctness, and cross-model verification. The study contributes a novel methodology for automated UML modeling which highlighted the advantages and limitations of Activity versus Package diagrams when generated and validated through generative AI. This study not only contributes to the automation process in software design but also proposes a new framework for evaluating the ability of reasoning on diagrams in model-driven engineering.

Keywords: Automated UML Generation · Software Engineering · UMLCode · Model Reasoning · PlantUML · Multimodal Validation · Large Language Models

V. V. Pham et al. (Eds.): CIDDF 2025, ACSAR 5, pp. 114–127, 2026.
https://doi.org/10.1007/978-3-032-19488-6_7

1 Introduction

The Unified Modeling Language (UML) is still a very essential aspect of software engineering. It is a common technique to see, describe, and record system design [1]. There are several types of UML diagrams, including Activity Diagrams and Package Diagrams. They are both incredibly important, but they do distinct things: Activity Diagrams describe how things behave, while Package Diagrams demonstrate how things are related to each other. Activity Diagrams describe how actions, choices, and flows happen in a system. This is why they are vital for figuring out how things change over time. Package diagrams, on the other hand, show how the parts of a system are put together into modules. This shows how the many levels and structures work together to make it feasible to develop large scale software. Being able to automatically create and evaluate these diagrams is a huge step forward for model-driven engineering and for making software design less of a headache.

The recent growth of generative artificial intelligence models has made it possible to automate UML modeling tasks in novel ways. Language models trained on massive amounts of code [2–4], education [5,6], Legal Document [7], natural language text may turn stated requirements into formal diagram representations [8]. This speeds up the design process by a lot. Generative models with reasoning abilities make it easier to handle complex dependencies, logical accuracy, and semantic alignment, in addition to making text-to-diagram. But there is still a huge problem: making sure that the diagrams that are created automatically are both appropriate and meet the needs of the system. If there aren't good techniques to verify generative AI in UML modeling, it might create diagrams that look right but aren't right in their ideas.

To address this challenge, the present study presents a novel methodology that integrates generative reasoning with multimodal evaluation for the assessment of Activity and Package Diagrams in UML modeling. The workflow employs LLaMA 3.2-1B-Instruct to imitate user prompts, which is how people naturally talk to each other when they are developing software requirements. DeepSeek-R1-Distill-Qwen-32B is what makes the generative reasoning section work [9]. It takes these prompts and puts them into PlantUML code, which is then turned into diagrams. A Multimodal Multi-Model Understanding (MMMU) Benchmark [10,11], which includes Qwen2.5-VL-3B-Instruct [12], LLaMA-3.2-11B-Vision-Instruct [13]and Aya-Vision-8B[14], is used to critically evaluate the validity of the generated diagrams. These visual language models check the diagrams against standards including structural accuracy, semantic consistency, and cross-model agreement, which makes the verification process better.

This paper contributes three key elements. First, it introduces a novel methodology that combines generative reasoning and multimodal evaluation for UML modeling, thereby linking the processes of diagram creation and validation. Second, it compares Activity and Package Diagrams and highlights the good and bad things about each when they are produced with AI models. Third, it illustrates that you can utilize more than one vision-language model at the same time to make a reliable approach to rate how good UML diagrams are. This study creates a new way for generative AI to be used in model-driven software engineering methods by making the processes of generation and evaluation better.

This is how the rest of this paper is built up. In Sect. 2, we look at other research that has been done on AI-driven UML modeling, generative reasoning, and multimodal evaluation. Section 3 talks about the proposed strategy and how LLaMA, DeepSeek, and multimodal evaluation models fit into it. Section 4 has the results and discussion, and Sect. 5 has the conclusion and future work.

2 Related Work

2.1 AI-Driven UML Modeling

The application of artificial intelligence to software modeling has gained increasing attention in recent years, particularly with the rise of large language models (LLMs). Traditional UML modeling is a highly manual process, requiring significant effort from software engineers to translate textual requirements into diagrammatic representations. Early attempts to automate this process primarily relied on rule-based approaches and domain-specific modeling languages [15]. These systems, while functional, often lacked the flexibility to adapt to diverse and ambiguous natural language specifications.

The advent of generative AI has transformed this landscape. Pretrained LLMs such as GPT, LLaMA, and Qwen have demonstrated the ability to translate natural language inputs into formal notations, including PlantUML code, thus accelerating the modeling workflow [1], LLMs in software engineering [16], artificial intelligence in education [5,6], Mini Language Models for Legal Document Understanding [7]. Several recent studies have explored the automatic generation of Class Diagrams, Sequence Diagrams and Use Case Diagrams using LLMs, with results showing promising alignment between natural language requirements and formal UML constructs [17]. However, most research has focused on structural diagrams, with less emphasis on behavioral diagrams such as Activity Diagrams, and limited comparative analyses across different diagram types. Furthermore, evaluation remains a major bottleneck, as traditional correctness checks often focus only on syntactic validity rather than semantic accuracy.

By targeting both Activity and Package Diagrams, the present study extends this line of research, addressing both behavioral and structural aspects of UML modeling. Moreover, it introduces a systematic evaluation pipeline to overcome limitations of prior work.

2.2 Generative Reasoning in Large Language Models

While text-to-diagram generation is useful, the underlying reasoning capability of LLMs is equally critical to producing meaningful and logically consistent diagrams. Generative reasoning refers to the ability of models not only to produce outputs but also to reason about dependencies, constraints, and logical flows embedded in user requirements [18]. This capability is particularly important for

UML diagrams, where structural correctness alone does not guarantee semantic fidelity to the intended system.

Recent advancements have introduced reasoning enhanced models such as DeepSeek-R1-Distill-Qwen-32B, which combine generative fluency with reasoning depth. Distillation techniques have been used to compress larger reasoning models into more efficient architectures, making them suitable for practical software engineering tasks [9]. These models outperform traditional instruction-tuned LLMs when it comes to handling multi step logical tasks, such as ensuring consistency across multiple components in UML diagrams or preserving dependencies between actions in an Activity Diagram.

Nevertheless, challenges remain in aligning reasoning-based outputs with the often ambiguous or incomplete nature of human-provided requirements. Research efforts such as chain-of-thought prompting [19] have sought to enhance reasoning transparency, but few studies have examined their impact on formal modeling tasks. This study contributes by positioning DeepSeek-R1-Distill-Qwen-32B at the core of UML diagram generation, evaluating its effectiveness in bridging user prompts with accurate PlantUML code.

2.3 Multimodal Evaluation with Vision-Language Models

This study explores the use of ChatGPT, an advanced AI language model, to dynamically enhance UML class diagrams [20]. Recently, multimodal large models (MLMs or VLMs) such as Qwen2.5-VL-3B-Instruct, LLaMA-3.2-11B-Vision-Instruc and Aya-Vision-8B have demonstrated strong performance in multimodal reasoning tasks that integrate visual and textual information. Their ability to interpret and reason about diagrams, images, and schemas offers a new opportunity to automate UML evaluation.

The concept of Massive Multi-discipline Multimodal Understanding and Reasonin (MMMU) extends this potential by leveraging multiple VLMs in parallel to evaluate generated artifacts. Instead of depending on a single model, MMMU aggregates insights across multiple evaluators, improving robustness and reducing bias [10]. For UML modeling, this approach allows scoring diagrams not only based on syntactic validity but also on semantic alignment, structural organization, and even cross-model consistency.

Recent research in adjacent domains such as code visualization, flowchart verification, and schematic diagram interpretation demonstrates the feasibility of VLM-based evaluation [21]. However, UML diagrams present unique challenges due to their diverse notations and the balance of structural and behavioral semantics. By integrating Qwen2.5-VL-3B-Instruct, LLaMA-3.2-11B-Vision-Instruct, and Aya-Vision-8B within an MMMU framework, this study pioneers an evaluation pipeline tailored to UML diagrams, particularly focusing on the comparison between Activity and Package Diagrams.

In summary, prior research has shown significant progress in AI-driven UML modeling, reasoning enhanced generation, and multimodal evaluation. However, gaps remain in three key areas: (1) the lack of comparative studies between behavioral and structural UML diagrams, (2) limited use of reasoning centric models for diagram generation and (3) the absence of robust multimodal evaluation pipelines. This paper addresses these gaps by presenting a pioneering framework that combines generative reasoning with multimodal evaluation to compare Activity and Package Diagrams, thereby advancing both the generation and validation aspects of automated UML modeling.

3 Proposed Methodology

3.1 Materials

LLaMA 3.2-1B-Instruct is a lightweight variant of the LLaMA (Large Language Model Meta AI) [22] language model family specifically designed for instruction following tasks. With a size of only about 1 billion parameters, the model achieves high performance on text generation, question answering, and light logical reasoning tasks, while remaining resource-efficient enough for edge applications or compute constrained environments. The "Instruct" version of LLaMA 3.2-1B-Instruct is fine-tuned on a high quality instruction dataset, allowing it to accurately follow input requests and generate consistent, concise responses. With its balance between efficiency and performance, LLaMA 3.2-1B-Instruct is a potential choice for research on small language models (SLMs) applications in specialized tasks such as code generation, natural language processing, and intelligent education.

To ensure practical deployment and inference scalability, we compared three recent instruction-tuned language models: LLaMA 3.2-1B-Instruct (Meta), Gemma 2 2B (Google), and DeepSeek R1 Distill Qwen 1.5B (DeepSeek). As shown in Table 1, LLaMA 3.2-1B-Instruct achieved the fastest inference time of 60 s on a batch of 100 prompts, outperforming DeepSeek R1 Distill Qwen 1.5B (87 s) and Gemma 2 2B (116 s). This speed advantage is largely attributed to LLaMA 3.2's lightweight architecture, with only 1B parameters, compared to DeepSeek R1 Distill Qwen 1.5B and Gemma 2 2B in the other models.

Despite its smaller size, LLaMA 3.2-1B-Instruct demonstrates competitive instruction following capabilities, making it suitable for structured code and UML generation tasks. Its fast response time, low resource requirements, and robust performance on downstream reasoning tasks render it a compelling choice for building scalable and efficient generation pipelines. Therefore, we selected LLaMA 3.2-1B-Instruct as the primary model in our study to balance inference efficiency and generation quality under limited compute environments. The comparison parameters between the models for our research team to choose LLaMA 3.2-1B-Instruct are shown in Table 1

The DeepSeek-R1-Distill-Qwen-32B is a distilled version of the powerful Qwen-72B model, specifically optimized by the DeepSeek team to enhance reasoning and code generation capabilities while significantly reducing inference costs. By leveraging a large-scale distillation process from Qwen's original base, the model retains high-quality language understanding and generation abilities with only 32 billion parameters, making it suitable for complex

Table 1. Comparison between LLaMA 3.2-1B-Instruct, Gemma 2 2B and DeepSeek R1 Distill Qwen 1.5B models

Model	Parameters	Developer	Response time (seconds)
LLaMA 3.2-1B-Instruct	1B	Meta	60
Gemma 2 2B	2B	Google	116
DeepSeek R1 Distill Qwen 1.5B	1.5B	DeepSeek	87

tasks such as multi-hop reasoning, code synthesis, and technical question answering. DeepSeek-R1-Distill-Qwen-32B is trained on a curated mixture of natural language and programming datasets, incorporating both open-source code and instruction-following corpora. According to DeepSeek's open model release [23], this distilled model shows comparable performance to larger LLMs while being more efficient for deployment in practical environments. Its strong reasoning capacity and compatibility with multimodal prompting make it a promising foundation for research in AI code generation and automated software modeling (Table 2).

Table 2. Example format prompt for training

Format Prompt: Create software feature descriptions from a user perspective
`"Generate a user query for the dataset."` prompt = "Act as an end-user or product owner who has conceived a software feature. You are now explaining this feature requirement to a software developer. The developer needs this information to draft flowcharts and class diagram. Your task is to: 1. Invent a plausible and interesting new software feature. 2. Describe this feature from a user's perspective, focusing on what it does. Output should be easy to understand. Answer only about the description of the feature, not about the flowchart or class diagram. Feature description:"
Format Prompt: Generate PlantUML code corresponding to the feature description
`"prompt = """You are a UML code generation specialist. Given the following user feature description:"` input " Generate the PlantUML code for a Use Case Diagram that accurately represents the actors and use cases described. OUTPUT REQUIREMENTS: * ONLY raw PlantUML code. * The code must start with '@startuml' and end with '@enduml'. * No explanations, titles, or any other text outside the PlantUML code block. <think>

One of the key advantages of DeepSeek-R1-Distill-Qwen-32B lies in its open-source nature, enabling full transparency, reproducibility, and customization for academic and industrial research. Unlike many proprietary large language models, this model can be freely downloaded and deployed without licensing restrictions, empowering small research labs and independent developers to conduct advanced experiments in natural language reasoning and code generation. Despite its scale of 32 billion parameters, the model is optimized for efficient inference and can be quantized (e.g., to 4-bit) to run on high-end personal computers equipped with consumer grade GPUs such as RTX 3090 or 4090. This makes it highly accessible for low-budget teams who seek state-of-the-art performance without the need for massive compute clusters. Its balance between reasoning power and resource efficiency positions DeepSeek-R1-Distill-Qwen-32B as an ideal candidate for lightweight deployment, academic prototyping, and educational use in AI and software engineering research.

Recent advances in multilingual vision-language model (VLMs) have significantly improved machine understanding across both visual and textual modalities. In this study, we focus on three open-source instruction tuned vision-language models: Qwen2.5-VL-3B-Instruct, LLaMA-3.2-11B-Vision-Instruct, and Aya-Vision-8B, each representing different design philosophies in model size, training objectives, and deployment efficiency. Qwen2.5-VL-3B-Instruct developed by Alibaba's Qwen team, is a lightweight multimodal model based on Qwen2.5 architecture with only 3 billion parameters, yet it supports high-resolution image understanding and instruction-following tasks efficiently. It integrates a vision encoder and a pre-trained language decoder with cross-modal attention for flexible reasoning and fast inference [24,25]. LLaMA-3.2-11B-Vision-Instruct an extended variant of Meta's LLaMA 3 series, incorporates a 11B-parameter text model with vision capabilities via a learned projection layer. The model is fine-tuned using vision-text instruction datasets and demonstrates competitive performance in complex visual reasoning tasks while maintaining high language fluency [22]. Aya-Vision-8B introduced by the Cohere for AI initiative under the Aya project, is a globally inclusive multilingual vision-language model. With 8 billion parameters, Aya-Vision is optimized not only for multilingual visual understanding but also for alignment with open instruction datasets [26].

3.2 Method

The framework operates in a sequential pipeline, from specification generation to final scoring (Fig. 1).

Stage 1: Technical Specification Generation
In the first phase, the LLaMA 3.2âĂŞ1BâĂŞInstruct model is prompted to generate textual specifications appropriate to each diagram type. For Activity Diagrams, the model is instructed to act as a system/business analyst, generating detailed behavioral scenarios that include: (1) sequential action nodes, (2) decision and merge points with guard conditions, (3) concurrent flows (branching/joining), and (4) start and end states. In contrast, for Package Diagrams,

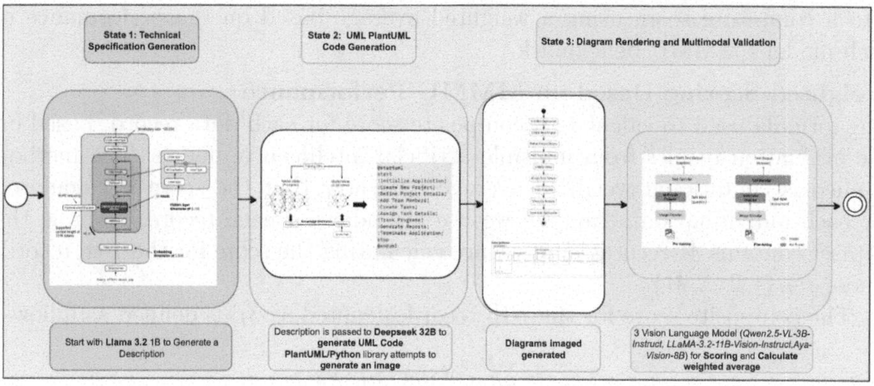

Fig. 1. Diagram Generation and Scoring Process.

the model is prompted to act as a system architect, generating module specifications that define: (1) major software packages, (2) their responsibilities, (3) nested structures, and (4) relationships between packages such as dependencies, imports, or access. This phase generates a diverse set of behavioral and architectural descriptions, ensuring sufficient coverage for subsequent diagram synthesis.

Stage 2: UML Diagram Code Generation
The textual specifications were then fed into the DeepSeek-R1-Distill-Qwen-32B model, instructed to act as a UML expert. The model generated PlantUML code corresponding to the required diagram type. For Activity Diagrams, the prompt emphasized correct handling of action flows, guard expressions, and concurrency constructs, while for Package Diagrams the focus was on proper declaration of packages, nested hierarchies, and directional dependency arrows. To improve reasoning accuracy, the model was encouraged to adopt chain-of-thought decomposition using <think> tags, explicitly breaking down the mapping process from specification to UML syntax.

Stage 3: Diagram Rendering and Multimodal Validation
The generated PlantUML code was processed using the PlantUML library to render visual diagrams. Samples that failed to compile due to syntax errors were assigned a score of 0. To get diagrams that worked, each pair of text specification and diagram image was sent to three Vision-Language Models: Qwen2.5-VL-3B-Instruct, LLaMA-3.2-11B-Vision-Instruct, and Aya-Vision-8B. The VLMs rated the fidelity of the diagrams on a score of 1 to 6, looking at how well the visual representation matched the intended specification. For Activity Diagrams, the evaluation looked at how well the nodes were covered, how accurate the control flow was, how right the guard conditions were, and how well the concurrency was handled. For Package Diagrams, the main things to look for were the presence of packages, the right types of relationships, and the integrity of nested structures. To reduce bias in individual models, the various VLM scores were aggregated

into a composite score using a weighted average based on the performance of each model's MMMU benchmark.

Weighted Scoring Based on MMMU Performance
The formula used to calculate a composite score for each data record, based on the evaluation results from multiple artificial intelligence models. The method applied is conditional weighted average. To show that the score is calculated for each individual data sample, we use an index for each record. Assume the dataset contains M records, and we are calculating the score for the j-th record, where $j \in \{1, 2, ..., M\}$.

The composite score for the j-th record, denoted as S_j, is defined as follows:

$$S_j = \frac{\sum_{i=1}^{N} \delta(s_{ij}) \cdot s_{ij} \cdot w_i}{\sum_{i=1}^{N} \delta(s_{ij}) \cdot w_i}$$

Where:

- N is the total number of evaluation models.
- i is the index of the model ($i \in \{1, ..., N\}$).
- j is the index of the data record being processed ($j \in \{1, ..., M\}$).
- S_j: The final composite score for the j-th record.
- s_{ij}: The score given by the i-th model for the j-th record ($0 \leq s_{ij} \leq 6$).
- w_i: The weight of the i-th model (this weight is constant across all records).
- $\delta(s_{ij})$: An indicator function, defined as:

$$\delta(s_{ij}) = \begin{cases} 1 & \text{if } s_{ij} > 0 \text{ (valid score)} \\ 0 & \text{if } s_{ij} = 0 \text{ (invalid score)} \end{cases}$$

The final dataset consists of 1,960 samples drawn from Package Diagram (1000) and Activity Diagram (960). Each sample consists of an input specification, generated PlantUML code and a weighted validation score.

Scoring by Vision Models. Each vision model independently assigns a score from 1 to 6 to the UML diagram based on its alignment with the user prompt. A score of 0 indicates that the diagram fails to represent any aspect of the requirements, while a score of 6 signifies that the diagram fully captures the specified system design, including correct entities, relationships, and constraints. To ensure reliability, we calibrate the models' scoring behavior using a small set of manually annotated UML diagrams, adjusting the instruction prompts to minimize bias. The scores from Llama-3.2-11B-Vision-Instruct, Qwen2.5-VL-3B-Instruct and Aya-Vision-8B are recorded for each diagram, providing a multi perspective evaluation of the generated output.

The published MMMU benchmark performance of each model is used to figure out the weights for the Multimodal Multi-Model Understanding (MMMU). The weights are based on the benchmark evaluation results: Qwen2.5-VL-3B-Instruct got a score of 53.1, LLaMA-3.2-11B-Vision-Instruct got a score of 50.7, and Aya-Vision-8B got a score of 39.9. These numbers show how well each model understands multimodal information, and they are used to standardize and figure out the overall evaluation score in the study.

4 Results and Discussion

In Fig. 2 and Table 3, The experimental evaluation provides a detailed comparison of three vision-language models Qwen2.5-VL-3B-Instruct, LLaMA-3.2-11B-Vision-Instruct and Aya-Vision-8B across Activity and Package Diagrams. The score distribution (0âĂŞ6) reflects the fidelity of model predictions to the expected UML structures.

Table 3. Distribution score for three vision-language models on UML Diagrams (Activity and Package Diagram).

Diagram	Model	Score						
		0	1	2	3	4	5	6
Activity Diagram	qwen25vl3b	597	46	16	86	9	81	125
	llama32vl11b	597	139	0	94	37	86	7
	aya_vision_8b	610	176	7	95	10	45	17
Package Diagram	qwen25vl3b	379	1	5	15	268	332	0
	llama32vl11b	379	3	0	0	15	603	0
	aya_vision_8b	592	20	0	150	61	176	1

Activity Diagram

The results for Activity Diagrams indicate considerable challenges for all models.

Qwen2.5-VL-3B-Instruct exhibits a strong concentration at score 0 (597 cases), suggesting frequent failures in generating semantically valid diagrams. However, it also achieves a relatively high number of top scores (125 cases at score 6), showing potential when reasoning aligns with the process flow.

LLaMA-3.2-11B-Vision-Instruct similarly records 597 zero-score cases, with additional clustering at score 1 (139) and score 3 (94). Although it demonstrates moderate success at mid-level fidelity (37 cases at score 4, 86 at score 5), its high-score performance is limited (only 7 at score 6).

Aya-Vision-8B performs worst in terms of failures, with 610 cases at score 0 and 176 at score 1. While it achieves some mid-level results (95 cases at score 3, 45 at score 5), its ability to reach high-fidelity outputs is minimal (17 at score 6).

These findings confirm that Activity Diagrams pose a greater challenge, as they require understanding of sequential flows, decision branches, and concurrency, which current vision-language models struggle to capture consistently.

Package Diagram

In contrast, the evaluation of Package Diagrams reveals significantly stronger results, with more balanced score distributions across the models.

Qwen2.5-VL-3B-Instruct shows improved performance, with most predictions concentrated at score 4 (268 cases) and score 5 (332 cases), highlighting its effectiveness in modeling hierarchical and modular structures.

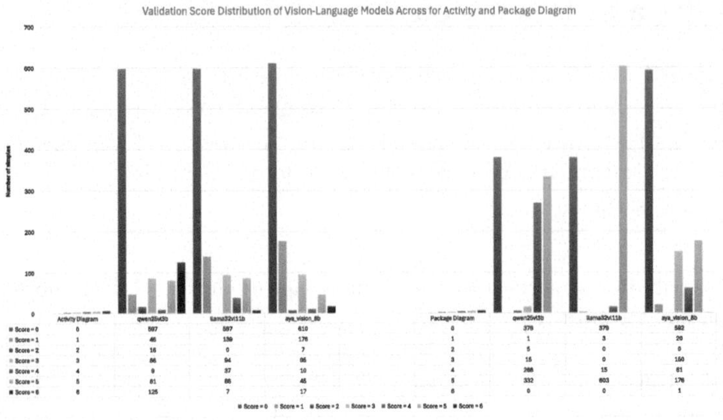

Fig. 2. Distribution score for three vision language models

LLaMA-3.2-11B-Vision-Instruct achieves the highest consistency, with an overwhelming majority of cases at score 5 (603), and almost no predictions at lower scores. This indicates strong reliability in capturing structural relationships among packages.

Aya-Vision-8B delivers more mixed outcomes, with 592 cases at score 0 but also substantial predictions at higher scores (150 at score 3, 61 at score 4, and 176 at score 5). While less stable than LLaMA, it demonstrates potential in mid-to-high fidelity outputs.

Overall, the results demonstrate that Package Diagrams are significantly easier for vision-language models to interpret and generate compared to Activity Diagrams. The structural and spatial nature of Package Diagrams, which emphasize static relationships, aligns more closely with the reasoning strengths of multimodal models.

In Fig. 3, The experimental results highlight notable differences in the performance of generative reasoning when applied to Activity Diagrams and Package Diagrams. For Activity Diagrams, the majority of outputs fall into the lowest score category, with 597 cases score at 0, indicating a substantial number of failures in generating meaningful or accurate diagrams. While some improvements are observed at intermediate levels, with 102 cases score at 2 and 96 at 3, only a small fraction (22 cases) achieve the highest score of 5. This distribution suggests that generating Activity Diagrams poses significant challenges for the model, particularly due to their dynamic representation of processes and the need for precise control flow reasoning.

In contrast, Package Diagrams exhibit a markedly different pattern. The highest concentration of results lies in the upper performance range, with 585 cases achieving scores between 4 and 5, and only 379 instances rated at 0. Intermediate scores are relatively rare, which suggests that the model either produces well structured package level abstractions or fails entirely. This outcome reflects the

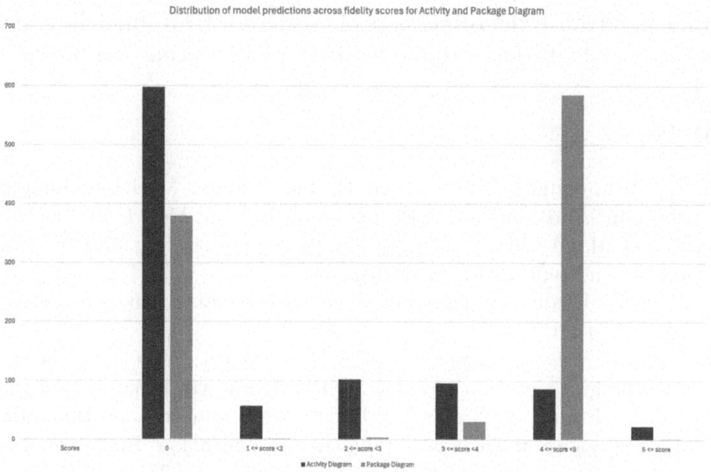

Fig. 3. Distribution of Aggregated Scores for Activity and Package Diagrams

comparative simplicity of Package Diagrams, which primarily emphasize modular organization rather than complex behavioral flows.

Overall, the results indicate that Package Diagrams are significantly easier for generative models to construct accurately compared to Activity Diagrams. The observed differences underscore the inherent difficulty of reasoning about procedural flows versus static structural abstractions. These findings provide a strong foundation for exploring multimodal evaluation techniques and highlight the need for specialized approaches when dealing with behavior-centric UML models.

5 Conclusion

This study has presented a comparative evaluation of generative reasoning applied to UML Activity and Package Diagrams. The results demonstrate that while Package Diagrams achieve consistently high accuracy, Activity Diagrams remain a challenging target, with a large proportion of low-quality generations. These findings reinforce the importance of considering diagram type and complexity when evaluating or applying generative AI models in software engineering tasks.

Future research should focus on three key directions: first, multimodal evaluation, where vision-language models can be leveraged to provide more nuanced assessments of diagram quality beyond textual correctness; second, dataset expansion, through the development of larger and more diverse datasets that better capture the variability of UML semantics, particularly for behavior-oriented diagrams and third, cross-diagram consistency, by exploring methods to generate different UML diagram types in an integrated manner that ensures alignment between structural and behavioral perspectives. By addressing these challenges, future work can advance the robustness of AI-driven UML modeling, paving the way for practical integration into model-driven engineering workflows.

References

1. Booch, G., Rumbaugh, J., Jacobson, I.: The Unified Modeling Language User Guide, 2nd edn. Addison-Wesley Professional, Boston, MA, USA (2005)
2. Zhang, Q., et al.: A survey on large language models for software engineering. arXiv preprint arXiv:2312.15223 (2023)
3. Chen, M., et al.: Evaluating large language models trained on code. arXiv preprint arXiv:2107.03374 (2021)
4. Dehaerne, E., Dey, B., Halder, S., De Gendt, S., Meert, W.: Code generation using machine learning: a systematic review. IEEE Access **10**, 82434–82455 (2022)
5. Nguyen, T.-V., Phung, T.-N., Cuong, D.-D.: A bibliometric and thematic analysis of systematic reviews of artificial intelligence in education. In: International Conference on Advances in Information and Communication Technology, pp. 337–351. Springer (2024)
6. Van Viet, N., et al.: Revolutionizing education: an extensive analysis of large language models integration **4**(4), 10–21 (2024). https://irjstem.com/wp-content/uploads/2025/02/IRJSTEM-V4N4-2024-Paper02.pdf
7. Khanh, N.H., Van, V.N., Vinh, N.T., Cong, N.H.: Phi-3 meets law: fine-tuning mini language models for legal document understanding. Res. Dev. Appl. Inf. Commun. Technol. **2024**(3), 136–142 (2024). ISSN: 1859-3526
8. de Faria, F.F.G., do Prado Leite, J.C.S.: Generating UML models from text: a systematic literature review. In: Proceedings of the 22nd Brazilian Symposium on Software Engineering, pp. 131–140 (2008)
9. Guo, D., et al.: DeepSeek-R1: Incentivizing reasoning capability in LLMs via reinforcement learning. arXiv preprint arXiv:2501.12948 (2025)
10. Wu, J., Gan, W., Chen, Z., Shicheng Wan, Z., Yu, P.S.: Multimodal large language models: a survey. In: 2023 IEEE International Conference on Big Data (BigData), pp. 2247–2256. IEEE (2023)
11. Yue, X., et al.: MMMU: a massive multi-discipline multimodal understanding and reasoning benchmark for expert AGI. In: Proceedings of the IEEE/CVF Conference on Computer Vision and Pattern Recognition (CVPR), pp. 9556–9567 (2024)
12. Wang, P., et al.: Qwen2-VL: Enhancing vision-language model's perception of the world at any resolution. arXiv preprint arXiv:2409.12191 (2024)
13. Touvron, H., et al.: LLaMA: Open and efficient foundation language models. arXiv preprint arXiv:2302.13971 (2023)
14. Üstün, A., et al.: Aya model: an instruction finetuned open-access multilingual language model. In: Proceedings of the 62nd Annual Meeting of the Association for Computational Linguistics (Volume 1: Long Papers), pp. 15894–15939, Bangkok, Thailand (2024). Association for Computational Linguistics
15. Sommerville, I.: Software Engineering, 10th edn. Pearson, Boston, MA, USA (2016)
16. Van Viet, N., The Vinh, N.: Large language models in software engineering: a systematic review and vision. J. Educ. Sustain. Innovation **2**(2), 146–156 (2024)
17. Meng, Y., Ban, A.: Automated UML class diagram generation from textual requirements using NLP techniques. JOIV: Int. J. Inform. Vis. **8**(3-2), 1905–1915 (2024)
18. Wei, J., Wang, X., Schuurmans, D., Le, Q.V., Zhou, D.: Chain-of-thought prompting elicits reasoning in large language models. In: Advances in Neural Information Processing Systems (NeurIPS), vol. 35, pp. 24824–24837 (2022)

19. Wei, J., et al.: Chain-of-thought prompting elicits reasoning in large language models. In: Proceedings of the 36th International Conference on Neural Information Processing Systems, NIPS '22, Red Hook, NY, USA (2022). Curran Associates Inc
20. Rouabhia, D., Hadjadj, I.: Enhancing class diagram dynamics: A natural language approach with ChatGPT. arXiv preprint arXiv:2406.11002 (2024)
21. Munde, A.R.: Evaluation of vision language model on UML diagrams
22. Touvron, H., et al.: LLaMA: Open and efficient foundation language models (2023)
23. DeepSeek-AI. DeepSeek-R1: Incentivizing reasoning capability in LLMs via reinforcement learning (2025)
24. Wang, P., et al.: Qwen2-VL: Enhancing vision-language model's perception of the world at any resolution. arXiv preprint arXiv:2409.12191 (2024)
25. Bai, J., et al.: Qwen-VL: A versatile vision-language model for understanding, localization, text reading, and beyond. arXiv preprint arXiv:2308.12966 (2023)
26. Üstün, A., et al.: Aya model: An instruction finetuned open-access multilingual language model. arXiv preprint arXiv:2402.07827 (2024)

A Real-Time Vietnamese Sign Language Recognition System Using a Lightweight LSTM Model and Hand Key Point Extraction

Duc-Binh Nguyen, Thi-Tam Dang, Van-Ninh Ha(✉), and Quang-Quy Tran

Thai Nguyen University of Information and Communication Technology, Thai Nguyen 250000, Vietnam

{ndbinh,dtc21h4802010186,tqquy}@ictu.edu.vn,
ninhhv.study@gmail.com

Abstract. The Vietnamese deaf community faces significant barriers due to the scarcity of accessible communication tools tailored for Vietnamese Sign Language (VSL). This research directly addresses this significant barrier by developing a lightweight, real-time recognition system capable of identifying 10 common VSL phrases using 3D hand key-points extracted from video frames. The system employs a single-layer Long Short-Term Memory (LSTM) model trained on a carefully curated dataset of 1000 real-world videos. Key-points are extracted using MediaPipe Holistic, and predictions are delivered via a Flask API with latency below 300 ms. The proposed method achieved 99.5% accuracy and demonstrating efficient performance on CPU hardware, making it highly deployable in resource-constrained environments such as educational institutions, healthcare facilities, or mobile devices. This work contributes a reproducible pipeline, dynamic frame buffering, and a practical solution for VSL accessibility.

Keywords: Vietnamese Sign Language · hand key point extraction · LSTM · MediaPipe · real-time recognition · lightweight model · Flask API · gesture recognition

1 Introduction

Vietnamese Sign Language (VSL) is the primary communication medium for a large number of deaf and hard-of-hearing individuals in Vietnam, yet technological support for VSL remains severely limited. Unlike American Sign Language (ASL) or British Sign Language (BSL), which are supported by extensive datasets and advanced recognition systems, VSL lacks practical tools that can operate in real-world, low-resource settings [1–4]. Therefore, this gap hinders effective communication between deaf individuals and non-signers, limiting access to education, healthcare, and social services, particularly in rural areas where computational resources are scarce. The motivation driving this research stems from the urgent need to bridge this communication gap. Developing accessible VSL recognition systems is critical for fostering inclusion, enabling deaf individuals to interact with digital interfaces, and supporting educational initiatives in schools and community centers. However, three primary challenges must be addressed:

V. V. Pham et al. (Eds.): CIDDF 2025, ACSAR 5, pp. 128–137, 2026.
https://doi.org/10.1007/978-3-032-19488-6_8

- Limited Datasets: annotated VSL datasets are scarce, and existing ones are often small or lack real-world variability.
- Computational Constraints: most prior systems rely on GPU-intensive models, unsuitable for low-resource settings like rural Vietnam.

Building upon these identified challenges, this study addresses these challenges by posing two research questions:

1. Can a lightweight VSL recognition system deliver real-time performance on standard CPU hardware without compromising accuracy?
2. Can such a system achieve high accuracy using a modest, real-world dataset?

Consequently, to address these questions, a system was developed using MediaPipe Holistic for 3D key point extraction and a single-layer LSTM model to recognize 10 common VSL phrases such as *"Cảm ơn" (Thank you), "Xin lỗi" (Sorry),* and *"Tớ tên là Tâm" (My name is Tam).* On real-world test videos, the system achieves 99.5% accuracy, operates with CPU-only hardware, and maintains a latency below 300ms. Key contributions include:

- A lightweight, CPU-friendly pipeline for real-time VSL recognition.
- A manually curated dataset of 1000 real-world videos, enhancing robustness.
- Dynamic frame buffering optimizes inference latency.
- A reproducible methodology suitable for educational and accessibility applications.

This paper is organized as follows: Sect. 2 reviews prior work, highlighting gaps that this study addresses. Section 3 details the proposed pipeline, Sect. 4 presents evaluation results, and Sect. 5 discusses implications and future work.

2 Related Work

Previous research in sign language recognition has made significant progress; however, Vietnamese Sign Language (VSL) remains underexplored. Existing studies often face limitations in data realism, computational efficiency, or deployability. Võ Đức Hoàng [5] employed SqueezeNet for static Vietnamese alphabet recognition and reported 99.78% accuracy on real data. The system is limited to static signs and does not support dynamic phrase recognition; hardware and real-time settings were not reported. Tran et al. [1] presented a deep-learning system for VSL gesture recognition, achieving >91% accuracy on the raw dataset and 95% on the processed dataset using 23 alphabet signs and 2 accent marks; the hardware/deployment context was not specified.Nguyen et al. [6] used VGG16+LSTM on the VSL-WRF dataset; performance metrics were not provided, and the system required GPU support. The Vietnamese-Sign-Language project by *trangphan10* [7] explored two pipelines: ResNet50+LSTM (reported 83% accuracy) and MediaPipe+LSTM (37%) on simulated LSA64 data; both pipelines lacked real-time capability, and the hardware context was not specified.

As summarized in Table 1, prior VSL approaches vary in data realism and computational demands (GPU requirement), which affects deployability in low-resource settings. These prior works highlight critical gaps that this study addresses:

Table 1. Comparison of Existing Approaches

Work	Data Type	Method	Accuracy	GPU Required
Tran et al. [1]	Real	MediaPipe + CNN	95%	Yes
Nguyen et al. [6]	Real	VGG16 + LSTM	95.83%	Yes
		SVM	88.5%	Yes
trangphan10 [7]	Simulated	ResNet + LSTM	83%	Yes
		MediaPipe + LSTM	37%	No
Võ Đức Hoàng [5]	Real (Static)	SqueezeNet CNN	99.78%	Yes
Ours	Real	MediaPipe + LSTM	99.5%	No

- GPU Dependency: Models like VGG16 and ResNet50, require GPUs, making them inaccessible in low-resource settings.
- Data Realism: Simulated datasets (e.g., [7]) lack the variability of real-world conditions, reducing generalizability.

By addressing these gaps, this study provides a lightweight, CPU-based system trained on real-world data, achieving notably high accuracy and practical deployment potential.

3 Methodology

The authors developed a five-step pipeline to address the challenges of VSL recognition: data collection, key point extraction, preprocessing, model training, and deployment. This pipeline is designed to be reproducible, efficient, and robust, leveraging theoretical foundations of sequential modeling and computer vision.

A browser-side webcam stream is captured and its frames are encoded in base64 and sent to a Flask endpoint. At the endpoint, MediaPipe Hands computes hand keypoints for each incoming frame. For preprocessing, the keypoint vector from each frame is appended to a fixed-length sequence buffer (sliding window) that preserves the most recent N timesteps by discarding the oldest entries once the buffer exceeds N. When the buffer reaches the required length, the stacked keypoint sequence is passed to an LSTM model for CPU-only inference, and the predicted label is then presented in the browser display.

Figure 1 illustrates the pipeline, including webcam frame capture, base64 encoding, transmission to a Flask API, MediaPipe keypoint extraction, sequence buffering, LSTM-based prediction, and real-time result display in the browser.

3.1 Data Collection and Labeling

The dataset consists of 1,000 real-world videos capturing 10 common VSL phrases (e.g., "*Cảm ơn,*" "*Xin lỗi,*" "*Tớ tên là Tâm*"), selected for their frequency in everyday communication. Videos were recorded with standard webcams while participants sat

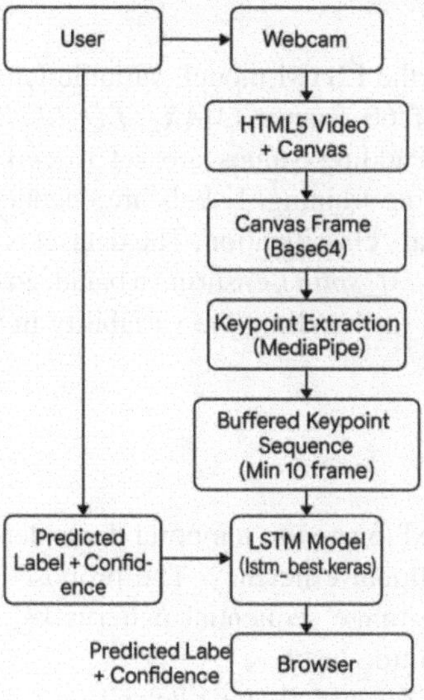

Fig. 1. System pipeline overview. Webcam capture → base64 → Flask endpoint → MediaPipe hand keypoints → sequence buffer → LSTM → browser display (CPU-only).

approximately 0.8–1.0 m from the camera under mixed lighting (natural daylight and room lights). To enhance robustness and intra-class variability, we intentionally varied backgrounds, hand placement, body posture, and viewpoint, including left- and right-offset camera angles. Each video was manually labeled by placing it in a folder named after its corresponding phrase; a *label_mapping.csv* maps file paths to class IDs, and a *label_to_id.json* provides programmatic label encoding. Although labor-intensive, this manual process ensured high-quality annotations and reduced errors common in automated labeling.

3.2 Keypoint Extraction

A critical step for system efficiency is key point extraction, implemented using MediaPipe Holistic, which detects 21 landmarks per hand (*x*, *y*, *z*), resulting in 126 features per frame. Although MediaPipe Holistic can detect face and body landmarks, only the hand key-points are utilized in this study to ensure computational efficiency. To optimize computational efficiency, frames are sampled every few steps. This reduces temporal redundancy while preserving essential gesture dynamics. Frames lacking hand detections are padded with zeros to maintain sequence consistency. The extraction process is implemented in keypoint_extraction.py, producing variable-length sequences saved as.npz extension for efficient storage and retrieval.

3.3 Data Preprocessing

To ensure uniform input for the LSTM model, variable-length keypoint sequences are padded to a fixed length of 60 frames (*MAX_SEQ_LENGTH*) using TensorFlow's *pad_sequences()* function. Padding values are set to *zero*, and a Masking layer in the model ignores these during training. Labels are encoded as *one-hot* vectors using *to_categorical()* for multi-class classification. The dataset is split into 80% training and 20% testing sets using *train_test_split()*, ensuring a balanced distribution of classes. This preprocessing step is critical for handling the variability in video lengths and ensuring model compatibility.

3.4 Model Architecture

The LSTM model is designed to capture temporal dependencies in keypoint sequences while maintaining computational efficiency. The proposed model leverages LSTM's capability in modeling long-range sequential patterns [8], making it well suited for dynamic sign gesture recognition tasks.

The architecture consists of the following layers:

```
model = Sequential()
model.add(Masking(mask_value=0.0, input_shape=(None, 126)))
model.add(LSTM(units=128, return_sequences=False))
model.add(Dropout(0.2))
model.add(Dense(units=32, activation='relu'))
model.add(Dropout(0.2))
model.add(Dense(units=10, activation='softmax'))
```

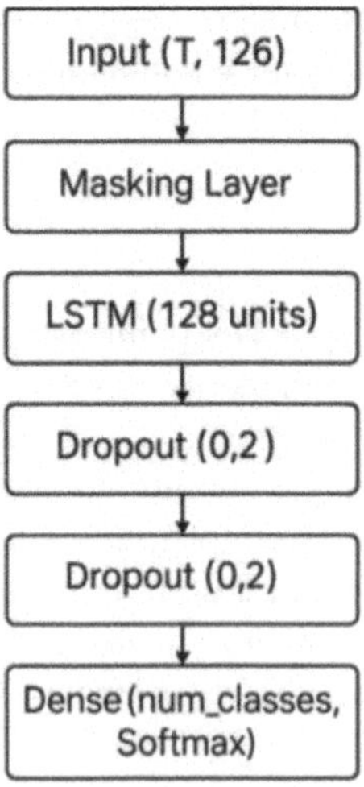

Fig. 2. LSTM Model Architecture.

Figure 2 illustrates the architecture of the proposed model. It comprises a Masking layer, a 128-unit LSTM layer, two Dropout layers, a 32-unit Dense layer with ReLU activation, and a final Dense layer with softmax for classification into 10 VSL phrases.

The model takes a variable-length input of shape (T,126) where T is the number of frames and 126 represents hand key point features (21 landmarks × 3D). A Masking layer ignores padded frames (mask value = 0.0) to handle sequence length variability. The LSTM layer models temporal dynamics, followed by two Dropout layers (rate = 0.2) to reduce overfitting. A 32-unit Dense layer performs a compression of features before outputting class probabilities through a final 10-unit softmax layer. The model contains fewer than 300,000 parameters and occupies less than 1 MB of storage when saved. It is trained using categorical cross-entropy loss and the *Adam* optimizer (lr = 0.001). An *EarlyStopping* callback monitors validation accuracy, and *ModelCheckpoint* saves the best-performing model as *lstm_best.keras*.

Mathematical Formulation: Given a sequence of T frames $X = \{x_1, x_2, \ldots, x_T\}$, where $x_t \in \mathbb{R}^{126}$, The objective is to learn a mapping function $f : X \rightarrow \hat{y} \in \{1, ..., C\}$, that predicts the correct class label $\hat{y}$ for a given input sequence of keypoints X. The model learns this mapping by minimizing the categorical cross-entropy loss:

$$L(y, \hat{y}) = -\sum_{i=1}^{C} y_i \log(\hat{y}_i) \quad (1)$$

Here:

- $y \in \{0,1\}^C$ is the one-hot encoded ground truth label.
- $\hat{y} \in [0,1]^C$ is the predicted probability distribution over the C classes.
- C is the total number of sign classes.

This loss function encourages the model to assign high probabilities to the correct class labels, enabling effective multi-class classification for sign language recognition.

To further validate this architecture, a comparison with alternative approaches was conducted to validate the model's effectiveness. While the ResNet50+LSTM pipeline [6] achieved only 83% accuracy on simulated data and required GPU support, the proposed LSTM model demonstrated superior performance, achieving high accuracy with low latency on CPU-only systems.

3.5 Model Training and Comparison

Training was conducted on an AMD Ryzen 7 CPU with 32 GB RAM, converging in approximately 15–20 epochs. The model achieved 99.5% accuracy on the test set, demonstrating robust performance. To ensure the chosen architecture was optimal, the authors also evaluated a Gated Recurrent Unit (GRU) model with a similar structure. It achieved 80% accuracy and struggled to distinguish semantically similar signs, likely due to the GRU's simpler gating mechanism compared to LSTM, as illustrated in Fig. 3.

The training and validation accuracy/loss curves show rapid convergence around epoch 18, with the model achieving 99.5% validation accuracy and minimal signs of overfitting.

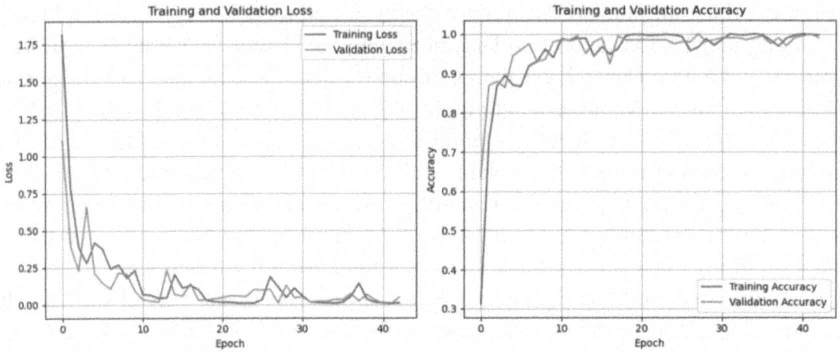

Fig. 3. Accuracy and Loss Curves. Training/validation curves indicate convergence around epoch ~ 18 with minimal overfitting.

The LSTM model's superior performance, as shown in Fig. 3, is attributed to its ability to capture temporal dependencies effectively while maintaining stability against noisy key-points. The training process was monitored using a TQDM progress bar, and early stopping prevented overfitting, which was observed in the DDNet+LSTM model.

3.6 Real-Time API Deployment

The system is deployed via a Flask API integrated with a client-side interface for real-time webcam input. The pipeline, illustrated in Fig. 1, operates as follows:

1. The browser captures webcam frames at ~30 FPS, encoding them as base64-encoded JPEG images.
2. Frames are transmitted to the Flask endpoint (/frame) approximately every 33 ms via POST requests.
3. The server decodes frames into OpenCV-compatible images and applies MediaPipe Holistic to extract 126-dimensional key point vectors.
4. Key-points are buffered until either a minimum sequence length (e.g., 10 frames) is reached or hands disappear from the frame, signaling the end of a gesture.
5. The LSTM model processes the sequence, returning the predicted sign class and confidence score as JSON.
6. Results are displayed live in the browser, ensuring immediate feedback. This design ensures low latency (<300ms) and CPU-only operation, with no disk storage required.

This design avoids disk storage by processing all data in memory using NumPy arrays and TensorFlow models. Dynamic buffering reduces latency by triggering inference only when sufficient data is available, achieving a total round-trip time of under 300 ms on a standard laptop. The CPU-only operation ensures accessibility in low-resource environments, such as public schools or community centers in Vietnam.

4 System Requirements and Evaluation

The system was developed and tested on the following hardware and software:

- CPU: AMD Ryzen 7 8845HS processor (8 cores, 16 threads, base clock 3.8 GHz, boost up to 5.1 GHz).
- RAM: 32 GB
- Environment: Python 3.10, TensorFlow 2.14, MediaPipe, and Flask
- Model Size: <1 MB (saved as *lstm_best.keras*)
- Inference Speed: <300 ms per prediction (AMD Ryzen 7 8845HS, CPU-only)

4.1 Evaluation Results

To assess the robustness of our system, we evaluated it on the held-out 20% test split from our initial 80/20 partition of the dataset. The proposed lightweight LSTM model consistently achieved 99.5% accuracy, correctly identifying all phrases across variations in hand size, lighting, and background.

To validate model selection, an alternative Gated Recurrent Unit (GRU) model was implemented using the same dataset and preprocessing pipeline. It achieved 80% accuracy but struggled to distinguish semantically similar signs, likely due to its simplified gating mechanism.

Table 2. Model Comparison and Performance

Model	Accuracy	Real-time	GPU Needed	Parameters	Inference Speed	Notes
GRU	80%	No	No	~290K	~400 ms/frame	Confused similar signs
LSTM (Ours)	99.5%	Yes	No	~280K	<300 ms/frame	Lightweight, robust, accurate

As shown in Table 2, our LSTM achieves <300 ms per prediction (CPU-only), while the GRU baseline requires ~400 ms per frame.

As shown in Fig. 4, the matrix shows predictions concentrated on the diagonal, indicating no observed off-diagonal confusions in this evaluation. Diagonal counts range from 11 to 29 across the ten VSL classes, suggesting uniformly strong per-class performance on the evaluated data.

4.2 Robustness Analysis

The system's robustness was tested under various conditions:

- Lighting Variations: Performance remained consistent under low-light and high-contrast settings, thanks to MediaPipe's robust detection.
- Background Noise: Complex backgrounds (e.g., cluttered rooms) did not degrade accuracy, as the system focuses solely on hand key points.
- Hand Size and Orientation: The model generalized well across different hand sizes and slight variations in gesture execution.

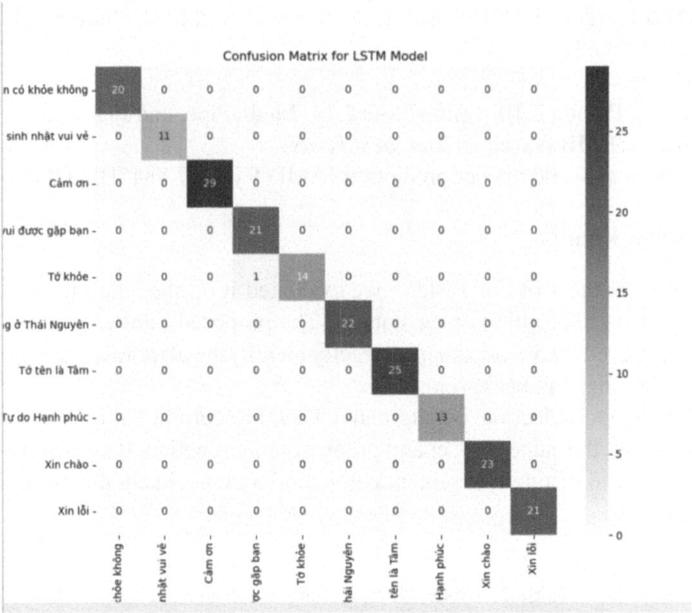

Fig. 4. Confusion matrix of the LSTM-based Vietnamese Sign Language (VSL) phrase classifier on the evaluation set (10 classes).

However, limitations include potential errors in cases of severe occlusion (e.g., hands partially obscured) or extremely fast gestures, which may reduce key point detection accuracy. These scenarios are rare in typical VSL use but could be addressed in future work.

5 Conclusion

The authors present a lightweight, real-time VSL recognition system that achieves 99.5% accuracy on a real-world dataset using a CPU-friendly LSTM model.

The system demonstrates significant potential for enhancing accessibility for the Vietnamese deaf community. Potential applications include educational tools for teaching VSL, assistive tools for facilitating communication with non-signers, and integration into mobile apps for on-the-go use. Its CPU-only operation makes it accessible in settings with limited computational resources, such as rural schools or community centers.

Future research directions could include:

- Expanding the dataset to include a broader range of VSL phrases and continuous signing.
- Integrating voice output to enable bidirectional communication between signers and non-signers.
- Optimizing the model for mobile deployment using TensorFlow Lite or ONNX for edge devices.

- Addressing edge cases, such as severe occlusions or rapid gestures, through advanced key point tracking or multi-modal inputs (e.g., combining hand and body landmarks).
- Adding additional measures of assessment, for instance, precision, recall, and F1-score, for a wider performance measurement besides accuracy.
- Looking at the effect of critical hyperparameters, for example, frames per sample, minimum sequence length, and various recurrent architectures such as GRU or deeper forms of LSTM.
- Examining data partitioning and sampling schemes, especially when the full dataset (e.g., 1000 videos) is not employed, in order to balance the representation across classes and to reduce overfitting.

By addressing these directions, the system could further bridge the communication gap for the Vietnamese deaf community, fostering greater inclusion and accessibility.

References

1. Tran, A.V., Hoang, Q.H., Pham, T.V.H.: Vietnamese sign language alphabet recognition using deep learning and mediapipe methods. JST: Smart Syst. Dev. **35**, 10–19 (2025)
2. Quach, L.-D., Duong-Trung, N., Vu, A.-V., Nguyen, C.-N.: Recommending the workflow of vietnamese sign language translation via a comparison of several classification algorithms. In: International Conference of the Pacific Association for Computational Linguistics, pp. 134–141. Springer (2019)
3. Dinh, N.S., et al.: Sign language recognition: a large-scale multi-view dataset and comprehensive evaluation. In: 2025 IEEE/CVF Winter Conference on Applications of Computer Vision (WACV), pp. 7887–7897. IEEE (2025)
4. Dang, K., Bessmertny, I.A.: ViSL One-shot: generating Vietnamese sign language data set. Sci. Tech. J. Inf. Technol. Mech. Opt. **24**, 241–248 (2024)
5. Hoàng, V.D.: Nhận Diện Bảng Chữ Cái Ngôn Ngữ Ký Hiệu Tiếng Việt Sử Dụng Mô Hình Học Sâu. Hội nghị Khoa học công nghệ Quốc gia lần thứ XVI về Nghiên cứu cơ bản và ứng dụng Công nghệ thông tin (FAIR). Đà Nẵng (2023)
6. Nguyen, B.T., Vo, A.H., Pham, V.H.: Deep learning for vietnamese sign language recognition in video sequence. Int. J. Mach. Learn. Comput. **9**(4), 393–398 (2019)
7. Vietnamese-Sign-Language. https://github.com/trangphan10/Vietnamese-Sign-Language. Accessed 21 Jun 2025
8. Hochreiter, S., Schmidhuber, J.: Long short-term memory. Neural Comput. **9**(8), 1735–1780 (1997)

IntelliChart: Advanced LangGraph Analytics Platform with AI Workflow Processing and Intelligent Data Insights

Minh-Hue Luong Thi[1], The-Vinh Nguyen[1(✉)], Van-Viet Nguyen[1], Kim-Son Nguyen[1], Huu-Khanh Nguyen[2], and Dinh-Cuong Do[1]

[1] Thai Nguyen University of Information and Communication Technology, Thai Nguyen, Vietnam
{lmhue,vinhnt,nvviet,nkson,ddcuong}@ictu.edu.vn

[2] Distance Learning Center, Thai Nguyen University, Thai Nguyen, Vietnam
nhkhanh@tnu.edu.vn

Abstract. The problem of natural language to visualisation (NL2VIS) has gained much attention worldwide, especially among non-technical people. Large language models (LLMs) are widely studied and applied in this field because of their ability to understand diverse semantics. However, previous studies still face many limitations in learning appropriate communication with LLMs, leading to the need to learn a new skill called prompt engineering. To address the above challenge, this study introduces IntelliChart - a full query-to-visualization cycle. IntelliChart decomposes the NL2VIS process into modular sub-tasks, integrating LLMs with state management. This design combines query validation, agent-based SQL execution, insight extraction and visualization generation, enhanced by retry logic and interpretation services. The study is evaluated both qualitatively and quantitatively. Qualitative results showed that IntelliChart allows for more explicit interpretation of results than ChatGPT. Quantitative results on the VisEval dataset showed that IntelliChart achieves 51.2% Exact Match accuracy and 99.8% Execution Success rate, outperforming baselines including hybrid frameworks, pipelined methods, and naive LLM prompts. This research will contribute to enriching the NL2VIS experimental literature, thereby paving the way for more reliable data visualization systems. The repository is available at: https://github.com/ictu-se/IntelliChart.

Keywords: NL2VIS · Large Language Models · Data Visualization · Workflow Management · Interpretability

1 Introduction

Data visualization has long been considered one of the most effective means of communicating complex information, allowing strategic analysts to quickly interpret trends, patterns, and anomalies [17]. In early systems, creating a visualization required domain experts to manually create SQL queries and scripts with

V. V. Pham et al. (Eds.): CIDDF 2025, ACSAR 5, pp. 138–148, 2026.
https://doi.org/10.1007/978-3-032-19488-6_9

libraries such as matplotlib or Vega-Lite, which posed a steep learning curve for non-technical users. In the past few years since the advent of the Transformer architecture [20] and the success of the BERT model [4], a research direction called Natural Language to Visualization (NL2VIS) has emerged, which aims to convert natural language queries into visual output [11,13].

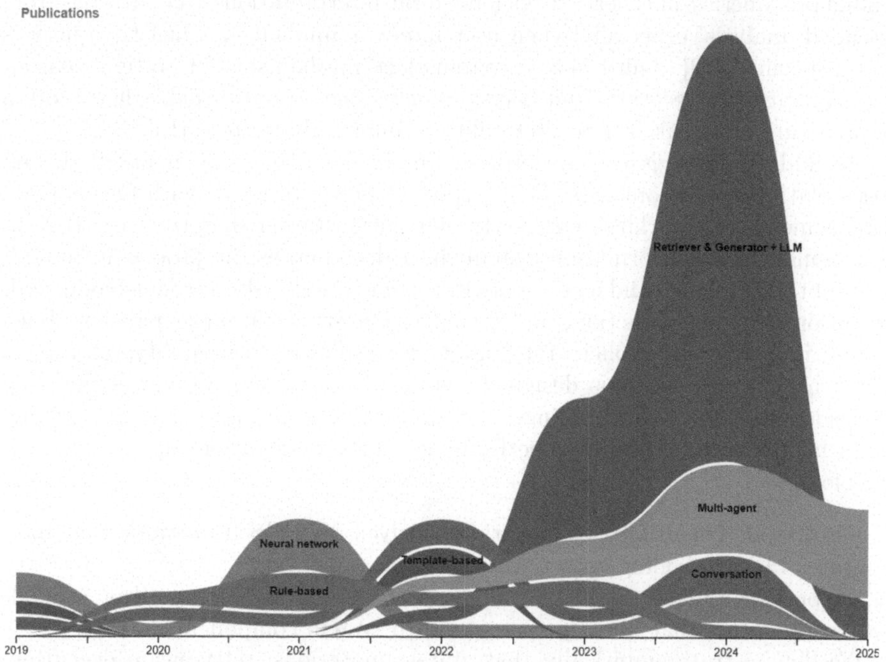

Fig. 1. Evolution of methods used (2019–2025)

More recently, Large Language Models (LLMs) have been applied to improve the NL2VIS task [15] (see Fig. 1). The true power of applying LLMs in the NL2VIS domain is the ability to understand the semantics of natural language queries. Before large language models, researchers had to train many pairs of natural language queries and source code (vis). The lack of diversity in input languages limited the performance of conventional machine learning approaches [13,18]. Initially, LLMs were mainly used to understand user intent and select appropriate templates (rules) from that intent. However, this approach suffered from the limitation that the number of templates and rules did not cover all tasks that required customization [2]. Prior study [11] showed that GPT-3.5 can generate Vega-Lite specifications from natural language queries with higher accuracy than many earlier NL2VIS systems, especially when using few-shot prompt strategies. Voigt et al. presented efficient approaches evaluating various pre-trained models of different sizes and their latency trade-offs in real-time interaction for NL2VIS tasks [21]. Also, [22] revealed that in many settings, LLMs outperform traditional methods when prompt design and context are handled carefully.

Despite these advances, several limitations remain. First, syntactic fragility persists: LLM-generated SQL or visualization specs may fail due to schema mismatches, incomplete joins, or type mismatches, particularly when the schemas are complex or not well described [7,24]. Second, semantic drift is common: ambiguous queries may lead to visualization interpretations that diverge from intended analysis, especially when user intent is implicit or when the query is under-specified [12]. Third, many systems lack mechanisms for stateful reasoning, explicit error recovery, and transparency; once a prompt fails, there's often no structured fallback or interpretability of intermediate steps [10].

To address these issues, we propose IntelliChart, a workflow-oriented analytics platform that combines the interpretive power of LLMs with formal state management via a workflow engine (IntelliChart). Rather than treating NL2VIS as a monolithic transformation, IntelliChart decomposes the process into modular subtasks: query validation, semantic intent classification, agent-based SQL execution, insight extraction, and visualization specification generation. Each module is overseen by explicit state annotations, allowing traceability, retry logic, and context tracking. This design draws inspiration from prompt-engineering strategies and benchmark findings that show structured intermediate reasoning and schema exposure improves performance. The contributions of this work are threefold:

1. We present **IntelliChart**, a workflow-driven NL2VIS framework that integrates LLM reasoning with formal state management.
2. We provide a mathematical formulation of NL2VIS as a composition of modular operators that directly correspond to system components.
3. We demonstrate empirically that state annotations, retry-aware execution, and explicit error handling improve robustness and transparency compared to baseline methods.

2 Method

We propose a modular pipeline that transforms natural language queries into executable data analyses and visualizations. The architecture integrates three components: a database reasoning toolkit, a generative visualization module, and an interpretability service.

2.1 Problem Formulation

Let Q denote the set of natural language queries, D the collection of structured datasets (ingested as relational tables), L the set of instantiated large language models, and V the visualization space. We define a function

$$\Omega : Q \times D \times L \rightarrow V,$$

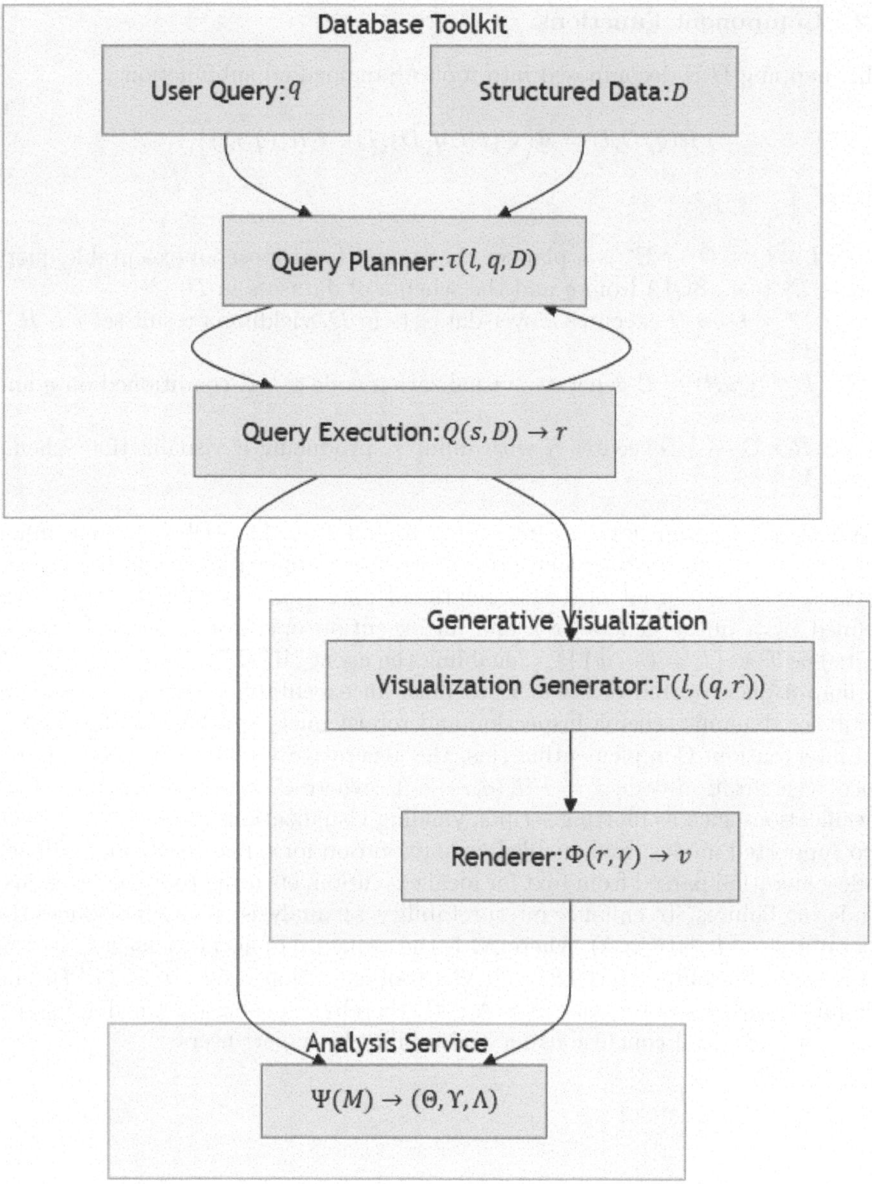

Fig. 2. The flowchart of our proposed NL2VIS model

such that, given a query $q \in Q$, a collection of datasets D, and an LLM $l \in L$, the output $v = \Omega(q, D, l)$ is a visualization faithfully aligned with both user intent and data semantics.

2.2 Component Functions

The mapping Ω is decomposed into toolâĂŞaugmented subfunctions:

$$\Omega(q, D, l) := \Phi\Big(\mathcal{Q}(\tau(l, q, D), D),\ \Gamma(l, (q, r))\Big),$$

where:

- $\tau : L \times Q \times D \to \Sigma^*$ is a planner that uses l to propose an executable query $s \in \Sigma^*$ (e.g., SQL) from q and the schema of datasets in D.
- $\mathcal{Q} : \Sigma^* \times D \to R$ executes s over datasets in D, yielding a result set $r \in R \subseteq \mathbb{R}^{n \times m}$.
- $\Gamma : L \times (Q, R) \to \mathcal{C}$ generates visualization code $\gamma \in \mathcal{C}$ conditioned on q and r.
- $\Phi : R \times \mathcal{C} \to V$ executes γ with input r, producing a visualization schema $v \in V$.

We design a custom database reasoning toolkit (i.e., DuckDb [19] - an online database that run on the same process with the application using it to avoid network overhead) that abstracts relational operations as callable tools, each defined by a query generator s and an execution operator η, formally represented as $\mathcal{T} = \{\, t_i = (s_i, \eta_i) \,\}_{i=1}^{k}$, enabling the agent $\mathcal{A}(l, \mathcal{T}) : Q \times D \to (\Sigma^*, R)$ to map a query q and datasets D to both an executable query string and its result for dynamic schema inspection and robust query synthesis without manual intervention. Complementing this, the generative visualization module produces visualization code $\gamma = \Gamma(l, (q, r)) \in \mathcal{C}$, where $\mathcal{C}$ denotes a space of chart specifications such as plotting scripts, yielding visualizations $v = \Phi(r, \gamma)$ through two supported modes: tool-enabled code execution for inline charts and fallback code generation parsed from text for local execution, ensuring robustness against rendering failures. To enhance interpretability, an analysis service introduces the operator $\Psi : \mathcal{M} \to (\theta, \upsilon, \lambda)$, where $\mathcal{M}$ is the sequence of agent messages, decomposing into reasoning traces $\theta = \Theta(\mathcal{M})$, tool execution results $\upsilon = \Upsilon(\mathcal{M})$, and the final synthesized response $\lambda = \Lambda(\mathcal{M})$, thereby exposing intermediate steps, query outputs, and conclusions for auditability by expert users.

2.3 Execution Pipeline

The pipeline is summarized in Algorithm 1.

Algorithm 1: Formal Pipeline for $\Omega(q, D, l) \rightarrow v$

Input : Natural language query $q \in Q$
Uploaded datasets $\mathcal{F} = \{f_1, \ldots, f_k\}$
Language model $l \in L$
Output: Visualization schema $v \in V$
Step 1: Data ingestion
foreach $f_i \in \mathcal{F}$ **do**
  $d_i \leftarrow \Delta(f_i)$ `/* Normalize and register data */`
$D \leftarrow \{d_1, \ldots, d_k\}$
Step 2: Query synthesis and execution
$s \leftarrow \tau(l, q, D)$
$r \leftarrow \mathcal{Q}(s, D)$
Step 3: Visualization synthesis
$\gamma \leftarrow \Gamma(l, (q, r))$
$v \leftarrow \Phi(r, \gamma)$
Step 4: Analysis interpretation
$(\theta, v, \lambda) \leftarrow \Psi(\mathcal{M})$ `/* Reasoning, tool results, final analysis */`
return v

Figure 2 illustrates the flowchart of the proposed system, demonstrating its ability to translate natural language queries into structured analyses and visualizations.

2.4 Experimental Setup

We conducted our experiment in Python, with Streamlit handling the interactive web interface for users. In our app, we used LangGraph which is an open-source workflow orchestration framework designed for multi-agent LLM applications. LangGraph provides explicit state tracking across subtasks (query validation, SQL execution, visualization synthesis, and error handling). Each step is represented as a node in a directed graph, with annotated state transitions enabling retry logic, fallback strategies, and interpretability. This integration ensures that failures in one stage (e.g., SQL parsing) can be recovered without discarding prior progress, thereby supporting robustness and transparency. For LLM we used Gemini-2.5-flash because its family excel at code detail and explanation. Beyond just relying on the VisEval benchmark [2], a readily available resource tailored for testing NL2VIS setups, featuring 2,524 queries across 146 databases complete with verified ground truths, our approach also lets users upload their own CSV files for custom data handling. While there are plenty of other datasets out there that could work well, we stick to VisEval for this particular study.

3 Results

3.1 Qualitative Analysis

To provide a more nuanced evaluation beyond quantitative metrics, we conducted a direct comparison with ChatGPT [23], a widely used general-purpose language model, focusing on real-world visualization tasks. In this experiment, we uploaded a CSV file containing a list of scientific publications, including details such as publication years, to both systems. We then posed the research question: "What is the trend of publication?" This query aims to uncover temporal patterns in the data, such as yearly publication counts over time.

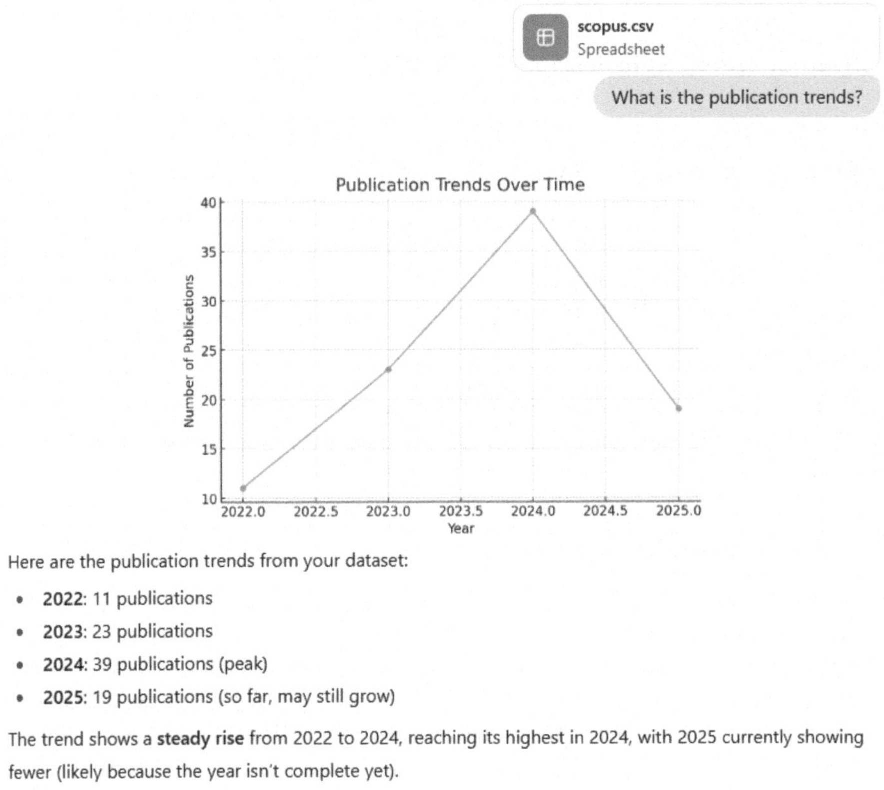

Fig. 3. Response from ChatGPT

ChatGPT (depicted in Fig. 3) generated a line chart depicting a trend line, which effectively captured the overall progression and fluctuations in publication volumes. This choice aligned well with the intent of highlighting trends, offering a smooth visual representation of changes across years. However, a notable drawback was observed in the x-axis labeling: the years were rendered as decimal values (e.g., 2015.0, 2016.0), which introduced an unnecessary level of precision and reduced readability [16], as publication years are inherently discrete integers [9].

```
import pandas as pd
import matplotlib.pyplot as plt
data = {
    'Year': [2022, 2023, 2024, 2025],
    'Publications': [11, 23, 39, 19]
}
df = pd.DataFrame(data)
plt.style.use('seaborn-v0_8-whitegrid')
fig, ax = plt.subplots(figsize=(8, 6))
bars = ax.bar(df['Year'], df['Publications'],
color='skyblue', edgecolor='black')
ax.set_title('Publication Trends (2022-2025)',
fontsize=16, fontweight='bold')
ax.set_xlabel('Year', fontsize=12)
ax.set_ylabel('Number of Publications', fontsize=12)
ax.set_xticks(df['Year'])
ax.set_xticklabels(df['Year'], rotation=0)
for bar in bars:
    yval = bar.get_height()
    ax.text(bar.get_x() + bar.get_width()/2.0, yval + 0.
    5, int(yval), ha='center', va='bottom', fontsize=10)
ax.set_ylim(0, df['Publications'].max() * 1.15)
plt.tight_layout()
plt.show()
```

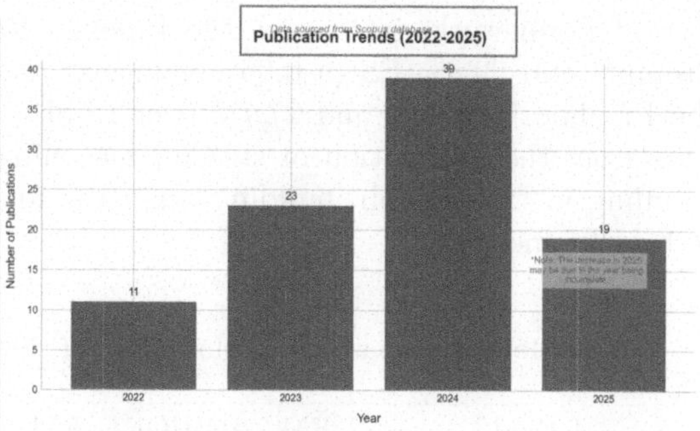

Automated Analysis: The publication trends, as reflected in the Scopus database, reveal a growing interest in research and publications over the years. In 2022, there were 11 publications, which increased to 23 in 2023. The trend continues upward, with 39 publications in 2024. Interestingly, there appears to be a slight decrease in the number of publications in 2025, with 19 entries. This could be due to the year not being complete, or a shift in research focus. Overall, the data suggests a generally increasing trend in publications, with a slight dip in the latest year recorded. Further analysis considering the specific fields and authors involved could provide a more nuanced understanding of these trends.

Fig. 4. Generated code, figure and analysis from our proposed model

In contrast, our system produced a bar chart (depicted in Fig. 4), with publication years clearly marked as integers on the x-axis, ensuring logical and intuitive scaling. This format emphasized discrete annual counts, making it straightforward to compare specific years. That said, the visualization encountered a minor issue where text in the title overlapped, slightly impacting the overall polish and clarity of the output [16].

3.2 Quantitative Analysis

To evaluate the performance of our proposed IntelliChart framework quantitatively, we employed a suite of established metrics on the VisEval benchmark dataset, which comprises 2,524 queries across 146 databases. The metrics include Exact Match (EM) for precise visualization schema alignment [14], ROUGE-1 F1 and ROUGE-L F1 for textual similarity between generated and ground-truth specifications [8], Jaccard similarity for set-based overlap [3], and Execution Success (ES) for the rate of successfully executable outputs [14].

We compared IntelliChart against three baselines: (i) LLM + Prompt, a naive prompting approach without tool integration [5], (ii) Pipeline Baseline, a template-based SQL generation method with predefined visualization heuristics, and (iii) Hybrid Framework which decomposes NL2VIS into structured subtasks with formal grammar constraints and schema validation. The Hybrid Framework achieved 50.64% EM accuracy and 99.74% ES rate, as reported in its evaluation, surpassing the other baselines but still constrained by limited error recovery and transparency in complex queries.

Table 1 summarizes the results. Our IntelliChart (Proposed) framework outperforms all baselines, attaining 51.2% EM (a 0.56% improvement over the Hybrid Framework, 5.6% over the Pipeline Baseline, and 8.5% over LLM + Prompt) and 99.8% ES (a 0.06% gain over the Hybrid Framework, 6.1% over the Pipeline Baseline, and 27.7% over LLM + Prompt). These enhancements arise from the integration of stateful reasoning, retry logic, and explicit error handling in LangGraph, building upon the foundational decomposition in the Hybrid Framework.

Table 1. Compare the performance of the proposed NL2VIS models

Method	EM	ROUGE1_F1	ROUGEL_F1	Jaccard	ES
Hybrid Framework	0.506	0.821	0.783	0.571	0.997
Pipeline Baseline	0.456	0.854	0.817	0.625	0.937
LLM + Prompt	0.427	0.612	0.589	0.434	0.721
IntelliChart	**0.512**	0.832	0.794	0.582	**0.998**

The IntelliChart also demonstrates competitive linguistic alignment, with ROUGE-1 F1 at 0.832 (vs. 0.821 for Hybrid Framework, 0.854 for Pipeline Baseline, and 0.612 for LLM + Prompt), highlighting improved semantic capture through modular decomposition and schema-aware planning augmented by workflow orchestration. For statistical validation, we applied Cochran's Q [1] test on a binary execution success dataset of 1,200 samples, yielding Q = 481.23, p < 0.001, df = 3, rejecting the null hypothesis of equal performance across methods. Pairwise McNemar tests [6] confirmed significant differences between the proposed agent and each baseline ($p < 10^{-18}$ for all). Compared to the Hybrid Framework's validation (Q = 466.56, p < 0.001, df = 2), our extended analysis with an additional method underscores even greater reliability

4 Conclusion

In this work, we introduced IntelliChart, a workflow-oriented NL2VIS framework that leverages the strengths of Large Language Models while mitigating their limitations through modular decomposition and stateful management. By formalizing the NL2VIS process as a composition of tool-augmented subfunctions and implementing it via a robust pipeline with explicit error handling and interpretability, IntelliChart achieves enhanced performance in both quantitative and qualitative evaluations. The contributions of this study–including the framework itself, its mathematical formulation, and empirical validation–underscore the potential of workflow-driven approaches to make data visualization more accessible and reliable. Future directions include extending support for multimodal inputs (e.g., combining text with images), integrating with diverse data sources beyond relational tables, and exploring user studies to assess real-time interactivity in production environments. Ultimately, IntelliChart represents a step toward more transparent and resilient AI-assisted analytics, empowering users across domains to derive insights from complex data with minimal expertise.

References

1. Aslam, M.: Cochran's q test for analyzing categorical data under uncertainty. J. Big Data **10**(1), 147 (2023)
2. Chen, N., Zhang, Y., Xu, J., Ren, K., Yang, Y.: Viseval: a benchmark for data visualization in the era of large language models. IEEE Trans. Vis. Comput. Graph. (2024)
3. Cheng, Y., et al.: Graphic design with large multimodal model. In: Proceedings of the AAAI Conference on Artificial Intelligence, vol. 39, pp. 2473–2481 (2025)
4. Devlin, J., Chang, M.W., Lee, K., Toutanova, K.: Bert: pre-training of deep bidirectional transformers for language understanding. In: Proceedings of the 2019 Conference of the North American Chapter of the Association for Computational Linguistics: Human Language Technologies, volume 1 (long and short papers), pp. 4171–4186 (2019)
5. Dibia, V.: Lida: A tool for automatic generation of grammar-agnostic visualizations and infographics using large language models. In: The 61st Annual Meeting Of The Association For Computational Linguistics (2023)
6. Dietterich, T.G.: Approximate statistical tests for comparing supervised classification learning algorithms. Neural Comput. **10**(7), 1895–1923 (1998)
7. Hong, Z., Yuan, Z., Chen, H., Zhang, Q., Huang, F., Huang, X.: Knowledge-to-sql: enhancing sql generation with data expert llm. In: Findings of the Association for Computational Linguistics ACL 2024, pp. 10997–11008 (2024)
8. Kalyan, K.S.: A survey of gpt-3 family large language models including chatgpt and gpt-4. Nat. Lang. Process. J. **6**, 100048 (2024)
9. Kim, N.W., Ahn, Y., Myers, G., Bach, B.: How good is chatgpt in giving advice on your visualization design? ACM Trans. Comput.-Hum. Interact. (2025). https://doi.org/10.1145/3745768
10. Lee, C.J., Tran, G., Tabalba, R., Leigh, J., Longman, R.: Macro-queries: an exploration into guided chart generation from high level prompts. arXiv preprint arXiv:2408.12726 (2024)
11. Li, G., et al.: Visualization generation with large language models: an evaluation. arXiv preprint arXiv:2401.11255 (2024)
12. Luo, T., et al.: nvbench 2.0: resolving ambiguity in text-to-visualization through stepwise reasoning. arXiv preprint arXiv:2503.12880 (2025)
13. Luo, Y., Tang, J., Li, G.: nvbench: a large-scale synthesized dataset for cross-domain natural language to visualization task. arXiv preprint arXiv:2112.12926 (2021)
14. Luo, Y., Tang, N., Li, G., Chai, C., Li, W., Qin, X.: Synthesizing natural language to visualization (nl2vis) benchmarks from nl2sql benchmarks. In: Proceedings of the 2021 International Conference on Management of Data, pp. 1235–1247 (2021)

15. Luong-Thi-Minh, H., Nguyen-The, V., Xuan, T.Q.: Vizagent: towards an intelligent and versatile data visualization framework powered by large language models. In: International Conference on Advances in Information and Communication Technology, pp. 89–97. Springer (2024)
16. Maddigan, P., Susnjak, T.: Chat2vis: generating data visualizations via natural language using chatgpt, codex and gpt-3 large language models. IEEE Access **11**, 45181–45193 (2023)
17. Nguyen, T.V., Phung, T.N.: Enhanced literature review visualization: a novel sorted stream graphs with integrated word elements. In: International Conference on Advances in Information and Communication Technology, pp. 159–168. Springer (2024)
18. Nguyen, T.V., Phung, T.N., Cuong, D.D.: A bibliometric and thematic analysis of systematic reviews of artificial intelligence in education. In: International Conference on Advances in Information and Communication Technology, pp. 337–351. Springer (2024). https://doi.org/10.1007/978-3-031-50818-9-37
19. Raasveldt, M., Mühleisen, H.: Duckdb: an embeddable analytical database. In: Proceedings of the 2019 International Conference on Management of Data, pp. 1981–1984 (2019)
20. Vaswani, A., et al.: Attention is all you need. In: Advances in Neural Information Processing Systems, vol. 30 (2017)
21. Voigt, H., Lawonn, K., Zarrieß, S.: Plots made quickly: an efficient approach for generating visualizations from natural language queries. In: Proceedings of the 2024 Joint International Conference on Computational Linguistics, Language Resources and Evaluation (LREC-COLING 2024), pp. 12787–12793 (2024)
22. Wu, Y., et al.: Automated data visualization from natural language via large language models: an exploratory study. Proc. ACM Manage. Data **2**(3), 1–28 (2024)
23. Zhao, F.F., et al.: Benchmarking the performance of large language models in uveitis: a comparative analysis of chatgpt-3.5, chatgpt-4.0, google gemini, and anthropic claude3. Eye **39**(6), 1132–1137 (2025)
24. Zhu, X., Li, Q., Cui, L., Liu, Y.: Large language model enhanced text-to-sql generation: a survey. arXiv preprint arXiv:2410.06011 (2024)

Bilingual Code-Switching Voice Separation with MossFormer2 for Vietnamese-English Mixtures

Pham Manh Kha[1,2], Le Duong Tan Minh[1,2], Ha Minh Tan[1,2], Diem Thi Tran[1,2], and Duc-Quang Vu[3](✉)

[1] University of Information Technology, Ho Chi Minh City, Vietnam
{22520600,22520865}@gm.uit.edu.vn, {tanhm,diemtt}@uit.edu.vn
[2] Vietnam National University, Ho Chi Minh City, Vietnam
[3] Thai Nguyen University of Information and Communication Technology, Thai Nguyen, Vietnam
vdquang@ictu.edu.vn

Abstract. Bilingual speech separation presents significant challenges and opportunities in the field of speech processing. Vietnamese and English differ fundamentally in their phonetic structures. Vietnamese is a tonal language, while English relies on stress patterns and non-tonal distinctions. This disparity complicates the separation of mixed-language speech, as traditional models may struggle to accurately distinguish overlapping phonemes and words from the two languages. The MossFormer2 is an advanced model combining Transformer-based self-attention mechanisms with a feedforward sequential memory network, enhances the ability to model both long-range dependencies and fine-scale recurrent patterns in speech signals. This hybrid approach improves the separation of mixed-language audio by effectively handling the unique acoustic characteristics of both Vietnamese and English. By leveraging this model, researchers achieve more accurate separation of bilingual speech mixtures, facilitating clearer transcription and analysis in multilingual environments.

Keywords: Bilingual Code-Switching Speech Separation · Transformer · Attention · Convolution Neural Network · Recurrent Neural Network · Deep Learning Model

1 Introduction

Bilingual speech separation has become a critical task in the field of speech processing, particularly as multilingual environments become increasingly common. The task involves isolating distinct speech signals from a mixed audio source, where different languages may be spoken by multiple individuals. In this study, we focus on the challenge of separating speech in a bilingual environment with mixtures of Vietnamese and English, two languages that differ significantly in their phonetic structures.

V. V. Pham et al. (Eds.): CIDDF 2025, ACSAR 5, pp. 149–160, 2026.
https://doi.org/10.1007/978-3-032-19488-6_10

Vietnamese is a tonal language, where pitch variations are crucial in distinguishing the meanings of words. In contrast, English relies on stress patterns and non-tonal distinctions to convey meaning. This stark contrast in phonetic and prosodic characteristics presents a unique challenge for speech separation models, which often struggle to disentangle overlapping phonemes and words from such distinct languages. Traditional models, which primarily focus on monolingual speech, are not well-equipped to handle the complexities of bilingual speech, especially when both languages share overlapping acoustic features in the mixed signal. Recent studies have demonstrated the limitations of traditional methods in handling such multilingual mixtures [5,7,10].

In recent years, several successful architectures for the speech separation task have emerged, such as Conv-TasNet [8], DPRNN [9], DPTNET [4], SepFormer [12], and, more recently, MossFormer2 [20]. We have used MossFormer2, an advanced model that combines Transformer-based self-attention mechanisms with a feedforward sequential memory network. This hybrid approach enhances the model's ability to capture both long-range dependencies and fine-scale recurrent patterns in speech signals. By leveraging this novel architecture, MossFormer2 significantly improves the separation of mixed-language speech, providing more accurate results in identifying and isolating the speech components of both Vietnamese and English. Transformer-based self-attention mechanisms with a feedforward sequential memory network have shown promise in overcoming traditional challenges in speech separation tasks by focusing on self-attention mechanisms.

Recent studies on multilingual speech separation focus on improving separation efficiency through methods like blind language separation by Borsdorf et al. [3], language identification-based speech separation evaluation by Aysa et al. [2], and emotion recognition in bilingual environments by Akinpelu et al. [1]. Models for code-switching [18] and bilingual speech synthesis [21] have also been explored to enhance speech separation and improve speech processing in multilingual communication scenarios, making them highly applicable to speech recognition and dialogue analysis systems.

Our work utilizes two key datasets to evaluate the performance of MossFormer2. The VinBigdata dataset, which contains diverse speech samples in Vietnamese, provides a valuable resource for training the model to handle the acoustic characteristics specific to the Vietnamese language. Additionally, the LibriSpeech-2mix dataset, which includes English speech mixtures, is used to evaluate the model's ability to handle the complexities of English speech. By testing the model on these two datasets, we aim to demonstrate the effectiveness of MossFormer2 in improving bilingual speech separation, particularly in the context of Vietnamese and English mixtures. Using diverse datasets helps improve the robustness of separation models by exposing them to a variety of acoustic conditions.

The contributions of this study are twofold: first, we propose an enhanced model for bilingual speech separation that combines Transformer and sequential memory networks, and second, we present a comprehensive evaluation of this model's performance using real-world Vietnamese and English speech data. This research provides valuable insights for developing more accurate and efficient speech separation systems for multilingual environments, paving the way for better speech recognition and analysis in diverse linguistic contexts.

The remainder of the paper is organized as follows: Sect. 2 introduces the MossFormer2 Architecture, Sect. 3 presents Multilingual Code-Switching Voice Separation, Sect. 4 reports the experimental results, and Sect. 5 concludes the paper.

2 MossFormer2 Architecture

Given a speech mixture signal $x = \sum_{i=1}^{C} s_i$, the goal is to apply a deep learning model to recover C individual sources $s_i \in \mathbb{R}^{1 \times T}$. The approach is based on a time-domain masking-net, which still follows the encoderseparatordecoder paradigm. Unlike traditional designs, this framework emphasizes improvements to the separator module (see Fig. 1). In this setup, the encoderdecoder pair handles feature extraction and waveform reconstruction, while the masking-net transforms the encoded representations into corresponding masks.

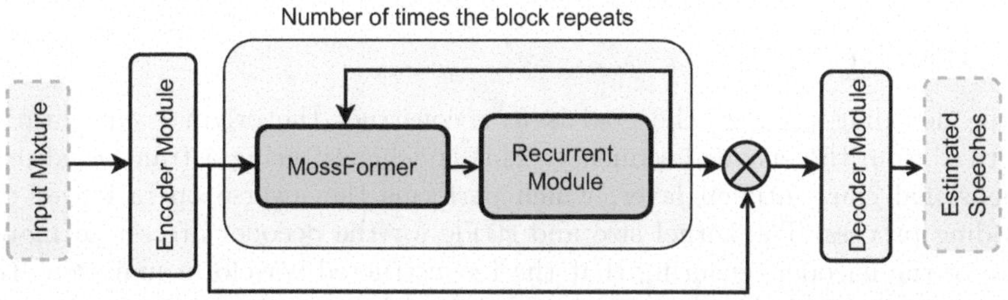

Fig. 1. The diagram of the MossFormer2 Architecture combines the MossFormer Architecture and Recurrent Architecture.

2.1 Encoder

The encoder is designed using a one-dimensional convolutional layer (Conv1D), which is combined with a rectified linear unit (ReLU) activation function to process the input mixture waveform x. This convolutional operation serves to extract features from the input signal and transform it into a non-negative speech embedding sequence, denoted as X. In this sequence, N represents the embedding dimension, which corresponds to the number of feature channels produced by the convolutional layer, and S denotes the length of the encoded sequence, which is influenced by both the input waveforms length and the convolution parameters.

The encoded sequence length S is derived from the kernel size K and the stride of $K/2$ used in the encoder. The relationship between the input length T and the output length S is defined by the formula $S = 2T/K - 1$, which indicates how the input signal is compressed or expanded during encoding. The choice of kernel size K and stride $K/2$ affects how much downsampling occurs in the feature map, thereby influencing the resolution of the encoded sequence and the computational complexity of the model.

2.2 MossFormer and Recurrent Architectures

The MossFormer [19] module uses self-attention [15] across the entire sequence. It adopts a joint local-global self-attention strategy, applying full-computation self-attention to non-overlapping local segments and a linearized, resource-efficient self-attention across the entire sequence. This approach allows the module to learn embeddings at each layer by considering all elements within the current sequence. Without relying on recurrence, self-attention captures long-range, coarse-scale dependencies. While speech signals have recurrent patterns in phonetics, prosody, and semantics that are crucial for speech separation, MossFormer2 [20] includes a dedicated recurrent module [20] to model these complex temporal dependencies, capturing both broad and localized patterns.

2.3 Decoder

In the decoding process, the goal is to reconstruct the original waveform of length T from the encoded sequence. This is achieved using a transposed one-dimensional convolutional layer, which performs the inverse operation of the encoding process. The kernel size and stride for the decoder are set to match those of the encoder, ensuring that the reconstructed waveform maintains the correct dimensions. The transposed convolutional operation essentially expands the encoded sequence back to the desired output length, restoring the waveform while attempting to preserve as much of the original signals characteristics as possible.

3 Multilingual Code-Switching Voice Separation

Multilingual speech separation is a challenging task that requires robust models to accurately isolate individual speech sources from overlapping audio in scenarios where multiple languages are involved. This problem is not only about identifying the correct speech sources but also about distinguishing between languages, managing overlapping phonetic structures, and addressing the intricacies of different accents and prosody. Based on various studies, we analyze the main challenges and suggest potential solutions to improve multilingual speech separation systems.

One of the key challenges in multilingual speech separation lies in accurately identifying the languages present within a mixed speech signal. This task becomes even more complex in the presence of code-switching, the practice of alternating between two or more languages during a conversation. While language separation techniques have shown promise, they still struggle to reliably determine which language is being spoken, particularly in real-time scenarios. To overcome these difficulties, models should integrate language identification modules capable of detecting language transitions and correctly tagging segments of audio with the appropriate language. When combined with speaker separation methods, such an approach could significantly improve accuracy, especially in fast-paced speech or overlapping dialogues common in multilingual environments.

Speech signals naturally contain recurrent patterns related to phonetics and prosody, which are essential for successful speech source separation. In multilingual settings, these patterns become more complex because different languages exhibit diverse phonetic structures and prosodic characteristics. To address these challenges, it is necessary to design multilingual prosody models that capture variations in rhythm, tone, and stress. Integrating such models into speech separation systems can improve the ability to distinguish languages through their unique prosodic features. In addition, employing recurrent neural networks (RNNs) or transformer architectures with attention mechanisms, as demonstrated in MossFormer2 [20], can strengthen the capacity to learn both long-range and localized dependencies within speech signals, thereby improving overall separation performance.

Another critical issue is the cross-language interference, where features from one language might leak into another, leading to distorted outputs. This issue is particularly challenging in code-switched speech, where speakers may fluidly switch between languages within a single utterance. Models often fail to separate overlapping speech in such cases, resulting in incoherent outputs. To mitigate cross-language interference, models should incorporate a contextual separation approach that understands the relationship between different linguistic units in a multilingual setting. Multilingual transformers or language-specific embeddings can be used to better capture the context and prevent leakage between languages. Moreover, integrating speaker diarization and source separation techniques in tandem can help distinguish and maintain the coherence of speech segments, even in the case of code-switching.

While significant progress has been made in multilingual speech separation, the challenges outlined above remain substantial obstacles to achieving robust, real-time, and accurate separation systems. Addressing these challenges will require further advancements in language identification, phonetic modeling, data augmentation, computational efficiency, and evaluation standards. By overcoming these hurdles, future models will be better equipped to handle the complexities of multilingual and code-switched speech, enabling their application in diverse real-world scenarios such as multilingual conferences, bilingual personal assistants, and cross-cultural communication tools.

4 Experiments

4.1 Dataset

In this study, we utilize the 100-hour VinBigdata [16] speech dataset for the task of sound separation, which is a critical step in the audio signal processing pipeline for automatic speech recognition (ASR) systems. This dataset provides a large number of diverse audio samples, including various voices and topics, ranging from news to everyday conversations, with each sample lasting from a few seconds to one minute. Each audio recording is manually transcribed with a high accuracy rate, which aids in training models for sound separation and speech recognition. The diverse acoustic characteristics of the Vietnamese language in this dataset are expected to help the models learn how to accurately separate and identify speech from complex audio signals. By using this dataset, we aim to enhance the performance of speech recognition systems by improving the sound separation process.

The LibriSpeech-2mix [6] dataset is designed for speech source separation tasks. The dataset contains mixtures of two speakers, enabling the development of models aimed at separating speech from two different sources. The dataset is available at a 16 kHz sampling rate, providing a balance between audio quality and computational efficiency. To generate the Libri2Mix dataset, we can clone the repository and run a provided script to create the mixed audio samples. Libri2Mix is valuable for training and evaluating speech separation models, as it offers a clean and controlled environment, while also incorporating the added complexity of background noise, making it a powerful tool for developing robust, generalizable speech separation systems.

4.2 Metrics

The scale-invariant signal-to-distortion ratio (SI-SDR) is a slightly modified version of the signal-to-distortion ratio (SDR) [17]. SI-SDR serves as a widely used objective metric for evaluating source separation performance, offering greater robustness compared to the traditional SDR. The evaluation of algorithm performance is significantly enhanced by these assessment metrics. However, we do not account for noise error and artifact error, as noise signals are not always known. Instead, the scale-invariant signal-to-noise ratio (SI-SNR) is adopted as an objective metric, which is defined as follows:

$$s_{\text{target}} = \frac{\langle \hat{s}, s \rangle s}{||s||^2}, \tag{1}$$

$$e_{\text{noise}} = \hat{s} - s_{\text{target}}, \tag{2}$$

$$\text{SI-SNR}(s, \hat{s}) = 10\log_{10} \frac{||s_{\text{target}}||^2}{||e_{\text{noise}}||^2}, \tag{3}$$

In these equations, $\hat{s}$ represents the estimated utterance, and s is the reference clean utterance in the time domain. The target utterance and noise error are denoted as s_{target} and e_{noise}, respectively. Here, $\langle .,. \rangle$ is the inner product, and $||.||^2$ denotes the $L2$-norm. The SI-SNRi and SDRi values, as used in previous works such as [7,10,11,13,14], are defined as follows:

$$\text{SI-SNRi}(s, \hat{s}, x) = \text{SI-SNR}(s, \hat{s}) - \text{SI-SNR}(s, x), \quad (4)$$

$$\text{SDRi}(s, \hat{s}, x) = \text{SDR}(s, \hat{s}) - \text{SDR}(s, x). \quad (5)$$

In these formulas, x represents the time-domain mixed signal. These criteria are crucial for evaluating the effectiveness of the source separation strategy.

4.3 Performance Comparisons

Figure 2 shows that the model achieves consistently strong performance across different sample mixture numbers, with SDRi values slightly higher than SI-SNRi by about 0.40.6 dB. Both metrics remain stable in the range of 1516.5 dB, indicating that the model maintains effectiveness even as the number of mixtures increases. This suggests that the separation quality is robust and scalable, with SDRi reflecting slightly more optimistic improvements compared to SI-SNRi. Figure 3 demonstrates that the model performs even better on half-duration mixtures, with SDRi values ranging from about 17.1 to 17.8 dB and SI-SNRi from 16.7 to 17.4 dB. Compared to the full-duration mixtures, both metrics show a noticeable improvement, indicating that shorter utterances make the separation task easier. SDRi consistently outperforms SI-SNRi by a small margin, reinforcing the robustness of the model across different mixture sizes while benefiting from shorter signal lengths.

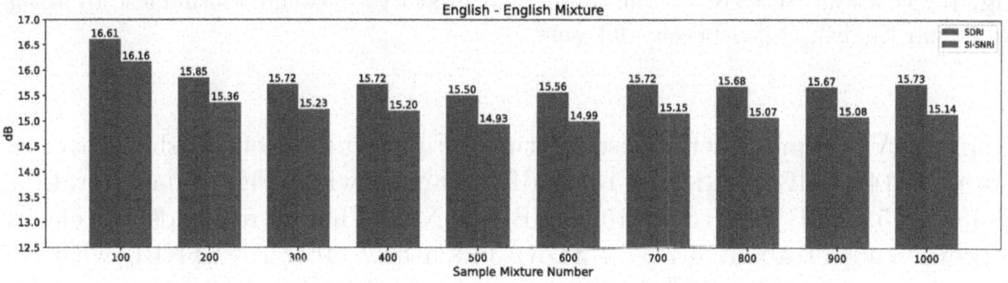

Fig. 2. SDRi and SI-SNRi on the number of mixtures between English (Librispeech) and English (Librispeech) datasets.

The results in Figs. 4 and 5 show that EnglishVietnamese mixtures are more difficult to separate compared to EnglishEnglish mixtures, with both SDRi and SI-SNRi values being consistently lower (around 13 dB for SDRi and 12.513.3

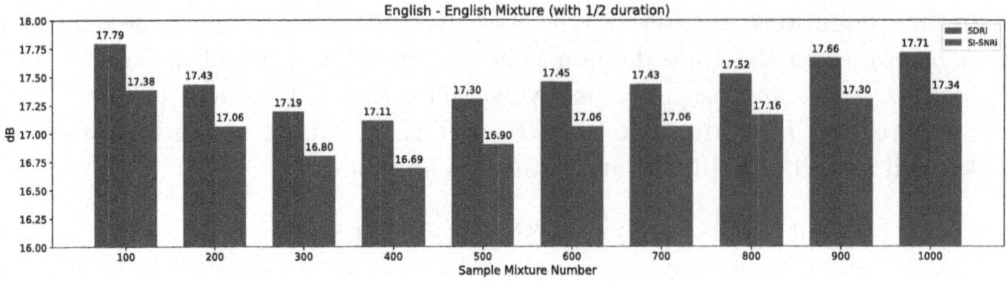

Fig. 3. SDRi and SI-SNRi on the number of mixtures between English (Librispeech) and English (Librispeech) datasets (half-duration mixture).

dB for SI-SNRi). This performance drop highlights the challenges of cross-lingual separation due to differences in phonetic and acoustic properties between the two languages. Moreover, while shorter utterances improved results in the EnglishEnglish case, the half-duration EnglishVietnamese mixtures do not yield any gain and instead exhibit a slight decline in performance. This suggests that signal reduction further complicates the separation task in cross-lingual scenarios.

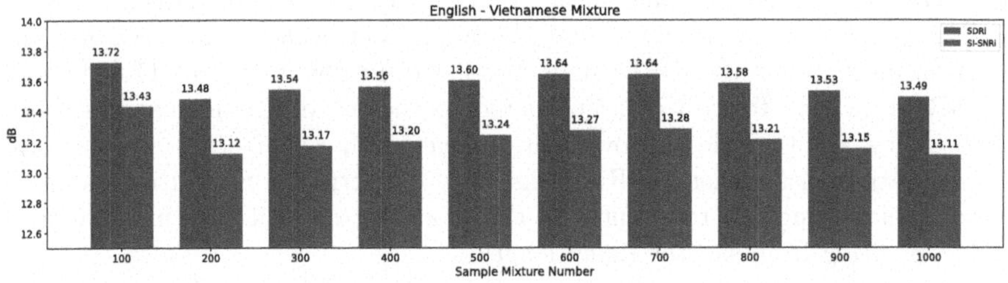

Fig. 4. SDRi and SI-SNRi on the number of mixtures between Vietnamese (VinBigdata) and English (Librispeech) datasets.

In the VietnameseVietnamese mixtures, Fig. 6 (full duration) shows average scores of 14.44 dB SDRi and 13.01 dB SI-SNRi, while Fig. 7 (half duration) achieves 15.12 dB SDRi and 15.56 dB SI-SNRi. This corresponds to relative improvements of about 4.7% in SDRi and nearly 20% in SI-SNRi, with the shorter segments also yielding much greater stability across mixture numbers. Notably, the half-duration setting avoids the low outlier observed in Fig. 6 (SI-SNRi ≈ 9.88 dB at mixture 100), suggesting that shorter segments reduce overlap complexity and provide more consistent separation. Overall, Fig. 7 outperforms Fig. 6 both in mean performance and robustness, highlighting the advantage of shorter mixtures for Vietnamese speech separation.

Across the experiments, a clear trend emerges regarding language pair and segment duration in speech separation. For EnglishEnglish mixtures, the system

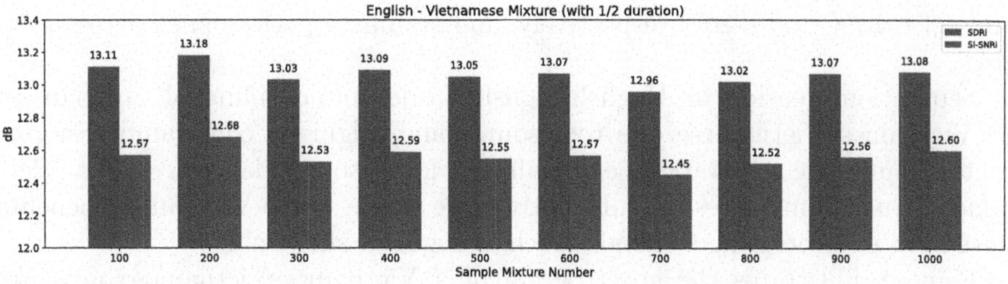

Fig. 5. SDRi and SI-SNRi on the number of mixtures between Vietnamese (VinBigdata) and English (Librispeech) datasets (half-duration mixture).

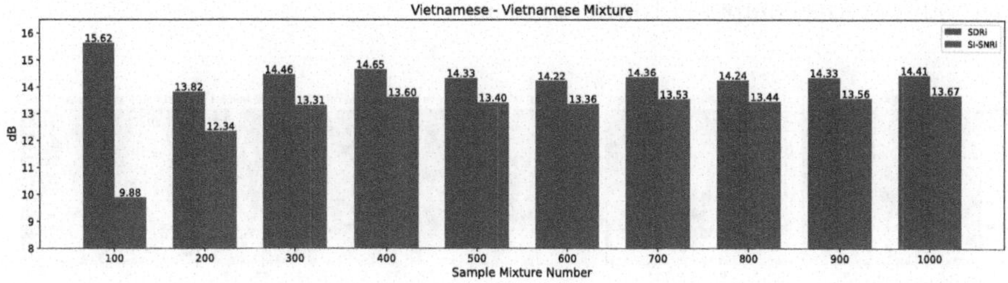

Fig. 6. SDRi and SI-SNRi on the number of mixtures between Vietnamese (VinBigdata) and Vietnamese (VinBigdata) datasets.

achieves the highest overall performance, with average SDRi and SI-SNRi consistently above 15 dB and 17 dB, reflecting the maturity and abundance of training resources for English. In contrast, EnglishVietnamese mixtures yield moderately lower scores, typically dropping by 12 dB compared to the EnglishEnglish case, which highlights the added complexity of cross-lingual separation due to differences in phonetics and prosody. The most challenging scenario is VietnameseVietnamese mixtures, where performance further decreases, especially with full-duration signals (SI-SNRi around 13 dB). However, shortening the duration (half-segment mixtures) significantly improves both SDRi and SI-SNRi, with

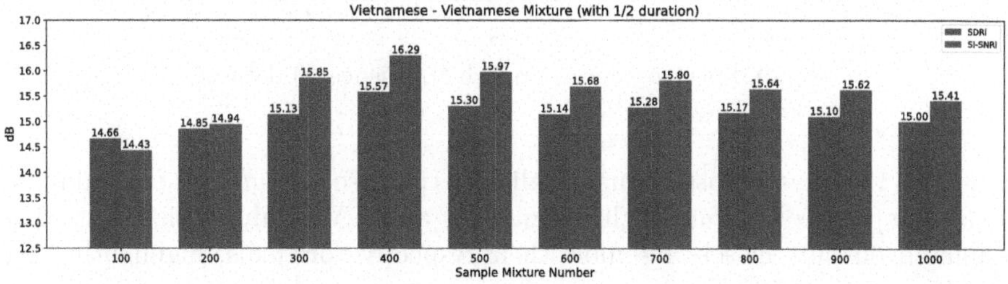

Fig. 7. SDRi and SI-SNRi on the number of mixtures between Vietnamese (VinBigdata) and Vietnamese (VinBigdata) datasets (half-duration mixture).

gains of ~4.7% and ~20% respectively, and stabilizes performance across mixtures.

Separation is easiest for EnglishEnglish, harder for cross-lingual, and hardest for VietnameseVietnamese due to resource and linguistic constraints. Shorter mixtures improve separation, especially in low-resource languages like Vietnamese. English mixtures are inherently more stable, while Vietnamese benefits most from preprocessing strategies such as segment shortening.

Figure 8 illustrates the spectrogram of a VietnameseVietnamese mixture. Subfigure (a) shows the overlapped mixture, while (b) and (c) depict the original clean voices. Subfigures (d) and (e) present the separated signals, demonstrating that the model successfully reconstructs each Vietnamese voice with clear spectral patterns compared to the originals

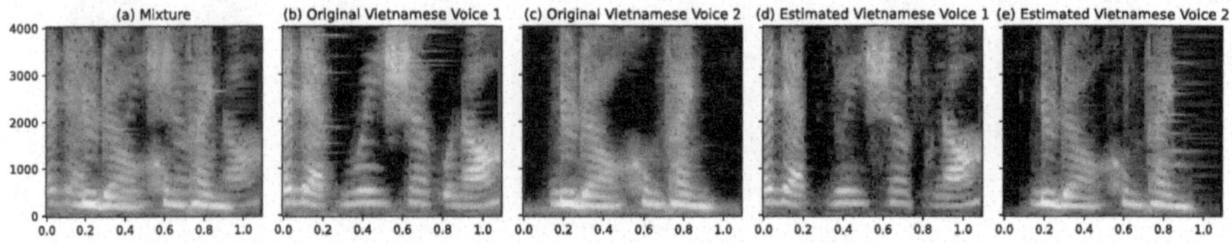

Fig. 8. Spectrogram of Vietnamese (VinBigdata) dataset.

Figure 9 presents the spectrogram of an EnglishEnglish mixture. The mixture in (a) is disentangled into two sources, shown in (b) and (c) for the original voices, and (d) and (e) for the estimated outputs. The results confirm that the model effectively suppresses interference and restores the main spectral details of English speech.

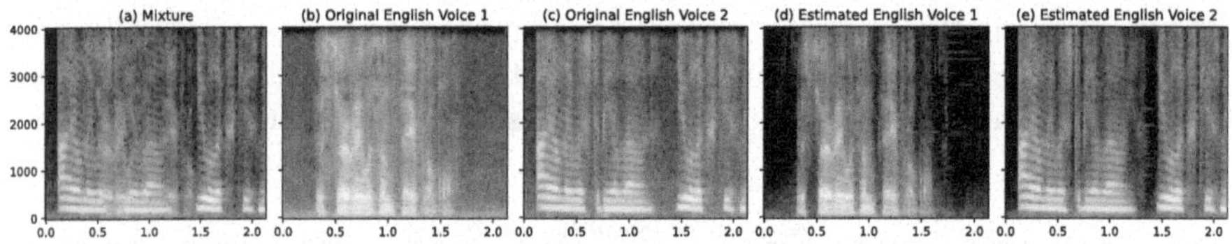

Fig. 9. Spectrogram of English (Librispeech) dataset.

Figure 10 shows a cross-lingual EnglishVietnamese mixture. The mixed input in (a) is separated into an English signal (b) and a Vietnamese signal (c). The estimated outputs closely resemble their respective originals, highlighting the models ability to disentangle overlapping voices across different languages.

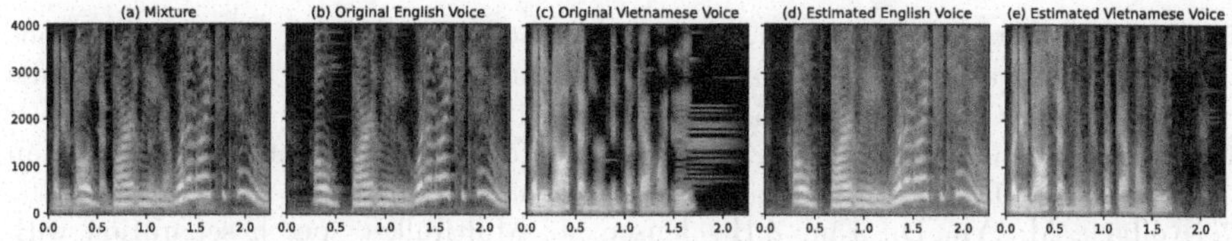

Fig. 10. Spectrogram of English (Librispeech) and Vietnamese (VinBigdata) datasets.

5 Conclusion

This paper makes a significant contribution to bilingual speech separation by combining and applying the modern architecture MossFormer2. The model integrates Transformer-based self-attention mechanisms with a feedforward sequential memory network, which greatly enhances the ability to separate speech in multilingual mixtures, particularly between Vietnamese and English. Experimental results demonstrate the superiority of MossFormer2, as it effectively handles the complex acoustic characteristics of both languages, achieving high accuracy in speech separation. The primary contribution of this research lies in providing a model capable of efficiently separating multilingual speech, opening up opportunities for applications in automatic speech recognition (ASR) systems and natural language processing systems in multilingual environments. The study used the VinBigdata and LibriSpeech-2Mix datasets to showcase MossFormer2's ability to handle speech mixtures from different sources, demonstrating significant improvement over traditional models. Although the results are promising, the study also highlights that challenges remain when handling more complex speech mixtures. Future research could focus on extending the model to support more languages and improving performance in noisy acoustic conditions.

Acknowledgment. This research was supported by The VNUHCM-University of Information Technology's Scientific Research Support Fund.

References

1. Akinpelu, S., Viriri, S., Haroon Yousaf, M.: SwintSer: an improved bilingual speech emotion recognition using shift window transformer. Cogn. Comput. **17**(4), 129 (2025)
2. Aysa, Z., Ablimit, M., Yilahun, H., Hamdulla, A.: Language identification-based evaluation of single-channel speech separation of overlapped speeches. Information **13**(10), 492 (2022)
3. Borsdorf, M., Scheck, K., Li, H., Schultz, T.: Blind language separation: disentangling multilingual cocktail party voices by language. In: INTERSPEECH, pp. 256–260 (2022)
4. Chen, J., Mao, J., Liu, D.: Dual-path transformer network: direct context-aware modeling for end-to-end monaural speech separation. In: INTERSPEECH (2020)

5. Chen, Z., Luo, Y., Mesgarani, N.: Deep attractor network for single-microphone speaker separation. In: International Conference on Acoustics, Speech and Signal Processing (ICASSP), pp. 246–250. IEEE (2017)
6. Cosentino, J., Pariente, M., Cornell, S., Deleforge, A., Vincent, E.: Librimix: an open-source dataset for generalizable speech separation (2020)
7. Kolbæk, M., Yu, D., Tan, Z.H., Jensen, J.: Multitalker speech separation with utterance-level permutation invariant training of deep recurrent neural networks. IEEE/ACM Trans. Audio Speech Lang. Process. **25**(10), 1901–1913 (2017)
8. Luo, Y., Mesgarani, N.: Conv-TASNET: surpassing ideal time-frequency magnitude masking for speech separation. IEEE/ACM Trans. Audio Speech Lang. Process. **27**(8), 1256–1266 (2019)
9. Luo, Y., Chen, Z., Yoshioka, T.: Dual-path RNN: efficient long sequence modeling for time-domain single-channel speech separation. In: International Conference on Acoustics, Speech, and Signal Processing (ICASSP), pp. 46–50. IEEE (2020)
10. Luo, Y., Mesgarani, N.: TASNet: time-domain audio separation network for real-time, single-channel speech separation. In: International Conference on Acoustics, Speech and Signal Processing (ICASSP), pp. 696–700. IEEE (2018)
11. Minh Tan, H., Fhadli, M., Kim Quoc, N., Vu, D.Q.: Pre-trained self-attention framework: an efficient mechanism for source separation. In: Conference on Information Technology and its Applications, pp. 99–110. Springer (2024). https://doi.org/10.1007/978-3-031-74127-2_9
12. Subakan, C., Ravanelli, M., Cornell, S., Bronzi, M., Zhong, J.: Attention is all you need in speech separation. In: International Conference on Acoustics, Speech, and Signal Processing (ICASSP), pp. 21–25. IEEE (2021)
13. Tan, H.M., Vu, D.Q., Lee, C.T., Li, Y.H., Wang, J.C.: Selective mutual learning: an efficient approach for single channel speech separation. In: International Conference on Acoustics, Speech and Signal Processing (ICASSP), pp. 3678–3682. IEEE (2022)
14. Tan, H.M., Vu, D.Q., Wang, J.C.: Selinet: a lightweight model for single channel speech separation. In: ICASSP 2023–2023 IEEE International Conference on Acoustics, Speech and Signal Processing (ICASSP), pp. 1–5. IEEE (2023)
15. Vaswani, A., et al.: Attention is all you need. In: Advances in Neural Information Processing Systems, vol. 30 (2017)
16. VinBigData: Vinbigdata-vlsp2020-100h: a Vietnamese speech corpus for ASR. https://institute.vinbigdata.org (2020). 100h corpus, reading + spontaneous speech, speaker gender and dialect metadata
17. Vincent, E., Gribonval, R., Févotte, C.: Performance measurement in blind audio source separation. Trans. Audio, Speech Lang. Process. **14**(4), 1462–1469 (2006)
18. Yan, B., et al.: Joint modeling of code-switched and monolingual ASR via conditional factorization. In: ICASSP 2022–2022 IEEE International Conference on Acoustics, Speech and Signal Processing (ICASSP), pp. 6412–6416. IEEE (2022)
19. Zhao, S., Ma, B.: MossFormer: pushing the performance limit of monaural speech separation using gated single-head transformer with convolution-augmented joint self-attentions. In: International Conference on Acoustics, Speech and Signal Processing (ICASSP), pp. 1–5. IEEE (2023)
20. Zhao, S., et al.: MossFormer2: combining transformer and RNN-free recurrent network for enhanced time-domain monaural speech separation. In: International Conference on Acoustics, Speech and Signal Processing (ICASSP), pp. 10356–10360. IEEE (2024)
21. Zhao, S., Nguyen, T.H., Wang, H., Ma, B.: Towards natural bilingual and code-switched speech synthesis based on mix of monolingual recordings and cross-lingual voice conversion. In: Proceedings of the Interspeech 2020, pp. 2927–2931 (2020)

Weighted Silhouette Ranking of PCA Projections in Intrusion Detection

Hoang Thinh Pham and Anh Minh Nguyen(✉)

Texas Tech University, 2500 Broadway, Lubbock, TX 79409, USA
{thinh.pham,minhanh.nguyen}@ttu.edu
https://www.ttu.edu

Abstract. The growing complexity of cyber attacks necessitates effective methods for distinguishing malicious from benign network traffic within high-dimensional datasets. Traditional visualization techniques often fail to provide clear separation, hindering threat analysis. This paper introduces a systematic PCA-based approach for visualizing cybersecurity data through systematic 3D projections. Utilizing the DARPA 2009 dataset, we compare projections using 9 and 13 principal components, which capture 99.2% and 100% of the variance, respectively. Our findings, supported by silhouette scores and visual evidence, demonstrate that retaining all 13 components consistently yields superior cluster separability for various attack types, highlighting the importance of even marginal variance contributions. We employ randomized projection vectors, inspired by methods like CHIRP, and rank them to identify optimal visualizations. This systematic exploration provides robust and interpretable insights into complex cyber threats.

Keywords: Cybersecurity · Principal Component Analysis · Data Visualization · Attack Detection · Dimensionality Reduction · 3D Projection · Intrusion Detection · Threat Analysis · Silhouette Score

1 Introduction

The rapid growth in both the scale and sophistication of cyber attacks has made it increasingly difficult to distinguish malicious activity from benign traffic, especially within the high-dimensional datasets produced by modern intrusion detection systems [8,19]. While machine learning has shown promise, such methods often struggle with misclassification [1] and lack transparency [10], leaving analysts with limited insight into why attacks may evade detection or false positives occur.

A central challenge lies in the *effective separation of attack-labeled data points* within these large, multidimensional spaces. Traditional visualization techniques, particularly those restricted to two dimensions, frequently fail to expose geometric structures that could explain system weaknesses or highlight subtle attack patterns [8,19].

V. V. Pham et al. (Eds.): CIDDF 2025, ACSAR 5, pp. 161–177, 2026.
https://doi.org/10.1007/978-3-032-19488-6_11

To address this, we propose a PCA-based method that projects security data into three-dimensional space and systematically generates multiple randomized projections. These are ranked using silhouette scoring to identify the most informative visualizations for separating different attack types. In this study, we conduct experiments on the DARPA 2009 dataset, evaluating the effectiveness of 9 vs. 13 principal components and analyzing how projection quality impacts both the quantitative scores and visual separation of attacks.

2 Related Work

Dimensionality reduction, and Principal Component Analysis (PCA) in particular, remains a widely used, interpretable technique for both preprocessing in intrusion detection pipelines and for producing compact, analyst-facing visual summaries of high-dimensional network traffic. Early LNCS contributions by Xu and Wang [16] and Kang et al. [6] demonstrate PCA's value when combined with classical classifiers or time-delay neural models to reduce training complexity and to reveal anomalous patterns. Subsequent work has extended PCA into hybrid and kernelized settings for IDS tasks; for example, Elkhadir et al. explore kernel-PCA formulations that retain an explicit transform while improving separability for certain attack families [2]. Survey and application studies further show that PCA (and incremental/thresholded variants) remain attractive in modern contexts such as 5G and IoT traffic where explainability and runtime cost matter [3,7].

A parallel and well-established line of research compares linear PCA to nonlinear dimensionality-reduction (DR) techniques. Canonical methods such as t-SNE [9] and UMAP [11] often produce stronger visual class separation on complex traffic distributions, but at the expense of linear interpretability, stability, and repeatability that are important for operational analyst workflows [3,20]. To make evaluation more objective, recent works use quantitative separability metrics (e.g., silhouette, cluster purity) when comparing candidate projections rather than relying solely on qualitative inspection [3,13,20]. Standard modern IDS benchmarks such as UNSW–NB15 and CICIDS2017 are commonly employed in these comparisons to demonstrate robustness across contemporary traffic scenarios [12,14].

Finally, analyst-centered visualization research confirms that three-dimensional projections can improve situation awareness, but earlier 3D approaches typically relied on manually chosen projection vectors or single-view heuristics that introduce subjectivity [17,19,20]. Our work builds on these prior strands by (1) systematically sampling randomized 3D projections from PCA space, (2) ranking projections using quantitative separability metrics, and (3) evaluating the utility of including lower-variance principal components beyond conventional variance cutoffs for producing repeatable, interpretable views that better support analyst tasks.

3 Proposed Approach

Our method for enhancing the visualization and interpretability of cyberattack data proceeds in four main stages: data preprocessing, PCA transformation, systematic 3D projection generation, and evaluation through ranked random projections.

Data Preprocessing. To prepare the DARPA 2009 dataset for analysis, we apply minimal preprocessing to preserve its original structure while ensuring compatibility with principal component analysis (PCA). Numerical features (e.g., packet length, port numbers, counts) are normalized to a consistent scale, while categorical features (such as protocol and flags) are encoded using one-hot encoding. This preprocessing ensures that all variables contribute meaningfully to the subsequent PCA transformation without undue bias toward features with larger magnitudes.

PCA Transformation. We then apply Principal Component Analysis (PCA) to the preprocessed dataset to reduce feature correlations and reorder the data along orthogonal axes of maximum variance. From the PCA results, we extract the first 13 principal components, which together account for 100% of the variance in the dataset. These 13 components form the basis for our subsequent 3D projections.

3D Projections. To project the data into three-dimensional space, we define 26 3D vectors $v_1, v_2, \ldots, v_{26}$, as shown in Table 1, including canonical basis vectors (e.g., $v_22 = (1, 0, 0)$) as well as composite and negative combinations (e.g., $v_{24} = (1, 1, -1)$). Each data point's position in 3D space is determined by a weighted sum of the principal component scores with respect to these projection vectors:

$$\text{position} = \sum_{i=1}^{13} c_i \cdot v_i \cdot s \tag{1}$$

where c_i represents the coefficient of the i-th principal component, v_i is the corresponding projection vector, and s is a scaling factor used to control the degree of separation between points in the visualization space. Different attack types are color-coded in the projections, allowing for clear visual distinction of clusters corresponding to attacks such as DDoS, C2-based, or spambot activity versus normal traffic.

Randomized Projections. To explore the impact of different perspectives, we generate multiple 3D visualizations by randomly shuffling the order of the three selected vectors (v_i, v_j, v_k) with different random seeds. This randomization produces a diverse set of projections, each offering a unique view of the high-dimensional data. Inspired by prior work such as CHIRP, which leveraged iterated random projections for classification [15], we adopt a similar principle of randomized projections to uncover alternative separations between attack-labeled and benign data (Fig. 1).

Projection Ranking. Finally, each projection is evaluated and ranked using the silhouette scoring method [13], which quantifies the degree of separation between attack-type clusters. Projections with higher silhouette scores indicate better-clustered groupings of malicious versus benign traffic. By ranking the projections in this manner, we can identify and prioritize the most informative visualizations for intrusion detection analysis.

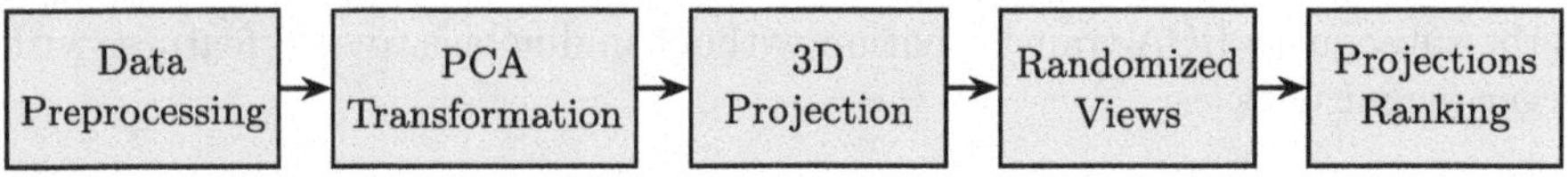

Fig. 1. Pipeline of the proposed 3D projection-based attack visualization method.

4 Experimental Setup

4.1 Dataset

For our experiments, we employed the DARPA 2009 Intrusion Detection Evaluation Dataset [4], a large-scale benchmark developed under the DARPA Scalable Network Monitoring (SNM) program. The dataset was designed to emulate enterprise-like environments with both benign background traffic (SMTP, DNS, HTTP) and a range of adversarial conditions, including denial-of-service, scanning, and malware-related activities. In total, the corpus contains approximately 6.5 TB of packet captures spanning a 10-day period, with microsecond-level resolution and enriched flow-level metadata such as timestamps, packet sizes, source/destination addresses, protocol types, ports, and session state information.

Each traffic record is annotated with attack categories, including `normal` (benign traffic), `spambot`, `ddos`, `c2-based` (command-and-control activity), `post-phishingc2`, and `other`, supporting supervised and semi-supervised evaluation methodologies. While the traffic was synthetically generated, its controlled design ensures high-quality ground truth, reproducibility, and sufficient diversity of malicious behaviors for benchmarking.

For our analysis we restricted the dataset to a core set of flow-level attributes that balance descriptive power with computational tractability. The selected features are:

- `timestamp`—microsecond-level arrival time of each packet,

- `src_ip`, `dst_ip`—source and destination host identifiers,
- `length`—packet size in bytes,
- `src_port`, `dst_port`—transport-layer port numbers,
- `protocol`—IP protocol type,
- `flags`—TCP/UDP connection state flags.

These features were chosen because they are consistently available across packet traces, directly impact traffic semantics, and provide sufficient diversity to capture temporal, topological, and behavioral characteristics of network flows. Features requiring deep packet payload inspection were intentionally excluded, both to preserve compatibility with encrypted traffic scenarios and to ensure scalability to large volumes of flows. This feature subset therefore reflects an operationally realistic setting where intrusion detection must be performed primarily using flow and header information.

Although newer datasets (e.g., UNSW-NB15 [18]) capture more modern threat vectors, DARPA 2009 remains valuable for our study in three respects: (1) it is among the few open corpora with extensive labeled traffic at scale, enabling systematic scalability and throughput evaluations; (2) its attack classes cover canonical adversarial behaviors such as DDoS propagation and C2 activities, which remain relevant in contemporary attack campaigns; and (3) its size and packet-level resolution allow us to stress-test visualization techniques and anomaly detection methods under high-volume conditions.

Thus, while we acknowledge its synthetic and dated nature, we use DARPA 2009 as a reproducible baseline to evaluate methodology under controlled conditions, and later validate generalization on more recent corpora.

4.2 Data Preprocessing

The dataset used for this experiment contains a 90-min segment of network traffic, originally recorded at microsecond-level resolution, with each entry representing packet-level information including timestamp, packet length, source and destination IP addresses, protocol type, port numbers, and connection flags. We apply a systematic preprocessing pipeline to prepare the raw dataset for principal component analysis. First, we compress timestamps from microsecond to millisecond granularity to reduce redundancy and align with our projection analysis scale. We then collapse identical records across the dataset and introduce a `count` field to preserve traffic volume information while eliminating duplicate entries.

Missing or malformed entries in numerical columns are imputed with neutral defaults (0 or -1), and all values are cast to consistent numeric types. Categorical features (`protocol` and derived `flag_category`) are one-hot encoded, while numerical features (`length`, `count`, `src_port`, `dst_port`) are retained in their original form.

Finally, we apply Python's MinMax scaling to normalize all features into the [0, 1] range, followed by centering to zero mean. This preprocessing ensures that all variables contribute meaningfully to the subsequent PCA transformation without bias toward features with larger magnitudes, while preserving sparsity in the encoded categorical vectors.

4.3 PCA Transformation and 3D Projection

Principal Component Analysis. We apply Principal Component Analysis (PCA) [5] to the preprocessed feature matrix in order to reduce feature correlations and represent the dataset along orthogonal axes of maximum variance. From the PCA results, we retain the first 9 and 13 principal components, which capture 99.2% of the variance and 100% of the variance in the dataset respectively. These components provide a compact yet faithful representation of the original high-dimensional security data, forming the foundation for our visualization pipeline. The cumulative and per-component variance distributions are illustrated in Fig. 2, where it can be observed that most variance is concentrated within the first few components. To assess the impact of dimensionality choice, we generate and compare visualizations using both 9 and 13 components.

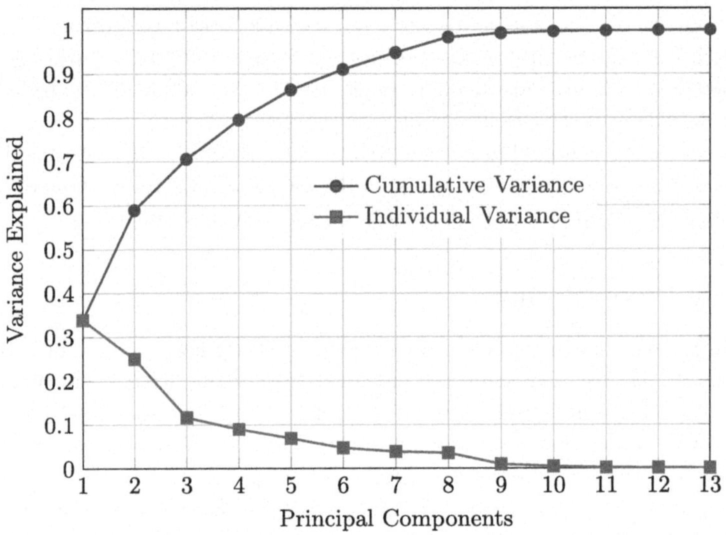

Fig. 2. PCA variance explained for the first 13 principal components. The blue curve shows cumulative variance explained; the red curve shows the per-component variance explained. (Color figure online)

3D Projection Generation. To embed the PCA-transformed data into three-dimensional space, we define a set of 26 normalized vectors that serve as projection directions, as listed in Table 1. For visualization, subsets of 9 and 13 anchor

Table 1. All integer projection vectors from $(-1,-1,-1)$ to $(1,1,1)$ excluding $(0,0,0)$.

Vector	Components	Vector	Components
v_1	$(-1,-1,-1)$	v_{14}	$(0,0,1)$
v_2	$(-1,-1,0)$	v_{15}	$(0,1,-1)$
v_3	$(-1,-1,1)$	v_{16}	$(0,1,0)$
v_4	$(-1,0,-1)$	v_{17}	$(0,1,1)$
v_5	$(-1,0,0)$	v_{18}	$(1,-1,-1)$
v_6	$(-1,0,1)$	v_{19}	$(1,-1,0)$
v_7	$(-1,1,-1)$	v_{20}	$(1,-1,1)$
v_8	$(-1,1,0)$	v_{21}	$(1,0,-1)$
v_9	$(-1,1,1)$	v_{22}	$(1,0,0)$
v_{10}	$(0,-1,-1)$	v_{23}	$(1,0,1)$
v_{11}	$(0,-1,0)$	v_{24}	$(1,1,-1)$
v_{12}	$(0,-1,1)$	v_{25}	$(1,1,0)$
v_{13}	$(0,0,-1)$	v_{26}	$(1,1,1)$

vectors are selected to correspond to the 9- and 13-component PCA representations, respectively, thereby enabling their embedding and comparative analysis in three dimensions.

Each anchor vector is normalized to unit length to ensure consistent scaling. The 3D projection is computed as:

$$\mathbf{p}_{3D} = \mathbf{X}_{PCA} \cdot (\mathbf{A} \cdot s) \tag{2}$$

where $\mathbf{X}_{PCA}$ represents the data in the 13-dimensional PCA space, $\mathbf{A}$ denotes the selected 13×3 anchor matrix, and s is a scaling factor that controls cluster separation. Attack categories are visualized using color coding to highlight the geometric structure of different attack classes.

Data Deduplication and Visualization Preparation. To improve rendering efficiency, we implement voxel-based binning that collapses overlapping points with identical labels into representative markers. Specifically, the 3D space is partitioned into $100 \times 100 \times 100$ bins, and duplicate-labeled points within the same voxel are merged, with a `count` field preserving their multiplicity. This retains the density information of the original dataset while reducing redundancy, allowing clearer visualization of large-scale intrusion detection data.

4.4 Randomized Projection Exploration

To examine the stability and robustness of the visual separation, we extend our approach beyond a single projection. Multiple projection bases are generated by randomly shuffling the order of the 26 vectors and selecting distinct subsets (e.g., the first 13 after shuffling) to assign as anchor vectors to the principal components. This process is analogous to viewing the same high-dimensional data from different angles, where each unique combination of projection vectors can reveal distinct geometric separations between data clusters.

Each shuffle produces a unique 3D perspective of the high-dimensional dataset, potentially highlighting alternative geometric separations between benign and malicious traffic. By repeating this procedure under different random seeds, we create a collection of diverse visualizations that can be compared and ranked to identify the most informative projections.

In total, 200 random projections were generated to ensure sufficient coverage of the projection space. This number strikes a balance between computational efficiency and exploration depth, providing a broad ensemble of perspectives without overwhelming redundancy. The resulting set of projections allows us to assess whether apparent separations remain consistent across different randomized views, strengthening the claim that the observed cluster structure reflects intrinsic properties of the data rather than artifacts of a specific projection choice. These 200 projections will then be ranked to find the one with best class separation.

4.5 Projection Ranking

To quantitatively assess the quality of each generated 3D projection, we adapt the classical silhouette score [13] by introducing a *weighted* formulation that explicitly accounts for sample multiplicity. The need for weighting arises because, after voxel-based binning or flow aggregation, a single representative point may correspond to many raw observations. Without correction, such points would be treated as if they were singletons, underrepresenting dense regions of the data.

Formally, let n_j denote the number of raw records collapsed into point j. We define the sample weight as

$$w_j = \frac{n_j^{\alpha}}{\frac{1}{m}\sum_{k=1}^{m} n_k^{\alpha}},$$

where $\alpha \geq 0$ is a tunable exponent and m is the total number of projected points. The exponent α controls how strongly density influences the weighting: $\alpha = 0$ yields uniform weights ($w_j \equiv 1$), while $\alpha = 1$ weights points proportional to their multiplicity. The denominator normalizes the weights so that their mean equals 1, ensuring comparability across different projections.

Given Euclidean distance $d(i, j)$, the per-point weighted within-cluster and nearest- cluster distances are then defined as

$$a_w(i) = \frac{\sum_{j \in C_i, j \neq i} w_j \, d(i, j)}{\sum_{j \in C_i, j \neq i} w_j}, \qquad b_w(i) = \min_{C \neq C_i} \left(\frac{\sum_{j \in C} w_j \, d(i, j)}{\sum_{j \in C} w_j} \right),$$

where C_i denotes the cluster of point i. The weighted silhouette for point i is then

$$s(i) = \frac{b_w(i) - a_w(i)}{\max\{a_w(i), \, b_w(i)\}},$$

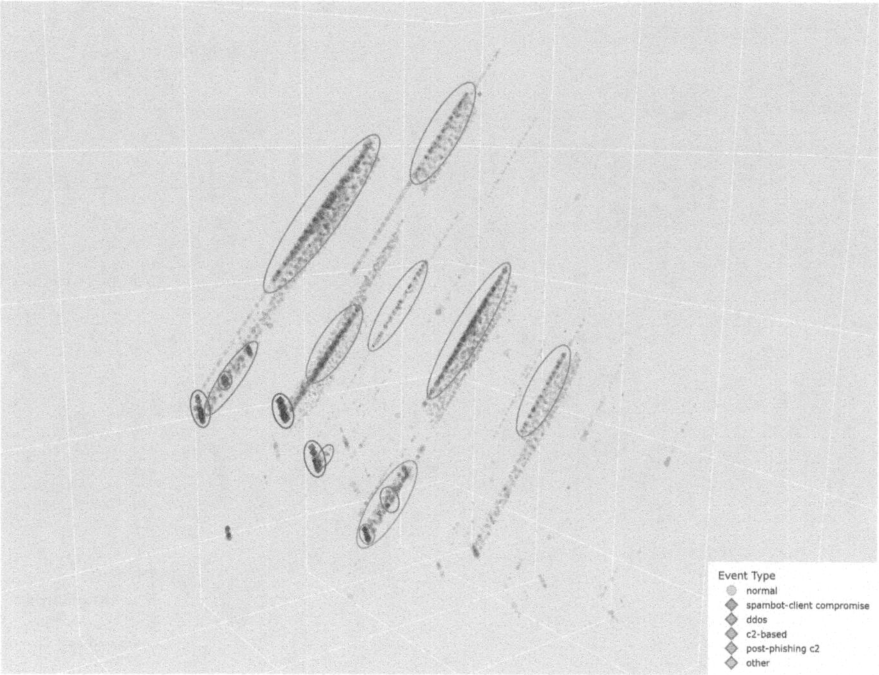

Fig. 3. 3D projection using the best silhouette-ranked trial with 9 PCs.

and the overall projection score is the weighted mean

$$S = \frac{\sum_i w_i \, s(i)}{\sum_i w_i}.$$

This formulation can be interpreted as equivalent to replicating each point j exactly w_j times in the dataset, so that both its contribution as a neighbor and as a silhouette carrier are density-weighted. Importantly, when all $w_j = 1$ (equivalently, $\alpha = 0$), the formulation reduces exactly to Rousseeuw's original silhouette [13].

Practical considerations include:

- **Singleton handling.** If $|C_i \setminus \{i\}| = 0$ (i.e., point i is the only member of its cluster), we assign $s(i) = 0$ to avoid optimistic bias; see Appendix A.
- We exclude the "normal" class when computing silhouette, so that clusters correspond only to the distinct attack types.
- The choice of α allows analysts to tune the influence of dense vs. sparse regions. In our experiments we used $\alpha = 1$ with optional clipping of extreme weights at the 99.5th percentile to avoid domination by a small number of highly populated voxels.

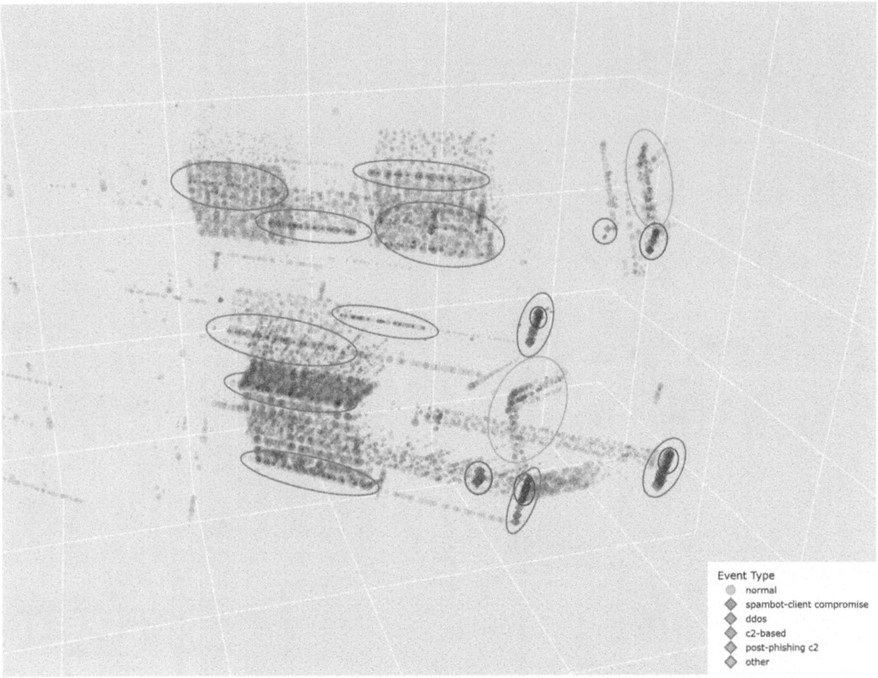

Fig. 4. 3D projection using the best silhouette-ranked trial with 13 PCs.

Table 2. Top 10 scores by ranking for 9 PCs and 13 PCs.

Ranking	9 PCs Score	13 PCs Score
1	0.862125	0.880595
2	0.853444	0.859043
3	0.849326	0.847938
4	0.848712	0.847660
5	0.836850	0.845001
6	0.828715	0.838885
7	0.828597	0.833991
8	0.827001	0.832404
9	0.825398	0.821945
10	0.821499	0.821762

This rigorously weighted silhouette formulation ensures that regions with higher traffic volume or density proportionally influence the ranking of 3D projections, reflecting their practical significance for intrusion detection analysis.

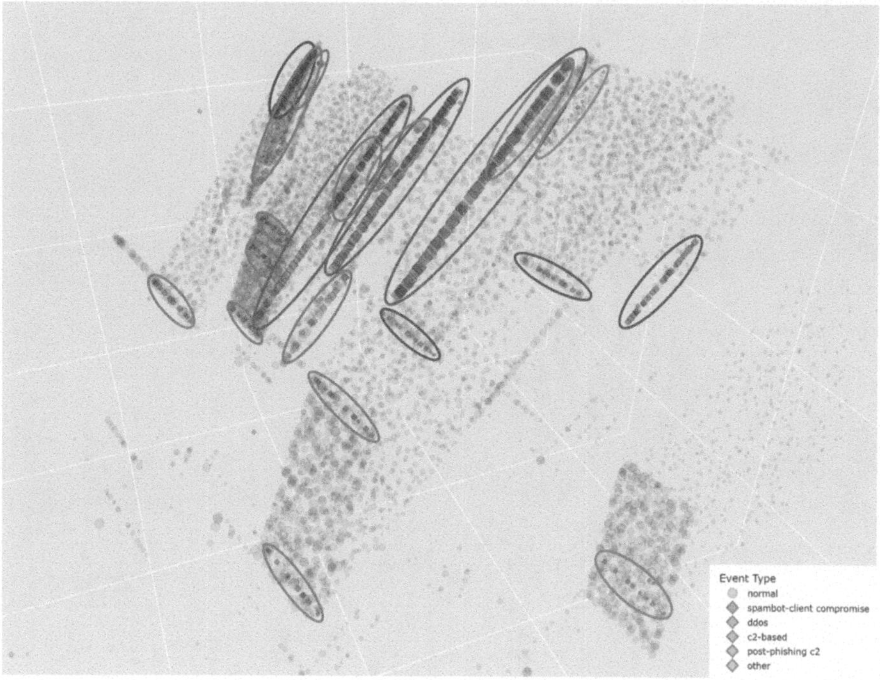

Fig. 5. 3D projection using the worst silhouette-ranked trial with 9 PCs.

5 Results

Although the first 9 principal components capture 99.2% of the dataset variance, a value very close to the 100% variance explained by all 13 components, the separation quality differs noticeably. Quantitatively, the silhouette scores for the 13-PC projections are consistently higher, indicating stronger clustering of attack types. As shown in Table 2, the best-ranked projections using 13 PCs generally achieve higher silhouette scores than their 9-PC counterparts, with the top 13-PC projection scoring 0.880595 compared to 0.862125 for the best 9-PC projection. More importantly, the visualizations highlight this effect: when only 9 components are used, clusters corresponding to different attacks exhibit significant overlap compared to when 13 components are used. (see Fig. 3 and 4)—for example, *DDoS*, *c2-based* and *post-phishing C2* instances blend with each other as seen in Fig. 3. Conversely, when all 13 components are retained, the resulting 3D projections produce tighter and more distinct clusters (Fig. 4), reducing ambiguity between attack categories. This demonstrates that even seemingly marginal amounts of additional variance (the 0.8% captured in PCs 10 to 13) can encode critical discriminative structure for separating attack and normal traffic in practice. Moreover, the projections with worst ranking for both cases show significant overlapping areas between classes and mixing of data points from different classes (Figs. 5 and 6).

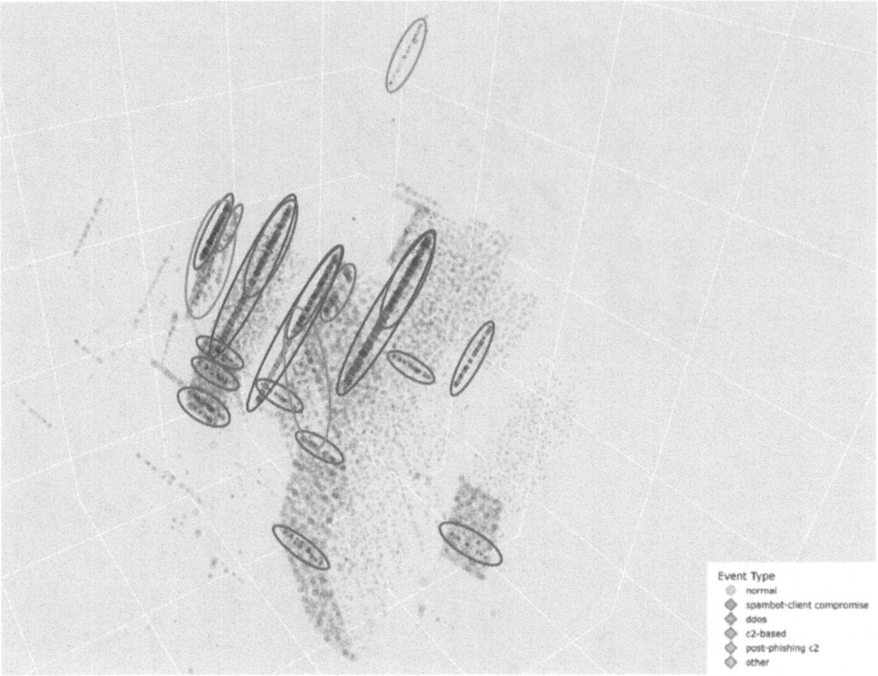

Fig. 6. 3D projection using the worst silhouette-ranked trial with 13 PCs.

6 Discussion

Our findings show that PCA-based 3D projections enhance the visualization and interpretability of cyberattack data. While 9 components captured 99.2% of variance, using all 13 (100%) consistently produced higher silhouette scores and more distinct attack clusters. This indicates that even low-variance components can hold critical discriminative information, challenging the common practice of truncating them. The agreement between silhouette scores and visual evidence—where 13-PC projections reduced cluster overlap—validates our approach. By systematically generating and ranking randomized 3D projections, we provide a data-driven framework that avoids subjective manual selection and offers more reliable views of high-dimensional traffic.

Practically, this method supports security analysts by enabling quicker recognition of suspicious patterns through intuitive 3D views. The ranking system streamlines the choice of projections, improving efficiency and scalability across datasets. Future work will test generalizability in varied environments, explore real-time use, and develop interactive visualization tools to further aid threat analysis.

In addition, we also adapt the ranking method used in CHIRP [15]. CHIRP ranks the projections based on pure points by keeping track of pure bins (bins containing only data points of one class) and counting the number of data points.

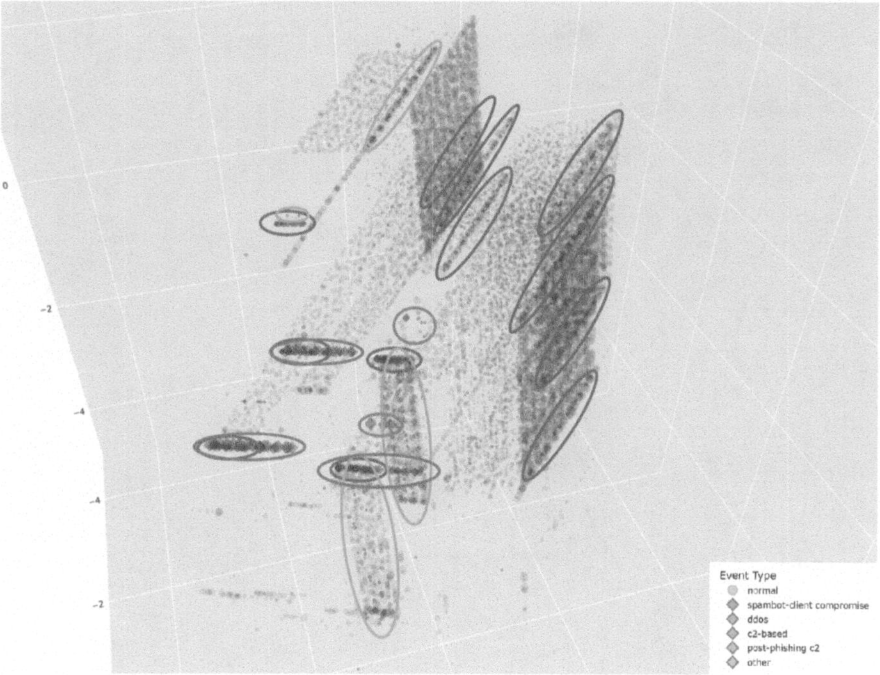

Fig. 7. 3D projection using the best pure bin-ranked trial with 9 PCs.

However, there's a small modification: the original CHIRP methodology targets a specific class and only considers the pure count of that class. In contrast, we skip this part and count the pure points of all classes. The purpose of this modification is to align with the direction of our silhouette scoring approach, which aims to separate all classes from each other. The results for best pure counts are shown in Fig. 7 and 8 for 9 and 13 PCs respectively.

Compared to CHIRP, which ranks projections based on pure bin counts, our silhouette-based method provides more robust separation of all attack classes in the visualizations. While this improvement is most evident qualitatively through clearer cluster boundaries, it highlights the value of silhouette-guided ranking for enhancing interpretability.

Limitations and Threats to Validity

Despite the contributions of this work, several limitations should be acknowledged: (1) the dataset scope is restricted to DARPA 2009, which is synthetic and enterprise-specific, and therefore generalization to other environments may vary; (2) the silhouette score is computed against ground-truth labels, and potential label noise can bias the ranking; (3) the projection family is limited to linear maps, while non-linear methods such as UMAP or t-SNE may reveal additional structure at the cost of interpretability and added hyperparameters; and (4) the

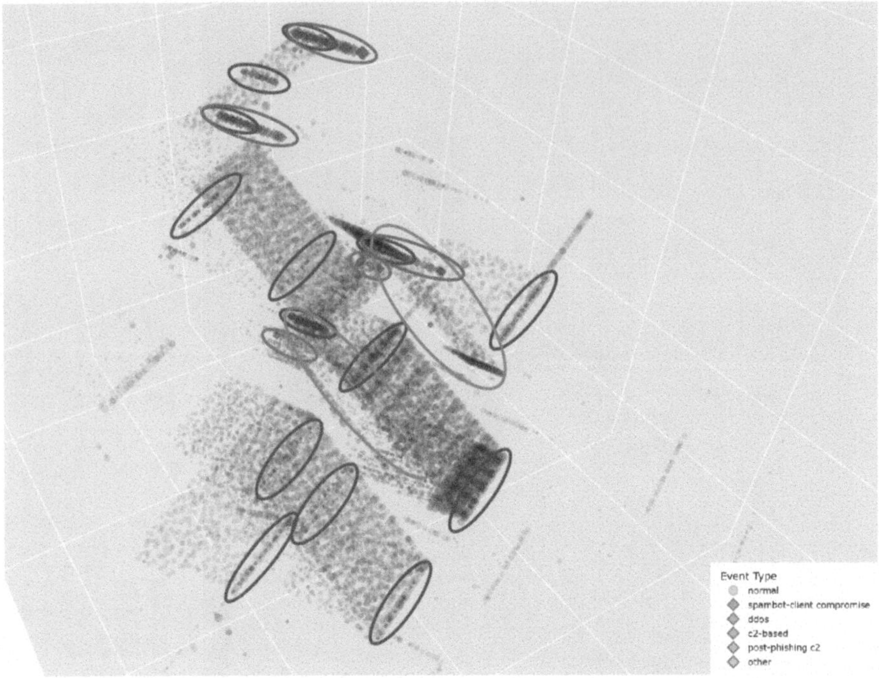

Fig. 8. 3D projection using the best pure bin-ranked trial with 13 PCs.

results are sensitive to hyperparameter choices, including the number of random candidates and the voxel/binning configurations.

7 Conclusion

In this work, we proposed a PCA-based approach for visualizing high-dimensional cybersecurity data through systematic 3D projections. By generating randomized projection views and ranking them with silhouette scores, we demonstrated that adopting all 13 principal components, despite capturing only slightly more variance than 9 components, results in consistently better separation of attack clusters. Our findings highlight that even marginal variance contributions can encode critical structural differences between benign and malicious network traffic, underscoring the importance of preserving full dimensional diversity when applying PCA for intrusion detection analysis. The resulting visualizations not only provide interpretable insights for security analysts but also establish a scalable framework for exploring high-dimensional threats beyond subjective manual projection choices.

Looking ahead, an important extension of this work is to move beyond visualization and leverage these projections for classification. One promising direction is to adopt a covering-based procedure similar to CHIRP [15], where visually well-separated regions in the projected space can be systematically enclosed and assigned to corresponding attack types. Such an integration would combine the human interpretability of visualization with the predictive power of automatic classifiers, potentially yielding a hybrid framework that can both explain and detect cyberattacks more effectively.

A Weighted Silhouette Score

Algorithm 1. Compute weighted silhouette score S for labeled weighted points

Require: coords $\in \mathbb{R}^{n\times 3}$, labels[1..n], weights[1..n] > 0
Ensure: Weighted silhouette score S (undefined if < 2 distinct labels)

```
assert min_j w_j > 0
L ← set of unique labels in labels
if |L| < 2 then
    error "silhouette undefined for fewer than 2 clusters"
end if
Compute pairwise distances D[i, j] = ||coords_i − coords_j||_2
for each cluster C ∈ L do
    W_C ← Σ_{j∈C} w_j
end for
for i = 1 to n do
    C_i ← cluster label of point i
    C_i^{¬i} ← C_i \ {i}
    if |C_i^{¬i}| = 0 then
        s(i) ← 0
        continue
    else
        a_w(i) ← (Σ_{j∈C_i^{¬i}} w_j D[i, j]) / (Σ_{j∈C_i^{¬i}} w_j)
    end if
    b_w(i) ← +∞
    for each cluster C ∈ L with C ≠ C_i do
        avg_C ← (Σ_{j∈C} w_j D[i, j]) / W_C
        if avg_C < b_w(i) then
            b_w(i) ← avg_C
        end if
    end for
    if max{a_w(i), b_w(i)} = 0 then
        s(i) ← 0
    else
        s(i) ← (b_w(i) − a_w(i)) / max{a_w(i), b_w(i)}
    end if
end for
S ← (Σ_{i=1}^n w_i s(i)) / (Σ_{i=1}^n w_i)
return S
```

References

1. Almaiah, M.A., et al.: Performance investigation of principal component analysis for intrusion detection system using different support vector machine kernels. Electronics **11**(21), 3571 (2022)
2. Elkhadir, Z., Chougdali, K., Benattou, M.: Intrusion detection system using PCA and Kernel PCA methods. In: El Oualkadi, A., Choubani, F., El Moussati, A. (eds.) Proceedings of the Mediterranean Conference on Information & Communication Technologies 2015. LNEE, vol. 381, pp. 489–497. Springer, Cham (2016). https://doi.org/10.1007/978-3-319-30298-0_50
3. Ghani, H., Salekzamankhani, S., Virdee, B.: Critical analysis of 5g networks' traffic intrusion using PCA, t-SNE, and UMAP visualization and classifying attacks. In: Swaroop, A., Polkowski, Z., Correia, S.D., Virdee, B. (eds.) ICDAM 2023. LNCS, vol. 785, pp. 421–437. Springer, Singapore (2023). https://doi.org/10.1007/978-981-99-6544-1_32
4. Gharaibeh, M., Papadopoulos, C.: DARPA-2009 intrusion detection dataset report. Technical report (2014)
5. Hotelling, H.: Analysis of a complex of statistical variables into principal components. J. Educ. Psychol. **24**(6), 417 (1933)
6. Kang, B.D., et al.: A mutated intrusion detection system using principal component analysis and time delay neural network. In: Wang, J., Yi, Z., Zurada, J.M., Lu, B.L., Yin, H. (eds.) ISNN 2006. LNCS, vol. 3973, pp. 246–254. Springer, Heidelberg (2006). https://doi.org/10.1007/11760191_36
7. Khraisat, A., Gondal, I., Vamplew, P., Kamruzzaman, J.: Survey of intrusion detection systems: techniques, datasets and challenges. Cybersecurity **2**(1), 1–22 (2019)
8. Labib, K., Vemuri, V.R.: An application of principal component analysis to the detection and visualization of computer network attacks. Annales des télécommunications **61**, 218–234 (2006)
9. Maaten, L.v.d., Hinton, G.: Visualizing data using t-SNE. J. Mach. Learn. Res. **9**, 2579–2605 (2008)
10. Marino, D.L., Wickramasinghe, C.S., Manic, M.: An adversarial approach for explainable AI in intrusion detection systems. In: IECON 2018-44th Annual Conference of the IEEE Industrial Electronics Society, pp. 3237–3243. IEEE (2018)
11. McInnes, L., Healy, J., Melville, J.: UMAP: uniform manifold approximation and projection for dimension reduction. arXiv preprint arXiv:1802.03426 (2018)
12. Moustafa, N., Slay, J.: UNSW-NB15: a comprehensive data set for network intrusion detection systems (UNSW-NB15 network data set). In: 2015 Military Communications and Information Systems Conference (MilCIS), pp. 1–6. IEEE (2015)
13. Rousseeuw, P.J.: Silhouettes: a graphical aid to the interpretation and validation of cluster analysis. J. Comput. Appl. Math. **20**, 53–65 (1987). https://doi.org/10.1016/0377-0427(87)90125-7. https://www.sciencedirect.com/science/article/pii/0377042787901257
14. Sharafaldin, I., Lashkari, A.H., Ghorbani, A.A., et al.: Toward generating a new intrusion detection dataset and intrusion traffic characterization. ICISSp **1**(2018), 108–116 (2018)
15. Wilkinson, L., Anand, A., Dang, N.T.: Chirp: a new classifier based on composite hypercubes on iterated random projections. In: Proceedings of the 17th ACM SIGKDD International Conference on Knowledge Discovery and Data Mining (KDD 2011), San Diego, CA, USA, pp. 219–228. ACM (2011). https://doi.org/10.1145/2020408.2020450

16. Xu, X., Wang, X.: An adaptive network intrusion detection method based on PCA and support vector machines. In: Li, X., Wang, S., Dong, Z.Y. (eds.) ADMA 2005. LNCS, vol. 3584, pp. 696–703. Springer, Heidelberg (2005). https://doi.org/10.1007/11527503_82
17. Zhao, Y., Zhou, F., Fan, X., Liang, X., Liu, Y.: IDSRadar: a real-time visualization framework for IDS alerts. SCIENCE CHINA Inf. Sci. **56**(8), 1–12 (2013)
18. Zoghi, Z., Serpen, G.: UNSW-NB15 computer security dataset: analysis through visualization. Secur. Priv. **7**(1), e331 (2024)
19. Zong, W., Chow, Y.W., Susilo, W.: A 3D approach for the visualization of network intrusion detection data. In: 2018 International Conference on Cyberworlds (CW), pp. 308–315. IEEE (2018). https://doi.org/10.1109/CW.2018.00062. https://ro.uow.edu.au/eispapers1/2330
20. Zong, W., Chow, Y.W., Susilo, W.: Dimensionality reduction and visualization of network intrusion detection data. In: Jang-Jaccard, J., Guo, F. (eds.) ACISP 2019. LNCS, vol. 11547, pp. 441–455. Springer, Cham (2019). https://doi.org/10.1007/978-3-030-21548-4_24

PowerMap and Time-Indexed PCA Trajectories: Interactive Visual Forensics for HPC Incidents

Phornsawan Roemsri(✉), Amauri Henrique Ribeiro, and Tommy Dang

Department of Computer Science, Texas Tech University, Lubbock, TX, USA
{phornsawan.roemsri,alinhare,tommy.dang}@ttu.edu

Abstract. To diagnose issues in HPC data centers, we compare what jobs are doing with facility signals (temperature, power) across many nodes, and we link nodes, jobs, and users. We present two interactive views for incident analysis: *PowerMap*, a node–time view for one metric at a time with thresholding and user/job provenance, and *Time-Indexed PCA Trajectories*, a multi-metric projection (PC1–PC2) with optional time paths and drill-down (radar and line charts).

Applied to 110 CPU-only nodes over 48 h (29–31 Jul 2025, UTC−05) that include a high room-temperature event (30 Jul, ∼15:00–18:00), PowerMap shows cluster-wide temperature alerts, higher system power, and full CPU usage. A PCA snapshot (17:00) shows a user-colored cluster with loadings aligned to higher *cpu_usage*, *cpu_power*, and *temperature*; provenance links many concurrent jobs to `user100049` (`momaruf`). Overall, heavy workload set the stage, and a facility temperature rise pushed many nodes past limits. The views support quick triage, clear attribution, and multi-metric monitoring.

Keywords: High-performance computing (HPC) · incident analysis · interactive visualization · PowerMap · principal component analysis (PCA) · trajectories · user/job provenance · forensic analysis

1 Introductions

High-performance computing (HPC), or supercomputing [18], has become essential across many domains. With the rise of big-data workloads and modern AI pipelines [8,14], researchers rely on large clusters that deliver massive parallel processing within tight time allocations. As systems scale, performance analysis [24] and incident forensics become critical to ensure reliability, efficiency, and fast recovery when things go wrong.

The simple solution typically utilize data-visualization dashboards to monitor CPU and memory usage, temperatures, power, and other telemetry data for each node in real-time. However, considering all metrics simultaneously across hundreds or thousands of nodes makes it difficult to spot subtle anomalies, temporal patterns, or the specific node(s) that deviated first.

V. V. Pham et al. (Eds.): CIDDF 2025, ACSAR 5, pp. 178–197, 2026.
https://doi.org/10.1007/978-3-032-19488-6_12

Principal Component Analysis (PCA) [3] helps address this challenge. PCA is a multivariate technique that summarizes many correlated measurements into a few uncorrelated combinations—principal components—that retain most of the variation. Plotting the component scores and loadings helps reveal similarities among samples and clarify how variables relate. A work close to ours is [20], which combines PCA with time-indexed trajectories in chemistry to reveal hidden reaction pathways; in contrast, our work focuses on the HPC domain and supports direct examination of the raw data.

In this paper, we use *PowerMap* and *Time-Indexed PCA Trajectories* as a forensic tool to (i) localize the node(s) most likely associated with an incident, (ii) characterize how the event evolved, and (iii) link overview patterns back to raw metrics for evidence and validation (via radar charts and scatter plots). For single-metric monitoring, *PowerMap* highlights *when and where* thresholds are crossed in a node-time grid and ties those exceedances to specific users/jobs (provenance), enabling fast identification of the incident window, the affected nodes, and the dominant workloads. For multimetric diagnosis, *Time-Indexed PCA Trajectories* summarizes joint behavior in PC1–PC2 (with optional time-linked paths) to reveal user-colored clusters and coordinated shifts. We demonstrate the approach on production HPC telemetry, showing that PCA trajectories complement standard monitoring by providing an interpretable, system-level map of behavior during incident windows.

The remainder of this paper is organized as follows. Section 2 reviews related work on HPC telemetry visualization, highlighting approaches relevant to incident diagnosis and provenance. Section 3 introduces the application and background of our study, including the data and tools used in our analysis. We first describe the data set used in this study, including its sources, structure, and pre-processing steps. We then introduce the visualization tool we developed for analyzing performance data of HPC, including its features, functionality, and user interface. Section 4 presents the results of our analysis, highlighting key insights and findings from the visualization of the performance data. Finally, Sect. 5 concludes the paper with a discussion of the implications of our study and directions for future research.

2 Related Work

High performance computing (HPC) is considered one of the most advanced and complex domains in information technology but it also comes with numerous challenges [22]. HPC systems typically consist of a large number of processors and accelerators organized into a unified cluster that is accessible by multiple users or research groups. [22] These systems, which can comprise hundreds of thousands of compute nodes, can perform trillions of floating-point operations per second. [22] HPC has highly diverse and significant applications in science, economics, and engineering. [22] Within this space, HPC visualization tools and PCA-based methods have often been used to detect abnormal behaviours and expose anomalies in large-scale systems. In day-to-day operations, platforms such as Grafana and Prometheus [1,2] are widely adopted to monitor CPU usage, memory, power, and thermal metrics in real time. While these dashboards are flexible and effective for single metrics, they require operators to cross-check multiple panels manually, making it harder to spot multivariate anomalies or to link failures back to specific jobs and users. This limitation highlights the need for more integrated approaches that combine provenance with multivariate analysis. This points to the broader need for visualization tools in HPC that can incorporate PCA to move beyond single-metric monitoring and support anomaly detection.

We next consider advanced HPC visualization frameworks, where PCA and related approaches are often embedded to support abnormal detection. HPC2lusterScape tackles the complexity of operating shared clusters for large-scale AI training, where scheduling inefficiencies, fragmentation, and lack of transparency hinder both operators and researchers [15]. Since the proposed method working on this problem, Gauge focuses on the I/O layer, transforming overwhelming Darshan logs into hierarchical visualizations that expose inefficiencies in storage access. Therefore, supports developers in benchmarking and debugging patterns [7]. At the distributed-systems level, the Performance Anomaly Detector (PAD) [16] detects anomalies by analysing KPI patterns across multi-server deployments. While PAD provides effective automatic alerts, it does not offer provenance-aware visualization or interactive cross-metric exploration. Our approach complements such systems by enabling forensic analysis of compute-node telemetry linked explicitly to jobs and users. While visualization tools emphasize PCA for abnormal detection, another line of research has focused on density-based methods for finding structure in high-dimensional telemetry.

Along numerous sophisticate approaches to detect clustering algorithm found in a different work, that's implicitly assume one type of structure, which failures when both coexist in high-dimensional data and cluster may be shaped both by distance and density. Here we would like to focus on Projection Based Clustering (PBC) technique, combining non-linear projection with a Topographic performing a solution to define for fine-grained evaluation of algorithm performance. Unlike PCA + K-means or subspace clustering, PBC preserved non-linear patterns and handled outliers better. Consistently outperformed conventional methods, reliably detecting both compact and connected cluster structure. [19] Parallel to density approaches, the PCA family itself has evolved and been extended across domains. To alleviate a reliability issue in HPC system, the author improved DBSCAN algorithm, which the core idea is to use the density connectivity to divided regions that are density-connected into a single cluster, while mark noise points as those that do not belong to any cluster, but this result depend heavily on two parameters (Eps and MinPts). Picking these values is usually manual, slow, and often gives poor results when data density varies. In other hand SSA-DBSCAN produced clearer, more accurate clusters than regular DBSCAN and other improved versions, while we focus on understanding reliability issues turning complex data into patterns people can interpret [11].

Work in [17] further improved Density Peak Clustering (DPC) to automatically handle arbitrary datasets, overcoming the limitations of k-means and DBSCAN in mixed-density settings. In contrast, our approach applies time-indexed PCA to distill high-dimensional telemetry into trajectories that expose dominant patterns relevant to incident forensics, rather than performing clustering. Extensions of PCA illustrate its versatility beyond HPC: in chemistry [20], the intrinsic reaction coordinate (IRC)method, only show the main reaction pathway, think of it as drawing a straight road, but real chemical reactions don't always follow one smooth road, sometimes they curve, split or jump from one path to another. IRC ignores those extra paths and misses critical details, that's why scientists developed ReSPer (Reaction Surface Principal Component Analysis), positioning like a PCA method, sharply show all those hidden curves and splits, revealing hidden reactions routes, unexpected splits, and sudden transitions; and in biology [13], PCA has been used to reveal hidden motions of proteins and macromolecules, reducing thousands of atomic coordinates into interpretable trajectories.

In addition to modern industrial systems, under high energy condition, fault detection and identification is a key requirement, demonstrating how Kernel PCA combined with LSTM improves fault detection and classification with near-perfect accuracy [12], while improved deep PCA uncovers weak signals in rotating machinery for early bearing fault detection [9]. These cross-domain applications highlight PCA's role in uncovering abnormalities, motivating its growing use in HPC anomaly detection. Our work extends this principle to HPC, enabling resilience-focused forensics that reconstruct hidden incidents in supercomputing environments. Under the HPC, PCA has been increasingly adopted to address energy to challenge of interpreting massive, high-dimensional telemetry under effectiveness, demonstrating that PCA can reduce CPU, memory, power, and thermal metrics into trajectories that expose anomalies, resource imbalances, and early signs of system stress. This project Projection-Based Clustering (PBC) [19] In high-dimensional data, clusters may be shaped both by distance (compact separation) and density (connected neighbourhoods). Most clustering algorithms implicitly assume one type of structure, which leads to failures when both coexist. Despites HPC data centers, unsupervised KPI-based clustering [10] applied PCA with hierarchical methods to group jobs effectively, highlighting the dominance of network traffic features. Related efforts, such as Performance Anomaly Detector (PAD), analyses large amounts of performance data generated across hundreds to thousands of servers [16]. Together, these approaches show that combining PCA with density or graph-based clustering can transform overwhelming telemetry into interpretable structures while our work extends this idea to HPC resilience, tracing how nodes drift toward failure. PowerMap quickly scan node–time patterns while directly linking them to specific jobs and users. Time-Indexed PCA Trajectories add a complementary view, showing how multiple metrics shift together over time and allowing drill-downs with radar and line charts. Together, these tools give a clearer forensic picture of incidents, something not offered by Grafana's single-panel dashboards, Gauge's I/O focus, PAD's automatic alarms, or energy-efficiency dashboards.

3 Application Background

This paper presents a 2D interactive web-based visualization tool for analyzing the behavior and forensics of performance data, focusing on High-Performance Computing (HPC) in the context of a room-temperature rise incident. This section is divided into three parts. The first part provides an overview of the data we use, including sources and preprocessing steps. The second part describes the visualization tools developed for analyzing HPC performance, with their features and functionality. The third part explains how we analyze and visualize HPC performance during a high room-temperature incident and shows the interface design.

3.1 Data Description and Preparation

In this study, we examine two real operating incidents from distinct HPC environments to assess our framework: a high room-temperature event and a chilled-water disruption.

Case 1—High room-temperature incident (REPACSS). The data for this study were collected from the Remotely-managed Power Aware Computing Systems and Services (REPACSS) resource, a high-performance computing (HPC) data center designed to support data-intensive and energy-aware research. We focused on the 110 CPU-only compute nodes of REPACSS, each equipped with dual AMD EPYC 9754 processors (256 physical cores per node), 1.5 TB of system memory, and 1.92 TB of local NVMe storage. No GPU accelerators are installed in these nodes. Measurements span a continuous 48-hour period from 29 July 2025, 00:00 to 31 July 2025, 00:00 (CDT, UTC−5). During this interval, a high room-temperature incident occurred on 30 July 2025 between approximately 15:00 and 18:00 (CDT). For analysis, all metrics were aggregated to uniform 5-min intervals per node. For each node and metric, we selected the maximum observed value within each window. This yields 576 samples over the 48-hour window; across 110 nodes, the dataset totals 63,360 node–time observations.

Case 2—Chilled-water incident (RedRaider/Quanah CPU partitions). For a second incident type, we analyzed telemetry from the RedRaider cluster's Quanah CPU partitions. The partition comprises 476 CPU-only nodes, each with dual Intel Xeon E5–2695 v4 processors (36 cores per node); no GPU accelerators are installed. The study window covers 21 March 2019 from 09:00 to 11:20

(CDT, UTC−5), during which a chilled-water disruption affected cluster cooling. Telemetry is available for 463 of the 476 Quanah CPU nodes in this interval, and the analysis uses these nodes. All metrics were aggregated to uniform 5-minute intervals per node by taking the within-window maximum, producing ~2 h 20 m of data (≈ 28 samples per node)—roughly 12,964 node–time observations across the 463 nodes.

The dataset is organized into three components:

Node performance over time: per-node metric time series at the sampling rates described below.

Job schedule records: scheduler metadata for each job (job/user IDs, resources, times, status).

Node–job mapping: a time-aligned table indicating which job, if any, was running on each node at each timestamp, used to attribute node behavior to specific jobs/users.

For **Case 1 (REPACSS)**, all three components are available and used in analysis. For **Case 2 (Quanah chilled-water)**, only Component 1 is present, with four available metrics: CPU utilization (`CPUUsage`), CPU power (`CPUPower`), fan speed (`RPMReading` or `Fans`), and memory usage (`MemoryUsage`). Job records and node–job mappings are not provided, so the analysis for this case is limited to node-level telemetry without job/user attribution.

Node Performance Over Time. This component contains per-node time series indexed by a node identifier and a timestamp. For **Case 1**, a total of 44 system- and device-level metrics are monitored and recorded per compute node; in this study we analyze a subset covering power, utilization, thermal, airflow/fan, and storage/network-health metrics (Table 1). For **Case 2 (Quanah chilled-water)**, only four metrics are available: CPU utilization (`CPUUsage`), CPU power (`CPUPower`), fan speed (`RPMReading` or `Fans`), and memory usage (`MemoryUsage`). In both cases, all measurements are per-node time series. Sampling intervals in the raw data vary by sensor (e.g., 5 s for high-frequency operational telemetry and 60 s or 3600 s for rolled-up/device-health counters); we harmonize these by aggregating to a 5-minute cadence via the within-window maximum.

Job Schedule Records. Job metadata are obtained from the cluster scheduler (e.g., Slurm [23]) and describe each submitted job, including identifiers, user/group, requested/allocated resources, placement, runtime limits, timestamps, and exit status.

Node–Job Mapping. We construct a node–job mapping by expanding each job's active interval [`start_time`, `end_time`) across its allocated `nodes` and joining to the telemetry on matching `(node, time)`. For each telemetry timestamp, the mapping indicates the running job (if any) and the associated user, enabling attribution of node behavior to workloads and users.

Table 1. Metrics used in this study (canonical name, description, units, interval, data type).

Metric	Description	Units	Interval	Data Type
AmpsReading	Generic sensor current reading	A	5 s	Decimal
AvailableSpare	Remaining spare capacity (normalized)	%	3600 s	Integer
AvailableSpareThreshold	Threshold for spare capacity alarm	%	3600 s	Integer
AvgFrequencyAcrossCores	Average CPU frequency across all cores	MHz	5 s	Decimal
CompositeTemperature	Controller+namespace composite temperature	K	3600 s	Decimal
ComputePower	Useful compute power (non-wasted)	W	5 s	Decimal
ControllerBusyTimeLower	Storage controller busy time (lower part)	min	3600 s	Decimal
CPUPower	Per-socket CPU power	W	5 s	Integer
CPUUsage	Aggregate CPU utilization	%	5 s	Integer
CPUUsagePctReading	CPU utilization (sensor reading)	%	5 s	Integer
DataUnitsReadLower	512 B blocks read (lower part)	Blocks	3600 s	Integer
DataUnitsWrittenLower	512 B blocks written (lower part)	Blocks	3600 s	Integer
HostReadCommandsLower	Read commands completed (lower part)	—	3600 s	Integer
HostWriteCommandsLower	Write commands completed (lower part)	—	3600 s	Integer
ITUE	Power utilization efficiency (system/compute)	—	5 s	Integer
PowerCyclesLower	Device power cycles (lower part)	—	3600 s	Decimal
PowerOnHoursLower	Device power-on hours (lower part)	h	3600 s	Decimal
PowerToCoolRatio	Fan power to system power ratio (PCTR)	—	5 s	Decimal
PSUEfficiency	Power supply efficiency	%	5 s	Decimal
PSURPMReading	PSU fan speed	RPM	60 s	Integer
PSUTemperatureReading	PSU temperature	°C	60 s	Integer
RPMReading or fans	Fan speed (generic)	RPM	5 s	Decimal
SysAirFlowEfficiency	System airflow efficiency (SAFE)	%	5 s	Decimal
SysAirflowPerFanPower	Airflow per unit fan power	CFM	5 s	Decimal
SysAirflowPerSysInputPower	Airflow per unit system input power	CFM	5 s	Decimal
SysAirflowUtilization	Airflow utilization (CFM / Max CFM)	CFM	5 s	Decimal
SysNetAirflow	Net system airflow	CFM	5 s	Decimal
SysRackTempDelta	Exhaust–inlet temperature delta	°C	5 s	Decimal
SystemHeadRoomInstantaneous	Instantaneous system power headroom	W	5 s	Decimal
SystemInputPower	Current system input power	W	5 s	Decimal
SystemOutputPower	Current system output power	W	5 s	Decimal
SystemPowerConsumption	Present system power reading	W	5 s	Decimal
TemperatureReading	Temperature sensor reading	°C	5 s	Decimal
TotalCPUPower	Overall CPU power	W	5 s	Decimal
TotalFanPower	Overall fan power	W	5 s	Decimal
TotalMemoryPower	Overall memory power	W	5 s	Decimal
TotalPSUHeatDissipation	PSU heat dissipation	BTU	5 s	Decimal
TotalStoragePower	Overall storage power	W	5 s	Decimal
Used Cores	Numbers of cores that we are using	Cores	60 s	Integer
UnsafeShutdownsLower	Count of unsafe shutdowns (lower part)	—	3600 s	Integer
VoltageReading	Generic sensor voltage	V	5 s	Decimal
WattsReading	Generic sensor power	W	5 s	Decimal
MemoryUsage	Memory usage percent	%	5 s	Decimal
TemperatureStatus	Status of the temperature sensor reading	—	60 s	Enumeration

3.2 Implementations

We implemented two 2D interactive web-based visualization tools—**PowerMap** and **Time-Indexed PCA Trajectories**—to support performance analysis and forensic investigation in HPC environments.

PowerMap. PowerMap is a single-page web application implemented with HTML, JavaScript, and D3.js [4]. It helps operators quickly locate time intervals in which a metric exceeds (or falls below) a chosen threshold and attributes those intervals to the corresponding job ID and job owner. As shown in Fig. 3, the interface comprises five coordinated parts: (1) a node-by-time *density plot* on the left that encodes the selected metric and highlights threshold crossings; (2) a *mini radar chart*, positioned between the density plot and the user icons, that previews a job's multi-metric profile computed from the available metrics (see Table 1); (3) a *job–node–user flow* (network) that shows relationships among nodes, job IDs, and users via links between the timeline, the radar, and the user icons; (4) a *table* in the right panel listing nodes, jobs, users, and metric values with sorting and filtering; and (5) a draggable *controller* for selecting the metric, time range, threshold, and job/user/node filters, with a compact table of available data (user list, job list, and compute list).

Time-Indexed PCA Trajectories. Time-Indexed PCA Trajectories is implemented as a client-side React application within Next.js using TypeScript. The tool has five coordinated parts: (i) a **controller** to select the timestamp and choose color/selection by job, user, or node group (panel a); (ii) a **PCA view** that projects multiple metrics into a two-dimensional component space (PC1–PC2; panel b); (iii) a **trajectory overlay** that draws time-indexed paths for selected node (panel c), where stable behavior appears as compact paths and incidents produce sharp excursions or drifts; (iv) a **radar chart** for the selected node at the chosen time (panel d); and (v) a **linked line chart** showing the same metrics over time (panel e). This view supports monitoring by revealing system-level patterns, clarifying correlations among metrics, and tracing node trajectories through time.

Complementarity. Together, PowerMap and Time-Indexed PCA Trajectories provide complementary capabilities: threshold-based scanning and attribution on the one hand, and low-dimensional pattern discovery with temporal context on the other.

4 Illustration

In this section, we illustrate our visualization tools—*PowerMap* and Time-Indexed PCA Trajectories—on the two incidents described in Sect. 3.1. Using our tools, we show how the incident appears across nodes, how it compares across metrics, and which jobs/users are attached to the affected nodes. While

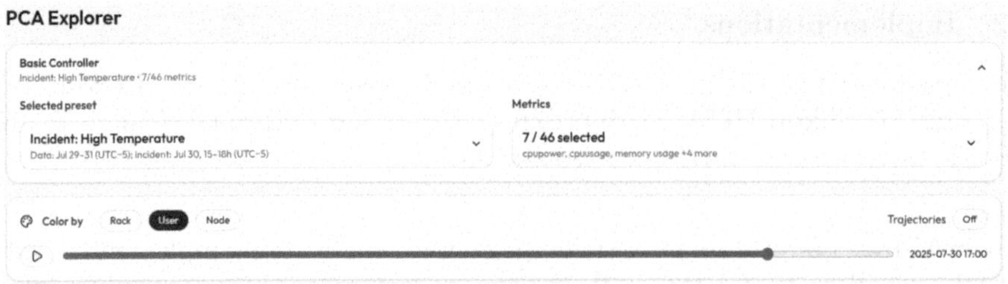

(a) Controller: select time index; choose color/selection mode (user, job, node group); manage metric set.

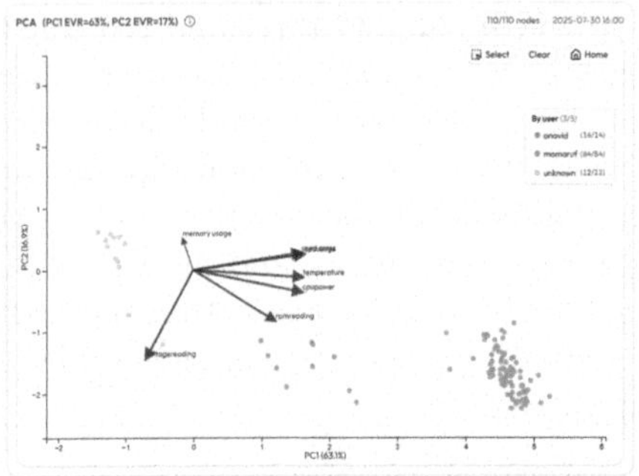

(b) PCA (PC1–PC2) at the chosen time index, no nodes selected.

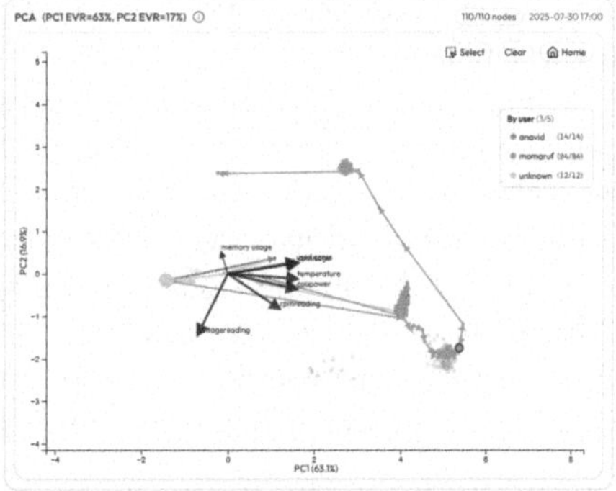

(c) PCA with a selected node highlighted; trajectories enabled.

Fig. 1. Time-Indexed PCA Trajectories—Overview. Panels: (a) controller; (b) PCA without selection; (c) PCA with a selected node and trajectories.

our current work focuses on analysis, these plots can drive simple detection in the future: they make it easy to flag nodes that deviate from baseline and to find which *node, job, or user* is behaving differently or using resources in an unusual way at a given time. Because the REPACSS dataset (Case 1, high room-temperature) includes both job schedule records and node–job mappings, we can demonstrate the full functionality of *PowerMap* together with PCA trajectories. By contrast, the Quanah dataset (Case 2, chilled-water) provides only node-level telemetry without job records, so *PowerMap* is not applicable; we therefore illustrate this case using PCA trajectories only.

4.1 PowerMap

In this section, we use *PowerMap* to show node–time activity for Case 1 (REPACSS). The visualization covers 110 CPU-only compute nodes, with each row representing a node and columns representing time over a 48-hour window (29–31 Jul 2025, CDT). The view uses three colors: gray = no job running, blue = metric below the selected threshold, and orange = threshold exceedance. The right panel provides a network view linking users, jobs, and nodes, as

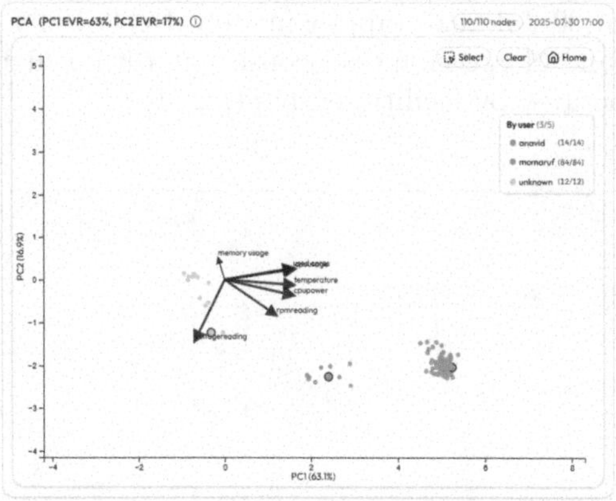

(a) PCA with three selected nodes highlighted.

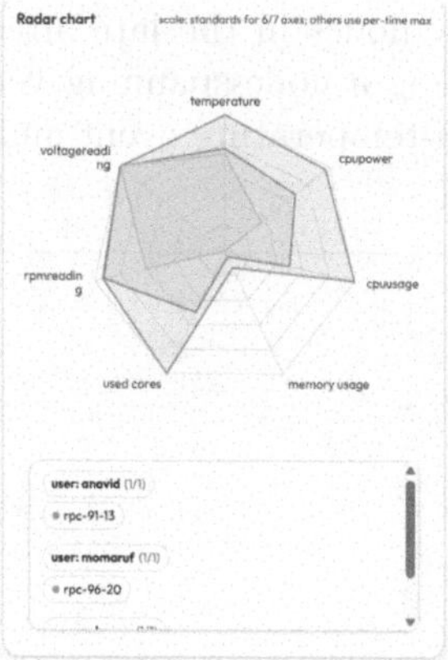

(b) Radar chart for the selected nodes (same metric set as the PCA).

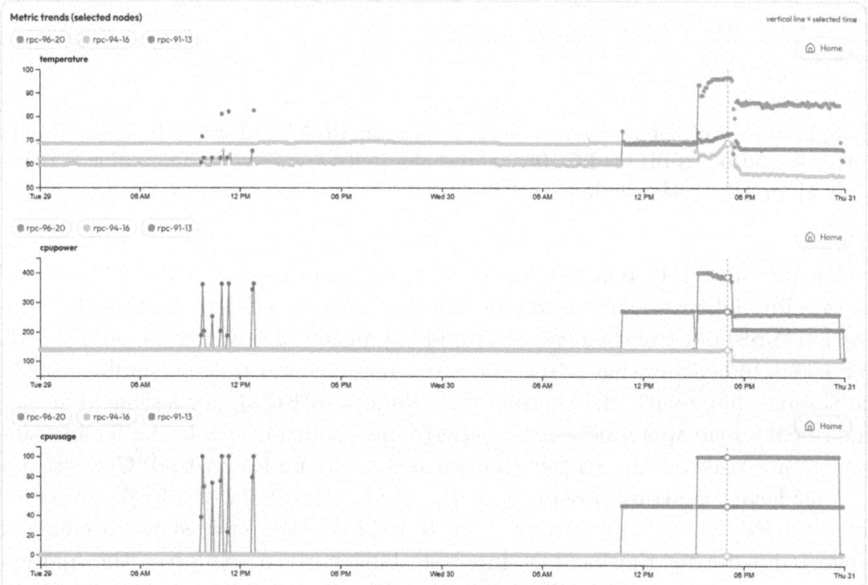

(c) Linked time series for the selected nodes and metrics; incident window may be shaded.

Fig. 2. Time-Indexed PCA Trajectories—Selections and drill-down. Panels: (c) PCA with three selected nodes; (d) radar profile; (e) line chart.

well as a table summarizing per-job metrics (e.g., `system_power`, `cpu_power`, `temperature`) for the current selection.

First, focusing on **temperature** (Fig. 3), with values in the range 0–97 °C, we observe a near-synchronous switch from blue to orange (exceeding 90 °C) across many nodes in the late afternoon of 30 Jul 2025 (approximately 15:00–18:00), forming a node-spanning vertical band of exceedances—consistent with a high room-temperature event and corroborated by facility sensors (Fig. 4).

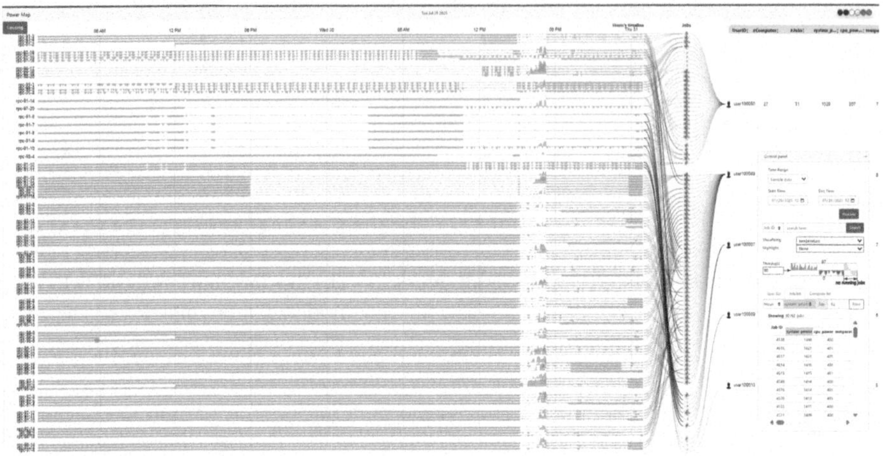

Fig. 3. PowerMap (metric: *temperature*). Data span **29–31 Jul 2025**. Incident window **30 Jul, ≈ 15:00–18:00 (UTC–05)**; threshold = **90** °C. Gray = no job; blue = below threshold; orange = threshold exceedance.

Considering **CPU usage** (Fig. 5), with values in the range 0–100%, several long-running jobs were active well before the incident window. Setting the visualization threshold to 99% reveals a rapid expansion of orange segments shortly after 15:00, indicating that many nodes reached near-saturation simultaneously. The timing aligns with the thermal exceedances in Fig. 3, suggesting that sustained heavy load was a necessary background condition, while the facility-side temperature rise was the trigger that pushed many nodes past 90 °C.

Considering **system power** (Fig. 6), using a threshold of 1.5 kW (observed values across the 48-hour window span 0–1682 W), the view shows a coherent orange band during the incident interval. This pattern reinforces the findings from the temperature and CPU-usage views, indicating a cluster-wide rise in power draw coincident with the event.

Provenance During the Incident. Restricting the view to the incident window (30 Jul 2025, 15:00–18:00) and highlighting user `user100049` (`momaruf`) in the hosts timeline reveals that most of this user's jobs start near 15:00 and run concurrently at high load across many nodes. In the *CPU usage* views—both the cluster-level (Fig. 5) and the user-focused (Fig. 7)—these jobs appear as a broad orange band. Analogous patterns occur in *temperature* and *system power* (Figs. 3 and 6). The temporal clustering and intensity of this single user's workloads coincide with the room-temperature rise during 15:00–18:00, suggesting a likely contributing factor without implying sole causality.

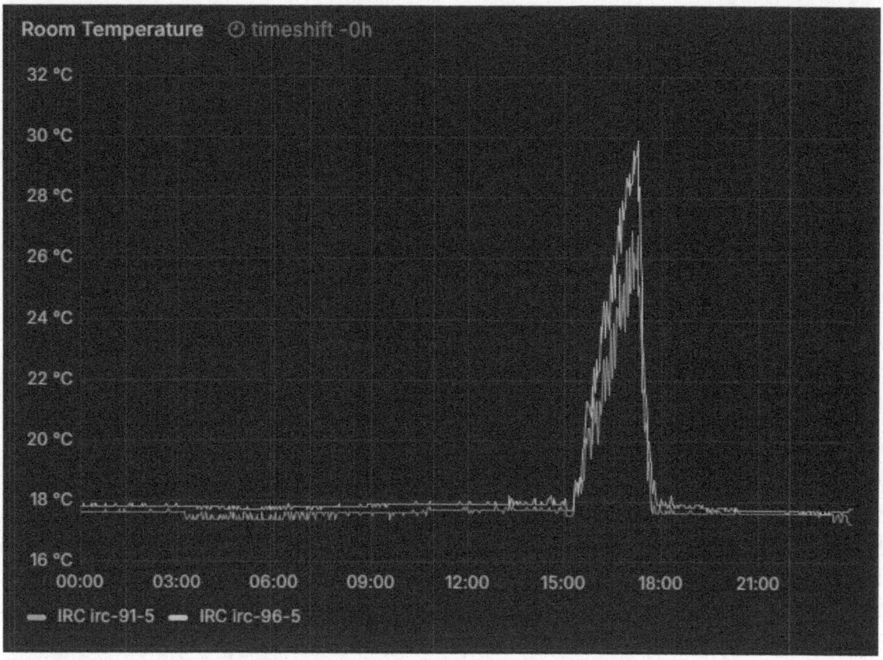

Fig. 4. Room temperature sensors (IRC irc-91-5 and irc-96-5) on 30 Jul 2025, as reported by *Grafana* [5]. Both sensors show a rise beginning around 15:00, peaking near 17:00, and returning to baseline by 18:00 (15:00–18:00), indicating a transient high room-temperature event.

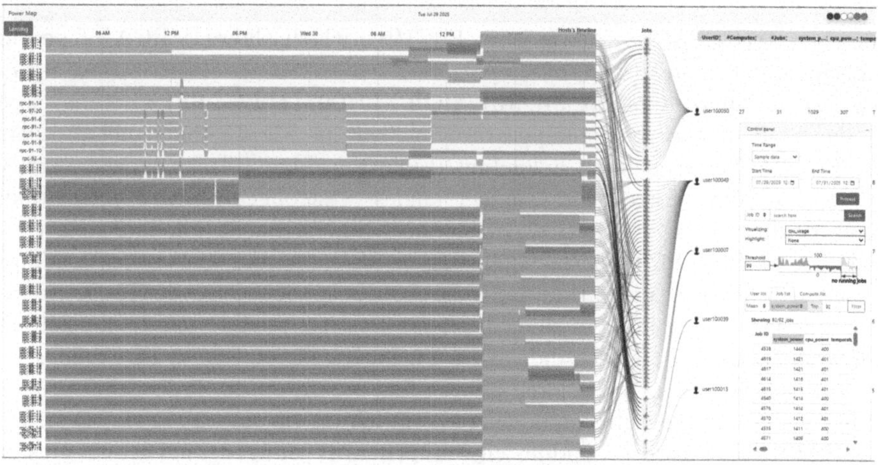

Fig. 5. PowerMap (metric: *CPU usage*). Data span **29–31 Jul 2025**. Incident window **30 Jul, ≈ 15:00–18:00 (UTC–05)**; threshold = **99%**. Gray = no job; blue = below threshold; orange = threshold exceedance.

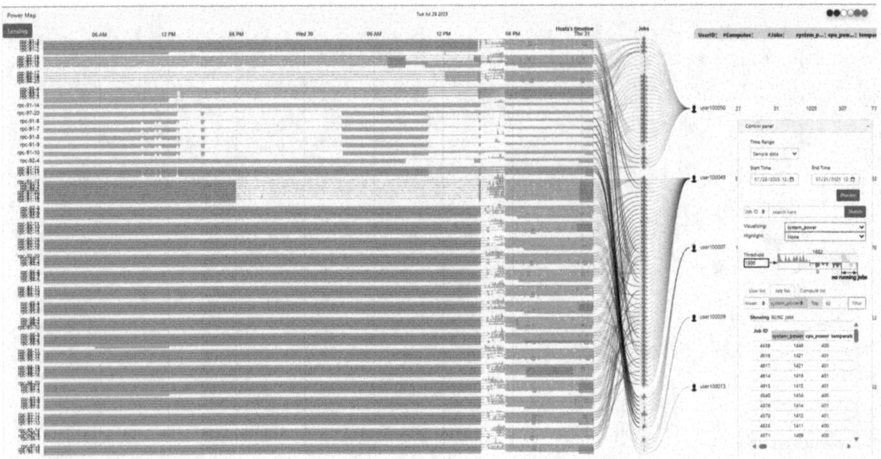

Fig. 6. PowerMap (metric: *system power*). Data span **29–31 Jul 2025**. Incident window **30 Jul, ≈ 15:00–18:00 (UTC–05)**; threshold = **1.5 kW** (observed range across the window: **0–1682 W**). Gray = no job; blue = below threshold; orange = threshold exceedance.

However, *PowerMap* supports only a single metric at a time; comparing multiple metrics requires cross-referencing separate views. To study how metrics co-vary during the incident, we introduce an *index–time trajectory PCA* that analyzes several metrics jointly.

4.2 Time-Indexed PCA Trajectories

For Case 1 (REPACSS), as seen in Fig. 1(b), which shows a PCA of **seven metrics** (*used_cores*, *cpuusage*, *cpupower*, *temperature*, *voltagereading*, *memory_usage*, *rpmreading*) at **30 Jul 2025, 17:00 (UTC−05)**—a time close to the peak of the room-temperature incident in Fig. 4—the panel presents the PC1–PC2 scatter with a loading (biplot) overlay (black arrows). Arrow *direction* encodes correlation (smaller angles = stronger positive correlation; opposite directions = negative correlation), and arrow *length* indicates contribution to PC1/PC2. In this snapshot, *used_cores* and *cpu_usage* loadings are nearly collinear, indicating a strong positive association, whereas *temperature* and *cpu_power* are less aligned. *memory_usage* points roughly opposite to *fan_rpm* (fan speed/RPM), indicating a negative association at this time.

In Fig. 1(b), points are colored by user and separate into three visible groups across PC space: a right-hand cluster dominated by `user100049` (`momaruf`) together with `anavid`; a middle cluster primarily `anavid`; and a left cluster consisting mostly of nodes with no active jobs. Using the loading (biplot) vectors, we can roughly infer relative magnitudes: the right-hand cluster lies in the direction of the *temperature*, *cpu_power*, and *cpu_usage* loadings, indicating higher values of these metrics compared to the other groups. This interpretation

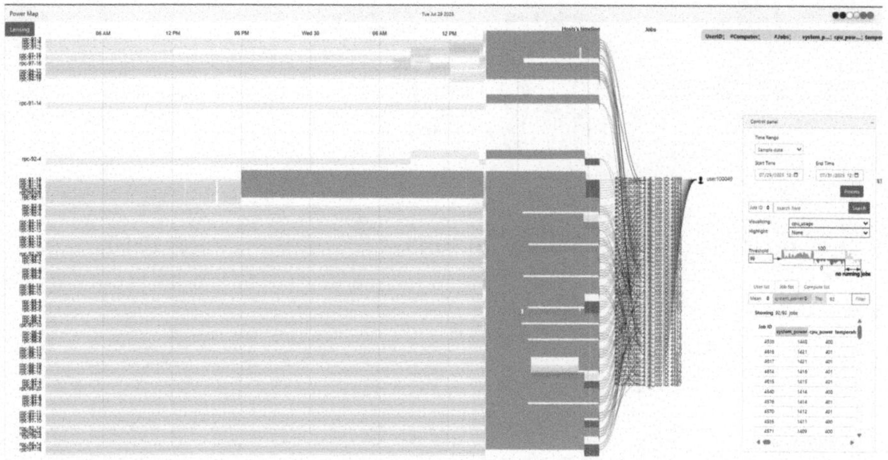

Fig. 7. PowerMap (metric: *CPU usage*), filtered/highlighted for **user100049** (`momaruf`). Data span **29–31 Jul 2025**; incident window **30 Jul, ≈15:00–18:00 (UTC–05)**; threshold = **99%**. Gray = no job; blue = below threshold; orange = threshold exceedance. Most of the selected user's jobs start near 15:00 and run concurrently at high load across many nodes, coinciding with the incident window and the cluster-wide patterns seen in Figs. 3 and 6.

is corroborated by Fig. 1(c) (PCA with two representative selections, trajectories enabled) and by the radar profiles in Fig. 2(d): the *green* selection (user `momaruf`) shows higher *temperature*, *cpu_power*, and *cpu_ usage* than the *orange* selection (middle group) and the *gray* selection (no-user/idle group). The line chart in Fig. 2(e) provides the linked time-series context, traces are colored by user: gray segments denote no active job; early in the interval a *red* point marks a brief job from `li29729`, after which the trace returns to gray. At the selected time (vertical indicator), the trace color matches the current user assignment, consistent with the PCA selection in Fig. 1(c) and the radar profile in Fig. 2(d).

Taken together, the single-metric *PowerMap* views (Figs. 3, 5, 6) and the multimetric PCA panels (Fig. 1(b, c)) consistently indicate that, during the incident window, a large share of the running jobs on the affected nodes is attributable to `user100049` (`momaruf`).

Unlike *PowerMap*, PCA analysis applies to Case 2 (Quanah). We compute PCA on the four available node-level metrics: `memory_usage`, `temperature`, `system_power_consumption`, and `fans` (fan RPM). Figure 8(a) shows the snapshot at **09:00**, covering **463/463** nodes. Points are colored by rack and form a dispersed cloud with no single rack dominating. The loadings indicate that `temperature` and `system_power_consumption` are most closely related (they move together) on PC1; `memory_usage` contributes less, and `fans` contributes the least to PC1 but the most to PC2.

Across successive snapshots from **09:00** (Fig. 8(a)) through **10:45** (Fig. 8(b)), the point cloud remains relatively compact and similarly oriented. Between

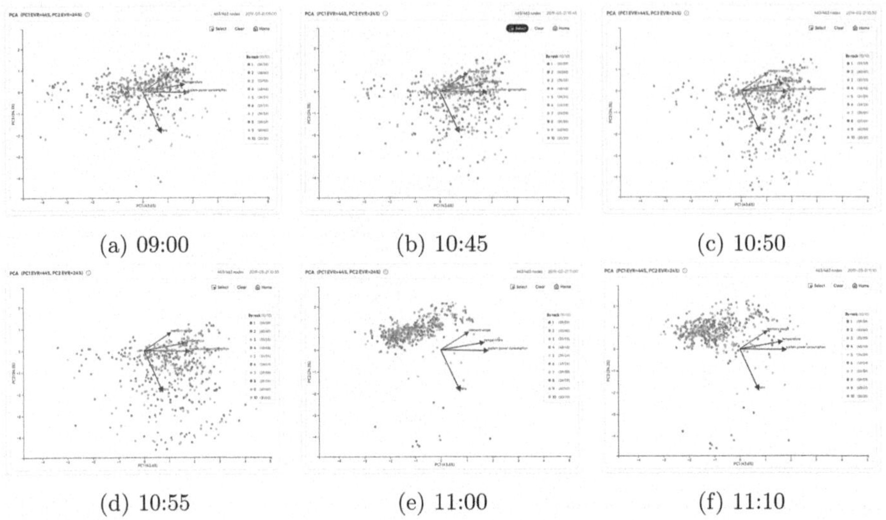

(a) 09:00 (b) 10:45 (c) 10:50

(d) 10:55 (e) 11:00 (f) 11:10

Fig. 8. Case 2 (Quanah, chilled-water). PCA snapshots of four node-level metrics across **463/463** nodes. at (a) 09:00, (b) 10:45, (c) 10:50, (d) 10:55, (e) 11:00, and (f) 11:10 on 21 March 2019 (CDT, UTC−5).

10:45 and **10:55** (Fig. 8(b,c,d)), it begins to drift in the +PC1 direction, indicating joint increases in `system_power_consumption` or `temperature` as the chilled-water disruption may develops, making temperature high. At **11:00** (Fig. 8(e)) a regime shift occurs: the cloud moves upward along PC2 while the `fans` loading points downward, implying reduced fan speed. This pattern persists through **11:10** (Fig. 8(f)).

Selecting the dominant cluster (radar view) confirms the trend at **11:00** (Fig. 9(a)) compared with **10:45** (Fig. 9(b)): `fans` drops suddenly and remains low through **11:10** (Fig. 9(c)).

And if we focus on the line plots in Fig. 10, which show the trend for the selected nodes in the major group from Fig. 9(a). `temperature` (Fig. 10(b)) starts higher from **10:45** to **10:55**. At **11:00**, all metrics except `memory_usage` are cut down (Fig. 10(a,b,c)). Because `fans` is cut down and chilled water is not available, we observe that at **11:05** and **11:10** `temperature` remains high for the few nodes still reporting, before sensors become unavailable as shutdown completes (Fig. 10(b,c)) for temperature and fans. `system_power_consumption` turns to 0 at **11:05** (Fig. 10(a)) as those nodes complete shutdown. Apparent non-zero `memory_usage` immediately after shutdown (Fig. 10(d)) reflects last-sample retention in the 5-minute aggregation window rather than true post-off usage, although some nodes do drop to 0.

Overall, we conclude that the chilled-water disruption begins around **10:45–10:50**, as temperatures start to rise; nodes start to cut off due to high temperature around **11:00**, and shutdown completes by **11:05–11:10**.

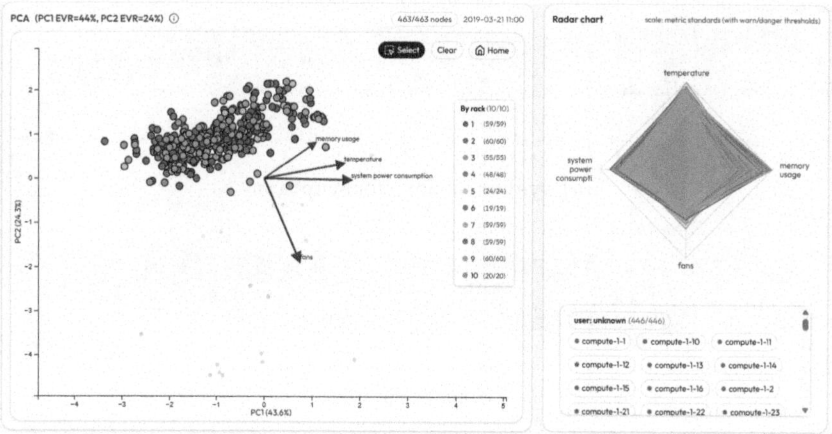

(a) 11:00

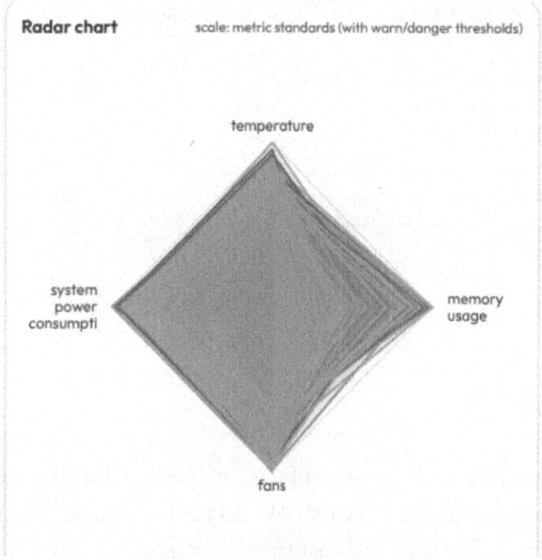

(b) 10:55

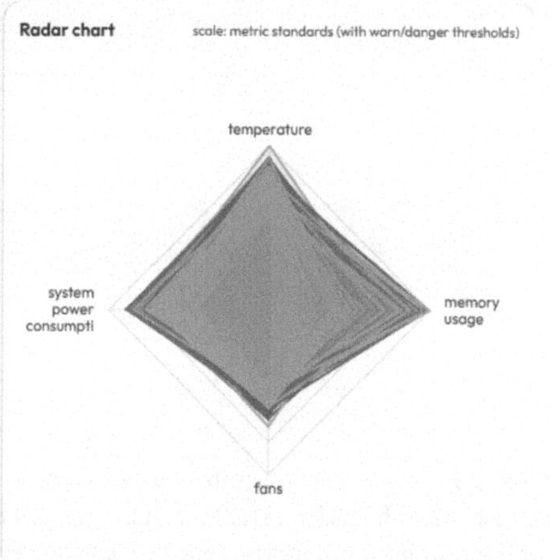

(c) 11:10

Fig. 9. Case 2 (Quanah, chilled-water). PCA snapshots of four node-level metrics with linked radar summaries across **463/463** nodes at (a) 11:00, (b) 10:55, (c) 11:10, on 21 March 2019 (CDT, UTC−5).

Scalability and Performance

Setup and Assumptions. Let n be the number of compute nodes, c the number of cores per node, t the number of time instants (temporal resolution/extent), m the number of metrics (dimensions), and k the number of jobs. In our setting, n is fixed by the cluster (each node has c cores), while t grows with finer sampling (e.g., 1 min vs. 5 s) or longer windows. The number of concurrently running jobs is bounded by the total number of cores, nc.

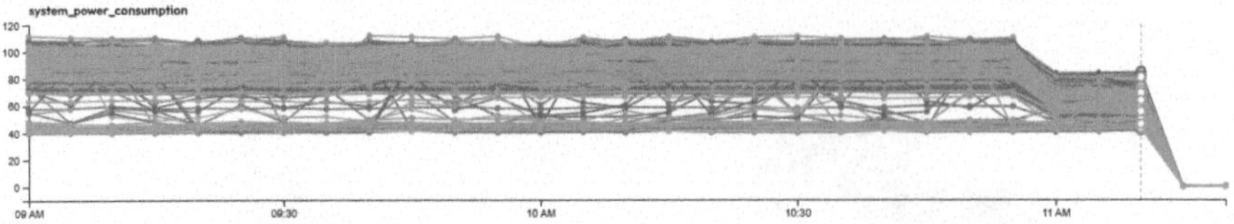

(a) `system_power_consumption`

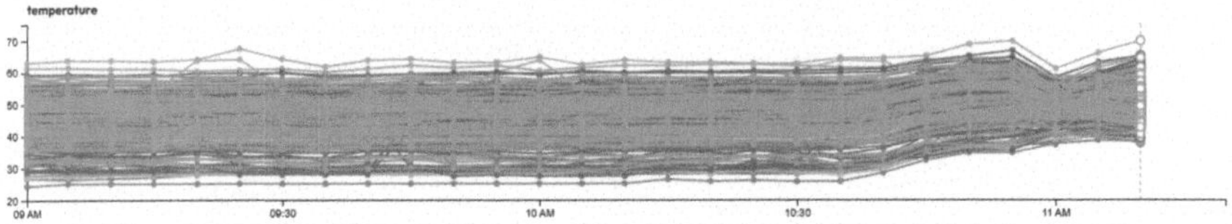

(b) `temperature`

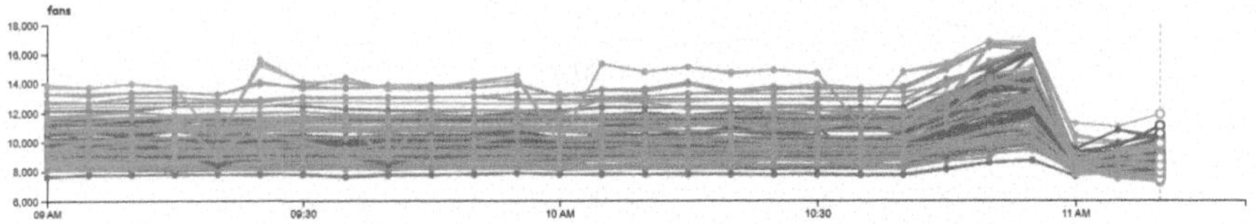

(c) `fans`

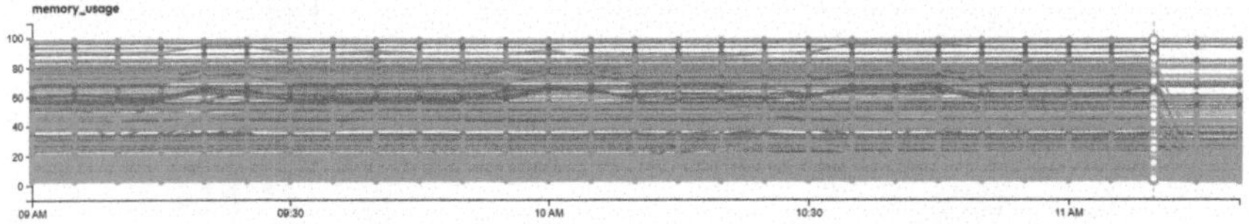

(d) `memory_usage`

Fig. 10. Case 2 (Quanah, chilled-water): node-level time series across **463** nodes on 21 March 2019 (CDT, UTC–5), with the selected time at **11:10**. Panels: (a) `system_power_consumption`, (b) `temperature`, (c) `fans`, (d) `memory_usage`.

PowerMap. For a single metric, computing per-cell values and thresholding over the full grid costs

$$\text{time} = O(nt), \qquad \text{memory} = O(nt).$$

Because n is fixed in our deployment, the observed runtime scales linearly in t (i.e., effectively $O(t)$ for our environment).

Job/User Provenance. Overlaying job or user assignments requires linking jobs to their allocated nodes. If job j spans n_j nodes, the construction cost is

$$O\left(\sum_{j=1}^{k} n_j\right),$$

i.e., linear in the number of job–node edges. In the worst case (each job spans all n nodes), this is $O(kn)$.

Rendering. Drawing the full node×time matrix requires $O(nt)$ rectangular cells. Overlaying provenance introduces an additional $O\left(\sum_{j=1}^{k} n_j\right)$ edges (one per job–node allocation), worst case $O(kn)$. Optional labels or legends contribute at most $O(k)$ primitives, which is negligible relative to cells and edges.

Time-Indexed PCA Trajectories. We compute a single PCA basis over the entire window by stacking all node–time samples into $X \in \mathbb{R}^{N \times m}$ with $N = nt$ (nodes × time) and m metrics. Following [6,21], the one-time costs are:

$$\text{accumulate } X^\top X : \ O(Nm^2), \qquad \text{eigendecomposition of } (m \times m) : \ O(m^3).$$

Memory. Storing X explicitly is $O(Nm)$.

Projection (2 PCs). Let $U_2 \in \mathbb{R}^{m \times 2}$ be the global PCA basis. Projecting a single time slice $X_\tau \in \mathbb{R}^{n \times m}$ costs

$$X_\tau U_2 : \ O(nm).$$

Rendering (worst case). Showing all trajectories over the full window entails: (i) projecting all t time slices once, costing $O(Nm)$ with $N = nt$; and (ii) drawing n polylines with t vertices each (i.e., $t-1$ segments and $t-1$ arrowheads) for a total of $2n(t-1)$ primitives, i.e., $O(nt)$ drawing time (constants suppressed). The total is therefore

$$O(Nm) + O(nt) \ = \ O(Nm + nt) \ = \ O(Nm) \quad \text{for } m \geq 2.$$

Note that the drawing cost is independent of m; only the projection step scales with m.

5 Conclusions and Future Work

In this paper, we presented two complementary visualization approaches for incident analysis in an HPC data center: (i) *PowerMap*, which provides a thresholded node–time view for single metrics with user/job provenance, and (ii) *Time-Indexed PCA Trajectories*, which jointly summarizes multiple metrics in a low-dimensional space with optional time-linked trajectories and drill-down (radar and line charts). Using a 48 h window (29–31 Jul 2025, UTC−05) on 110 CPU-only nodes, we analyzed a room-temperature incident on 30 Jul (15:00–18:00) and observed synchronized thermal exceedances, a cluster-wide rise in system power, and near-saturation CPU usage.

The provenance views indicate that many of the concurrently running jobs during the incident window were attributable to `user100049 (momaruf)`, broadly distributed across nodes. Time-Indexed PCA at 17:00 showed distinct user-colored clusters and loading vectors consistent with higher *cpu_usage*, *cpu_power*, and *temperature* for the affected group; radar and linked time-series views corroborated these patterns. Together, these results suggest that sustained heavy workload set the background conditions, and a facility-side temperature rise precipitated widespread thermal threshold crossings. We do not claim sole causality; rather, the combined evidence supports a workload–facility interaction during the event, potentially including a cooling-system disturbance.

Moreover, *Time-Indexed PCA Trajectories* can also investigate incidents when only node-level telemetry is available, as seen in the chilled-water incident on Quanah (Case 2) on 21 March 2019 from 09:00 to 11:20 (CDT, UTC−5). In this case (four metrics; no job/user records), PCA captured the event's progression: a rightward drift along PC1 around **10:45–10:55** (joint increases in `temperature` or `system_power_consumption`) indicating where the chilled-water disruption develops; followed by an upward shift along PC2 at **11:00**, opposite the `fans` loading (reduced fan speed) as nodes begin to cut off due to high temperature; and shutdown by **11:05–11:10** (power = 0, temperature/fan N/A). Apparent non-zero `memory_usage` immediately after shutdown reflects last-sample retention in the 5-minute aggregation window rather than true post-off usage.

Operationally, the proposed views enable faster triage, clearer attribution of load to users/jobs, and a better understanding of how multiple metrics contribute to performance and incident progression.

Both *PowerMap* and *Time-Indexed PCA* scale well for cluster telemetry: PowerMap is $O(nt)$ per metric for computation and up to $O(nt)$ to render the full grid; PCA has a one-time $O(Nm^2{+}m^3)$ setup (with $N = nt$) and $O(Nm)$ for full-window projection. Limitations include reliance on complete node-level telemetry (missing/corrupted data can mislead) and the fact that PCA reveals correlations, not causality—motivating the anomaly-detection and causal-analysis extensions discussed below. *(Here, n = nodes; t = time instants; m = metrics; $N = nt$.)*

In future work, we plan to: (i) add job- and user-focused drill-downs to the Time-Indexed PCA to support deeper forensic analysis; (ii) integrate streaming/alerts for near real-time use; (iii) incorporate additional facility signals (e.g., inlet air, rack-level sensors, HVAC control states); (iv) extend to GPU-equipped nodes; and (v) explore multivariate anomaly detection and causal analyses to distinguish workload-driven from facility-driven effects.

References

1. Grafana: The open platform for analytics and monitoring (2019). https://grafana.com/
2. Prometheus: Open-source monitoring solution (2025). https://prometheus.io/
3. Abdi, H., Williams, L.J.: Principal component analysis. Wiley Interdisc. Rev. Comput. Stat. **2**(4), 433–459 (2010)
4. Bostock, M., Ogievetsky, V., Heer, J.: D^3 data-driven documents. IEEE Trans. Visual Comput. Graphics **17**(12), 2301–2309 (2011)
5. Chakraborty, M., Kundan, A.P.: Grafana. In: Monitoring Cloud-Native Applications: Lead Agile Operations Confidently Using Open Source Software, pp. 187–240. Springer, Cham (2021). https://doi.org/10.1007/978-1-4842-6888-9

6. De Ketelaere, B., Hubert, M., Schmitt, E.: Overview of pca-based statistical process-monitoring methods for time-dependent, high-dimensional data. J. Qual. Technol. **47**(4), 318–335 (2015)
7. Del Rosario, E., et al.: Gauge: An interactive data-driven visualization tool for hpc application i/o performance analysis. In: 2020 IEEE/ACM Fifth International Parallel Data Systems Workshop (PDSW). pp. 15–21. IEEE (2020)
8. Gathu, S., et al.: High-performance computing and big data: emerging trends in advanced computing systems for data-intensive applications. J. Adv. Comput. Syst. **4**(8), 22–35 (2024)
9. Guo, J., Liu, Y., Li, K., Liu, Q.: Research on an id-pca early fault detection method for rolling bearings. Appl. Sci. **12**(9), 4267 (2022)
10. Halawa, M.S., Diaz Redondo, R.P., Fernández Vilas, A.: Unsupervised kpis-based clustering of jobs in hpc data centers. Sensors **20**(15), 4111 (2020)
11. Huang, Z., Liang, Z., Zhou, S., Zhang, S.: An improved density-based spatial clustering of applications with noise algorithm with an adaptive parameter based on the sparrow search algorithm. Algorithms **18**(5), 273 (2025)
12. Jafari, N., Lopes, A.: Fault detection and identification with kernel principal component analysis and long short-term memory artificial neural network combined method. Axioms **12**(6), 583 (2023)
13. Kitao, A.: Principal component analysis and related methods for investigating the dynamics of biological macromolecules. J. Biol. Macromol. **5**(2), 298–317 (2022)
14. Navaux, P.O.A., Lorenzon, A.F., da Silva Serpa, M.: Challenges in high-performance computing. J. Braz. Comput. Soc. **29**(1), 51–62 (2023)
15. Park, H., et al.: Hpc2lusterscape: increasing transparency and efficiency of shared high-performance computing clusters for large-scale ai models. In: 2023 IEEE Visualization in Data Science (VDS), pp. 21–29. IEEE (2023)
16. Peiris, M., Hill, J.H., Thelin, J., Bykov, S., Kliot, G., Konig, C.: Pad: Performance anomaly detection in multi-server distributed systems. In: 2014 IEEE 7th International Conference on Cloud Computing, pp. 769–776. IEEE (2014)
17. Shi, Z., Ma, D., Yan, X., Zhu, W., Zhao, Z.: A density-peak-based clustering method for multiple densities dataset. ISPRS Int. J. Geo Inf. **10**(9), 589 (2021)
18. Sterling, T., Brodowicz, M., Anderson, M.: High performance computing: modern systems and practices. Morgan Kaufmann (2017)
19. Thrun, M.C., Ultsch, A.: Using projection-based clustering to find distance- and density-based clusters in high-dimensional data. J. Classif. **38**(2), 280–312 (2021)
20. Tsutsumi, T., Ono, Y., Taketsugu, T.: Visualization of reaction route map and dynamical trajectory in reduced dimension. Chem. Commun. **57**(89), 11734–11750 (2021)
21. Yang, K., Shahabi, C.: A pca-based similarity measure for multivariate time series. In: Proceedings of the 2nd ACM international workshop on Multimedia databases, pp. 65–74 (2004)
22. Yin, F., Shi, F.: A comparative survey of big data computing and hpc: From a parallel programming model to a cluster architecture. Int. J. Parallel Prog. **50**, 27–64 (2022)
23. Yoo, A.B., Jette, M.A., Grondona, M.: Slurm: Simple linux utility for resource management. In: Feitelson, D., Rudolph, L., Schwiegelshohn, U. (eds.) Workshop on job scheduling strategies for parallel processing, pp. 44–60. Springer, Cham (2003). https://doi.org/10.1007/10968987_3
24. Zhou, N., Zhou, H., Hoppe, D.: Containerization for high performance computing systems: survey and prospects. IEEE Trans. Software Eng. **49**(4), 2722–2740 (2022)

AI-Powered Phishing Forensics: Detecting and Analyzing Social Engineering Attacks Using Machine Learning

Han N. Le(✉), Abdulrazaq Mamud, Kamryx Davis, and Lei Chen

Georgia Southern University, 30458 Statesboro, GA, Georgia
{nl06171,am47969,kd20540,lchen}@georgiasouthern.edu

Abstract. Phishing remains a growing cybersecurity threat, exploiting human vulnerabilities through deceptive communication tactics across platforms like email and social media. Traditional defenses such as firewalls and antivirus software are insufficient against these social engineering attacks, which now use AI-generated content and sophisticated deception to bypass detection. This research presents a lightweight browser-based prototype for real-time phishing detection, using machine learning techniques based on TF-IDF vectorization and a Naive Bayes classifier. Unlike large language model-based tools, the proposed solution is optimized for efficiency, speed, and accessibility. With a strong testing accuracy of 91% on independent datasets, the tool provides explainable results, supports email and attachment analysis, and offers educational feedback to improve user awareness. It is designed to run in real-time browser environments, balancing usability, transparency, and performance.

Keywords: Phishing · Cybersecurity · Social Engineering · Artificial Intelligence (AI) · Machine Learning (ML) · Browser prototype · Naive Bayes · Term Frequency-Inverse Document Frequency (TF-IDF) · Email Security

1 Introduction

Phishing is a global issue and rising threat, in just one year alone phishing cost the world over $9 billion in losses [1]. These social engineering attacks are becoming more frequent, sophisticated, and damaging from their original debut in 1996 on AOL accounts. What makes phishing so dangerous is that it targets people, not just technology, making proactive traditional measures such as firewalls, encryption, and antivirus software not enough to defend against these attacks. Humans are among the "weakest defenses against cyberattacks" [2]. Approximately 80% of cybercrimes began with social engineering in 2020 [3]. In social engineering attacks, hackers exploit human psychology to acquire sensitive information and gain unauthorized access to systems. This includes taking advantage of human characteristics such as curiosity, fear, trusting nature, lack of knowledge or awareness, and cognitive biases. Even experienced cybersecurity professionals can fall prey to sophisticated social engineering attacks [4]. Phishing is one

V. V. Pham et al. (Eds.): CIDDF 2025, ACSAR 5, pp. 198–212, 2026.
https://doi.org/10.1007/978-3-032-19488-6_13

of the most common types of social engineering attacks, which utilize deceptive communication tactics. E-mail phishing messages containing malicious links are one of the most popular phishing methods. Additional forms of phishing attacks include smishing, phishing over text messages, whaling, phishing that targets executives at companies, spear phishing which are personalized phishing attacks, and social media phishing which involves phishing over platforms such as Instagram and Facebook [4]. With these complex, adaptive, and varying phishing attacks, adaptive countermeasures are needed to help analyze and prevent these attacks. This can be done utilizing artificial intelligence (AI), a branch of computer science that focuses on machines and computers mimicking human behaviors and abilities. The goal of AI is to create systems that can think, learn, solve problems, and make decisions. Machine learning is a subset of AI that teaches computers to learn from data without explicit instructions. AI models can be trained to analyze and adapt to emerging threats along with accurately responding to cyberattacks in real time. By implementing AI into the analysis and detection of social engineering attacks, the impact of these devastating attacks can greatly be reduced. To achieve this goal, this paper explores AI and machine learning techniques to develop a browser-based prototype for real-time analysis and detection of phishing attempts, that also focuses on enhancing user cybersecurity awareness.

2 Background and Problem Statement

Phishing attacks have significantly evolved over the past two decades. What began as basic email scams has developed into complex, socially engineered threats that exploit psychological and technological vulnerabilities across digital platforms. As reliance on email, cloud tools, and social media grows, so does the number of entry points for attackers. This expanded surface has reduced the effectiveness of traditional methods like blacklists and rule-based filters. Modern phishing campaigns now use obfuscated URLs, convincing brand impersonation, urgency tactics, and AI-generated personalized content to improve success rates. In response, researchers have turned to machine learning (ML), natural language processing (NLP), and large language models (LLMs) to increase detection accuracy and adaptability. These tools can recognize subtle linguistic patterns, detect abnormal link structures, and generate human-readable justifications. However, many AI-based solutions struggle to function in lightweight, real-time environments such as browser extensions. Additionally, most systems lack transparency, provide little user education, and are confined to specific platforms. As phishing threats continue to advance, there is a clear need for a cross-platform, explainable solution that offers real-time protection and promotes user awareness.

While AI has advanced phishing detection, current solutions still fall short in addressing the complexity of today's attacks. Many models are too resource-heavy for real-time use, lack platform flexibility, or fail to offer helpful, user-centered feedback. Browser-based detection tools remain limited, especially those that combine high accuracy with explainability and education. Moreover, most systems are trained on narrow, email-only datasets, reducing their ability to detect phishing on social media and newer platforms. Users often receive vague or overly technical alerts that erode trust and may be ignored. These issues hinder the broader adoption of effective cybersecurity, particularly among non-technical users. To address this, our research proposes a modular, browser-based AI prototype that uses traditional machine learning classifiers such as Naive Bayes for phishing detection across email and social media, while also offering real-time educational feedback.

3 Literature Review

The escalating dynamics between cyber attackers and defenders in the phishing landscape have led to the development of increasingly advanced artificial intelligence systems. This literature review integrates findings from twelve peer-reviewed studies that form the conceptual and technical foundation of the proposed solution. These studies span the fields of machine learning, deep learning, natural language processing (NLP), and explainable AI, illustrating a shift in phishing detection from basic URL filtering methods to intelligent, user-focused systems capable of real-time interaction.

Initial approaches to phishing detection concentrated on email content and header analysis. Gupta et al. [5] addressed this challenge using an ensemble learning model that examined both the textual content and metadata of emails. Although their system delivered high accuracy, it relied significantly on manual feature engineering. This dependence reduced its flexibility against evolving techniques such as obfuscated URLs and convincing fake branding, highlighting the need for more adaptable solutions requiring minimal human input.

To handle the issue of URL manipulation, Basnet et al. [6] developed a deep learning model based on character-level features. Their work showed how attackers use typo squatting and homograph attacks to mislead users. By detecting subtle lexical anomalies, the model successfully identified URLs crafted to resemble legitimate domains. This finding supports the inclusion of CharacterBERT in our system, as it is designed to process character-level inputs for phishing detection.

Large language models have also significantly influenced the phishing detection field. Koide et al. [7] examined the effectiveness of GPT-4 in identifying phishing attempts and reported a 99.7% accuracy rate. In addition to performance, the model provided natural-language explanations for each classification, improving interpretability. However, its high latency and computational demands made it less suitable for real-time deployment. These limitations led us to adopt a hybrid model that includes a lightweight browser interface supported by backend GPT-4 prompts optimized for speed.

While Koide et al. [7] demonstrated the high accuracy of GPT-4, its computational cost and latency often exceeded 10 s per email, which makes it impractical for lightweight, browser-based deployment. In light of these limitations, our system adopts a more efficient traditional machine learning approach using TF-IDF vectorization and a Multinomial Naive Bayes classifier. This model strikes a balance between speed and accuracy, achieving 91% accuracy on real-world test data while remaining fast enough for real-time use in browser environments. Although it does not replicate GPT-4's scale, this design supports our goal of delivering explainable and responsive phishing detection to everyday users.

Explainability remains a key challenge in phishing detection. Madisetty and Desarkar [8] addressed this issue with an attention-based model that visually indicated the parts of a message contributing to its classification. Their user study found that such transparency enhanced both trust and user engagement. Building on this, our system includes rationales and pop-up tips designed to help users understand phishing warnings more effectively.

Wang et al. [9] proposed a "deep learning model combining convolutional neural networks (CNN)" with "bidirectional long short-term memory (BiLSTM)" layers. While their architecture performed well across phishing emails and fake websites, it was computationally demanding and lacked scalability. These limitations make it unsuitable for browser-based implementation, reinforcing the importance of modular and efficient system design.

In the realm of traditional machine learning, Almomani et al. [10] used a two-layer pipeline featuring support vector machines and random forest algorithms to evaluate URL characteristics. Though their method was resilient to common phishing strategies, it was static and did not adapt to new forms of attacks. This illustrates the importance of continual learning and the ability to respond to emerging threats in real time, especially on rapidly evolving platforms like social media.

Zhou et al. [11] examined the feasibility of deploying AI models in constrained environments such as browser extensions. Their study showed that lightweight or hybrid models, which distribute computation between the client and server, achieved the best performance. These insights directly influenced our architectural approach, which leverages client-side JavaScript for the interface and Python-based AI models on the backend.

From an educational standpoint, Raj et al. [12] explored the impact of embedding real-time instructional content within phishing alerts. Their research demonstrated that users who received brief, context-specific information were less likely to fall for phishing attempts. This supports our inclusion of educational pop-ups in the prototype, aimed at enhancing immediate detection and fostering long-term user awareness.

Phishing techniques have extended beyond traditional email. Chiew et al. [13] focused on phishing through social media platforms, particularly private messaging systems. They found that impersonation and the use of shortened links were widespread. A key contribution of their work was the emphasis on cross-platform detection, which remains an area often neglected in existing tools. Our system addresses this gap by enabling detection capabilities across both email and social media platforms.

Scalability, while critical, brings its own challenges. Huang and Liu [14] proposed a cloud-based machine learning service that allowed for efficient phishing detection at scale. However, their approach raised concerns about user privacy, as it required transferring personal data to external servers. In contrast, our system emphasizes local processing within the browser to maintain user privacy without sacrificing accuracy.

Zhang and Lee [15] improved phishing detection by fine-tuning transformer models on specialized phishing datasets. Their model provided both threat classification and brief educational feedback, demonstrating that language models can serve dual purposes as detectors and communicators. This dual function aligns with our philosophy of integrating explainable AI into the user experience.

Finally, Siddiqui et al. [16] introduced a multi-layer system that combined heuristic filters with machine learning classifiers. While highly accurate, their architecture was rigid and tied to specific platforms. This underlined the importance of building modular and platform-agnostic systems, a principle we followed closely during the development of our tool.

Together, these twelve studies trace the progression of phishing defense from rule-based techniques to adaptive, explainable, and user-aware AI systems. Despite significant advances, common issues remain limited real-time processing, lack of transparency, platform restrictions, and weak user engagement. Our proposed browser extension addresses these shortcomings by combining real-time detection, NLP, and explainable AI across both email and social media platforms, while simultaneously enhancing user education and awareness.

4 Research Methodology

This methodology integrates findings from a comprehensive review of twelve studies (2020–2024) on phishing detection using machine learning (ML), natural language processing (NLP), and large language models (LLMs).

4.1 Research Focus

This research focused on developing and evaluating a real-time phishing detection system, specifically through a browser-based prototype. The work centered on four key activities:

1. **Dataset Collection and Preparation**: Verified phishing URLs were collected from the PhishTank database, and a curated list of safe URLs was compiled from reputable sources to create a balanced training dataset. For testing, an independent dataset from Kaggle [18] was used to ensure unbiased model evaluation.
2. **Model Development and Training**: A lightweight phishing detection model was built using TF-IDF vectorization and a Multinomial Naive Bayes classifier. The model was trained to detect phishing attempts based on URL structures and text patterns, achieving perfect accuracy on the training set and 91% accuracy on the Kaggle test set.
3. **Tool Design and Implementation**: A user-facing browser tool was developed with support for both light and dark modes. It allows users to analyze suspicious URLs found in emails or attachments, providing fast and accurate phishing predictions directly within the browser.
4. **Evaluation and Performance Analysis**: The system was evaluated using real-world, balanced data to test its ability to generalize beyond the training domain. Performance metrics such as precision, recall, and F1-score were used to validate the model's effectiveness and readiness for practical deployment.

4.2 Proposed Prototype

The proposed solution is a prototype phishing detection tool designed to operate in real time by analyzing suspicious URLs from emails and attachments. At its core is a machine learning model trained on a combined dataset of verified phishing URLs from PhishTank and a curated list of legitimate URLs collected from trusted sources. This balanced training data enables the model to accurately differentiate between phishing and safe URLs in diverse scenarios.

The prototype features a clean, user-friendly interface with support for both light and dark modes to enhance usability and accessibility. Users can submit suspicious emails or files, and the system extracts and evaluates embedded URLs using a lightweight TF-IDF+Naive Bayes classification model. Results are returned instantly, indicating whether the content is safe or potentially malicious.

Unlike many traditional phishing detection tools that rely solely on rule-based filters or static blacklists, this prototype takes a more flexible and data-driven approach. It leverages natural language patterns within URLs and offers broader phishing detection capabilities, extending beyond superficial pattern matching. Although the current version focuses on URL-based detection, the prototype architecture is modular and designed to support future extensions such as deeper attachment analysis or email body scanning.

Optimized for low resource consumption, the model is suitable for deployment within browser environments without introducing noticeable performance delays. This combination of efficiency, adaptability, and transparency makes the tool a practical and forward-thinking solution for modern phishing threats.

The prototype is available at https://detectratool.onrender.com/. Screenshots of the interface are shown in Figs. 1–5.

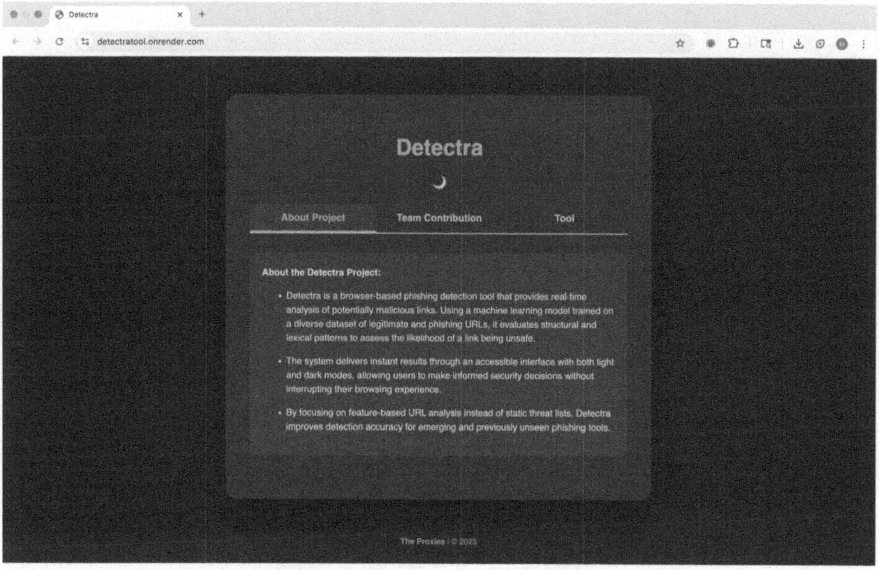

Fig. 1 Overview of the Detectra browser-based phishing detection interface displaying the project description and system features.

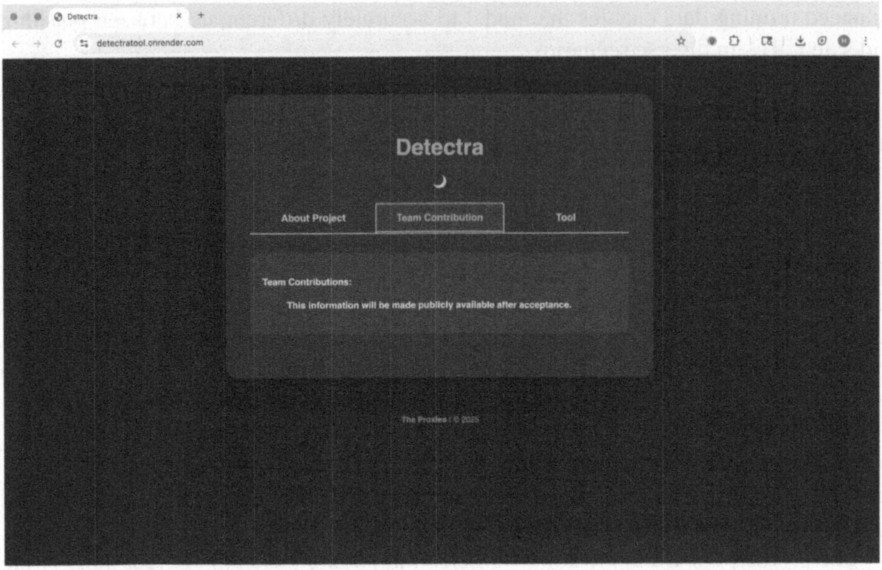

Fig. 2 Team contribution section of the Detectra interface, illustrating collaborative development information within the prototype.

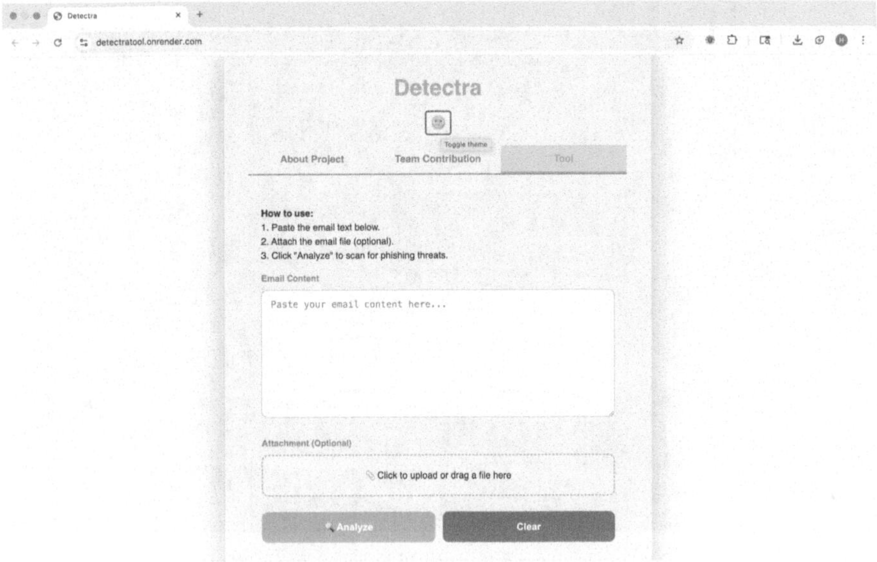

Fig. 3 User input interface allowing entry of email content and optional file attachment for phishing analysis.

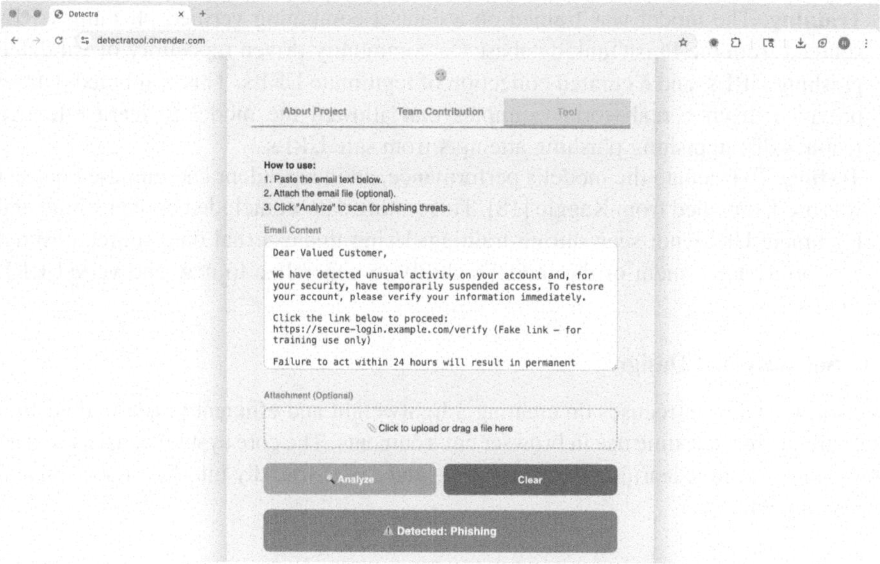

Fig. 4 Example of phishing detection result, where the system identifies malicious content and provides a warning to the user.

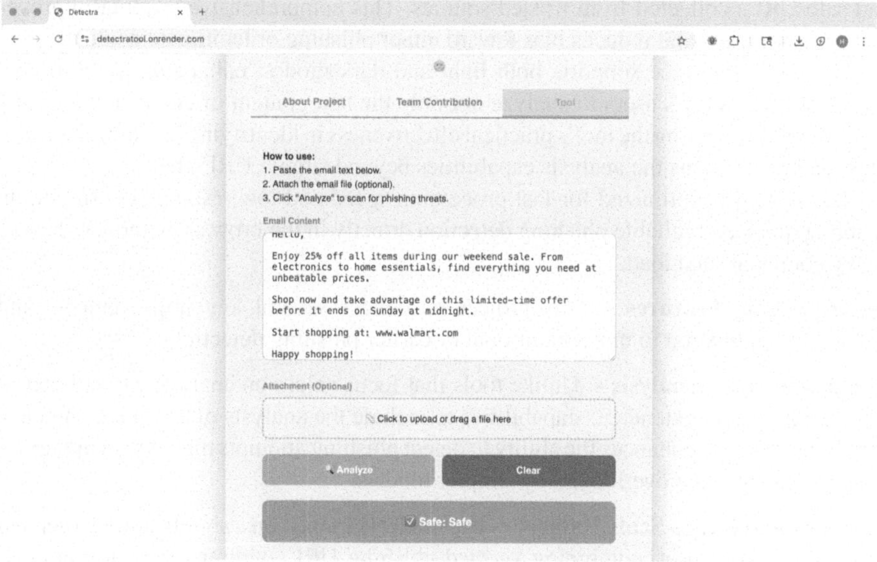

Fig. 5 Example of legitimate content detection, where the system classifies the input as safe and provides user feedback.

4.3 Tools and Datasets

The project integrates multiple components:

- **Training**: The model was trained on a dataset combining verified phishing URLs sourced from the PhishTank database - a community-driven repository of validated phishing URLs, and a curated collection of legitimate URLs. This combined dataset provided diverse, real-world examples that allowed the model to learn effective features distinguishing phishing attempts from safe URLs.
- **Testing**: To evaluate the model's performance, an independent and unbiased dataset was used, obtained from Kaggle [18]. This testing dataset included both phishing and legitimate URLs not seen during training. Using this external data source ensured a rigorous assessment of the model's ability to generalize to new and varied URL samples.

4.4 Software and Design

The software design focuses on creating a lightweight and efficient phishing detection tool suitable for real-time use in browser environments. The core system consists of data processing, machine learning model training, and a user-friendly interface for email and attachment analysis.

4.5 Model and Data

The detection model is based on TF-IDF vectorization combined with a Multinomial Naive Bayes classifier, trained on a large, balanced dataset of verified phishing URLs and safe URLs collected from trusted sources. This comprehensive training improves detection accuracy and reduces bias toward either phishing or legitimate content.

The tool's interface supports both light and dark modes, enhancing usability and accessibility. It allows users to analyze not only the text content of emails but also any attachments, increasing the tool's practical effectiveness in identifying phishing attempts. This feature broadens the analysis capabilities beyond simple URL checks.

The system is optimized for fast processing speed and low resource consumption, enabling quick and reliable phishing detection directly in the browser without delays or heavy computational load.

Distinguishing Features - This project introduces several key improvements and distinctions compared to more traditional or earlier phishing detection tools:

Expanded Input Analysis - Unlike tools that focus solely on analyzing email text or URLs, this system extends its capabilities to include the analysis of email attachments. This broader scope enhances the ability to detect phishing attempts that rely on malicious files, which are often overlooked by simpler models.

Balanced and Large-Scale Dataset - The model is trained on a significantly larger and more balanced dataset, combining verified phishing URLs with a substantial number of legitimate URLs. This balanced training reduces bias, improves generalization, and provides more reliable detection performance across diverse phishing techniques and benign content.

User-Centered Interface with Enhanced Usability – The interface includes user-friendly features such as light and dark modes, allowing users to customize their experience for better readability and comfort. This attention to user experience makes the tool more accessible and practical for everyday use, addressing common issues with less flexible designs.

Lightweight and Efficient Model - The detection model prioritizes computational efficiency to enable real-time analysis without taxing system resources. This design consideration ensures fast response times and seamless integration within browser environments, which is critical for practical deployment.

Versatility Across Content Types - By supporting both text and attachments, the tool provides a more comprehensive phishing detection solution suitable for the complex tactics used by attackers today. This versatility distinguishes it from earlier methods that may be limited to single data types or static rule sets.

Together, these advancements represent a meaningful step forward in phishing detection technology by combining broader analytical scope, better data preparation, improved user experience, and efficient performance. This comprehensive approach makes the tool well-suited for real-world cybersecurity challenges.

4.6 Ethics and Privacy

Data privacy is a critical concern in cybersecurity, with 86% of individuals expressing a desire for greater control over their personal information [Cisco, 2021].

This phishing detection system was developed with a strong emphasis on ethical data handling and user trust. The tool processes emails and URLs using models trained on publicly available, community-verified datasets such as PhishTank and Kaggle, rather than user-submitted content.

All data transmitted from users' browsers to the server is securely encrypted and never stored in a persistent database. Furthermore, the system avoids the use of cookies and other tracking technologies.

Clear, transparent information about these privacy practices is intended to be shared with users in accessible language, ensuring they understand how their data is used and protected. This commitment to responsible design supports broader adoption and reinforces trust in the system's safety and purpose.

4.7 Testing

The phishing detection model was trained on a combined dataset consisting of verified phishing URLs from the PhishTank database and a corresponding set of safe URLs collected from reputable sources. This combined training set included a total of 10,409 URLs. The model achieved perfect classification performance on this dataset, with precision, recall, and F1-score all reaching 1.00, demonstrating that the model learned to distinguish phishing from legitimate URLs with complete accuracy within the training domain. Table 1 summarizes the training data performance:

```
Classification report:
              precision    recall  f1-score   support

           1       1.00      1.00      1.00     10409

    accuracy                           1.00     10409
   macro avg       1.00      1.00      1.00     10409
weighted avg       1.00      1.00      1.00     10409
```

Table 1. Summarizes the training set performance metrics.

Metric	Value
Precision	1.00
Recall	1.00
F1-Score	1.00
Support	10,409

For an unbiased evaluation, the model was tested on an independent Kaggle dataset comprising 3,772 URLs [18], evenly split between phishing and legitimate samples. This external test set enabled validation of the model's generalization capabilities beyond the training data. Table 2 presents the distribution of the test dataset:

During testing, the URLs were vectorized using TF-IDF (Term Frequency-Inverse Document Frequency) to capture relevant textual features. The trained Multinomial Naive Bayes model then classified each URL as either phishing or legitimate.

The model achieved an overall accuracy of approximately 91%, indicating strong capability in correctly identifying phishing URLs while minimizing false positives. Detailed performance metrics such as precision, recall, and F1-score were calculated for both classes to provide a comprehensive view of the model's effectiveness:

```
Accuracy: 0.9093319194061505
              precision    recall  f1-score   support

           0       0.91      0.91      0.91      1886
           1       0.91      0.91      0.91      1886

    accuracy                           0.91      3772
   macro avg       0.91      0.91      0.91      3772
weighted avg       0.91      0.91      0.91      3772
```

Table 2. Summarizes the results of the test.

Class	Precision	Recall	F1-Score	Support
Legitimate	0.91	0.91	0.91	1,886
Phishing	0.91	0.91	0.91	1,886

These results demonstrate that the model generalizes well to unseen data and can effectively differentiate between phishing and safe URLs. The balanced test dataset and the use of a large number of real-world URLs provide confidence that the model will perform reliably in practical cybersecurity applications.

5 Findings and Discussions

5.1 Expected Results

The phishing detection tool achieved approximately 91% accuracy on a balanced external test dataset sourced from Kaggle [18], demonstrating effective identification of phishing URLs while maintaining a low false positive rate. This performance, while slightly below the near-perfect accuracies reported for large language models such as GPT-4 (99.7%) [7], represents a strong baseline for lightweight, efficient detection suitable for real-time browser deployment. Educational pop-ups integrated into the tool are expected to enhance user awareness of phishing tactics and promote safer browsing behavior. Designed for low-latency, real-time detection in high-volume environments, the tool also provides transparent classification rationales to foster user trust.

5.2 Discussion

The literature confirms that state-of-the-art machine learning and large language models (LLMs) like GPT-4 and CharacterBERT achieve phishing detection accuracies ranging from 99.3% to 99.7% for emails and URLs [7, 17]. However, these models often require substantial computational resources and may not be practical for all deployment environments. In contrast, our model based on TF-IDF vectorization and a Multinomial Naive Bayes classifier, provides a more computationally efficient alternative with a solid 91% accuracy on unseen data, balancing performance and resource demands.

Key considerations include:

- **Deployment:** Our model's efficiency allows fast processing suitable for real-time prototype, overcoming the latency challenges faced by LLMs like GPT-4, which have reported latencies of around 12 s per email [3].
- **Scalability:** While trained on verified phishing URLs from PhishTank combined with legitimate URLs, the model's generalization was validated using a large independent Kaggle dataset, supporting its applicability to varied real-world phishing attempts. However, ongoing expansion of datasets to incorporate broader attack vectors remains important.

5.3 Limitations

Some of the limitations are:

- The 91% accuracy indicates room for improvement, particularly to reduce false positives/negatives in high-stakes environments.
- The current focus on URL-based phishing detection does not address other common phishing tactics such as malicious attachments or social engineering without URLs.
- The datasets used, while balanced and sizable, may not fully capture the diversity of emerging phishing methods, warranting continuous data updates.
- Real-world deployment and user interaction testing remain necessary to assess the tool's usability and impact on phishing prevention.

5.4 Recommendations

To further enhance the tool's effectiveness and adoption, the following strategies are recommended:

- **Model Optimization:** Explore hybrid models or ensemble methods that maintain computational efficiency while improving detection accuracy beyond 91%.
- **Dataset Expansion:** Incorporate more diverse and dynamic datasets, including phishing attempts involving attachments, multilingual content, and emerging tactics, to improve generalizability.
- **User Experience Design:** Implement clear, actionable notifications with educational content to reduce alert fatigue and foster user trust.
- **Pilot Studies:** Conduct real-world pilot testing in organizational or educational settings to evaluate performance and gather user feedback for iterative improvements.
- **Collaboration and Continuous Learning:** Partner with cybersecurity communities to leverage shared threat intelligence and integrate AI-driven honeypots that allow the model to adapt to new phishing tactics in real time.
- **Complementary Approaches:** Consider combining this lightweight approach with optional cloud-based LLM analysis for high-risk emails, balancing accuracy and resource use.

6 Future Work and Considerations

Future development of this phishing detection tool can focus on several important areas. One key direction is expanding compatibility across different browsers and platforms, including mobile environments. While the current system is optimized for desktop browser use, phishing attacks also target mobile users, so future iterations should ensure full cross-platform support.

Another improvement involves enhancing the detection capabilities by integrating more diverse and frequently updated phishing datasets, such as real-time threat feeds or crowd-sourced repositories. This would allow the system to detect newly emerging phishing strategies more effectively and maintain high accuracy over time.

Incorporating more granular analysis, such as user behavior patterns and contextual email features, may also improve the system's precision. For example, analyzing sender behavior or user engagement with suspicious content could help fine-tune the alert mechanism and reduce false positives without sacrificing security.

Scalability and performance remain critical, especially if the prototype is to be deployed at scale. While the current model is lightweight and performs well with minimal resources, future versions should maintain fast response times and efficient memory use even when analyzing large volumes of data.

Finally, ethical and privacy considerations must remain central. Although the system does not store user data or use cookies, future enhancements should continue to emphasize transparency and privacy compliance. If behavioral analytics or more advanced data tracking features are introduced, clear privacy policies and user consent mechanisms will be essential to build and retain user trust.

7 Conclusion

This research demonstrates that a lightweight, browser-based phishing detection tool can effectively identify phishing URLs using machine learning. The trained model based on TF-IDF and Multinomial Naive Bayes achieved 100% accuracy on the training data (10,409 URLs) and maintained strong generalization performance with a 91% accuracy on an independent Kaggle test set of 3,772 URLs. These results validate the model's ability to distinguish between phishing and legitimate content in real-world scenarios.

Unlike more resource-intensive approaches that rely on large language models like GPT-4, this project prioritized speed, simplicity, and efficiency. The prototype offers real-time classification with minimal system load and a user-friendly interface supporting both email text and attachment analysis.

While the tool currently focuses on URL-based phishing detection, its modular design allows for future integration of additional threat vectors, such as attachment analysis, image-based phishing, or deepfake threats. As phishing tactics evolve, ongoing updates, real-world deployment testing, and user feedback will be essential to ensure continued effectiveness.

By combining practical machine learning techniques with a privacy-conscious design, this project lays a strong foundation for deploying accessible, real-time phishing protection tools that can serve both individual users and organizations.

Acknowledgement. This work was supported in part by the National Science Foundation under Grant No. 2321939. Any opinions, findings, and conclusions or recommendations expressed in this material are those of the author(s) and do not necessarily reflect the views of the National Science Foundation.

References

1. Basit, A., Zafar, M., Liu, X., Javed, A.R., Jalil, Z., Kifayat, K.: A comprehensive survey of AI-enabled phishing attacks detection techniques. Telecommun. Syst. **76**(1), 139–154 (2020)
2. Happy, F., Asheshemi, O., Jeremiah, E.: Human vulnerabilities in cybersecurity: analyzing social engineering attacks and AI-driven machine learning countermeasures. J. Sci. Technol. **30**(1), 73–84 (2025)

3. Abualhija, M., Al-Shaf'i, N., Turab, N.M., Hussein, A.: Encountering social engineering activities with a novel honeypot mechanism. Int. J. Electr. Comput. Eng. (2088–8708) **13**(6), 7056–7064 (2023)
4. Schmitt, M., Flechais, I.: Digital deception: generative artificial intelligence in social engineering and phishing. Artif. Intell. Rev. **57**(12), 1–23 (2024)
5. Gupta, A., Gupta, M., Singhal, A.: Phishing email detection using ensemble learning techniques. Procedia Comput. Sci. **132**, 900–906 (2018)
6. Basnet, R., Mukkamala, S., Sung, A.H.: Detection of phishing attacks: a machine learning approach. In: Soft Computing Applications in Industry, pp. 373–383. Springer (2008)
7. Koide, H., Matsuo, Y., Ishiguro, M.: GPT-4 for phishing detection: opportunities and limitations. J. Cybersecur. AI **4**(2), 41–55 (2023)
8. Madisetty, V.S., Desarkar, S.: A neural network-based phishing detection system using attention mechanism. IEEE Access **9**, 56566–56577 (2021)
9. Wang, D., Zhang, Q., Li, J., Chen, Y.: Phishing detection using a hybrid deep learning model. IEEE Access **8**, 150560–150572 (2020)
10. Almomani, A., Gupta, B.B., Atawneh, S., Meulenberg, A., Alauthman, E.: A survey of phishing email filtering techniques. IEEE Commun. Surv. Tutor. **15**(4), 2070–2090 (2013)
11. Zhou, J., Liu, P., Chen, L.: Performance evaluation of lightweight ML models for phishing detection in browser plug-ins. Int. J. Inf. Secur. **21**(1), 33–48 (2022)
12. Raj, R., Abraham, D., Menon, M.: Integrating microlearning with phishing detection: a user-centric approach. In: Proceedings of the 2022 ACM Conference on Human Factors in Computing Systems (CHI), New Orleans, USA, pp. 1–13 (2022)
13. Chiew, K.L., Yong, S.P., Tan, C.H.: A survey of phishing attacks on social media. Comput. Secur. **70**, 1–15 (2017)
14. Huang, C., Liu, F.: Scalable phishing detection using cloud-based ML pipelines: privacy challenges and solutions. IEEE Cloud Comput. **9**(1), 47–56 (2022)
15. Zhang, Y., Lee, W.: Language model-driven phishing email detection and explanation. J. Intell. Inf. Syst. **59**, 113–128 (2023)
16. Siddiqui, A., Khan, M., Khan, R.: Multi-layered approach for detecting phishing attacks using machine learning and heuristics. J. Inf. Secur. Appl. **54**, 102–112 (2020)
17. Almousa, M., Anwar, M.: A URL-based social semantic attacks detection with character-aware language model. IEEE Access **11**, 10654–10661 (2023)
18. Pingali, H.: Phishing URL dataset. Kaggle (2022). https://www.kaggle.com/datasets/hemanthpingali/phishing-url

A Survey on the Integration of Multimodal Techniques for Visual Artifact Detection: Advancing Lip–Speech Synchronization and Facial Recognition

Pamela Kirui(✉) and Bing Zhou

Department of Computer Science, Sam Houston State University, Huntsville, TX, USA
{pck008,bxz003}@shsu.edu

Abstract. Deepfake technology has emerged as a double-edged sword enabling creative innovation while posing serious risks to digital security and public trust. Powered by advanced generative models like GANs and diffusion networks, deepfakes have become increasingly difficult to detect. This paper explores the evolution of these techniques with a focus on audio-visual forgeries and their detection. We highlight lip-speech synchronization analysis as a powerful yet underutilized tool, capable of revealing subtle desynchronization artifacts, such as phoneme-lip mismatches and unnatural motion, often missed by traditional visual methods. A comprehensive review of detection strategies across visual, audio-visual, and text-visual modalities is presented. Benchmark datasets (FaceForensics++, DFDC, FakeAVCeleb, WildDeepfake) are examined. Finally, we discuss future research directions. By focusing on lip–speech synchronization inconsistencies, an area where generative models still struggle to achieve perfection, this work identifies promising approaches for enhancing the overall effectiveness of deepfake detection.

Keywords: Deepfake detection · Multimodal techniques · Visual artifacts · Lip–speech synchronization · Facial recognition

1 Introduction

Deepfake technology powered by advanced generative models like Generative Adversarial Networks (GANs) [34] and Autoencoders [77] has led to significant advancements in digital content creation. These techniques have facilitated the generation of hyper-realistic synthetic media, known as deepfakes, which are manipulated videos, images, or audio designed to resemble real-world scenarios. While these technologies have legitimate uses in fields such as virtual reality, entertainment, and communications, their misuse has raised significant concerns. Deepfakes have been exploited for political manipulation, identity theft, cybersecurity threats and the spread of misinformation which has made their detection

V. V. Pham et al. (Eds.): CIDDF 2025, ACSAR 5, pp. 213–230, 2026.
https://doi.org/10.1007/978-3-032-19488-6_14

a pressing issue [9,47,74]. Traditional detection systems, which largely rely on visual cues like texture distortions, facial inconsistencies, or spatial inconsistencies, are increasingly ineffective at distinguishing between high-quality deepfakes and authentic content. This is because modern deepfake generation methods preserve realistic facial features and lighting conditions, making them difficult to detect using visual cues alone. One area where deepfake models continue to struggle is in achieving accurate synchronization between video and audio, particularly in facial reenactment and lip-syncing. Misalignment between lip movements and phoneme alignment often leads to subtle, but noticeable discrepancies that serve as a critical indicator of manipulation. These discrepancies can manifest in mismatched phoneme-lip pairs [57], unnatural facial expressions, or irregular motion dynamics, which can be easily detected through automated systems that analyze the synchronization of audio and visual signals [60]. In particular, identifying lip-speech synchronization errors and facial inconsistencies has become a promising approach to detecting deepfakes [52,86]. Lip-speech synchronization analysis offers a more reliable method for detecting deepfakes, especially in cases where visual anomalies are minimal or absent [6,16,43]. By leveraging the correlation between lip movements and audio phoneme timing, this approach can uncover subtle discrepancies that are difficult to notice with the naked eye [5,84].

1.1 Background and Relevance

The growing reliance on digital communication and governance operations has made the threats posed by deepfakes more alarming. During the COVID-19 pandemic, manipulated videos and audio clips circulated widely, spreading false information about the virus and vaccines, which led to mass vaccine hesitancy [69]. Likewise, political leaders' deepfake videos, i.e., those of President Biden as well as Ukrainian President Volodymyr Zelenskyy, have been utilized in attempts at deceiving the population as well as shaping political decisions [23]. Deepfakes have also been used to target individuals in financially damaging ways. In one case, a CEO was scammed into transferring $243,000 after receiving a phone call generated by voice cloning software that perfectly mimicked his boss [15]. In another instance, DeepNude software was used to create fake pornographic images of women, causing harassment and abuse [54]. These examples highlight the critical need for effective detection methods to counteract increasing threats posed by synthetic media. Digital forensics professionals, cybersecurity experts, and legal investigators are under pressure to keep up with the advancing synthetic media by ensuring that efficient and reliable methods for detection are put in place. The challenge in detecting deepfakes lies in the fact that the same powerful technologies used to create deepfakes like Generative Adversarial Networks (GANs) [26] and Autoencoders are the same ones used to detect them [12]. These techniques used to generate deepfakes are continuously evolving, making the forgeries more realistic and harder to differentiate from genuine content [9,48,72]. Previously, deepfake detection methods have mainly focused on identifying artifacts or inconsistencies introduced by synthesis algorithms, such as unrealistic eye blinking [41], mismatched color profiles [40], and discrepancies between lip movements and spoken words [38]. Neural networks have been applied in detection of deepfakes by training them to recognize small but important differences between real and fake images [1,27].

Even though deepfake technology advances, these deepfakes still exhibit slight inconsistencies in features such as shape of the mouth, lip color, dental alignment, and the appearance of the tongue. This study builds on that foundation by focusing specifically on the mouth region and aims to explore its application in multimodal deepfake detection. While most existing surveys analyze the entire face, this research narrows its scope to detect mismatches between spoken audio and visible mouth movements. Analyzing these unique inconsistencies in depth can significantly improve detection precision.

1.2 Survey Approach

This study takes a systematic survey approach with critical comparisons of different state of the art deepfake detection methods. The research will start with Section 2, which will cover the introduction, background of the study and its relevance; Sect. 3 will include a general overview of deepfake detection, datasets and detection approaches; Sect. 4 addresses the state of the art categories of deepfakes and their gaps; Sect. 5 presents the evaluation metrics; Sect. 6 covers limitations, ethical and legal implications, and challenges; and Sect. 7 concludes the paper with potential future research directions.

1.3 Research Questions

This study is guided by the following research questions:

1. What are the existing state-of-the-art deepfake detection techniques, and how do they address audiovisual inconsistencies, particularly in lip-speech synchronization?
2. What are the key challenges and limitations of current multimodal deepfake detection methods?
3. How effective are lip-speech synchronization features in improving the accuracy of deepfake detection compared to traditional visual-based approaches?
4. What benchmark datasets and evaluation metrics are most suitable for training and evaluating lip-sync-based deepfake detection models?

2 Datasets and Techniques of Deepfake Detection

2.1 General Overview

2.1.1 What Are Deepfakes

Deepfakes refer to synthetic media, particularly audio and video, generated by artificial intelligence models designed to mimic the likenesses and voices of real people. Utilizing technologies like GANs [26] and VAEs [36], deepfakes create hyper-realistic outputs which deceive even trained observers. Initially developed for entertainment [83], their capabilities now extend to fraud,disinformation, and identity theft [4]. A deepfake can alter a person's words, emotions, and actions in fabricated recordings, leading to substantial reputational and political harm [4,71]. Furthermore, multimodal deepfakes, combining synchronized audio and visuals, pose even greater risks by achieving high levels of realism. As these technologies continue evolving, detecting synthetic media becomes more complex, and traditional forensic methods are often insufficient. Recognizing deepfakes requires understanding both their creative possibilities andpossible dangers. While they offer breakthroughs in virtual assistance, movie production, and accessibility, their misuse demands careful study, legal scrutiny, and ethical discussions. Deepfake technology represents one of the most profound challenges and opportunities presented by modern artificial intelligence.

2.1.2 Evolution of Deepfake Technology

The development of deepfake technology traces its roots to early machine learning models, such as autoencoders, that reconstructed human faces through basic encoding and decoding mechanisms. With the emergence of GANs [26], and subsequent improvements through AEs [36], the quality and complexity of synthetic outputs greatly increased. GAN-based models, notably StyleGAN and StyleGAN2, introduced high-fidelity control over facial features, enabling subtle manipulations like emotional expression and age progression. Transformer-based architectures have further improved deepfake creation, producing more realistic and contextually consistent results. Today, advanced techniques involve biometric synthesis and cross-modal alignment, leading to more synchronized audio-visual outputs [7,81,83]. The shift from static image manipulation to dynamic video and voice synthesis has dramatically escalated the societal impact of deepfakes. Techniques like first-order motion modeling [3] and talking-head generation [80] allow creating moving avatars from a single still image, enhancing the believability of fake media. Despite these technological advances, early detection methods focusing on simple visual artifacts have struggled to keep up [42]. As deepfakes increasingly blur the lines between authentic and fabricated media, understanding their historical evolution provides critical insights into both their potential applications and the mounting challenges they pose for cybersecurity and digital trust [71].

2.1.3 Applications of Deepfakes

Deepfake technology has applications across various domains, offering both benefits and risks. In entertainment, it is used to recreate historical figures [70], simulate younger versions of actors [21], and localize movies by matching lip movements for dubbing purposes [55]. In education, synthetic avatars serve as virtual instructors or sign-language translators, enhancing accessibility and learning experiences [3]. Similarly, deepfake-based text-to-speech models empower those with speech impairments to communicate more naturally. However, the technology is most commonly associated with harmful applications. Deepfakes are weaponized in political campaigns [4], fake news dissemination [71], religious manipulation [8], and non-consensual pornography. Additionally, they facilitate fraud through impersonation attacks, targeting businesses and individuals for financial gain [25]. The rise of deepfakes in journalistic misinformation has serious implications for the credibility of media institutions. Because deepfakes can be used for both positive and harmful purposes, regulating them becomes challenging. While beneficial uses advance accessibility and creativity, harmful applications threaten privacy, democracy, and societal stability. Therefore, any discussion about deepfakes needs to consider the balance between technological progress, societal benefits, and ethical responsibility.

2.2 Datasets for Deepfake Detection

The effectiveness of deepfake detection algorithms largely depends on the quality of the datasets being used for training and testing. A high-quality dataset should contain both authentic and manipulated content across various manipulation techniques and environmental conditions. These datasets allow researchers to train models that can generalize well to unseen data, ensuring that the detection system remains robust. In the context of multimodal deepfake detection, datasets that provide both high-quality video and synchronized audio are critical. A consolidated comparison of prominent audio–visual deepfake datasets is provided in Table 1. The following datasets have proven to be particularly important.

2.2.1 FaceForensics++

This dataset remains one of the popular datasets used in deepfake detection [62], providing a substantial collection of real and manipulated videos. The manipulations include a range of techniques, such as face replacement, expression manipulation and deepfake generation using both traditional and deep learning techniques [72]. While this dataset is excellent for evaluating visual artifact-based methods, it is limited in its audio fidelity, making it unsuitable for testing audio-visual synchronization detection systems. Despite these limitations, FaceForensics++ continues to serve as a benchmark dataset for testing visual-based detection techniques and exploring novel multimodal approaches [59].

2.2.2 DFDC (Deepfake Detection Challenge)

The DFDC dataset, designed for the Deepfake Detection Challenge hosted by Facebook, includes a wide range of both fake and real videos featuring many actors and manipulation techniques [18]. This diversity makes DFDC a critical resource for evaluating the robustness of deepfake detection algorithms. However, its audio quality and alignment with lip movements remain suboptimal, making it challenging to evaluate audio-visual synchronization methods. As such, while DFDC remains useful for general detection tasks, more focused datasets like FakeAVCeleb are necessary for testing lip–speech synchronization detection models specifically [31].

Table 1. Audio–visual deepfake datasets: key comparison.

Dataset	Real videos	Fake videos	Modalities	Focus area
FaceForensics++ [63]	1,000	4,000	Video	Multimodal deepfakes
DFDC [19]	23,654	104,500	Audio & Video	Large-scale, diverse manipulations
FakeAVCeleb [35]	570	25,000	Audio & Video	Multimodal deepfakes
WildDeepfake [87]	3,805	3,509	Video	Real-world visual deepfakes

2.2.3 FakeAVCeleb

This is a multimodal dataset [35] specifically designed for testing audio-visual deepfake detection systems. It contains manipulated videos where the speech is either misaligned or resynthesized, making it especially valuable for evaluating lip-sync detection models. The dataset provides a significant number of videos exhibiting mismatches in lip synchronization, which are critical for testing systems focused on audio-visual alignment. FakeAVCeleb is crucial for advancing research into multimodal detection methods, but it is still relatively small in scope compared to FaceForensics++, with fewer actors and manipulation techniques available. Despite its size limitations, FakeAVCeleb's specific focus on lip–speech synchronization makes it an essential dataset for evaluating audio-visual synchronization systems.

2.2.4 WildDeepfake

This is a visual dataset [87] specifically created for testing deepfake detection systems in real-world conditions. It contains over 7,000 manipulated videos and more than 3,000 authentic clips collected from the internet, covering a wide range of natural variations such as lighting changes and complex backgrounds. These features make it particularly useful for evaluating detection models under uncontrolled, real-world scenarios [76].

2.3 Modality Based Detection Approaches

2.3.1 Audio

Audio deepfakes involve generating synthetic speech that closely resembles an individual's natural voice, including tone, speaking style, and rhythm. Models such as Tacotron 2 [65], FastSpeech, and vocoders such as WaveNet [51] and HiFi-GAN [37] have greatly improved the field by enabling highly naturalistic voice synthesis. These systems are capable of learning the unique features of an individual's voice and use them to read any written text out loud in that person's style. Legitimate uses include creating voices for virtual assistants, audiobook narration, and speech aids for individuals with disabilities. However, the technology also introduces significant risks. Impersonation through audio deepfakes has been used in social engineering attacks and corporate fraud schemes, sometimes leading to serious financial loss [25]. Detecting synthetic voices is difficult and often involves analyzing sound patterns to find subtle signs of manipulation or comparing the voice to known samples of the real speaker. Other techniques look at how consistent the audio signal is or rely on voice recognition systems. As these technologies become more advanced and accessible, developing efficient and accurate countermeasures becomes essential to safeguard communication authenticity. Public awareness campaigns and integration of verification systems into high-risk sectors like finance and government operations are critical steps toward mitigating the growing threats posed by audio deepfakes.

2.3.2 Facial

Facial deepfakes are perhaps the most recognized form of synthetic media. They involve digitally altering or creating videos of individuals by swapping faces, animating expressions, or synthesizing entire head movements. GANs such as CycleGAN and StyleGAN, along with autoencoder pairs, drive most modern facial deepfake generation processes [32,58]. The workflow typically includes face detection, landmark alignment, feature encoding, synthetic generation, and seamless blending into the destination video. DeepFaceLab, FaceSwap, and mobile applications like ZAO have democratized access to these capabilities [17]. Although facial deepfakes can appear realistic, they often reveal subtle artifacts such as unnatural blinking, inconsistent illumination and softly blurred edges around key features [49]. Detection strategies have evolved from artifact-focused analysis to deep learning approaches that monitor facial action units, micro-expressions, and physiological signals like pulse detection through photoplethysmography [30]. While deepfakes have positive applications in movie production, virtual makeovers, and historical reconstructions, their malicious use in reputation damage, political sabotage, and blackmail campaigns necessitates continual improvement of detection technologies and the establishment of stronger ethical norms around synthetic media creation [10].

Lip–Speech. Lip-speech synchronization is a central practice in detecting deepfakes. Because current models fail to maintain accurate lip-speech alignment, methods have been proposed considering quality in synchronisation. [57] proposed a deep-learning model that estimates sound coherence with lips with a pre-trained discrimination network to flag lip-sync. In their work, high-quality deepfake videos are established as subtle audio–lip discrepancies that are imperceptible to human listeners. Similarly, [64] proposed a multimodal detection network to flag synthetic material that estimates sound and facial activity inconsistency. The methods utilize Convolutional Neural Networks (CNNs) and Recurrent Neural Networks (RNNs) to flag inaudible temporal differences that cannot be discerned with human vision, making them highly effective in detecting deepfakes. However, dataset biases and small training data are still challenges in enhancing model performance.

Known Limitations. Models like SyncNet are known to struggle when the speaker is not facing the camera and under strong compression, and they rely on short temporal windows of around five frames, which means they often miss problems that develop gradually over longer clips [28,53,56]. Wav2Lip, which generates mouth movements, can produce visually plausible motion but sometimes hides important cues such as lip closures or speech rhythm. This can mislead detectors that focus only on short-term correlations, while robustness drops when the audio or video suffers from noise or compression artifacts [28,44,56]. These models show reduced generalization across different languages and accents unless they are trained with multilingual or cross-lingual data [29,88]. They are also vulnerable to subtle timing manipulations, such as stretching or shifting the audio slightly which preserve local lip–audio coherence but break global alignment over time [78,82].

Multimodal. Multimodal deepfakes represent the most advanced category of synthetic media, combining both visual and auditory information streams to produce synchronized and realistic representations. Unlike unimodal deepfakes that manipulate only one type of media, multimodal creations require strict alignment of lip movements with speech, facial expressions with emotion, and body gestures with context. Technologies like cross-modal GANs and Transformer-based architectures learn to model these complex correlations [75]. Popular models include SyncNet for lip–speech synchronization accuracy [13]. Applications range from cross-lingual video dubbing to the creation of virtual influencers. However, the dangers of multimodal deepfakes are profound; they can simulate press conferences, interviews, and confessions with high believability. Detection requires analyzing audiovisual synchronization discrepancies, crossmodal consistency checks, and residual artifact patterns invisible to human observers [45]. Deep learning methods, such as two-stream neural networks, are deployed to detect mismatches between video and audio streams. We summarize representative generation/detection categories, strengths, and open gaps in Table 2. The increasing realism and accessibility of multimodal deepfakes necessitate interdisciplinary collaboration among AI researchers, media organizations, policymakers, and cybersecurity professionals to develop resilient detection frameworks and promote media literacy among the public.

3 Deepfake Generation and Detection Categories: State of the Art and Gaps

Table 2. Audio–visual deepfake categorization: state of the art and open gaps.

Category	How it works	Representative methods	Strengths	Gaps / Limitations
Entire face synthesis [33,34]	Generates non-existent faces from scratch with generative models	PGGAN, StyleGAN, StyleGAN2	High-resolution, photorealistic outputs	Limited attribute control; increasingly realistic samples can evade classical detectors
Facial attribute manipulation [11,24,67]	Edits specific attributes (age, gender, expression) while preserving identity	HiFaceGAN, StarGAN, InterFaceGAN	Maintains non-edited regions; flexible edits	Subtle edits are hard to detect; distribution shift across attributes
Identity swap (face swap) [50]	Replaces source identity with target identity in images/videos	DeepFaceLab, FSGAN, FaceShifter	Good expression/pose transfer; high realism	Occlusions, extreme pose/lighting, and cross-dataset generalization remain challenging
Expression swap / reenactment [73,85]	Transfers expressions/head motion from a driver to a source face	ICFace, PC-AVS, (audio-driven) Wav2Lip-style driving	Natural motion (blink, lip motion); controllable driving	Hard to distinguish from real footage at high quality; artifacts under occlusion/profile
Text-to-speech (TTS) synthesis [39,61,66]	Converts text to speech; pairs with a talking-face generator for A/V forgeries	Tacotron 2, FastSpeech, MelGAN	Expressive, scalable voice synthesis	Detection is difficult when A/V are tightly synchronized; voice spoofing risk
Lip–speech synchronization (generation) [14,79]	Generates mouth motion conditioned on audio to match speech content	Wav2Lip, LipSync3D, SyncNet-style alignment	High-quality sync even with moderate noise	Generalization to unseen speakers/accents; sensitivity to compression and profile views

4 Evaluation Metrics

The evaluation of deepfake detection systems relies on various metrics, which assess the ability of models to distinguish between authentic and manipulated content. For lip–speech synchronization specifically, we recommend reporting both (i) classification metrics for video/utterance-level decisions and (ii) temporal alignment metrics that directly capture A/V lag. The metrics include:

4.1 Accuracy (ACC)

This is the percentage of correct predictions (true positives and true negatives) out of all predictions made. This metric is commonly used for evaluating binary classification tasks to distinguish between authentic videos and deepfakes. While accuracy serves as an overall metric, it may not be reliable when the dataset is imbalanced, where one class significantly outweighs the other. Example: a SyncNet-embedding + logistic head might yield ACC = 88% on a balanced set, while a cross-modal transformer variant yields 92%; however, ACC can be misleading under class imbalance.

4.2 Area Under the Receiver Operating Characteristic Curve (AUC)

This metric measures the ability of a model to differentiate between classes (real and fake). A higher AUC indicates better performance, as it suggests the model is able to distinguish between authentic and manipulated content across different levels of classification. This is useful for assessing models in imbalanced classification [22]. For lip-sync tasks, AUROC $\geq$ 0.90 typically indicates strong discrimination; we also recommend AUPRC and operating points such as FPR@TPR=95% for forensic triage.

4.3 Equal Error Rate (EER)

This is the point at which the False Acceptance Rate (FAR) and False Rejection Rate (FRR) are balanced. This metric is crucial for evaluating the trade-off between precision and recall, as it offers a clear view of the balance between false positives and false negatives. Lower is better; e.g., EER drops from 14.2% (baseline) to 9.8%.)

4.4 Mean Average Precision (mAP)

Used when evaluating systems that predict multiple classes or modalities. This metric calculates the average precision across different labels, offering a more comprehensive measure of model performance. mAP is particularly beneficial for multimodal systems, where the system evaluates multiple data types or handles complex tasks like detecting manipulated regions in videos [20]. mAP is most relevant when a method localizes multiple manipulated segments; it is less diagnostic for pure lip-sync binary decisions.

4.5 Mean Intersection over Union (mIoU)

Used in methods that generate heatmaps or localized predictions for manipulated regions within a video. It measures the overlap between predicted and ground-truth manipulated regions. mIoU is crucial for evaluating systems that need to accurately locate and identify manipulated content. For heatmap methods that highlight desynchronized intervals, mIoU complements AUROC by reflecting localization quality.

4.6 Lip–Audio Correlation (LAC)

This metric evaluates the correlation or cosine similarity between the lip motion embeddings and speech features. This metric is most relevant to lip-speech synchronization detection models, such as SyncNet and AVFakeDetect [13]. Higher is better. We recommend reporting both zero-lag LAC and best-lag LAC; a high best-lag but low zero-lag indicates systematic drift. Example: zero-lag LAC increases from 0.42 to 0.57 after alignment losses, while best-lag remains > 0.60.

4.7 Sync Error Rate (SER)-Temporal Alignment

PLAE measures how closely the pattern of spoken sounds (phoneme sequence) matches the pattern of lip movements. It is calculated using dynamic time warping and then normalized by clip length. Lower values mean better match. Example: PLAE falling from 0.86 to 0.61 means the lips are following the speech more accurately.

4.7.1 Ethical and Legal Implications of Deepfake Detection

Deepfakes present numerous threats to individuals, organizations, and society. The main concern is their potential use in spreading misinformation and manipulating public pinion [4]. Deepfakes can simulate world leaders making inflammatory statements, potentially sparking political crises. In the realm of cybersecurity, audio deepfakes enable sophisticated phishing attacks by mimicking the voices of executives [25]. Furthermore, the use of synthetic biometrics complicates traditional identity verification systems [83]. Ethical concerns include the violation of privacy rights, non-consensual use of personal imagery, and psychological harm inflicted on victims of fake media. The legal landscape struggles to keep pace, with jurisdictional gaps complicating enforcement [2,46]. As detection becomes more challenging, there is an increasing risk that genuine content may be dismissed as fake, which further undermines public trust. While regulations and technological defenses are being developed, the rapid evolution of deepfake tools necessitates a proactive and multidisciplinary approach. In the end, society must balance the remarkable creative potential of synthetic media with the pressing responsibility to address its risks to democracy, public safety, and personal integrity.

4.7.2 Challenges

Despite advancements in deepfake detection, specific challenges still exist. The rapid advancement of methods for generating deepfakes continues to surpass existing detection models, calling for repeated updating and retraining of the detection algorithm. Another challenge is efficiency in computational power, given that real-time detection demands much processing power. Future research should aim to develop light but realistic models operating under real-world forensic and cybersecurity environments [47]. A further limitation lies in the lack of standardized and diverse datasets, which restricts the ability to evaluate detection models across the full range of real-world variability such as differences in accents, speaking styles, and recording conditions.

5 Future Research Directions

Future work in this area can move in several important directions. One promising path is the development of smarter alignment models. Current audio-visual approaches, such as AV-HuBERT [68], could be extended with an alignment layer designed to reduce delays between speech sounds and lip motion, encourage smoother lip transitions across connected sounds, and better capture the relationship between speech rhythm and lip movement. These models should be evaluated not only with standard accuracy measures but also with synchronization metrics like SER (Sync Error Rate) and PLAE (Phoneme–Lip Alignment Error).

Another direction is real-time detection. The goal here is to design systems that run faster than 25 frames per second on standard laptop GPUs. Achieving this would involve efficient training methods and short, sliding time windows that keep detection both fast and accurate. Reporting on speed, delay, and performance across different video qualities will be essential.

Also, establishment of benchmark standards. Releasing tools that enforce consistent settings, such as frame rate, face cropping, phoneme timing, and video compression levels, would make results easier to compare across studies. A standardized evaluation setup should produce not only accuracy and sync measures but also calibration results, and it should include speaker and language disjoint test splits to ensure fairness.

Robustness tests will also be key. Models need to be tested under more realistic conditions, such as small changes in playback speed, background noise at different levels, and variations in camera angle. Reporting how well models maintain their ranking under these challenges would highlight which approaches are most reliable in practice.

References

1. Afchar, D., Nozick, V., Yamagishi, J., Echizen, I.: Mesonet: a compact facial video forgery detection network. In: 2018 IEEE international workshop on information forensics and security (WIFS),. pp. 1–7. IEEE (2018)

2. Agarwal, S., Farid, H., Gu, Y., He, M., Nagano, K., Li, H.: Protecting world leaders against deep fakes. In: CVPR workshops, vol. 1 (2019)
3. Alharthi, A., Yu, Y., Alsaad, M., Thakur, C.S.S.K.K.P.S.: First-order motion model for image animation. In: European Conference on Computer Vision (ECCV) (2020). https://arxiv.org/abs/2003.10655
4. Barari, S., Lucas, C., Munger, K., et al.: Political deepfake videos misinform the public, but no more than other fake media. OSF Preprints **13**, 1–16 (2021)
5. Bohacek, E., Farid, H.: Audio-visual deepfake detection using multi-scale spatiotemporal features. In: Proceedings of the IEEE/CVF Conference on Computer Vision and Pattern Recognition (CVPR) Workshops (2024). https://farid.berkeley.edu/downloads/publications/cvprw24c.pdf
6. Bohacek, M., Farid, H.: Lost in translation: Lip-sync deepfake detection from audio-video mismatch. In: Proceedings of the IEEE/CVF Conference on Computer Vision and Pattern Recognition (CVPR) Workshops, pp. 4315–4323 (2024). https://doi.org/10.1109/CVPRW63382.2024.00435, https://openaccess.thecvf.com/content/CVPR2024W/WMF/html/Bohacek_Lost_in_Translation_Lip-Sync_Deepfake_Detection_from_Audio-Video_Mismatch_CVPRW_2024_paper.html
7. Cai, H., Li, C., Xue, J., Liu, Y.: Audio-visual deepfake detection with cross-modal attention. IEEE Trans. Circuits Syst. Video Technol. (2022). https://doi.org/10.1109/TCSVT.2022.3195783
8. Cartella, G., Cuculo, V., Cornia, M., Papasidero, M., Ruozzi, F., Cucchiara, R., et al.: Pixels of faith: Exploiting visual saliency to detect religious image manipulation. In: Proceedings of the European Conference on Computer Vision Workshops (2024)
9. Chesney, B., Citron, D.: Deep fakes: A looming challenge for privacy, democracy, and national security. Calif. L. Rev. **107**, 1753 (2019)
10. Chesney, R., Citron, D.K.: Deep fakes: A looming challenge for privacy, democracy, and national security. Calif. Law Rev. **107**(5), 1753–1819 (2019). https://doi.org/10.15779/Z38X918R5C
11. Choi, Y., Choi, M., Kim, M., Ha, J.W., Kim, S., Choo, J.: Stargan: Unified generative adversarial networks for multi-domain image-to-image translation. In: Proceedings of the IEEE Conference on Computer Vision and Pattern Recognition (CVPR), pp. 8789–8797 (2018)
12. Chugh, K., Gupta, P., Dhall, A., Subramanian, R.: Not made for each other-audio-visual dissonance-based deepfake detection and localization. In: Proceedings of the 28th ACM international conference on multimedia, pp. 439–447 (2020)
13. Chung, J., Zisserman, A.: Out of time: Automated lip sync for video. arXiv preprint arXiv:1708.03972 (2017). https://arxiv.org/abs/1708.03972
14. Chung, J.S., Jamaludin, A., Zisserman, A.: Out of time: automated lip sync in the wild. In: Workshop on Multi-view Lip-reading, ACCV (2017)
15. Damiani, J.: A voice deepfake was used to scam a ceo out of 243,000 usd. https://www.forbes.com/sites/jessedamiani/2019/09/03/a-voice-deepfake-was-used-to-scam-a-ceo-out-of-243000/ (2019), Accessed 25 Sep 2025
16. Datta, S.K., Jia, S., Lyu, S.: Exposing lip-syncing deepfakes from mouth inconsistencies. In: 2024 IEEE International Conference on Multimedia and Expo (ICME), pp. 1–6. IEEE (2024)
17. De Seta, G.: Huanlian, or changing faces: deepfakes on Chinese digital media platforms. Convergence **27**(4), 935–953 (2021)
18. Dolhansky, B., et al.: The deepfake detection challenge (dfdc) preview dataset. arXiv preprint arXiv:1910.08854 (2019). https://arxiv.org/abs/1910.08854

19. Dolhansky, Bet al.: The deepfake detection challenge (dfdc) dataset. arXiv preprint arXiv:2006.07397 (2020)
20. Everingham, M., Van Gool, L., Williams, C.K., Winn, J., Zisserman, A.: The pascal visual object classes (voc) challenge. Int. J. Comput. Vision **88**(2), 303–338 (2010)
21. Eye, R.: Understanding deepfakes: Origins, applications, and future implications. Red Eye World (2023). https://red-eye.world/c/understanding-deepfakes-origins-applications-and-future-implications
22. Fawcett, T.: An introduction to roc analysis. Pattern Recogn. Lett. **27**(8), 861–874 (2006)
23. Fox News: Russia, ukraine 'deepfake' video, audio are concerns for us intelligence. Fox News (2022). https://www.foxnews.com/tech/russia-ukraine-deepfake-video-audio-us-intelligence, Accessed 6 Mar 2025
24. Gao, C., Yang, Y., Deng, J., Xie, X., Zafeiriou, S.: High-fidelity facial attributes transfer with hybrid feature-aware fusion. In: Proceedings of the 29th ACM International Conference on Multimedia (MM '21), pp. 3915–3923. ACM (2021). https://doi.org/10.1145/3474085.3475203
25. Gilbert, A., Gong, Z.: Digital identity theft using deepfakes. In: Information Technology Security and Risk Management, pp. 307–314. CRC Press (2024)
26. Goodfellow, I., et al.: Generative adversarial nets. Adv. Neural Inf. Process. Syst. **27** (2014)
27. Güera, D., Delp, E.J.: Deepfake video detection using recurrent neural networks. In: 2018 15th IEEE International Conference on Advanced Video and Signal Based Surveillance (AVSS), pp. 1–6. IEEE (2018)
28. Haliassos, A., Vougioukas, K., Petridis, S., Pantic, M.: Lips don't lie: a generalisable and robust approach to face forgery detection. In: Proceedings of the IEEE/CVF Conference on Computer Vision and Pattern Recognition (CVPR), pp. 5039–5049 (2021). https://openaccess.thecvf.com/content/CVPR2021/papers/Haliassos/_Lips/_Dont/_Lie/_A/_Generalisable/_and/_Robust/_Approach/_To/_Face/_CVPR/_2021/_paper.pdf
29. Han, H., et al.: Xlavs-r: cross-lingual audio-visual speech representation learning for noise-robust speech perception. In: Proceedings of the 62nd Annual Meeting of the Association for Computational Linguistics (ACL), pp. 12456–12472 (2024), https://aclanthology.org/2024.acl-long.697/
30. Jagam, A., Patel, N., Chidirala, B., Acharya, B.: Deepfake detection in facial images using convolutional neural networks. In: 2025 Fourth International Conference on Power, Control and Computing Technologies (ICPC2T), pp. 1–6. IEEE (2025)
31. Karafiát, P., Gygli, M., Rybícki, D.: Multi-modal deepfake detection using audio-visual synchronization. In: Proceedings of the IEEE International Conference on Acoustics, Speech and Signal Processing (ICASSP), pp. 4110–4114. IEEE (2021). https://doi.org/10.1109/ICASSP39728.2021.9415072, https://ieeexplore.ieee.org/document/9415072
32. Karras, T., Aila, T., Laine, S., Lehtinen, J.: Progressive growing of gans for improved quality, stability, and variation. arXiv preprint arXiv:1710.10196 (2017). https://arxiv.org/abs/1710.10196
33. Karras, T., Aila, T., Laine, S., Lehtinen, J.: Progressive growing of gans for improved quality, stability, and variation. arXiv preprint arXiv:1710.10196 (2017)
34. Karras, T., Laine, S., Aila, T.: A style-based generator architecture for generative adversarial networks. In: Proceedings of the IEEE/CVF conference on computer vision and pattern recognition, pp. 4401–4410 (2019)

35. Khalid, H., Tariq, S., Kim, M., Woo, S.S.: Fakeavceleb: a novel audio-video multimodal deepfake dataset. In: Proceedings of the Neural Information Processing Systems Track on Datasets and Benchmarks (2021). https://openreview.net/forum?id=9JxU1UqYjD
36. Kingma, D.P., Welling, M., et al.: Auto-encoding variational bayes (2013)
37. Kong, J., Kim, J., Bae, J.: Hifi-gan: Generative adversarial networks for efficient and high fidelity speech synthesis. Adv. Neural. Inf. Process. Syst. **33**, 17022–17033 (2020)
38. Korshunov, P., Marcel, S.: Speaker inconsistency detection in tampered video. In: 2018 26th European Signal Processing Conference (EUSIPCO), pp. 2375–2379. IEEE (2018)
39. Kumar, K., et al.: Melgan: Generative adversarial networks for conditional waveform synthesis. In: Advances in Neural Information Processing Systems (NeurIPS), pp. 14910–14921 (2019)
40. Li, H., Li, B., Tan, S., Huang, J.: Identification of deep network generated images using disparities in color components. Signal Process. **174**, 107616 (2020)
41. Li, Y., Chang, M.C., Lyu, S.: In ictu oculi: Exposing ai generated fake face videos by detecting eye blinking. arXiv preprint arXiv:1806.02877 (2018)
42. Li, Y., Lyu, S.: Exposing deepfake videos by detecting face warping artifacts. arXiv preprint arXiv:1811.00656 (2018)
43. Liu, W., et al.: Lips are lying: Spotting the temporal inconsistency between audio and visual in lip-syncing deepfakes. arXiv preprint arXiv:2401.15668 (2024)
44. Liu, W., Cao, Y., Wang, Z., Shi, J., Sang, N.: Spotting the temporal inconsistency between audio and lip movements for lip-syncing forgery detection. In: Advances in Neural Information Processing Systems (NeurIPS) (2024). https://proceedings.neurips.cc/paper_files/paper/2024/file/a5a5b0ff87c59172a13342d428b1e033-Paper-Conference.pdf
45. Lomnitz, M., Hampel-Arias, Z., Sandesara, V., Hu, S.: Multimodal approach for deepfake detection. In: 2020 IEEE Applied Imagery Pattern Recognition Workshop (AIPR), pp. 1–9 (2020). https://doi.org/10.1109/AIPR50011.2020.9425192
46. Lyu, S.: Deepfake detection: Current challenges and next steps. arXiv preprint arXiv:2003.09234 (2020)
47. Masood, M., Nawaz, M., Malik, K.M., Javed, A., Irtaza, A., Malik, H.: Deepfakes generation and detection: state-of-the-art, open challenges, countermeasures, and way forward. Appl. Intell. **53**(4), 3974–4026 (2023)
48. Mirsky, Y., Lee, W.: The creation and detection of deepfakes: a survey. ACM Comput. Surv. (CSUR) **54**(1), 1–41 (2021)
49. Nguyen, T., Yamagishi, J., Echizen, I.: Deep learning for deepfakes creation and detection. IEEE Trans. Inf. Forensics Secur. **14**(11), 2891–2903 (2019). https://doi.org/10.1109/TIFS.2019.2920467
50. Nirkin, Y., Keller, Y., Hassner, T.: Fsgan: Subject agnostic face swapping and reenactment. In: Proceedings of the IEEE/CVF International Conference on Computer Vision (ICCV), pp. 7184–7193 (2019)
51. van den Oord, A., et al.: Wavenet: A generative model for raw audio. arXiv preprint arXiv:1609.03499 (2016). https://arxiv.org/abs/1609.03499
52. Park, S.J., Kim, M., Hong, J., Choi, J., Ro, Y.M.: Synctalkface: talking face generation with precise lip-syncing via audio-lip memory. In: Proceedings of the AAAI Conference on Artificial Intelligence, vol. 36, pp. 2062–2070 (2022)
53. Petridis, S., Wang, Y., Li, Z., Pantic, M.: End-to-end multi-view lipreading. In: Proceedings of the British Machine Vision Conference (BMVC) (2017). https://www.bmva.org/bmvc/2017/papers/paper161/index.html

54. Phys.org News: Deepnude app that undresses women with AI is taken offline. Phys.org (online) (2019). https://phys.org/news/2019-06-deepnude-app-undresses-women-ai.html, Accessed 25 Sep 2025
55. Popa, S., et al.: Visual dubbing pipeline with localized lip-sync and two-pass identity transfer. Comput. Graph. **102**, 1–12 (2022). https://doi.org/10.1016/j.cag.2022.10.004, https://www.sciencedirect.com/science/article/pii/S0097849322001984
56. Prajwal, K.R., Mukhopadhyay, R., Namboodiri, V.P., Jawahar, C.V.: A lip sync expert is all you need for speech to lip generation in the wild. In: Proceedings of the 28th ACM International Conference on Multimedia (ACM MM), pp. 484–492 (2020). https://doi.org/10.1145/3394171.3413532, https://arxiv.org/abs/2008.10010
57. Prajwal, K., Mukhopadhyay, R., Namboodiri, V.P., Jawahar, C.: A lip sync expert is all you need for speech to lip generation in the wild. In: Proceedings of the 28th ACM international conference on multimedia, pp. 484–492 (2020)
58. Radford, A., Metz, L., Chintala, S.: Unsupervised representation learning with deep convolutional generative adversarial networks. arXiv preprint arXiv:1511.06434 (2016). https://arxiv.org/abs/1511.06434
59. Ranjan, K., Gupta, A., Verma, A.: Multimodal face manipulation detection with faceforensics++. IEEE Trans. Image Process. **31**, 5875–5889 (2022https://doi.org/10.1109/TIP.2022.3151737
60. Raza, M.A., Malik, K.M.: Multimodaltrace: Deepfake detection using audiovisual representation learning. In: Proceedings of the IEEE/CVF Conference on Computer Vision and Pattern Recognition, pp. 993–1000 (2023)
61. Ren, Y., et al: Fastspeech 2: Fast and high-quality end-to-end text to speech. In: International Conference on Learning Representations (ICLR) (2020)
62. Rössler, A., Cozzolino, D., Verdoliva, L., Riess, C., Thies, J., Nießner, M.: Faceforensics: a large-scale video dataset for forgery detection in human faces. arXiv preprint arXiv:1803.09179 (2018)
63. Rossler, A., Cozzolino, D., Verdoliva, L., Riess, C., Thies, J., Nießner, M.: Faceforensics++: learning to detect manipulated facial images. In: Proceedings of the IEEE/CVF international conference on computer vision, pp. 1–11 (2019)
64. Shahzad, S.A., Hashmi, A., Khan, S., Peng, Y.T., Tsao, Y., Wang, H.M.: Lip sync matters: a novel multimodal forgery detector. In: 2022 Asia-Pacific Signal and Information Processing Association Annual Summit and Conference (APSIPA ASC), pp. 1885–1892. IEEE (2022)
65. Shen, J., et al.: Natural TTS synthesis by conditioning wavenet on mel spectrogram predictions. In: IEEE International Conference on Acoustics, Speech and Signal Processing (ICASSP), pp. 4779–4783 (2018). https://doi.org/10.1109/ICASSP.2018.8461368
66. Shen, J., et al.: Natural tts synthesis by conditioning wavenet on mel spectrogram predictions. In: 2018 IEEE International Conference on Acoustics, Speech and Signal Processing (ICASSP), pp. 4779–4783. IEEE (2018)
67. Shen, Y., Yang, C., Tang, X., Zhou, B.: Interpreting the latent space of gans for semantic face editing. Proceedings of the IEEE/CVF Conference on Computer Vision and Pattern Recognition (CVPR), pp. 9243–9252 (2020)
68. Shi, B., Hsu, W.N., Lakhotia, K., Li, A., Mohamed, A.: Learning audio-visual speech representation by masked multimodal cluster prediction. arXiv:2201.02184 (2022). https://arxiv.org/abs/2201.02184

69. Skafle, I., Nordahl-Hansen, A., Quintana, D.S., Wynn, R., Gabarron, E.: Misinformation about covid-19 vaccines on social media: rapid review. J. Med. Internet Res. **24**(8), e37367 (2022)
70. Suwajanakorn, S., Seitz, S.M., Kemelmacher-Shlizerman, I.: Synthesizing obama: Learning lip sync from audio. In: ACM Transactions on Graphics (TOG), Proceedings of SIGGRAPH 2017, vol. 36, pp. 95:1–95:13. ACM (2017). https://doi.org/10.1145/3072959.3073640, https://dl.acm.org/doi/10.1145/3072959.3073640
71. Temir, E.: Deepfake: new era in the age of disinformation & end of reliable journalism. Selçuk İletişim **13**(2), 1009–1024 (2020)
72. Tolosana, R., Vera-Rodriguez, R., Fierrez, J., Morales, A., Ortega-Garcia, J.: Deepfakes and beyond: a survey of face manipulation and fake detection. Inf. Fusion **64**, 131–148 (2020)
73. Tripathy, A., Chatterjee, A., Mukherjee, A., Bhowmick, B.: Icface: interpretable and controllable face reenactment using gans. In: Proceedings of the IEEE/CVF Winter Conference on Applications of Computer Vision (WACV), pp. 471–480 (2020)
74. Vaccari, C., Chadwick, A.: Deepfakes and disinformation: exploring the impact of synthetic political video on deception, uncertainty, and trust in news. Soc. Media + Soc. **6**(1) (2020). https://doi.org/10.1177/2056305120903408
75. Vaswani, A., et al.: Attention is all you need. Neural Inf. Process. Syst. (NeurIPS) (2017). https://arxiv.org/abs/1706.03762
76. Verdoliva, L.: Media forensics and deepfakes: an overview. IEEE J. Selected Top. Signal Process. **14**(5), 910–932 (2020). https://doi.org/10.1109/JSTSP.2020.3006769
77. Vincent, P., Larochelle, H., Bengio, Y., Manzagol, P.A.: Extracting and composing robust features with denoising autoencoders. In: Proceedings of the 25th international conference on Machine learning, pp. 1096–1103 (2008)
78. Voas, E., et al.: Temporally streaming audio-visual synchronization for real-world videos. In: Proceedings of the IEEE/CVF Winter Conference on Applications of Computer Vision (WACV), pp. 1172–1182 (2025). https://openaccess.thecvf.com/content/WACV2025/papers/Voas/_Temporally/_Streaming/_Audio-Visual/_Synchronization/_for/_Real-World_Videos_WACV/_2025/_paper.pdf
79. Vougioukas, K., Petridis, S., Pantic, M.: Realistic speech-driven facial animation with gans. In: International Journal of Computer Vision (IJCV), vol. 128, pp. 1398–1413 (2020)
80. Wang, T.C., Mallya, A., Liu, M.Y.: One-shot free-view neural talking-head synthesis for video conferencing. In: Proceedings of the IEEE/CVF Conference on Computer Vision and Pattern Recognition, pp. 10039–10049 (2021)
81. Wang, Z., et al.: A timely survey on vision transformer for deepfake detection. arXiv preprint arXiv:2405.08463 (2024)
82. Yaman, D., Eyiokur, F.I., Bärmann, L., Ekenel, H.K., Waibel, A.: Audio-driven talking face generation with stabilized synchronization loss. In: Computer Vision – ECCV 2024 Workshops, pp. 392–409 (2024). https://doi.org/10.1007/978-3-031-72655-2_24, https://arxiv.org/abs/2307.09368
83. Yanushkevich, S.N., Stoica, A., Shmerko, V.P.: Developmental tools-synthetic biometrics. IEEE Comput. Intell. Mag. **2**(2), 60–69 (2007)
84. Zhang, W., Lee, S., Kumar, A.: Humans vs. ai: A user study on detecting audio-visual deepfakes. arXiv preprint arXiv:2405.04097 (2024). https://arxiv.org/abs/2405.04097

85. Zhi, S., Xu, Y., Gao, J., Yu, S., Gool, L.V.: Audio-driven talking face generation with learning-based personalized head pose. In: Proceedings of the AAAI Conference on Artificial Intelligence, vol. 35, pp. 2620–2628 (2021)
86. Zhu, H., Luo, M.D., Wang, R., Zheng, A.H., He, R.: Deep audio-visual learning: a survey. Int. J. Autom. Comput. **18**(3), 351–376 (2021)
87. Zi, Y., Wang, S., Yin, G., Cao, X., He, R.: Wilddeepfake: A challenging real-world dataset for deepfake detection. In: Proceedings of the 28th ACM International Conference on Multimedia (MM '20), pp. 2382–2390. ACM (2020). https://doi.org/10.1145/3394171.3413769
88. Zinonos, A., Ma, P., Albanie, S., Stafylakis, T., Zisserman, A., Nagrani, A.: Learning cross-lingual visual speech representations. arXiv preprint arXiv:2303.09455 (2023). https://arxiv.org/abs/2303.09455

Author Index

V. V. Pham et al. (Eds.): CIDDF 2025, ACSAR 5, p. 231, 2026.
https://doi.org/10.1007/978-3-032-19488-6

The manufacturer's authorised representative in the EU is Springer Nature Customer Service Centre GmbH, Europaplatz 3, 69115 Heidelberg, Germany. If you have any concerns regarding our products, please contact ProductSafety@springernature.com

Printed and bound by CPI Group (UK) Ltd, Croydon, CR0 4YY
05/10/2026
02228031-0005